D0214645

Reform or Repression

AMERICAN BUSINESS, POLITICS, AND SOCIETY

Series editors
Andrew Wender Cohen, Pamela Walker Laird, Mark H. Rose,
and Elizabeth Tandy Shermer

Books in the series American Business, Politics, and Society explore the
relationships over time between governmental institutions and the creation and
performance of markets, firms, and industries large and small. The central theme
of this series is that politics, law, and public policy—understood broadly to
embrace not only lawmaking but also the structuring presence of governmental
institutions—has been fundamental to the evolution of American business
from the colonial era to the present. The series aims to explore, in particular,
developments that have enduring consequences.

A complete list of books in the series is available from the publisher.

arson, Chad,
form or repression :
ganizing America's ant
016]
234531
08/04/16

Reform or Repression

Organizing America's Anti-Union Movement

Chad Pearson

PENN

UNIVERSITY OF PENNSYLVANIA PRESS

PHILADELPHIA

Copyright © 2016 University of Pennsylvania Press

All rights reserved. Except for brief quotations used for purposes of review or scholarly citation, none of this book may be reproduced in any form by any means without written permission from the publisher.

Published by
University of Pennsylvania Press
Philadelphia, Pennsylvania 19104-4112
www.upenn.edu/pennpress

Printed in the United States of America
on acid-free paper

10 9 8 7 6 5 4 3 2 1

Library of Congress Cataloging-in-Publication Data
ISBN 978-0-8122-4776-3

To Sandra and Lucia

Contents

Introduction. Reformers and Fighters: Employers and the Labor Problem

> Those who have given any thought to the labor question must see
> that it is a very inadequate statement to make that it is merely a
> controversy between employers and employes.
> —David M. Parry, 1904

The period between 1890 and 1917 in the United States was shaped by both far-reaching reforms and episodic cases of violence and repression. Reform-minded citizens fought corruption and vice in cities and in official politics, sought to make our food and water supplies safer, denounced the role of alcohol in society, and campaigned for protective labor laws. Some reformers were motivated to improve efficiency; others were troubled by what they considered expressions of immorality in communities and workplaces. In that same era, dramatic strikes pitted militant workers against obstinate employers. Middle-class campaigners helped win legislation designed to protect some workers—namely women and children—at roughly the same time that immigrant anarchists, western miners, and socialists of various stripes preached the need for a working-class-led revolution. Picket-line violence was commonplace, and the state responded to the most aggressive examples of working-class combativeness and acts of sabotage with arrests, and sometimes even executions. The era truly was, as the names of two influential books about the period suggest, both an *Age of Reform* and America's *First Age of Terror*.[1]

This project investigates the ways an often overlooked and under-explored group, employers and their allies, helped shape this period of contrasts. Why study the history of American employers and their organizations? The reason is straightforward: historically, they have wielded a tremendous amount of authority over the lives of millions of people. They hired, fired, disciplined, rewarded, promoted, set pay rates, decided what, if any, benefits to offer, and fought trade unionists and working-class activists. Turn-of-the-century employers representing different types and sizes of workplaces also joined with one another in unprecedented ways to build powerful organizations designed to alleviate the "labor problem," which Americans from all classes viewed as one of the era's most pressing concerns. Defined largely by clergymen, lawyers, journalists, and employers in the years after the Civil War, the labor problem consisted of a set of working class-led activities, including union organizing campaigns, boycotts, and strikes, that threatened to destabilize American capitalism.[2] How, reform-seeking employers demanded to know, could they best respond to expressions of insubordination like strikes and workers' demands for recognition, which in practice meant the establishment of closed shops—workplaces where all wage earners held union membership cards and bargained collectively with management?[3] Hundreds of employers' organizations, established at both the local and national levels, worked to solve these multilayered challenges at the point of production, in politics, and in society more generally. This study reveals that an employer-centered analysis offers an especially fruitful way of understanding the dynamics of class relations, the rhetorical power of progressivism, and the workings of the era's political economy.

What was, from employers' collective perspective, the long-term labor *solution*? Their answer was the widespread creation of workplaces filled with loyal, industrious, and law-abiding employees who sincerely respected America's industrial and political institutions. Above all, employers and their allies generally believed that wage earners must embrace individualism over collectivism, and hence resist the temptations to join anarchist or socialist organizations or the more numerous "labor trusts"—the term employers and their allies used to describe what they considered the many powerful, intemperate, and subversive unions that demanded recognition and collective bargaining rights. Reinforcing a commonly held opinion among employers, George B. Hugo—owner of a modest-sized Boston-based wholesale liquor and beer bottling company, head of the Employers' Association of Massachusetts, and a former leader of the influential Citizens' Industrial Association of America (CIAA)—drew an especially stark contrast between the two basic choices facing workers in 1909: "Properly defined, individualism means progressive civilization, order, and liberty. Collectivism means retrogression, chaos, compulsion, and, at its best, state servitude."[4] In an effort to find solutions to the many-sided labor problem, employers like Hugo had built alliances with one another and with members of their communities, lobbied politicians, organized public lectures, published and distributed pamphlets, and fired and blacklisted working-class activists who demanded collective bargaining rights.[5] Paradoxically, early twentieth-century employers, including many self-identified reformers, established hundreds of "defense" organizations—both restrictive employers' associations and the more inclusive "citizens'" alliances—largely to discourage workers from participating in their own confrontational, class-based associations.

No issue better highlights employers' combination of reformist and combative tendencies, this study maintains, than their widespread involvement in establishing open-shop workplaces—workplaces run by employers who refused to recognize or negotiate with labor unions—and in creating a well-organized and mostly effective open-shop movement. Organized employers, many of whom were stalwart Republicans, invented and popularized the anti-labor union open-shop theory—which they presented as a nondiscriminatory managerial principle, welcoming both union and nonunion "free" men—in the aftermath of the late nineteenth-century labor actions that rocked much of the nation.[6] Soon, thousands embraced the theory and took part in the open-shop movement, which was designed to liberate employers and nonunionists from what they considered the burdens of collective bargaining, labor unrest, and "class dictation." In short, employers demanded greater freedom to hire and fire.[7] By the early post-World War I period, 1,665 separate employers and business associations throughout the country officially supported the open-shop movement and enforced this managerial policy in their workplaces.[8] This study examines the origins, character, growth, and limitations of the first-wave open-shop movement—which emerged at the turn of the century and concluded when the United States entered World War I—by exploring the colorful figures behind it and the ideas and events that influenced them.

Who exactly were these figures? One cannot offer a perfectly exhaustive sociological portrait of the thousands of merchants, manufacturers, coal mine bosses, bankers, railroad executives, clergymen, lawyers, journalists, academics, and nonunion workers who gave the movement its character and direction. But this study does explore some of the most influential, outspoken, and visible open-shop proponents, examining their involvement in campaigns against the labor problem both nationally and in several important industrial centers: Cleveland, Buffalo, Worcester, Massachusetts, and southern areas of the United States. Indeed, this book, in part because of its spatial approach, illuminates both the national and regional dimensions of the open-shop movement's foundational history.[9]

We can actually make some generalizations about many of the individuals who participated in the assorted groups that helped launch and lead this movement. A glance at the membership of the National Metal Trades Association (NMTA), the National Founders' Association (NFA), and the National Association of Manufacturers (NAM)—influential business organizations that emerged in the late nineteenth century—reveals that numerous members identified with the Republican Party, resided in northern and midwestern cities, and shared a profound appreciation for America's economic vibrancy. Some had fought as Union soldiers during the Civil War, and most held the nation's political history and institutions in high esteem. Many were engineers, managed various-sized specialized manufacturing establishments, celebrated periods of prosperity, and coped, as best as they could, with periodic economic downturns. These relatively privileged men, residing in cities like Boston, Buffalo, Chicago, Cincinnati, Cleveland, Detroit, Indianapolis, Kansas City, Milwaukee, Minneapolis, New York, Omaha, Philadelphia, Pittsburgh, St. Louis, and Worcester, also joined commercial clubs, engineering societies, higher education alumni groups, Republican leagues, and English-style gentlemen's associations—organizations that offered intellectual and social stimulation and thus fostered class-based bonds of friendship and solidarity. By century's end, these figures—the architects and beneficiaries of what historians have long called the second industrial revolution—had ultimately developed a common concern with the labor problem, the primary force that they believed threatened to undermine their collective goals of financial prosperity, industrial progress, and managerial stability.[10] In 1903, Frank Vanderlip, a New York banker and open-shop proponent summed up these fears succinctly, warning that "the only serious obstacle" to these objectives "will be our labor organizations."[11]

This study brings to light the efforts of the numerous activists who helped convince employers to join with one another to confront this "serious obstacle." One of the most influential individuals we will meet was an ambitious and talented Cincinnati-based organizer named Ernest F. Du Brul, a partner in the large Miller, Du Brul, and Peters Manufacturing Company, a highly productive and internationally recognized cigar mold manufacturing establishment. Beginning in 1902, the Notre Dame and Johns Hopkins educated Du Brul organized numerous recruitment trips and met with audiences of engineers and manufacturers in cities throughout the Northeast and Midwest. In early 1903, Du Brul expressed enormous satisfaction with the results of his enlistment campaigns in a newspaper interview: "in about 100 different places central bodies of employers are now flourishing."[12] Du Brul helped motivate many fellow union critics, including David M. Parry, the Indianapolis-based carriage manufacturer who helped turn the NAM into the nation's most recognized open-shop organization in spring 1903. Speaking to an excited crowd of 400 like-minded open-shop proponents, including Du Brul, in Indianapolis in early 1904, Parry explained that "the cry is going up in every part of the country: 'we want to be organized'."[13]

This book does not limit itself to members of manufacturers' associations in the Northeast or Midwest. As Parry noted, not all open-shop activists lived in highly industrialized cities in these regions, and some preferred to join one of the hundreds of "citizens' associations" rather than one or more of the less inclusive employers' organizations. For example, an additional noteworthy labor movement foe, Wilbur F. Sanders—western pioneer, 1860s vigilante, and one of Montana's first two U.S. senators—helped lead both the Citizens' Alliance of Helena and the larger, more powerful CIAA in the early twentieth century. The CIAA—comprised of open-shop activists from throughout the nation, including many from small and moderate-sized western cities—campaigned for "the maintenance of industrial peace, the preservation of constitutional rights, and the creation of public sentiment against all forms of violence, coercion and intimidation," wrote George Creel, a Kansas City newspaperman and one of its spokespersons, in 1903.[14]

Union opponents were especially successful in the South. And another prominent CIAA member we will meet is Birmingham's N. F. Thompson, an enthusiastic regional booster, Confederate veteran, and one of the first Ku Klux Klan heads. Thompson had earned a reputation for his unapologetic condemnations of labor unrest at the turn of the century. In 1900, for example, the former Klansman called for the enactment of "justifiable homicide" laws in the context of labor-management disputes. Such laws would provide employers with the legal right to murder those who threatened, in Thompson's words, the "right [of Americans] to earn an honest living."[15] By exploring the activities of individuals like Sanders and Thompson, this study draws fresh connections between nineteenth-century vigilantism and racial violence on the one hand and early twentieth-century anti-union activism on the other. Indeed, both Sanders and Thompson invoked the politics of law and order in the context of confrontations with labor in the 1900s, just as they had previously during their respective struggles against gold thieves and insubordinate former slaves in the 1860s. A proper analysis of the movement's activists and leaders, as this study demonstrates, requires that we reckon with this deep history.

Many open-shop activists did not start their adult lives as businessmen or elite politicians. Some, like NFA chief organizer John A. Penton, were even once active in the labor movement before switching sides. Well before he worked for the NFA at the turn of the century, Penton headed the International Brotherhood of Machinery Molders of North America—a union that engaged in numerous jurisdictional disputes with the substantially larger Iron Molders Union (IMU) in the late 1880s and early 1890s. Penton abandoned the labor movement in the 1890s, and in 1900 played a critical role in helping Cleveland's foundry operators recruit strikebreakers during a dramatic work stoppage staged by his old IMU adversaries. Shortly afterward, the Cleveland-based Penton—who rivaled Du Brul as the period's most ambitious employer organizer—established the Penton Publishing Company, which produced and circulated a half-dozen trade publications nationally that frequently covered the open-shop movement's challenges and successes.

Movement participants were somewhat diverse with respect to race, ethnicity, and religion. Most open-shop advocates were Protestant whites, but certainly not all. Elite African Americans like Booker T. Washington, head of the Tuskegee Institute in southern Alabama, and William H. Councill, top administrator at Alabama Agricultural and Mechanical College in Huntsville, played their own roles in assisting their mostly white colleagues by encouraging southern black students and graduates to stay away from labor unions. And several leading employer activists were Catholic by religion, including Du Brul and Thompson. Jews were also present in the movement, especially in the garment industry. As we will discover, a shared dislike of closed shops combined with a pervasive fear of labor unrest helped unite dissimilar groups of economically privileged elites.

In an effort to protect themselves, business interests generally, and non-union workers, Creel, Du Brul, Parry, Penton, Sanders, Thompson, and many others had concluded that they needed their own organizations to effectively challenge what CIAA activist C. W. Post called in 1906 "the greatest trust with which the people have had to contend."[16] Together, they became active in what one newspaper in 1902 called "missionary work."[17]

The nation's variety of open-shop advocates realized that effectively framing the movement's agenda and goals remained a critical task from its birth to the 1910s and beyond. As Creel put it in 1903, "public opinion is the great arbitrator."[18] By this time, a diverse set of employers and their supporters had insisted that the open-shop principle, the idea that workers must be allowed access to jobs irrespective of union status, constituted a fundamentally fair, progressive, economically sound, and ultimately *American* alternative to closed shops. "The union label," Thompson complained in 1907, "no longer stands for skill or merit in any particular way, but it has become a weapon with which to fight independent workmen and a club to destroy freedom in a free land."[19] Writing in 1910, one NAM leader, reinforcing Thompson, referred to the membership of his organization as "the progressive employers of the United States."[20] By highlighting such rhetoric—including statements that connected open shops to American patriotism, workplace competence, and merit—this study aims to heighten our understanding of this forceful movement's reformist tendencies. After all, those in the crusade's front line presented themselves, first and foremost, as mainstream campaigners, defenders of ordinary people, and representatives of technological and managerial progress, "not," Creel argued in 1903, "a body of 'Labor Crushers,' or 'Strike Busters'."[21] In other words, those in the movement sought to show that they were far from the profit-driven reactionaries and union busters depicted by labor union and leftist activists.

Open-shop advocates claimed that they stood squarely in favor of what we have come to call a system of meritocracy, and they argued that open-shop workplaces rewarded employees for their loyalty, skill, and efficiency, not whether or not they belonged to unions. Writing in 1902, Chattanooga's E. H. Putnam, a foundry operator and one of the original organizers of the NFA, insisted that well-trained independent workmen "are better molders than some of the fellows who are drifting about the country with union cards in their pockets."[22] These "better" employees, open-shop proponents claimed, deserved the right to employment without confronting pressures to join labor organizations as a precondition. As Putnam's colleague Philadelphia's William H. Pfahler explained in early 1903, the individual job hunter must "be free to seek employment wherever and under whatsoever conditions he may prefer, without regard to his politics, his religion, or his affiliation with organizations based on principles which he cannot endure."[23] For industrial leaders like Pfahler, discrimination against nonunionists, a central feature of closed shops, was no less immoral than any other form of intolerance.

Employers and their allies often complained that closed shops suffered from inefficiencies and were plagued by unnecessary rules, as well as challenging, unreasonable union leaders—individuals who, open-shop proponents believed, stubbornly held on to outdated ideas. Such leaders routinely demanded across-the-board wage increases for all, irrespective of skill, behavior, or productivity levels, and periodically launched crippling work stoppages, which, union critics insisted, threatened manufacturing and technological progress. "Striking as a means of redressing wrongs," Creel's *Independent* newspaper declared in late 1901, "is a thing of the past."[24] Indeed, employers maintained that demanding unionists, unlike themselves, behaved anachronistically. Writing about one union during a 1906 strike against the introduction of open-shop conditions, a commentator in a trade publication noted, "Sentiment has moved on, but the Iron Molders Union has refused to move with it. Its failure to catch step with the modern industrial movement has demonstrated its unfitness for the control of the instruments of production at which it aims."[25] Closed shops were, as another open-shop magazine asserted in 1908, "tyrannical and reactionary."[26]

This study illustrates that open-shop advocates hungered for an industrial relations system that allowed them greater freedom to manage, insisting that they must enjoy the unalloyed authority to employ nonunionists and reward ambitious individuals with financial bonuses and attractive working conditions while also enjoying the flexibility to dismiss those they deemed lazy, inefficient, or insubordinate. Wage rates, workload, hours, benefits, and employment itself, open-shop defenders maintained, needed to be tied to the output and reliability of employees, to the overall state of the economy, and ultimately to the judgment of managers, not to onerous collective bargaining agreements or to pressure from trade unions. Why, employers and their allies asked, would employees want to labor in closed shops, workplaces that apparently suppressed their individual talents and restricted their ability to choose whether they wanted to belong to a labor organization?

But, as we know, hundreds of thousands of workers in various industries *did* join unions, demanding the establishment of closed shops, the ability to negotiate contracts, and the right to secure regular across-the-board pay increases. Facing a determined employer class, workers frequently disrupted production and joined picket lines in their efforts to achieve these aims. In the face of such pressure, employers often responded collectively, fired protestors, recruited strikebreakers, attempted to influence public opinion, and collaborated with lawyers—many of whom held membership in employers' associations—to secure injunctions and thus resume production. For the most part, organized employers had enormous faith in the nation's public institutions, expecting that the courts and police had a responsibility to protect businesses, property, and nonunionists in confrontations with protestors. But they also believed that the private sector had a crucial role to play in these efforts, and many employers from the metal-working, foundry, garment, coal mining, railroad, retail, timber, and numerous other industries used their connections with one another and with law enforcement to fill struck workplaces with nonunionists. They often referred to nonunionists as "free men," individuals unburdened by union rules, unwilling to participate in coercive picket-line activities, and uninterested in fostering the development of what Thompson referred to in 1903 as "class dictation, class interference, and class rule."[27] Employers, seeking to both contain the labor problem and remove the concept of class from the consciousness of as many workers as possible, routinely defended their often heavy-handed managerial policies.[28] A spokesperson from the NMTA summed up the fight apocalyptically in 1903: "The devil must be fought with fire."[29] Thus employers and their allies became flamethrowers, they maintained, out of necessity. In the face of labor unrest, they used a common phrase to justify their actions: "Do Right—Then Fight."[30]

As they sought to "do right," union fighters repeatedly claimed to place the interests of the nation above their own particular economic and class concerns. They denounced strike leaders and unionists generally who used coercion to build unions, presenting themselves, most importantly, as class-neutral defenders of the American people's long-term interests, not merely protectors of the business community.[31] As Parry put it in April 1903, employers had opted to act decisively because union activists had simply become too powerful, "dominating to a dangerous degree the whole social, political and governmental systems of the Nation."[32]

The commanding, straight-talking Parry, building on the efforts of union antagonists like Du Brul, Sanders, Thompson, Penton, Pfahler, Putnam, and others, had helped give voice and direction to growing numbers of employers who had long struggled with restive, closed-shop-demanding workers. By the time Parry had assisted in turning the NAM into a robust union-fighting outfit in 1903—a year when organized labor staged close to 3,500 strikes nationally—thousands had already flocked to the hundreds of national and local employers' associations. By mid-decade, groups like the NAM, the NFA, the NMTA, the American Anti-Boycott Association (AABA), the many locally based employers' associations, and the considerably more inclusive CIAA had transformed labor relations by providing union opponents with numerous perks: access to strikebreakers and spies, managerial training, legal assistance, greater confidence, comradeship, and a set of progressive-sounding talking points as they struggled against what appeared to be an overwhelming labor problem. In the face of this problem, they sought to, as the CIAA put it on its letterhead, protect "the common people"—no one narrow group or class.

Employers, many of whom identified themselves as enlightened visionaries partially responsible for the welfare of "the common people," repeatedly showed a willingness to protect individual nonunion workers against challenges from a "monopoly-imposing," often hostile, and sometimes lawless labor movement. They promised to offer a genuine alternative to closed shops, insisting, as veteran open-shop activist Walter Gordon Merritt put it in 1919, that "factory solidarity" was far superior to "class solidarity."[33] And indeed, many employers offered benefits beyond pay to their workers and engaged in philanthropic activities in their communities. As so-called welfare capitalists, employers, especially those who oversaw large multi-campus workplaces, sought to improve industrial life by investing in sports teams, theater clubs, seasonal outings, and measures intended to improve shop floor safety. Additionally, a number offered their employees health insurance and subsidized housing. Some employer activists insisted that all owners and managers must demonstrate kindness to their wage earners, and they criticized those who failed to treat their employees fairly. For example, a spokesperson for the employer-led Citizens' Industrial Association of St. Louis, which claimed a membership of 8,500, declared in 1907 that "Our Association has no worse enemy than the unfair employer."[34] Members of this association, like others, held the view that benevolent expressions from above proved that workers had no need for their own oppositional organizations from below.[35] Numerous manufacturers, merchants, mine owners, and retail heads—holding membership in national and local organizations—positioned themselves as principled opponents of both "the labor trust" and "unfair employers."

In fact, the open-shop principle enjoyed enormous popularity across a range of locations and industries. An organization that would come to play a leadership role in the movement, the NAM, for instance, welcomed and assisted, as this group put it in 1895, "manufacturing industries of all classes throughout the country."[36] Furthermore, locally based employers' associations in places like Cleveland, Buffalo, and Worcester and in cities throughout the nation included men who represented a diversity of workplaces in terms of both size and type. Even those who opted not to join employers' or citizens' associations typically preferred the open-shop system of management. As the *New York Times* explained in 1904, "the open-shop is the first issue ever presented to employers upon which they could combine in entire agreement."[37]

Yet, although the era's business owners and managers were attracted to the open-shop philosophy and often promoted it, many, under certain circumstances, negotiated with unions in closed shops. For example, those who required skilled workers, including managers of construction sites, foundries, printing presses, and specialized manufacturing establishments, employed union members in contexts in which there were shortages of comparably adept nonunionists. Others, under pressure during work stoppages, bargained with unions simply because they could not afford expensive and inconvenient strikes. They typically did so grudgingly. In fact, as we will see, more than a dozen NFA members and small shop owners continued to identify as open-shop proponents after reluctantly granting wage increases to striking IMU members in 1906. But these Buffalo-based employers, annoyed by idled factories and harassing picketers, would have certainly preferred managing unilaterally without the nuisances of collective bargaining agreements and repeated union demands.[38] Combative and effective protests at the point of production reinforced, rather than altered, their underlying managerial philosophy.

Many non-employers shared this outlook. Indeed, members of open-shop organizations were far from the era's only reform-minded group to express displeasure with outbreaks of working-class conflict, revulsion with the hard left's ideology and militancy, fear of labor violence, and discomfort with the subject of class itself. Most prominent reform organizations, including the American Association for Labor Legislation, the National Consumers' League, the National Child Labor Committee, the National Conference of Charities and Corrections, and an assortment of settlement house volunteers, remained consistently unwilling to challenge the roots of economic and social inequality in the nation's communities or work-places.[39] And several high-profile individuals who participated in these types of reform-oriented groups found themselves siding with open-shop employers and nonunion workers during periods of industrial disputes. That a surprisingly large and varied range of Americans, including President Theodore Roosevelt, journalist Ray Stannard Baker, social gospeler Washington Gladden, Harvard University president Charles W. Eliot, lawyer Louis D. Brandeis, and numerous other, lesser-known reformers, endorsed the open-shop principle is a testament to organized employers' networking and public relations effectiveness.

A number of mainstream reformers, like open-shop employers, were unquestionably supportive of the rights of individuals to reject unionization in the context of labor-management conflicts and often expressed horror at the extent to which unyielding unionists carried out their organizing campaigns.[40] Commenting on a series of belligerent miners' strikes in 1904 in the pages of the NAM's monthly magazine, *American Industries*, Gladden, a high-profile Protestant reformer, advised labor activists that they "must learn to be reasonable and decent" and cease the harassment of nonunionists by enforcing "a policy of live and let live."[41] Gladden was one of numerous reformers to share his views of the labor problem in the pages of employers' association magazines. The same magazine applauded Roosevelt in 1905 for taking "the position that every man, whether union or nonunion, should have an equal chance in the United States."[42] Employers' association publications were far from the only source to enthusiastically tout the open-shop principle's virtues. *The New Encyclopedia of Social Reform* 1908 edition, edited by Christian socialist William Dwight Porter Bliss, honored open-shop workplaces for promoting "individual freedom," which, it insisted, "is the cardinal principle of American life."[43]

Why did prominent reformers, including muckrakers, social gospelers, good government proponents, and consumer advocates, embrace the open-shop movement's goals? One somewhat obvious reason: they generally shared a similar class background with the movement's employers. But reductionist explanations alone are insufficient; we must dig deeper by also considering how late nineteenth-century opinion makers depicted the multiple clashes between unions, on the one hand, and employers, police, and nonunion workers, on the other. Certainly many middle-class observers sympathized with the plight of nonunionists and found picket line violence directed against these "free men," repeatedly conveyed—often exaggeratedly—in the press, intensely unnerving. Starting in the second part of the nineteenth century, newspaper reporters began providing their mostly middle-class readership with dreadful, attention-grabbing reports of ill-behaved unionists, rebels guilty of riotously destroying property, attacking police officers, harassing nonunionists, and threatening employers with bodily harm. Such sources were much less inclined to highlight the considerably more powerful and effective forms of state repression aimed at protestors. In its coverage of the 1877 railroad strike, for example, the *New York Times* condemned the "lawlessness" and "the incendiary and inflammatory speeches" delivered by working-class demonstrators.[44] In the following decade, the *Chicago Times* referred to the anarchists present during the Haymarket Square bombing in 1886 as "arch counselors of riot, pillage, incendiarism, and murder."[45] And the *Richmond Dispatch* mocked Eugene Debs, American Railway Union head and leader of the 1894 Pullman strike, for failing to preserve peace despite promising to do so: "This 'peaceful' strike has attained the proportions of a war upon the entire people, and the interest on which their very lives are dependent."[46] Picket-line activities were, to be sure, not always violent, but judges, employers, and much of the press tended to portray most as pernicious expressions of intimidation and brutality—and as a result helped to generate a pervasive atmosphere of terror.[47] By the early twentieth century, many bourgeois Americans had concluded that, in the words of Eliot, "there is no such thing as peaceful picketing."[48]

Organized employers, many of whom shared Eliot's analysis, sincerely cherished the support that they received from well-known reformers and the mainstream press, but they were especially thankful for state assistance, including direct help from judges and police forces during labor conflicts. As they campaigned to reform workplaces and communities by pitting what they considered uncontrollable and demanding unionists against hardworking "free" employees, open-shop advocates saw themselves as firmly embedded in the political mainstream and securely allied with the nation's lawmakers and enforcers.[49] Judges were particularly helpful. Altogether, state and municipal courts issued 2,095 injunctions against trade unions between 1890 and 1920.[50] The legal establishment, including the Supreme Court, even legitimized employers' use of blacklists against union supporters, and numerous judges invoked the Sherman Antitrust Act, which punished strikers for restraining interstate trade.[51] By policing labor and issuing rulings against working-class activists and the unions that represented them, the legal establishment gave employers greater peace of mind, inspiration, and intellectual ammunition for their campaigns.[52]

The court system and influential reformers certainly helped to legitimize the open-shop movement by providing its practitioners with legal assistance and moral support. This study emphasizes that a wide spectrum of figures—both from within and outside industrial relations settings— offered a set of multidimensional antiunion critiques, which involved a mix of tough-minded economic logic, flag waving, and a moral concern with the welfare of "free workers," business owners, and citizens generally. In essence, a broad range of mostly privileged Americans, intolerant of labor solidarity and fearful of working-class militancy, provided a hearty defense of "the common people."

Large numbers of influential people supported the open-shop principle in the name of fairness and progress, but there were definitely exceptions. Certainly not all open-shop managers saw themselves as progressive actors fighting to improve the livelihoods of the "common people." Furthermore, this book does not claim that all reformers were advocates of open-shop workplaces and supporters of the men who refused to bargain collectively with organized labor. We can undoubtedly identify several influential progressive campaigners, including settlement house pioneer Jane Addams and lawyer Clarence Darrow, for example, who had, at various points in their lives, stood in solidarity with unions at marches and on picket lines.

Additionally, this book largely, though not entirely, avoids labels like "conservative" and "liberal" in the context of labor-management conflicts mainly because such terms are historically contingent. After all, we can surely point to plenty of historical scenarios that defy such political categorizations. Consider some questions. Were the employers who demanded that nonunionists—including African Americans, Mexicans, and Chinese— enjoy the right to work during periods of strikes staged by white laborers liberal or conservative? How should we label the union members who defiantly refused to toil next to those without union cards? Were they closed-minded conservatives, principled liberals, or perhaps something else? Of course, different observers, prioritizing dissimilar values, will offer various responses to questions like these. We must acknowledge, in other words, the lack of a political consensus with respect to these questions.[53]

Yet, as we look back on them, we should not perceive employers' fundamental supervisory interests as controversial or mysterious. Although they frequently presented themselves as committed to "doing right" by protecting the "common people" in the name of community harmony, patriotism, and industrial peace, employers were primarily interested in earning profits and maintaining unfettered managerial control. Of course, they seldom expressed their objectives in such a crass way. This does not mean that they were uninterested in their workers' welfare; many certainly acknowledged the diversity of grievances harbored by wage earners, but consistently claimed that they could respond meaningfully to them without recognizing unions. For many employers, providing benefits beyond paychecks, drawing attention to what they considered the virtues of America's economic and political institutions, and joining "defense" organizations constituted a considerably more cost-effective, empowering, and emotionally satisfying set of responses than relinquishing any managerial control by formally bargaining with trade unions.

The open-shop principle itself was enormously comforting to the nation's diversity of employers both during periods of labor peace and in the context of industrial disputes. Its advocates were unwilling, with very few exceptions, to question the logic or limitations of this managerial principle, even in the face of intense labor unrest, protests from the radical left, and critical journalistic exposés. For most, this managerial system was absolutely nonnegotiable, even though, in the short term, open-shop campaigns often intensified, rather than alleviated, working-class discontent and community strife. Given the profound impact it had on their collective consciousness, employers were naturally disinclined to address one of the root causes of labor's restlessness: demands for closed shops and collective bargaining rights. Employers' ideological blind spots and stubbornness are entirely understandable—even rational—given their primary interests as managers and profit maximizers in a capitalist economy. As novelist Upton Sinclair famously put it, "It is difficult to get a man to understand something, when his salary depends upon his not understanding it."[54]

This study explores employers and their embrace of the open-shop system both nationally and locally. The first two chapters demonstrate the birth, growth, and influence of open-shop ideas and employer-led activism throughout much of the nation. The final four are regional case studies that investigate at the ground level the ways in which the open-shop philosophy influenced workplace relations, urban politics, and local identities. The most intense confrontations, including strikes and anti-strike campaigns, occurred in, and left lasting impacts on, individual communities. Indeed, a multiregional focus allows us to better appreciate the ways in which employers responded to different-sized labor movements, to various types of political challenges, and to each other. Context certainly mattered, and to obtain a suitable understanding of the drama of open-shop campaigns, one must explore the particular ways in which local level employers established relationships with municipal authorities, including judges and police forces, and attempted to mobilize public opinion. After all, "the Open-Shop war," as historian Howell Harris has observed, "was prosecuted at the grass roots."[55]

The regional portion of this study moves from the Midwest to the East, and concludes in the South. Open-shop proponents were usually very active in their communities, and they identified closely with their regions. The most ardent "labor trust" critics and champions of the rights of independent workers were also civic boosters, proudly wearing the open-shop badge on their sleeves as they advertised what they considered the almost limitless virtues of their communities. Spokespersons in Cleveland, Buffalo, Worcester, and the southern areas of the United States insisted that their communities were progressive, prosperous, vibrant, and inviting in part because of the broad, multi-industry, and cross-class support for the open-shop principle. Public relations activities were an essential part of the movement.

These urban-based open-shop boosters were actually indebted to a long history of public relations efforts. Beginning in the early antebellum period, developers, promoters, and newspaper editors, especially in cities and towns throughout the South, the Great Lakes Region, and the West, enthusiastically advertised—even embellished—the financial and political promises of their nascent communities. Such spokespersons, hoping to lure additional settlers and investors, often pointed to the availability of convenient railway lines, productive manufacturing establishments, nearby natural resources, visionary political leaders, and the enduring promise of shared prosperity.[56] Years later, promoters added the presence of both lawful wage earners and magnanimous employers, joined together amicably in productive open shops, to the list of municipal virtues. Countless regional pamphlets and journals advertised this cooperative spirit of progress, but the reality, of course, was always more complicated. The periodic eruption of strikes and union organizing campaigns certainly represented a fundamental challenge to these boosterish narratives, demonstrating an alternative way of interpreting the collective views of the "common people."

The particular regions I have chosen to explore enable us to better understand the open-shop movement's propagandistic, boosterish, reformist, and confrontational dimensions while helping us to appreciate a series of regionally specific challenges and opportunities faced by a colorful cast of characters. Many of these characters appear throughout the book; others appear only in individual chapters. Importantly, I tell different, though equally significant, stories without losing sight of the larger picture. In the process, I have sought to illustrate the open-shop movement kaleidoscopically.

I selected Cleveland for two reasons. First, I wanted to know how strong open-shop campaigns found expression in a city that enjoyed a national reputation as a bastion of progressivism under the leadership of Mayor Tom L. Johnson. In 1905, muckraker Lincoln Steffens, for instance, famously called Johnson "the best Mayor of the best-governed city in the United States."[57] How did this municipal luminary and his administration respond to the labor struggles and growing open-shop movement in his backyard? His public record is actually silent on the movement itself, but a look at his own public sector managerial policies at the end of his career demonstrate that he actually shared much with the city's financially privileged open-shop proponents. And the movement grew under his watch. Johnson himself infamously helped break a strike of unionized streetcar workers in 1908. During the course of it, he dispatched hundreds of police officers to picket lines and demanded that protestors refrain from harassing nonunionists, promising that "disorder will be met with force adequate to suppress it."[58]

Second, Cleveland was home to several nationally prominent open-shop activists, including former trade unionist Penton and one-time president of the Cleveland Employers' Association turned union supporter Jay P. Dawley. These two immensely influential men helped the city's employers break a series of strikes while presenting themselves as forward-thinking reformers concerned with protecting the well-being of nonunionists, the interests of business owners, and the overall welfare of the city itself. In 1911, during an exceptionally bitter garment workers' strike, Dawley, a successful defense lawyer who had spent much of the previous decade representing numerous employers in court, no longer believed that the open-shop principle was fair or progressive, severed his relationships with members of Cleveland's business community, and began working for union-seeking garment laborers. This chapter explores their remarkable changes in a context of broad reform activities, strikes, and strikebreaking campaigns.

A second case study focuses on activities in Buffalo, another useful setting that teaches us much about employers' reformist, repressive, and public relations activities. How, I wanted to know, did sections of Buffalo's business community respond to threats from left-wing activists and demanding unionists in the years after anarchist Leon Czolgosz, inspired in part by Emma Goldman's radical doctrines, killed President William McKinley—a longtime ally of employers, both in Buffalo and nationally—on the grounds of the city's Pan-American Exposition? Coincidentally, the head juror in Czolgosz's trial was Henry W. Wendt, an influential NFA leader. I discovered that Buffalo's foundry operators, like their counterparts nationally, became increasingly attracted to the politics of law and order and to the open-shop principle in the aftermath of the president's murder. And in 1906, with indispensable assistance from judges and the police, NFA members, including Wendt, fought—and in most cases defeated—a city-wide IMU-initiated strike. The city's outstandingly loyal police force also prevented anarchist Goldman from speaking to Buffalo's protestors. In the victory's aftermath, members of Buffalo's business community, including leaders of the union-breaking campaign, trumpeted their city in the same way that they publicly celebrated it during the Pan-American Exposition. And spokespersons from national employers' associations praised Buffalo's foundry operators for their accomplishments. By exploring the struggles of Buffalo's employers, we can better comprehend how they helped overcome the closed-shop challenge, assisted in halting the spread of anarchism, and ultimately regained confidence in the years after McKinley's death.

Worcester's open-shop campaigns deserve close attention for several reasons. Above all, Worcester, the smallest city in this study, was home to one of the NMTA's most active and successful branches. It grew considerably after a half dozen of the city's metal-working manufacturers defeated a machinists' strike in 1902. In the strike's aftermath, the city's metal-working employers developed what became one of the NMTA's busiest labor bureaus, the central headquarters that coordinated hiring, firing, and blacklisting. The labor bureau, run by diligent clerks, earned considerable praise nationally and attracted the attention of employers and reformers from as far away as Australia. Additionally, Worcester's employers were widely recognized for their welfare capitalist programs, which, according to city spokespersons, reduced the appeal of unions. For these reasons, Worcester's open-shop activists saw themselves as national leaders in the struggle against the labor problem, and the NMTA's chapter secretary, Donald Tulloch, even projected in 1914 that the city would enjoy a "strikeless future." Wage earners certainly did not share this vision: in 1915, 3,000 workers left their workstations and mobilized on city streets while demanding that managers cut their hours, raise their wages, and recognize their unions. This chapter investigates the ways in which the city's open-shop proponents and industrial reformers engaged in excessive myth-making, noting the tensions between what they said about labor relations in Worcester and the reality of how workers thought and acted.

Of course, not all open-shop advocates resided in the North, and this study devotes much attention to Thompson and the South. Thompson—the Middle Tennessee-born former Klansman, diehard temperance activist, editor of the boosterish and widely circulated *Tradesman*, and CIAA leader—was the region's most effective and recognizable open-shop developer and spokesperson. He played a critical role in luring steel mills, textile factories, and railroads to several southern cities, including Birmingham, Huntsville, and Chattanooga, insisting that these communities—headed by forward-looking paternalistic managers who oversaw racially divided workforces—were largely free of labor troubles, which contrasted with much of the North. Thompson, who had earned a considerable amount of attention nationally for delivering an electrifying anti-union speech before the U.S. Industrial Commission in 1900, offered a simple solution to northern industrialists: flight rather than fight. As the president of the Thompson Land and Investment Company, an industrial real estate concern, Thompson and his regional allies were actually, this chapter demonstrates, beneficiaries of the mostly northern-based labor problem. Exploring Thompson's life helps us to better recognize the connections between southern economic development and the northern labor problem.

The process of confronting the labor problem was often difficult and complex. And indeed, this work underlines the ways in which a diverse set of employers and their partners in the areas of law, journalism, higher education, and politics approached a challenging set of questions, including how best to respond to labor unrest, how to effectively build organizations, how to secure state support, and how to establish public legitimacy. Of course, employers and their allies did not always meet their goals, but they won far more battles than they lost. It is my hope this study provides a deeper understanding of their ideas and struggles, as well as a better appreciation for the enduring power, elasticity, and significance of the open-shop principle.

Finally, this study does not limit itself to the views and behavior of employers and their allies; it also takes very seriously the struggles of their primary victims: defeated strikers, blacklisted unionists, and at-will employees. By considering the collective plight of the movement's many casualties, we cannot help but recognize that the boosterish and flowery rhetoric persistently used by open-shop activists was quite obviously self-serving, intended to fundamentally legitimize an often repressive, largely successful movement that created an enormous amount of frustration and insecurity for millions of ordinary people. Therefore, we must remember those in the movement's vanguard not primarily as defenders of "free workers," "the common people," or "progressive individualism," but instead as the nation's foremost champions of an economic system designed to protect the most privileged classes of Americans at the expense of those who had demanded a more democratic say over their lives.

PART I

Nation

Chapter 1

Fighting "Union Dictation": Birth of the Open-Shop Movement

In no case with which I am familiar has the demand for a union shop
been accompanied by a proposition for benefit to the employer,
except perhaps that he may, by conceding to the demand, hope to
avoid the persecution of the local union to which his men belong.
    —William H. Pfahler, "Free Shops for Free Men," 1903

To properly understand the open-shop movement's birth, one must explore
the lives of the colorful individuals who built the organizations that drove
it, shaped labor-management relations, and impacted community and
national affairs. These employer-activists presented themselves publicly as
concerned not only with their own economic challenges, but also with the
interests of the country, their communities, and their workers. They organized open-shop groups because they believed that unionists were selfish,
often lawless figures responsible for creating a host of problems for independent workers, business owners, and the economy generally. In the public sphere, practically all open-shop proponents claimed they wanted to
establish and oversee profitable workplaces built around principles of fairness and meritocracy. One can generalize further: they tended to be ambitious, community-oriented, socially conscious, and uncompromising in
their belief that, as employers, they must have final say over matters of
management. Yet they seldom presented themselves as, say, purely self-
interested figures disconnected from the masses of wage earners or from
the public generally. Overall, they believed that confronting labor union

excesses, lawlessness, and monopolies was a community rather than an individual undertaking. Some held the opinion that their collective efforts represented the very best traditions of American patriotism. As proud defenders of open shops, they saw themselves as fair-minded Americans determined to find solutions to community, national, and industry problems.

This chapter explores the contexts in which these forward-thinking individuals emerged. It examines the local, national, and trade-based origins of the open-shop movement, noting its multiple roots, which can be traced to the ideas and actions of employers from numerous regions. It also illustrates the widespread popularity and effectiveness of the movement across industries. The movement grew relatively quickly, and most employers across a range of industries agreed with its central message. The clearest sociological pattern that emerges from an examination of turn-of-the-century organized employers is that they tended to share a belief in the importance of defending private property and management rights while insisting that workers must enjoy the freedom to refuse membership in labor unions. They believed that, by working together, they could achieve these goals and help reform American society generally.

"A force for good": Employers in the Foundry and Metal-Working Industries

The final years of the nineteenth century are an appropriate starting point to understand both employers' collective frustration with, and nationwide attempts to solve, labor unrest. Historians have written extensively about the massive, often destructive, and frequently violent strikes that unsettled the nation in the decades after the Civil War. There is no reason to revisit the causes, characteristics, and results of these titanic battles, but it is worth pointing out that, taken together, these protests forced observers to confront what many Gilded Agers called "the labor question."[1] For mostly self-interested reasons, employers often took the lead in addressing what was undoubtedly one of the central concerns of the period.

Consider first the case of the American Foundrymen's Association (AFA), a trade organization comprising foundry owners and managers principally concerned with matters related to research, innovation, production, and profits. Formed in 1896, the AFA was not chiefly interested in labor-management matters, but much of its membership, in the face of an emboldened labor movement, was forced to come to terms with, in the words of a *Foundry* magazine writer in 1897, "the inconveniences insepara-ble from labor troubles."[2] As union protests spread, foundry owners discov-ered that there was a genuine need for the establishment of a professional, rigorous, and well-focused organization because the AFA had, according to an *Iron Trade Review* article in 1898, "limited itself to the discussion of technical questions and the betterment of practice in the shop."[3] In prac-tice, labor troubles meant serious production- and distribution-related dif-ficulties, which in turn harmfully impacted customers and reduced earnings. Solution-minded AFA members responded to such troubles by beginning the process of building what they called a "defense association" in 1896.[4] They had models to emulate. Stove builders, for instance, had previously illustrated how to establish labor peace with iron molders as a result of creating the Stove Founders National Defense Association (SFNDA), which emerged in 1886 in the face of a nationwide strike wave. That organization, the first national employers' association, enjoyed years of give-and-take negotiations with leaders from the Iron Molders Union (IMU), which resulted in long-lasting peace and stability.[5]

In late 1896, three AFA members, Pittsburgh's William Yagle, E. H. Putnam of Chattanooga, and Philadelphia's William H. Pfahler, began the formal process of building a new, more inclusive organization, one that promised to effectively respond to the nagging labor problem. All three came from highly industrialized communities that experienced periodic outbursts of labor troubles, which in practice generally meant momentary periods of social unrest, loss of income, and a breakdown of goodwill between workers and their bosses. Each of the men saw themselves as capa-ble and resilient leaders, determined to find solutions to these managerial and financial challenges, set an example through their leadership, and ulti-mately inspire others to follow their examples. They met privately, dis-cussed labor-management matters at length, prepared a report, and submitted it to the AFA's general delegation. According to an 1897 article in *Railway Age and Northwestern Railroader*, AFA delegates responded favorably to the organizers' efforts, unanimously holding the view that the creation of an effective defense association "would be of greater importance to the foundry business and possess greater possibilities for good than any-thing else that could be suggested at this time."[6]

As the three conducted their tasks, AFA affiliates, including the Phila-delphia Foundrymen's Association, continued to discuss labor matters. One member spelled out the problem explicitly in early 1898: "When we realize that 90 per cent of all that enters into the cost of our products is labor, we must take it seriously into consideration. If we can convince labor that lower prices must prevail, then we are all right for the future."[7] From their collective viewpoint, the central problem was that labor unions naturally functioned, in part, to raise wages for their members, which, very simply, tied the employer's hand and ultimately hurt his bottom line. Simply put, they felt a sense of urgency to do something meaningful to reduce labor costs and increase profits.

Their conclusions, detailed in trade publications, suggest their preparedness to approach the labor question diplomatically in ways that mirrored the SFNDA's strategy.[8] They believed there was little reason to antagonize their employees because many, though hardly all, held membership in the IMU, a politically moderate union with a long history of representing craftsmen. Labor-management relations were hardly perfect, but foundry operators and union leaders tended to believe in compromise, recognizing the benefits, fairness, and long-term stability of cooperation. The three men wanted, at first, to perfect a system of negotiations in order to ensure mutual rewards and thus reduce workplace strife. At the AFA annual meeting in May 1897 in Detroit, they spoke boldly about "the necessity of meeting organization with organization" and "adding strength and dignity to any arrangements that might be amicably concluded between all parties." Above all, the committee sought to persuade the delegation to support the creation of an organization that would, in essence, help reduce the number of strikes and ultimately give manufacturers greater peace of mind. Collective action made good sense, they realized, because strikes often caused "a host of indirect disasters" that created "false conditions, utterly unwarranted by the general state of trade or by any principle of abstract justice." In other words, labor unionists engaged in activities that threatened the fundamental laws of economics and thus challenged the expertise of diligent managers. To avoid these unfavorable consequences, the committee proposed finding ways to build trust with union leaders, full-time figures who negotiated with employers, helped enforce contracts, and in the process often established friendships with management. This solution was commonsensical: one could reduce workplace conflict by taking "a few hours or a few days for calm deliberation."[9] The general body agreed, and the National Founders' Association (NFA), as a writer for *The Iron Trade Review* explained in 1898, had become "a fruit of the American Foundrymen's Association's efforts."[10]

It is worth looking more closely at the men behind the NFA's creation. As established business owners and community leaders, they had earned admiration from the AFA general membership. Pfahler served as an officer and treasurer of the Abram Cox Stove Company, a vast, five-story manufacturing establishment in Philadelphia's densely populated and heavily industrialized north end. The company's 400 employees built stoves and furnaces that were sold, according to an 1890 issue of *Manufacturer and Builder*, throughout "the entire country from Maine to California."[11] Yagle stood on the other side of Pennsylvania, where he led the Yagle Foundry and Machine Company, near the Allegheny River that received industry-wide admiration for its "original Black crusher."[12] In the somewhat sparsely industrialized South, Putnam held a high-level management position at the Chattanooga Plow Company, one of East Tennessee's most productive, profitable, and sizable manufacturing establishments. A structurally imposing worksite spread over six acres, the Chattanooga Plow Company supplied cane mills, chilled plows, evaporators, and hay presses to markets throughout the globe. According to a 1913 book on Tennessee industries, this company, which began operations in 1878, was "the largest industry of its kind in the south, and may be considered one of the corner-stones of Chattanooga's industrial prosperity." The same source bragged that "the sun never sets upon Chattanooga plows."[13]

It appears that Pfahler, Yagle, and Putnam had their eyes on more than their own immediate economic successes. They each displayed a sincere desire to assist the industry, their colleagues, and their communities. Accounts of their lives suggest that they were not exclusively inspired by the supposed joys of materialistic individualism or the emotional pleasures of ego building. Yet they certainly were ambitious. In addition to holding an AFA leadership position, Yagle had served on the Pittsburgh Board of Education and was highly active in the Pittsburgh Foundrymen's Association.[14] Seeking to share his deep knowledge of the industry, Putnam wrote for the *Tradesman*, a Chattanooga-based trade publication that promoted economic development throughout the South. Founded by future *New York Times* owner Adolph Ochs in 1879, the *Tradesman* contained statistics and detailed information about innovations and industrial output as well as details regarding the establishment of new factories and the accomplishments of older industrial plants within the borders of the numerous jewels of the "new South": Atlanta, Birmingham, Charlotte, Jacksonville, Louisville, New Orleans, and, above all, Chattanooga. According to an 1897 article in the *Chattanooga Daily Times*, also owned by Ochs, the *Tradesman* offered "the most complete, exhaustive, and valuable review of the South."[15] And finally, Pfahler was a visible social reformer in his community. This public-spirited individual played a leadership role in Philadelphia's Committee of Seventy, a municipal reform organization that, in its own words, sought to "keep watch and ward over the public interest."[16]

The NFA did not emerge to "fight" labor. Instead, its members initially promised to negotiate honorably and dispassionately with union heads while offering fair working conditions to employees irrespective of union status. They sought to establish an atmosphere of shared trust and cooperation at their worksites, and they occasionally distanced themselves from the nation's most excessively exploitative employers. Putnam, for instance, strongly criticized those who presumably felt no shame in employing young females in heavy industry. Writing in 1899, he lashed out at "The man who can be satisfied with industrial conditions that drive girls into the foundry in the struggle for existence." In the *Tradesman*'s pages, Putnam complained that such a manager "certainly ought not to be satisfied with his own moral condition; and if he is satisfied therewith, society ought to be so dissatisfied with him as to make it known in no uncertain terms." Putnam, echoing the moral outrage expressed by growing numbers of gender-conscious reformers, realized that a minority of these immoral employers "would work their own grandmothers in the foundry if they could make a little profit by it. This is the most mischievous class of people in industrial society. They are much harder to manage and far more injurious in their influence upon trade than the trades-union can be when under unwise direction."[17]

Fellow employers, Putnam held, had an obligation to use sound judgment, which in part meant barring women, children, and the elderly from laboring in grimy and often hazardous foundries. By mentioning the malevolent deeds of these "unjust" employers—the unnamed members of the "mischievous class"—Putnam illustrated that he was not merely interested in leading an organization designed to minimize labor unrest; he also sent a clear message that he was wholly unafraid to sharply criticize examples of what he called "scavenger business" practices.[18] The new employers' association, led by righteous critics of both labor radicalism and employer abuses, professed that it had no tolerance for the "mischievous class."

The most pressing dilemma facing these agents of industrial change was effectively making and sustaining lasting peace with a mostly grown-up workforce of men. NFA leaders believed that offering benefits and creating a respectful rapport with wage earners made for sound policy in a context in which fewer employees enjoyed upward mobility of the sort that was apparently commonplace for hardworking men in the nineteenth century's first half. Consider the words of Pfahler, a Civil War veteran who served as first NFA president—his 1908 obituary credited him for "first propagating the theory of defense associations of manufacturers."[19] By 1898, when the NFA officially started, Pfahler had come to realize the sharp decline in the number of top managerial positions in the country—and this process seemed irreversible. No longer could every focused, diligent man climb his way to the top. "With that incentive taken away," Pfahler argued, "it was important that conciliation should prevail."[20] Such structural changes, including the growing concentration of wealth in the hands of the few—a process accelerated by the turn of the century's great merger movement—meant that employers needed to play their part in modifying, even lowering, the workforce's expectations. The fifty-six-year-old Pfahler, whose devotion to the Republican Party had been put to the ultimate test on the battlefields in the 1860s, no longer unconditionally believed that the party's early free labor ideology—a doctrine professing that hard work in a free, non-slaveholding society would eventually translate into financial success and independence, including business ownership—reflected the reality of late nineteenth-century America. Yet workers' lower prospects, he reasoned, must not translate into frustration, misery, cynicism, or, worst of all, raw outbreaks of workplace conflict. Pfahler, who would soon serve as a leader of the National Civic Federation (NCF)—an organization comprising leaders from business, labor, and the general public that promoted union-management cooperation—did not break with free labor ideology completely; he continued to believe that ambition, efficiency, and skill mattered. But "reward" signified something markedly different at the end of the century from what it meant in the era of the Civil War. Simply put, Pfahler had come to accept the limits of upward class mobility.[21] *The Iron Trade Review* recommended that workers take Pfalher's assessment seriously: "Let us hear more of the desirability of being successful as an employe."[22]

Pfahler, like Putnam, sympathized with the predicaments of shop floor employees and rejected the harshest features of Social Darwinism, the cutthroat theory shared by numerous corporate moguls and their elite friends on both sides of the Atlantic. This cold-hearted concept, which applied the eminent biologist Charles Darwin's famous views to the free market, stressed that only the fittest economic actors, a tiny minority, could achieve extraordinary financial success—and such success came at the expense of ordinary people. The theory, in essence, helped legitimize an industrial society shaped by stark class divisions. Social Darwinists, including both business leaders and a handful of elite academics, sought to justify their own wealth and power, believing they essentially owed nothing to the laboring masses.[23] Pfahler, unlike insensitive Social Darwinists, believed employers needed to show goodwill by reaching out to employees, patiently listening to them, and, when possible, helping resolve their grievances. In essence, he wanted fellow NFA members, some of whom stood near, but not at, the apex of industrial society, to ensure they were basically fair to their employees.[24] Rather than view wage laborers as, in the words of historian Sven Beckert, " 'the dangerous classes' who threatened the rights of property holders," Pfahler's public statements suggest he perceived employees, both unionists and nonunionists, as potential partners—albeit junior ones—in a future shaped by cross-class harmony and prosperity.[25] One of his colleagues even claimed in 1903 that this Philadelphian was "one of the most earnest friends of organized labor."[26]

But creating an atmosphere in which employees thrived and experienced feelings of fulfillment was not enough. Pfahler and his comrades realized the importance of building and maintaining trust with the IMU leadership, relatively privileged individuals who tended to conduct their tasks from comfortable offices, not grubby shop floors. These individuals, Pfahler realized, were critical, even necessary, to ensuring industrial peace. And meetings between the NFA and the IMU culminated in the 1899 New York Agreement, a labor-management settlement promising to usher in years of industrywide harmony similar to the arrangements reached by the SFNDA. In other words, Pfahler, in consultation with his colleagues, realized that routine, courteous conferences with labor representatives served a productive purpose. Pfahler, writing in 1903, understood that the NFA must use its connections with the union leadership wisely to prevent rebellious rank-and-filers from violating labor-management agreements and disrupting the production process:

> It is true that at first the members of local unions, led by some wild agitator, would make a demand upon their employer, and, failing to enforce the demand, would quit work; but the national officers of

the union would require them to return to work at once and await the usual and proper means of adjustment.[27]

Union leaders, Pfahler acknowledged, were often largely responsible, fair-minded figures who exercised a certain amount of control over the potentially "wild" rank and file. The labor leadership, by ensuring contract enforcement, were colleagues, rather than adversaries.

This leadership also saw the benefits of industrial peace. Writing about the NFA's development, the *Locomotive Firemen's Magazine* explained in 1901, "This splendid situation is indeed a rift in the clouds that have lowered over the industrial world throughout a generation in most lines of business."[28] And an IMU spokesperson, writing in early 1898, affectionately welcomed the new employers' association partially because of Pfahler's involvement:

we have looked with favor upon the efforts of Mr. Wm. H. Pfahler and his colleagues of the American Foundrymen's Association to organize a protective organization among the foundrymen, which, working in harmony with the Iron Molders' Union, would endeavor to fix yearly, or otherwise, the wage rate and thus avoid the possibility of a strike and its attendant inconvenience to both parties.[29]

While the NFA leadership recognized the value of meeting and negotiating with union leaders, Pfahler and his colleagues also held firm to the belief that the employers must have the option of hiring and firing men irrespective of union status. In practice, foundry operators employed mostly unionists because local IMU chapters often represented the majority of the skilled employees in the industry. Yet NFA members were perfectly willing to hire nonunionists, including strikebreakers, during industrial disputes.[30]

At the same time, most had peace on their minds. And several AFA activists, understanding the need for workplace stability and the necessity of collaborating with politically moderate labor leaders, followed Pfahler's lead by helping to build the new defense association. In a short period, the NFA had become a formidable team, consisting of, in the 1916 words of its early chronicler, Margaret Loomis Stecker, "some of the best-known manufacturers of heavy machinery and other casting iron specialties."[31] The organization included, for example, executives from General Electric and the American Locomotive Company, two large, highly prosperous, multi-location workplaces. Employers attached to more modest-sized, stand-alone establishments also paid their membership dues and volunteered their time to the cause. Numerous figures joined the association apparently because, as *The Iron Trade Review* explained in 1898, they took a liking to Pfahler's "affable and charming manner" and because they shared his faith "that bringing together all the brains that have developed the manufacturing interests of this country, must be a force for good."[32]

The recruitment process was fairly straightforward, involving face-to-face contacts between men from roughly the same class. In meetings with foundry owners, many of whom were clubby, AFA-affiliated individuals, recruiters provided membership cards and requested assistance as they built this "force for good." Some organizers were paid; others donated their time. In 1898, Pfahler hired John A. Penton, the AFA secretary and the former president of the Detroit-based International Brotherhood of Machinery Molders Union, a rival to the IMU before the two unions merged in 1893, to organize full time.[33] By most accounts, the Paris, Ontario-born Penton was a sensible pick. The *New York Times* explained in 1902 that he was once "a practical molder and consequently understands every question of the foundry as one without a knowledge of the work could not."[34] His union-organizing experience gave him a degree of credibility possessed by few others, and he used his connections wisely, recruiting dozens from the AFA. One NFA member named Penton "the early propagandist" in 1903.[35] Yet his former IMU adversaries, recalling previous conflicts, called him "something of a hustler" in 1897.[36]

Penton certainly hustled, enlisted many, and received help in the process. He explained in 1899 that "if your secretary has achieved any measure of success in the work of obtaining new members, it has been in the main owing to the very substantial assistance he has received from time to time from our other members and officers."[37] Volunteers from Buffalo, Birmingham, Cincinnati, Cleveland, Chicago, Detroit, Milwaukee, New York, Pittsburgh, and Pfahler's home town of Philadelphia also played a key part in this process, conducting what some referred to as "missionary work."[38] Audiences in these and other locations heard Penton, Pfahler and their colleagues deliver impassioned speeches about the necessity of joining together in order to protect themselves and their workmen from demanding unionists and the notorious walking delegates, the labor leaders responsible for calling strikes and therefore creating unnecessary turbulence and economic hardships.[39] P. W. Gates, NFA president after Pfahler's brief term and head of the Chicago-based Gates Iron Works, a successful manufacturer of mining machinery, performed "yeoman service in strengthening the association and making it a force in the foundry world."[40] Pittsburgh's Isaac W. Frank, owner of the large United Engineering and Foundry Company, which employed about 2,000 men, helped by meeting with his contacts in foundries and social clubs throughout Western Pennsylvania. In addition to his business activities, Frank, a prominent individual in the city's Jewish community, earned a reputation as a generous philanthropist.[41] Ogden P. Letchworth, director of the giant Pratt and Letchworth Company, a malleable iron and steel castings manufacturing establishment in Buffalo, convinced dozens to join in his community. In Buffalo, Letchworth enjoyed a reputation as a socialite and as a benevolent welfare capitalist.[42] As a result of the organizing carried out by Pfahler, Yagle, Putnam, Penton, Gates, Frank, Letchworth, and others, the NFA "added to its membership many of the most extensive foundries in the country."[43] Their traveling, networking, agitation, promises of greener pastures, and occasional good humor paid off handsomely: the NFA tripled in size from 1899 to 1900. The NFA gave voice and support to the nation's leading manufacturers and community leaders. These "men of affairs" were fully "determined," as *The Iron Trade Review* insisted in 1900, "to oppose injustice by employers and employes."[44] Together, NFA members promoted themselves as honest brokers, promising to challenge both working-class troublemakers and management's most abusive exploiters.

Some activities were unavoidably messy. Strikebreaking coordination, usually orchestrated by Penton, was considerably more challenging than recruitment. The organization's leadership recognized that breakdowns in negotiations often resulted in temporary work stoppages, which led to financial inconveniences and social disorder, forcing managers to scramble. Yet strikes did not mean that production must cease altogether. Penton had requested that the membership help out during these emergencies, explaining at the NFA's second annual conference in 1899, "When men are wanted to take the place of strikers, much assistance can be rendered if each member will take it upon himself to offer the secretary the services of any volunteers whom they may secure in their own establishments, or of those applying for work who are willing to go to such positions."[45] Penton wanted his colleagues to remain vigilant by carefully monitoring the job market structure, recognizing that labor surpluses in one region could very possibly help beleaguered employers facing strike-related shortages in other sections. Managers could aid considerably, Penton maintained, by establishing relationships with loyal workmen willing to travel distances to break strikes. By pointing out how to resume production during industrial emergencies, the former union chief helped foundry owners understand the value of collective problem solving.

Recognizing the labor problem's widespread adverse impacts on a variety of workplaces, NFA members sought to build defense networks beyond the foundry industry. Pfahler remained especially critical. In fact, he was principally responsible for laying the groundwork for the establishment of the National Metal Trades Association (NMTA), which included employers active in all types of metal-working activities and emerged in late August 1899 in response to a New York City pattern-makers strike. At the NMTA's 1905 conference, the Philadelphian reminisced about the context surrounding the association's creation. But instead of presenting a clear, detailed explanation of the specific conversations, disagreements, and strategies adopted by the men present at these initial meetings held in English-style gentlemen's clubs, Pfahler noted that they came together because they developed "a feeling" about the usefulness of working "collectively."[46] Pfahler's rather vague, yet upbeat, comments should not be surprising. The era's reporters noted that NMTA members, a group of sentimental joiners, ambitious industrialists, and forward-looking reformers, concealed most of the details of their activities from the general public, "pledging themselves to secrecy."[47]

The two organizations shared much in common. While the NFA and the NMTA believed that they must enjoy the right to hire whomever they wanted irrespective of union status, members initially chose to bargain with organized labor's representatives. They acknowledged that they could both negotiate with "responsible" union leaders and insist on the right to employ nonunionists. For years, the two groups, seeking to resolve grievances in mutually satisfactory and peaceful ways, met regularly with union leaders to discuss issues relating to workloads, hours, wages, and recognition. But an undercurrent of dissatisfaction recurrently afflicted each side during bargaining sessions. Union heads often made demands that irritated employers' association leaders, and rank-and-file workers regularly staged strikes, failing to uphold their contractual obligations. In light of these tensions, both the NMTA and the NFA, unlike the SFNDA—which continued to bargain with unionists—ultimately decided to reject negotiations altogether following intense strikes in 1901 and 1904 respectively.

It is worth considering the two agreements before more fully exploring the individuals behind these organizations. The Murray Hill Agreement, signed by the NMTA and the International Association of Machinists (IAM) in May 1900, called for a nine-hour day to take effect the following year. Questions of wages were to be determined individually between workers and employers in their respective workplaces. Yet shortly before the agreement was to go into effect, the IAM's James O'Connell demanded that the employers also provide an across-the-board pay raise of twelve and a half cents per hour and accept national arbitration. The NMTA flatly refused, prompting 45,000 machinists to leave their stations; this national work stoppage lasted from late May to June 1901. In the face of this insurgency, the NMTA's Henry F. Devens nonchalantly summed up the employers' response: "This will close our relations with the International Association of Machinists. We are not going to bother with them further."[48]

The NFA's New York Agreement, signed with the IMU in 1899, lasted longer. The organization continued meeting with IMU leaders ritualistically until spring 1904, when the leadership became too annoyed to continue in the face of repeated demands from union leaders and routine eruptions of strikes. In fact, the agreement called for a prohibition on strikes and lockouts, but walkouts over pay and hours broke out regularly before the agreement ended. Over the course of four years, leaders from both sides, illustrating various levels of patience, had sought to resolve their differences through negotiations. Yet the meetings became increasingly acrimonious as the two sides found themselves disagreeing over a host of issues, including wages, hours, the number of apprentices employed in shops, the subject of labor saving technology, and the employment of strikebreakers—the most contentious issue of all. Under the leadership of the Minneapolis-based Otis P. Briggs, one of the owners of the sprawling Minneapolis Steel and Machinery Company, the NFA decided to put a formal stop to negotiations following an especially aggressive molders' strike in Utica, New York, in 1904.[49] Briggs, Penton's successor, had come to regret the years of cooperation:

The entire undertaking was a complete failure so far as concerns arriving at any agreement whatever with the Iron Molders' Union—a sad commentary upon the boasted broadmindedness of the union leaders. At the close of these conferences it was plainly

evident that instead of meeting the foundrymen in any spirit of conciliation whatever it was the union's sole purpose to force still more
unreasonable conditions upon them.[50]

Both the NMTA and the NFA had become, in the face of a growing,
more militant labor movement—one that seemed to them to have been
directed by both unmanageable rank-and-file activists and "unreasonable"
leaders—what Clarence E. Bonnett called in 1922 "belligerent" associations.[51] Amid this uptick in working-class combativeness, employers,
unambiguously and passionately asserting their preference for undimin-
ished control, sought to provide their members with helpful services: ship-
ments of strikebreakers during periods of labor unrest, management
consultants, attorneys, and spies. They also circulated joint publications,
including the aptly named *Open Shop*, which began in 1903. Speaking in
1910, Dayton's John Kirby, Jr., who had helped develop one of the nation's
first citywide open-shop organizations ten years earlier, explained that
"these two great National organizations of employers stand as a unit for
the open-shop, and against union dictation in their shops."[52]

Hundreds of metal-working and foundry employers found the era's
upsurge of working-class protests worrisome, joined these self-proclaimed
defense associations, paid their dues, lent a hand in union avoidance campaigns, and spoke favorably to their colleagues about the open-shop principle's emancipatory potential. Started in 1899, the NMTA, the slightly larger
of the two groups, leaped from 423 firms in March 1905 to 523 in March
1906. By March 1907, under the leadership of Cleveland's Walter D. Sayle,
the membership grew to 755. The NFA remained a more modest-sized
group, growing to a peak of 536 in 1903. Its numbers fell in subsequent
years, but the organization remained a formidable outfit committed to solving the labor question in the nation's foundries.[53]

Yet despite Bonnett's claim, few members saw themselves as "belligerents" after declaring their refusal to negotiate with organized labor's representatives. Instead, they viewed themselves as agents of managerial and
technological progress, publicly spirited men eager to help the nation reap
the benefits of industrial improvements and an expanding economy. Biographical sketches reveal that many were respected civic leaders and well-
regarded members of the engineering elite. For instance, one of the

Table 1: NFA and NMTA, 1899–1914: Growth and Consolidation

	NFA firms	Operatives	Average	NMTA firms	Operatives	Average
1899	94	5,500	59			
1900	369	16,646	45	108		
1901	377	20,434	54	125		
1902	494	27,389	55	148	18,524	125
1903	536	27,242	51	220	25,366	115
1904	456	24,281	53	324	28,145	87
1905	456	23,359	51	423	36,844	87
1906	475	23,764	50	523	44,978	86
1907	421	22,295	53	755	65,000	86
1908	419	14,373	34	736	48,460	66
1909	408	18,585	46	718	32,671	46
1910	426	22,039	52	738	50,967	69
1911	454	20,142	44	732	53,669	73
1912	484	23,593	49	733	56,889	78
1913	500	25,930	52	740	64,000	86
1914	484	21,598	45	719	63,808	89
Average			50			84

Source: Howell J. Harris, "Research Note": https://docs.google.com/document/d/1dipyO77UdrOk27Vhq CSFYHITw7NcpAUoIvsIK4Y1jEg/edit?pli = 1.

NMTA's first presidents, Edwin Reynolds, also served as head of the American Society of Mechanical Engineers (ASME), the preeminent society of professional engineers.[54] Reynolds, the general manager of Milwaukee's sizable and profitable Allis-Chalmers Company, developed the company's popular immobile pumping engines. "All of the large builders," a fellow ASME member explained in 1899, "have adopted Reynolds's pumping engines."[55] He became NMTA president in 1901, and served as one of three chief negotiators responsible for the short-lived Murray Hill Agreement.[56] Equally notable was John E. Sweet, an ASME founder, former Cornell University mechanical engineering professor, and inventor of the Sweet Measuring Machine. In 1879, following his teaching career, Sweet began running the Straight Line Engine Company, a machine shop in Syracuse specializing in gray iron castings. Under Sweet's management, the Straight Line Engine Company received numerous prizes for its impressive castings, including a gold medal at the 1895 Atlanta Exposition. In Syracuse, Sweet headed the NMTA branch and held membership in the NFA.[57]

Reynolds, Sweet, and numerous other engineers most likely hungered for the prestige and financial compensation that resulted from their hard work and technological innovations, and their involvement in employer-led defense organizations indicates their profound desire to help prevent the many types of union troubles—boycotts, organizing campaigns, nettlesome shop floor demands, and strikes—from interfering with their goals. After all, like the NFA's original organizers, they had businesses to run, patents to develop, clubs to visit, and money to make. Yet their active involvement in research and development, combined with their participation in employers' associations, demonstrates their broader commitment to what they most certainly believed benefited the general public.

Some in this growing movement apparently went above and beyond the call of duty, including Henry N. Covell, a well-connected engineer who had attended the original meeting that launched the NMTA. Born in Troy, New York, in 1862, Covell was reportedly a prominent NFA member and, since 1889, superintendent of the large and enormously lucrative Brooklyn-based Lidgerwood Manufacturing Company, a producer of steam engine castings and logging machinery that formed in 1873. A Yale University graduate and former National Guard member, Covell hobnobbed with several economically privileged, intellectually curious, and socially active individuals as a young man; he held memberships in various organizations, including the Brooklyn Engineers Club. He was also involved in the more socially oriented Brooklyn, Hamilton, and Midwood Clubs, where he participated on various entertainment committees. His business and social pursuits naturally brought him into contact with other prominent Brooklynites and occasional outside visitors. Some fellow clubmen joined him as he helped build and lead the NMTA's New York City branch.[58]

Yet Covell did not limit his activities to Brooklyn or Manhattan, and union opponents from outside New York treasured his sociability, community services, foresight, and involvement in the NMTA's formative period. Speaking at the association's 1903 conference in Buffalo, British-born William Lodge, an illustrious engineer himself and president of the Cincinnati-based Lodge and Shipley Company, praised the sacrifices and "brains [Covell put] into the inceptionary work of this Association." Lodge, who was partially responsible for forming the Machine Tool Builders Association in 1902, explained that Covell could have made "thousands of dollars if he had spent the same time in his business" that he spent organizing the NMTA.[59] Here Lodge emphasized Covell's apparent selflessness, noting that he had broader goals than his own financial achievements. Lodge clearly saw Covell as fundamentally duty-bound, compelled to act in order to protect the interests of a virtuous, forward-thinking brotherhood, one that was interrelated by layers of educational, economic, military, and social networks. Indeed, Lodge himself was a core member of this honorable partnership, which was led by, as the NMTA's *Bulletin* declared in 1903, "the wisest heads and the most skillful hands."[60]

One of the movement's "wisest heads" was Ernest F. Du Brul, the NMTA's principal organizer. He often gave stirring speeches, including one at the 1903 ASME convention in Saratoga Springs, New York. Here he spoke shortly after Frederick W. Taylor presented one of his influential talks on "Shop Management" to the group. An observer noted that Du Brul "made a strong plea for the organization of employers."[61] While Taylor spoke methodically, Du Brul talked passionately, insisting that those without an NMTA membership card needed to fill one out immediately and contribute to the employer-led open-shop movement, a campaign designed to transform America's workplaces by helping employers reestablish full control, profitability, and ultimately harmony. Too many workmen, Du Brul and his colleagues realized, had not become, as *The Iron Trade Review* had put it, "successful as employees." Their acts of insubordination, expressed most sharply by demands for exclusive bargaining rights often accompanied by outright rebellion, meant employers needed to take a tough stance. Instead of employing and negotiating with unionized labor, open-shop supporters like Du Brul insisted on the need to secure "free men," individuals who, as Pfahler had explained earlier that year, "prefer to control the sale of their own labor according to its value, rather than at a price fixed by a body of men whose purpose is to create a standard of wages based upon the ability of the incompetent workman."[62] By the time Du Brul gave his talk, NMTA activists had uniformly come to oppose closed shops, which they found costly and burdensome to themselves, and fundamentally unfair to their "free men." How, Du Brul implied, could one talk about "shop management" without first responding to a more profound crisis—the aggressive and utterly unwelcome penetration of trade unions into America's workplaces?

In 1903, the year Du Brul delivered his ASME address, organized labor staged roughly 3,500 work stoppages nationally. The immediate question facing employers from across industries was how best to respond, regain workplace control, and set a moral example for others to follow. In Du

Brul's plainspoken words, "To-day we must take into account a very important factor, and one which did not enter very largely into shop questions until recent years: the factor of unionism." He continued, "Individually the manufacturer cannot oppose the Unions excepting at a tremendous cost, and even if he wins his fight alone he establishes no precedents and he has peace only for a time." Organized manufacturers, Du Brul believed, needed to begin the process of looking to one another for support and thus realize their potential to stop strikes and hence minimize their economic consequences. Du Brul offered three reasons why, in his opinion, holding NMTA membership was necessary: "First, for the purpose of defense. Second, for purposes of educating themselves, their workmen and their foremen." And finally, "From motives of patriotism. In the matter of defense it is self-evident that with the whole power of organized labor concentrated on one individual firm there is much danger to that firm in individual resistance; collective resistance to injustice, however, has never yet failed." A careful observer of economic developments and industrial relations throughout the western world, Du Brul often invoked history and used fear tactics, arguing that if American manufacturers failed to unite against trade unionism, then labor relations would soon resemble the poor state of conditions in England, where "industrial prosperity" was "disappearing" in the face of merciless strikes.[63] Though it is unclear how many engineers Du Brul converted, his influence at this meeting eclipsed that of Taylor's.[64]

It is possible that Du Brul garnered more interest at this gathering than Taylor, whose influence on workplace management has interested multiple generations of scholars, because the open-shop advocate spoke to a problem that concerned practically all manufacturers, not just those interested in adopting scientific management techniques. Indeed, some employers organized their workplaces on Taylor's methods, but plenty of others did not. In the midst of the 1903 strike wave, the open-shop system promised to address the more immediate needs of managers overseeing workforces of various sizes and types. One could not make the same point about Taylor's ideas, even though, as historian Hugh G. J. Aitken claimed, Taylor's methods constituted "an allegedly complete *system* of management."[65] The multifaceted labor problem, experienced intimately and often agonizingly by the nation's manufacturers, united both disciples of Taylor's methods and those with no, or only a passing, interest in his ideas.

Observers of the nascent open-shop movement recognized that Du Brul was a gifted leader and organizer, called "an enthusiast in the employers' association movement" by *The Iron Trade Review* in 1903.[66] Born in 1873, he, like Pfahler, Penton, and Covell, traveled considerable distances and devoted enormous amounts of time to establishing the movement principally by offering talks like the one he delivered in Saratoga Springs. With an undergraduate degree from the University of Notre Dame, where he obtained a classical liberal arts education and played football, and graduate course work under his belt from Johns Hopkins University, where he studied politics and economics under some of the country's most distinguished scholars—including future president Woodrow Wilson—Du Brul became the NMTA's first vice president and commissioner in 1902, impressing his colleagues with his values, educational background, good character, and strong opinions.[67] He was a partner of the Cincinnati-based firm Miller, Du Brul, and Peters Manufacturing Company, a very large plant that specialized in the construction of cigar and cigarette machines, established partially by his father, Napoleon.[68] Napoleon Du Brul's oldest son quickly became an influential leader in what was, at the time, one of the nation's most productive centers of machine tool manufacturing.[69] Ernest F. Du Brul's interest in collective endeavors was likely influenced, at least in part, by his peers, men who created a number of elite organizations during the nineteenth century.[70]

It is noteworthy that Du Brul was a devoted follower of the Catholic faith leading a largely, though hardly exclusively, Protestant membership. In a previous generation, Du Brul's Catholicism would have likely barred him from participating in elite organizations; many Protestants in the 1850s, for example, believed the growing Catholic community in the United States placed their devotion to the Pope above their respect for the nation's republican values. This was certainly not the case half a century later with respect to the open-shop movement. The ambitious Cincinnatian's central involvement in open-shop campaigns, like the participation of Frank, a Jew, demonstrates the movement's cultural and religious pluralism. In short, White Anglo Saxon Protestants (WASPs) hardly commanded total control over the nation's prominent businessmen-led organizations at this time. One's religious beliefs and practices clearly mattered less than one's commitment to a managerial philosophy that called for the full protection of business owners and independent workmen against "union dictation."[71]

Du Brul shared the lessons he learned in northern Indiana, Baltimore, and Cincinnati with manufacturers throughout much of the country, vigorously proselytizing about the open-shop principle's defensive, educational,

Figure 1. Ernest F. Du Brul as a student at Notre Dame University. Courtesy of Notre Dame University archives.

and patriotic virtues. He traveled long distances, lectured on matters related to the political economy, and pressured manufacturers to join the NMTA. He visited factories, gentlemen's clubs, and meetings of professional groups, sharing his deep knowledge of economics, history, and business etiquette. "Probably more than the average manufacturer," *The Iron Trade Review* observed in 1902, "Mr. Du Brul has acquainted himself with the history of industrial and social movements."[72] He was confident, and occasionally even arrogant. Following several trips, Du Brul boasted about the NMTA's righteousness and influence. "We have been tried by the fire," he declared in early 1903, "and found true steel."[73] "When they [trade unionists] tangle up in a fight with this association," he remarked less than a year after addressing the ASME meeting, "they are in for a fight to the finish, and the finish has only been one way, and that is our way."[74]

Certainly nothing helped the movement grow more than effective battles, which involved both the direct breaking of labor protests at the point of production and the use of propaganda to legitimize such actions. Open-shop proponents tended to portray trade union campaigners as incurable troublemakers while almost always insisting that employers and independent workers were innocent victims. But the movement succeeded in minimizing casualties, and spokespersons further illustrated that salaried members of employers' associations, enjoying access to large supplies of nonunion strikebreakers, constituted a consistent source of enormous help. And the grateful and often community-spirited beneficiaries of their mobilizations, excited by the prospects of long-term labor peace, then joined the movement. The lessons embedded in these tedious narratives are unambiguous and rather simple: led by noble warriors, the open-shop movement was fundamentally a force of good against evil.

A few cases illustrate this point. For instance, managers at Columbus, Indiana's Reeves Pulley Company, a wood split pulley manufacturing establishment that occupied over 300,000 square feet, expressed a great amount of indebtedness for the NMTA's services after it helped transform their city from a place plagued by trade union radicalism to a center of labor peace and affluence. How? Faced with labor troubles in 1903, a Reeves manager "went personally to Cincinnati," where he requested Du Brul's assistance. After Du Brul promised help, the manager "immediately made application for membership." The thrilled man, a beneficiary of trainloads of strikebreakers, shared his experiences with fellow manufacturers. "Our labor troubles," he proclaimed to a room full of supporters, "began to subside, and the unions have decided to carry the labor agitation in Columbus no further." Like civic boosters speaking in the aftermath of natural disasters, Reeves, no longer hampered by labor troubles, promised long-term calm and prosperity for manufacturers and community members.[75]

Other victims joined the movement for similar reasons. W. O. Bates of the Joliet, Illinois-based Bates Machine Company, constructors of power-transmitting machinery and the Bates-Corliss Engine, became a dedicated NMTA member, "thanks to the association's successful efforts in the handling" of a strike.[76] In 1904, strikebreakers and guards, dispatched from the NMTA's Cincinnati headquarters, kept Bates's factory, one of Joliet's largest, running consistently during the conflict. The demoralized unionized workforce, confronted by formidable strikebreaking actions, had lost its bargaining power. For several years, the IAM maintained a strong presence in the shop. In 1901, before Bates joined the NMTA, IAM activists forced him to accept a closed union shop, which granted workers the nine-hour day.[77] Now an NMTA member, Bates was emboldened, no longer willing to make costly and inconvenient concessions. Backed by a network of professional union-fighters, he now managed unilaterally, voiding previous agreements that had covered pay rates and hours, a practice that presumably became contagious in this community. Spokespersons were confident of a future free of union-provoked mayhem, proclaiming that "Joliet is today in a position to practically guarantee industrial peace not only to her own manufacturers, but also to future site-seekers." Those who harbored a desire to invest in Joliet had Bates and the NMTA to thank for creating inviting and peaceful business conditions. Like Reeves, Bates and movement spokespersons interpreted successful union breaking as a community accomplishment rather than as a narrow workplace victory.[78]

Not all recruits became members because they heard speeches by organizers or because they contacted activists after reading the movement's voluminous output of antiunion propaganda. Nevertheless, the NMTA played a part in helping such employers caught up in labor troubles. Sometimes "free men," wage earners who rejected unionism, encouraged employers to discover the virtues of the open-shop philosophy. In the South, J. W. Glover, head of the Marietta, Georgia-based Glover Machine Works, the region's foremost maker of locomotives and hoisting engines, joined the NMTA shortly after suffering through what appears to have been an especially debilitating strike. Yet no NMTA organizers engaged in any recruitment campaigns in this part of the nation prior to Glover's conflict.

Nevertheless, in a matter of a few short years, Glover became a regional leader.

An ostensibly timid industrialist who had never before given a public speech, Glover addressed the NMTA annual conference in Cleveland in 1906 about the profound impact the group had on his career and morale after his IAM encounter. Alarmed by the viciousness of the strikers, Glover complained his factory nearly closed down. "I have tried to build up my little business down in a small town in Georgia," he remarked in an exaggeratedly humble fashion, "and the Machinists' Union tackled me last July." Unionists were ruthless, he reported: "they laughed at me like a little chicken." Glover needed assistance—and a renewed sense of confidence—but knew nothing about the NMTA until an unnamed antiunion employee told him about the group in the midst of the conflict. After learning about its vision and services, Glover traveled to the association's Cincinnati headquarters, where he spent hours talking to William Eagan and Robert Wuest, the NMTA's commissioner and secretary respectively, pleading for aid.[79]

Eagan and Wuest agreed to help, ordering nonunionists from two of the association's hardest-working secretaries, Philadelphia's D. H. McPherson, a former NMTA organizer, and New York's Henry C. Hunter, an activist who had mastered the craft of strikebreaking in New York and New Jersey shipyards.[80] The leadership's generosity, combined with the organization's efficient and reliable union-busting services, warmed Glover's heart and transformed him into an open-shop ideologue: "I feel that you gentlemen ought to know what a good work you have done for a poor little devil like me." In reply, the audience, consisting principally of mechanical engineers, proprietary capitalists, and veteran union fighters, broke into laughter.[81]

Glover learned that his largely northern-based comrades were a supportive and amusing bunch. That Glover lived hundreds of miles from the majority of the NMTA's membership did not matter; the NMTA was organized on class and industry rather than geographic lines. The IAM established locals and staged nationwide protests; the NMTA leadership learned that, in order to perform its union fighting effectively, it too needed to maintain chapters in southern cities. It appears that Glover had less self-assurance and fewer acquaintances than his more educated, seemingly more experienced and cosmopolitan Yankee brothers, though he shared their concern over the labor movement's growth and combativeness. More importantly, he shared a willingness to fight and reform his community.

One certainly did not need a Ph.D. in mechanical engineering to hold membership in the NMTA and win battles against trade unions.

Glover had become a dedicated NMTA member, served on committees, and recruited fellow employers in his home state of Georgia. In 1906, he began serving as secretary of the newly formed southern district, based in Atlanta, where he helped build an open-shop presence in the heart of the "New South." No longer intimidated by abusive labor activists, he was now part of a proud alliance enjoying the discretionary power of managing unilaterally. By testifying about the association's help, Glover reinforced the organizing by Du Brul and his successor, Eagan.[82]

The movement's successes continued to multiply in the second part of the decade. According to NMTA secretary Wuest, the association responded to 126 strikes in 1907, winning all but four.[83] Not coincidentally, 1907 was a year of significant growth. Of course, such effective strikebreaking and membership increases occurred in the context of a deep recession. High levels of unemployment meant a larger pool of potential strikebreakers, which certainly assisted the organization's union-breaking operations. In July of that year, Wuest, who had helped place many nonunionists in struck workplaces, reported that "practically all of the strikes called in the shops of our members have failed in their purpose."[84] Victory rates of over 90 percent compelled employers, both organized and independent, to take notice. After triumphant campaigns, numerous employers became eager open-shop advocates, acknowledging that their labor problems could be solved with help from professional antiunionists. Employers like Reeves, Bates, and especially Glover, toughened and educated by their experiences, became collaborators in this national movement because they profited personally from it. They were in awe of the NMTA's strikebreaking operations, thankful to the panoply of participants, and grateful to have managerial hegemony restored, and as members, they too were prepared to engage in further campaigns designed to reform their communities against "union dictation." And Bates, Reeves, Glover, and hundreds of others saved money in the process. According to Cleveland's Sayle, a leader of both the NFA and the NMTA, members paid their union-free workforces "a low average rate of $2.50 per day."[85] The NMTA, effectively using strikebreakers, guards, and management consultants in the interests of its members, had proved itself a central player in the open-shop movement. Writing about the NMTA in 1922, Bonnett observed that "the Association has reduced the combating of strikes to a science." Other historians have more recently referred to its activities as an "art."[86]

"We too must organize": The Movement Spreads

Employers from other sectors of the economy demonstrated equal annoyance with organized labor's activities. And by mid-decade, large numbers from coast to coast had elected to follow the lead of the NMTA and the NFA. Organizers formed both city- and trade-based associations. Some of the more influential groups included the National Association of Manufacturers, the Laundrymen's National Association, the National Association of Employing Lithographers, the National Erectors' Association, the Building Trades Employers' Association (BTEA), and the American Anti-Boycott Association (AABA), led by lawyers determined to use the courts against organized labor's boycott drives and demands for closed shops.[87]

The AABA chief organizer, Bridgeport, Connecticut-based attorney Daniel Davenport, was especially active, pointing out, as he asserted to a room full of employers in 1904 "the duty, the importance, and the necessity of standing firmly for the right of the individual to run his own business." Davenport, known in part for his endorsement of women's suffrage rights, insisted that employers must feel no obligation to succumb to union pressure because the courts had routinely upheld the legality of the open-shop system of management. By providing legal support and by pointing out the significance of decades of judicial backing, Davenport had reminded employers they were far from alone.[88]

But the presence of anti-union laws did little to discourage labor leaders from making what open-shop proponents believed were outlandish demands. And few felt more overwhelmed by such demands than building contractors in places like New York City. Take, for instance, the circumstances surrounding the BTEA's decision to follow in the NMTA's footsteps. Like the NMTA, it spent the twentieth century's first few years bargaining with union leaders. But its members increasingly found the process unnecessarily laborious, frustrating, and ultimately fruitless. In 1903, speaking in front of a crowd of over 700 men, Charles L. Eidlitz, a well-known building architect and NCF leader, pointed to what he considered the repetitiveness of preposterous union demands:

At first you were asked simply to take down the bar from the door. Later the chain was to be taken off. Still later the key must be left on the outside. All these demands and many others were granted. And now, what is asked of you? That the door shall be taken off the hinges and thrown into the street. What will be your answer to this request?[89]

Inspired by his colorful and dramatic analogy, the men in attendance, who, according to its *Bulletin*, had links to "various building trades representing eighty percent of all the building interests of New York," had finally recognized the slippery slope nature of negotiations and thus reached the same conclusions drawn by the NMTA two years earlier: "By a unanimous vote it was determined to solidly unite and stand for the rights of employers to manage their own business."[90]

This same impulse inspired thousands of others to form locally based employers' associations. Defense associations of the sort that Pfahler, Penton, Davenport, Du Brul, and Eidlitz helped build had sprung up in large and small cities throughout the country. By late 1903, Birmingham, Chattanooga, Chicago, Cincinnati, Cleveland, Dayton, Denver, Detroit, Indianapolis, Kansas City, Los Angeles, Louisville, Minneapolis, Omaha, Philadelphia, St. Louis, and Worcester had become movement hubs.[91] And some of these urban-based employers' associations were led by individuals outside the heavy manufacturing and the building trades. The Chicago Employers' Association, for instance, was launched largely by John G. Shedd of department store Marshall Field's in 1902. "Labor is organized," Shedd announced. "We, too, must organize."[92]

There was, from the perspective of Chicago's merchants and manufacturers, a profound sense of urgency. Chicago's participating employers obtained the help of attorney Frederick W. Job, a former member of the Illinois State Board of Arbitration. As ambitious as Penton and Du Brul, Job sent notices to Chicago's employers, explaining the importance of unity in the face of a relentless uptick in strikes, boycotts, and organizing campaigns. His persistent activities bore fruit, resulting in the creation of forty "sub-associations," including the Building Owners' Association, the Laundry Owners' Association, and the Manufacturing Confectioners' Association. All functioned under the umbrella of the larger Chicago Employers' Association. With a growing and increasingly confident membership behind them, Job and Shedd promised to supply struck workplaces with "independent" replacement workers, and they appealed to local politicians, such as Mayor Carter Henry Harrison Jr., to provide police protection. Harrison, once organized labor's ally, honored their request, and in April 1904, more than 1,000 members of Chicago's police force helped strike-breakers travel to struck workplaces. In the period of just a few months, this employers' association, numbering about 1,000 firms by early 1904, had helped give renewed confidence to the city's diverse business community. According to the magazine *World's Work*, "The employer has been educated to appreciate the value of organization."[93]

One of the most powerful, inclusive, and effective groups to support the open-shop principle and spread its underlying message was the NAM. Formed in response to the 1893 depression, the NAM held its initial meeting in 1895 in Cincinnati, where delegates, including future president William McKinley, discussed the necessity of expanding economic development in part by increasing foreign trade. The organization, representing mostly locally controlled, midsized workplaces that employed somewhere between 30 to 50 percent of the nation's manufacturing wage earners, enjoyed a close relationship with the Republican Party. Chroniclers of the NAM's early history have long pointed out that the membership under its first two presidents neither formally discussed, nor took positions on, matters related to the management of labor.[94] Unlike others, it did not develop as a labor-fighting, or union-containing, "defense association."

Yet under the leadership of Indianapolis's David M. Parry, the organization, in response to widespread labor unrest and agitation from recruiters like Du Brul, had established itself as a leading participant in the movement. Parry had clear, class-based reasons to oppose organized labor. Immensely wealthy and well connected, he headed Indianapolis's enormous Parry Manufacturing Company, which built several different types of wagons and employed roughly 2,000 employees, including at least some union sympathizers. According to a historian of Indiana, his towering, capital-intensive workplace was "bigger than the next five biggest carriage factories in the world."[95]

The NAM's anti-union activities officially began in 1902 and involved intensive political lobbying and letter writing directed at policy-makers in Washington, where it ultimately succeeded in blocking the American Federation of Labor-backed proposal for an eight-hour workday on government contracts. Parry and his colleagues, some of whom enjoyed profitable contracts with the U.S. navy, found the prospect of such "class legislation" wholly obnoxious. "The right to say how long men shall work," Parry declared, "is a right which belongs to private agreement between employer and employe, and we deny the justice of government endeavoring to regulate those matters which come within the province of industrial adjustment."[96]

The NAM's aggressive anti-union efforts under Parry's leadership, defended under the banner of protecting personal "rights," should not surprise us in part because Parry himself had confronted several organizing drives orchestrated by Indianapolis's Central Labor Union. In 1901, a union spokesperson, citing low pay, frequent firings, and a generally dispiriting atmosphere, claimed "that conditions there are worse than in any factory in the city." And by August of that year, the union stated that it had the support of 75 percent of the labor force. Insisting that he compensated his men "better" than most employers, Parry dismissed the union's number as simply absurd, doubting that its lead organizer, John Blue, could identify "1 per cent of the men ready to go into a union."[97]

This seems more like wishful thinking on Parry's part than a truly honest appraisal of his workforce's views on the matter. While it may be correct that fewer than 75 percent signed union cards, it is difficult to believe Parry's claim that only 1 percent supported the organizing effort. But Parry wanted observers to believe that he took the high road, insisting that, as a good-hearted American, he did not care if the individual worker joined a labor union, "the Odd Fellows," or "The Presbyterian Church," provided "he does not molest anybody else." That "anybody else" did not merely mean him. Yet as the owner, he felt a responsibility to prevent the creation of a closed shop—a truly nightmarish industrial relations scenario that, in his view, would lead to falling levels of productivity and the growth of an increasingly incompetent labor force. As he explained, "I do not propose to have it run by any labor union or these fakers who never did an honest day's work in their lives." For Parry, unscrupulous outside dissenters and charlatans, rather than grievance-holding workmen, were responsible for triggering the unnecessary controversy. Whatever its source, Parry succeeded, demonstrating his unwillingness to "tolerate [the union's] dictatorial policy."[98]

Less than two years later at the NAM annual conference in New Orleans, Parry forcefully professed that his organization was committed to solving the labor problem nationally by strenuously backing efforts to establish thousands of open-shop workplaces like his own. Here he helped to usher in a period that labor leaders disparagingly called "Parryism."[99] In front of over 200 delegates, including Pfahler and Du Brul, Parry delivered a speech as passionate and as pointed as anything given by Du Brul, insisting that organized labor posed a singular threat to "liberty-loving people" and thus challenged "the whole social, political, and governmental systems of the Nation." He made his points almost selflessly, explaining that the reinvented organization's principal goal was emancipatory, designed to help "thousands of men to shake off the shackles of unionism."[100]

Figures from both sides of the open-shop question immediately understood the significance of the NAM's evolution under Parry's tenure. According to one labor activist, "Trade unionists who imagine that Mr. Parry and his colleagues have merely organized to give pink teas or chowder parties will find that they are sadly misinformed."[101] Employers at this momentous event, reflecting on what they considered onerous contracts, organized labor's unreasonable demands, pushy business agents, and occasional outbreaks of labor turmoil, affectionately greeted this development. Indeed, the fervent responses to Parry's speech in Tulane Hall, which found expression in repeated eruptions of loud applause, indicate that the delegates understood the extent of the problem and saw the possibilities of resolving it. Parry's thunderous declarations gave inspiration to many rank-and-file employers who sincerely cherished his bold and steady leadership. As word spread of the organization's transformation into a confident, union-fighting outfit, hundreds of employers flocked to it. The organization counted 1,900 dues-paying members in 1902; a year later, that number climbed to 2,700.[102] Dayton's Kirby, excited that the NAM had placed union breaking at the center of its program, called Parry "the Abraham Lincoln of the twentieth century."[103]

At first glance, this comparison seems far-fetched. Yet Kirby was apparently dead serious in making it, noting that Parry was one of the most vocal, visible, and determined proponents of the emancipation of independent wage earners and employers from what they viewed as the burdensome reality of closed-shop unionism. Like antebellum slaves, business owners and nonunion workers were, according to his logic, unfairly, even brutally, constrained by the oppressive rules that prevented them from achieving their economic goals and full freedom, which laissez-faire capitalism was supposed to ensure. The movement activists who catapulted Parry to this elevated position clearly saw him as a transformative visionary capable of leading employers away from the morass of union-run corruption and closed-shop oppression.

By invoking Lincoln, Kirby demonstrated consistency with other reformers in this period. Lincoln's strong leadership at a time of an unprecedented national crisis inspired several prominent early twentieth-century figures, including Theodore Roosevelt. As historical sociologist Barry Schwartz notes, "Progressives promoted Lincoln as a model for their era of reform."[104] In the eyes of Kirby, and presumably other employers, Parry, by helping to lead the movement, had reached the conclusion that provocative language and industrial warfare constituted the soundest, and perhaps only, choice in the face of an increasingly rebellious and radical labor movement intolerant of the rights of the "free worker."

The movement took on a new urgency around the time of the NAM's transformation. No longer did organized employers merely complain about what a member of the AFA called in 1897 "the inconveniences inseparable from labor troubles."[105] By 1903, employer activists, led partly by Lincoln-esque visionaries like Parry, viewed the labor problem, expressed most sharply by demands for closed shops, as more than simply "inconvenient." Rather, they warned about the creeping threats of dictation and domination, and argued that the nation's rich diversity of employers—corporate heads, proprietary capitalists, practitioners of scientific management, self-made men, and products of nepotism—had a moral "duty" to fight back. C. W. Post, multimillionaire breakfast cereal mogul, explained the urgency at the NAM historic New Orleans conference. "That duty," Post maintained, "lies toward the innocent children made fatherless by the tyranny of union laborers; toward the wives made widows from the same cause; towards the small tradesmen throughout the country, whose business has been ruined; towards manufacturers whose property has been destroyed."[106]

Du Brul described his "duty" in patriotic terms, declaring that he joined the open-shop movement because it was "a call on my patriotism, just as much as if it were a call to shoulder arms in defense of our country's institutions from any other sort of an attack."[107] The stakes involved were, as Du Brul, Post, Parry, and others made abundantly clear, significantly weightier than their own inconvenient financial struggles. In this spirit, organizers sought to recruit and motivate hundreds more, explaining to them that, together, they had the power to stop the irredeemable forces of immorality and economic destruction by building organizations that publicly prioritized the interests of ordinary people and the nation as a whole over the demands of any particular class. Their statements clearly indicate that they chose to fight unions not because they wanted to limit their employees' rights while maximizing profits, but rather because they felt a moral obligation to defend what they defined as the labor movement's most vulnerable targets: innocent children, widows, small tradesmen, modest-sized business owners, and, above all, "free" workers.

The movement leaders announced that they were especially active in defending nonunionists. Open-shop employers from coast to coast, Parry eagerly told his colleagues in 1904, had finally stepped up and come to the rescue of these "liberty loving people":

> Shop after shop has been opened to the non-union man, and protection has been given him against the sluggers in most of our industrial centers. I believe that fully one thousand manufacturing establishments have, in the last year, abandoned the closed shop and thrown their doors open to workmen without regard to their membership or non-membership in a union.[108]

These victories ignited renewed feelings of confidence and clarity of vision. And there was little public disagreement about the overall soundness of the open-shop system in management circles across the country's diverse industrial landscape. As one unnamed observer explained in *The Iron Trade Review* the following year,

> the "open-shop" idea is becoming very much more prominent in the minds of all manufacturers. They no longer debate the question; they have given up feeling timid over the issue, and when the alternative of the open-shop is placed before them they are ready to make whatever sacrifice is necessary to maintain the open-shop and will not listen to any other method of conducting their business.[109]

Importantly, the movement's primary contribution was not that it was somehow responsible for educating thousands of diverse employers about the magnitude of the problem; in most cases, they were painfully aware of it. Instead, Davenport, Du Brul, Job, Parry, Pfahler, Post, and many others contributed most meaningfully by providing their likeminded colleagues with practical resources, emotional reassurance, and strategic guidance as they charted a new course. They had, essentially, armed their comrades with the confidence and the tools necessary to solve this many-sided problem. And in return, together, they enthusiastically welcomed the development of an advanced stage of employer empowerment. The optimism was immensely contagious.

But what about the NCF, a joint labor-management organization formed in 1900 committed—at least publicly—to trade agreements and peaceful collective bargaining in a spirit of mutual respect? Did its merchants, manufacturers, corporate moguls, and railroad operators—a very prosperous fraternity—abandon closed-shop agreements like so many others? Based on the conclusions reached by generations of scholars, it would appear that it was the least inclined of any association of employers to support the open-shop movement's efforts.[110]

We must resist the temptation to view the NCF businessmen as genuine supporters of organized labor's main, workplace-centered goals in light of both the documentary record and simple common sense. In essence, like other organized businessmen, the NCF employer members believed that union demands for exclusive bargaining rights were unfair to nonunionists and, like all employers, dreaded eruptions of labor militancy. Of course, this class-collaborationist organization hardly spoke with one voice on the issue of the open versus closed shop—its union representatives understandably wanted recognition and collective bargaining rights. But a number of its employer members were unrepentant Parryites, holding overlapping membership in hardcore open-shop associations, including the NFA, the NMTA, and the NAM.[111] Pfahler, for example, was an especially influential open-shop proselytizer. He actually spoke positively about trade unions and defended the employer's right to employ nonunionists. In fact, few of these people publicly said that unions should not exist; yet they still tended to insist that closed shops were un-American, dictatorial, tyrannical, and so on.

But let us consider additional evidence, including the role played by the NCF's full-time secretary and strategist, Ralph M. Easley, who occasionally sought assistance from leaders in the emerging open-shop movement to help suppress strikes. For example, in summer 1902 he secured Du Brul's aid in settling a New York City strike of skilled blacksmiths; Du Brul made the lengthy trip from Cincinnati shortly after becoming NMTA commissioner.[112] The circumstances surrounding Easley's hire are noteworthy: the NCF secretary decided to employ Du Brul a year after the NMTA ceased all formal negotiations with the IAM. Indeed, it is highly difficult to imagine that Easley, who was well-connected in the world of business and had studied labor questions carefully, was somehow unaware of Du Brul's principled and vocal opposition to closed-shop unionism.[113]

Finally, we must ponder the words and actions of the NCF's employers at meetings. Writing about the organization's fall 1903 gathering in Chicago, the journal *World's Work*, for example, described an absolutely polarized atmosphere, noting that "every employer [at the conference] favored the open shop, and every union man opposed it."[114] Furthermore, consider the case of Eidlitz, a leader of both the BTEA and the NCF. Eidlitz apparently felt only mildly reluctant about making a provocative speech in front of mixed company, including the AFL's Samuel Gompers and the United Mine Workers of America's John Mitchell, in late 1903. "Gentlemen," he began, "I have been told to make it funny, but I can't be humorous, for I have something that I am boiling to say." Recognizing the controversial nature of his subject, Eidlitz claimed that "I am speaking my personal views." Less confident and combative than Du Brul or Parry, Eidlitz nevertheless went on: "when organized labor interferes with the rights of a free white man over twenty-one who lives in this country something must be done, and I hope the Civic Federation is going to do it." As an NCF member, perhaps Eidlitz appreciated organized labor's campaigns against child labor, but he believed that the same forces were misguided to interfere with the rights of nonunion white adults. Echoing Du Brul, Parry, and Post, Eidlitz called on fellow employers to offer them protection. In essence, he wanted the businessmen in the room, many of whom had experienced their own rather unpleasant brushes with strikes and boycotts, to acknowledge what growing numbers had already concluded: that the open-shop principle constituted a progressive and just solution that promised to protect the individual rights of employers, workers, and Americans generally. How did the crowd respond? Rather favorably, according to a report in the *Building Trades Employers' Association Bulletin*: "There was a sharp buzz of comment when Mr. Eidlitz sat down. He got considerable applause, and there were one or two cries of 'You're right'!"[115]

"For the Protection of the Common People": Citizens, Progressives, and "Free Workers"

> American public opinion is more liable to be with the underdog. In other words, it is more apt to sympathize with the demands of organized labor than with the demands of organized capital, because of an indefinable feeling that capitalists are able to take care of themselves, while labor is less able to do so. For this reason the employers' associations usually make studious and intelligent efforts to so regulate their conduct as to inspire the sympathy and assistance of public opinion as reflected by the Citizens' Alliance.
>
> —J. C. Craig, *Proceedings of the Second Annual Convention of the Citizens' Industrial Association of America*, 1904

Although the open-shop movement was led chiefly by employers with recognizable financial and managerial interests, numerous others from outside industrial relations settings played their own important roles in strengthening it. This chapter describes the multiple ways well-known reformers in the areas of higher education, journalism, law, politics, and religion, combined with nonunion workers, assisted management by embracing policies, joining organizations, and making statements that promoted what they considered the open-shop principle's virtues. Together, broad coalitions of citizens, led by employers, sought to illustrate that this principle was fundamentally fair to Americans as a whole, rather than simply serving the interests of the elite. What follows below is a series of biographical sketches and case studies, beginning with the 1902 anthracite coal strike and its immediate aftermath, that highlight efforts to convince the general public of the open-shop principle's evenhanded, class-neutral, and reformist character.

The Square Deal?

The 1902 anthracite coal mine strike, an enormous protest that dragged on for more than five months and involved as many as 147,000 demonstrators in northeastern Pennsylvania, was undoubtedly one of American history's most significant labor-management confrontations. Protestors, represented by the United Mine Workers of America (UMWA), harbored numerous grievances—low pay, irregular work schedules, long workday hours, and the inability to bargain collectively. They demanded a 20 percent wage increase, an eight-hour workday, and closed shops. The region's mightiest railroad and coal companies, embroiled in this conflict, flatly refused these demands. They were especially unwilling to recognize the UMWA as the miners' exclusive bargaining unit. As attorney Clarence Darrow, who represented the UMWA during the conflict, explained, the owners were motivated by more than a desire to save money and maintain existing work hours; fundamentally, the showdown was based on "a question of mastery—nothing else; because they felt and they believed that upon this contest depended the question of whether they should be the masters or whether the men should be the masters."[1]

The coal company employers were accustomed to winning strikes, but they typically had to battle for their victories. Consider the words of the Philadelphia and Reading Coal and Iron Company president, George Baer, whose workplaces were affected by this, and previous, strikes. In 1901, he claimed that labor conflicts always have "and, perhaps, always will result in the 'survival of the fittest'."[2] During the 1902 strike, Baer, who served as a spokesperson for a number of the besieged mine managers and owners, including J. P. Morgan, remained confident that his side, by effectively employing strikebreakers and guards while ensuring class solidarity, would, yet again, demonstrate that it was indeed the country's economically fittest. The coal miners, Baer arrogantly wrote in 1902, "will be protected and cared for—not by labor agitators, but by the Christian gentlemen to whom God has given control of the property rights of the country."[3]

As the disruptive, increasingly violent, and seemingly intractable conflict continued into the fall, reformers took notice. The *(Kansas City) Independent*, annoyed by both sides, contended that "the public interest in this
and similar struggles is paramount to that of either employers or workmen." Above all, the newspaper argued, the public needed "to protect itself
against either or both parties to the controversy."[4] It maintained that ordinary people, particularly consumers, were hurt by both the strikers' actions
and "the stubborn Baer and his associates."[5]

Not all commentators faulted both sides. And few captured the strike's
sense of drama better than muckraker Ray Stannard Baker, whose somewhat probing and lengthy article about the conflict was published in
McClure's, a widely circulated magazine popular with a middle-class readership. Baker was one of *McClure's* most prolific writers, and he established
a reputation for himself partially by writing "The Right to Work"—a
decades-old slogan that some employers and their allies had used as an
attempt to personalize the plight of non-strikers, individuals who faced
organized labor's unforgiving wrath on picket lines.[6] Rather than draw
attention to northeastern Pennsylvania's widespread poverty, stark class
divisions, the repressive coal mine police, or the undiluted arrogance articulated by Social Darwinists like Baer, Baker's fourteen-page article—which
appeared in print shortly after the strike's conclusion—focused on the ways
nonunion men, numbering approximately 17,000, faced what Baker called
the multiple "tragedies of the great coal strike."[7] Baker depicted cases of
unrelenting viciousness, describing how strikers verbally and physically
abused strikebreakers. He offered many anecdotes, allowing the nonunionists to speak for themselves; such victims faced multiple horrors, including
aggressive attacks against themselves, their homes, and their families. He
discovered that the nonunion workmen were loyal to their employers,
proudly independent, lawful, and patriotic. Baker sincerely believed that
these humble sufferers, who "did not believe in the strike," needed protection from union activists.[8]

Baker, whose article added a layer of legitimacy to the burgeoning open-
shop movement, was not the only well-known figure concerned with protecting the rights of nonunionists in and around the tumultuous coalfields.
President Theodore Roosevelt, distressed by picketers' interference with
nonunionists and fearing the devastating consequences of a prolonged
strike involving the winter fuel supply, was determined to end the strife.
After all, major cities relied on anthracite coal as a heating source. There

was, from Roosevelt's perspective, a profound sense of urgency, and like others before him, he could have opted to mobilize federal troops to break the protest. Instead of following the examples of earlier presidents like Rutherford B. Hayes or Grover Cleveland, executives who had dispatched armed forces against railroad strikers in 1877 and 1894 respectively and thus played a critical part in ensuring that the affected capitalists were, in the context of these disputes, "the fittest," Roosevelt plotted a significantly more diplomatic path, one that considered the workers' grievances, the owners' interests, and the public's overall well-being.[9] Roosevelt and his administration reached out to J. P. Morgan—who owned most of the coal mines affected by the strike—and oversaw the establishment of a commission, which was designed to put pressure on both the union and management, including the cantankerous Baer, to resolve the conflict amicably.[10] Roosevelt's intervention, historian Perry Blatz notes, marked "the first time in American history" the federal government responded evenhandedly to a private sector labor-management conflict.[11] Impressed by Roosevelt's willingness to get the warring sides to find common ground, the UMWA's John Mitchell, a leading member of the class-collaborationist National Civic Federation (NCF), called off the strike in mid-October. He had come to believe that the seven-person body, consisting of Judge George Gray, General John M. Wilson, E. W. Parker, Thomas H. Watkins, Bishop John L. Spalding, Carroll D. Wright, and E. E. Clark of the Order of Railway Conductors—a union with a long history of opposing strikes—would resolve the issues fairly.[12]

Several high-profile reformers, including Boston-based attorney Louis D. Brandeis, sought to help the commission—led by Gray, a former U.S. senator, corporate lawyer, and millionaire from Delaware—reach a mutually acceptable settlement. Brandeis was certainly no stranger to the labor question. More than twenty-five years earlier, while in Louisville in the summer of 1877, the recent Harvard University law school graduate joined a businessmen-led volunteer militia, carried a rifle, and helped guard the city's railroad property from hordes of ill-tempered striking Louisville and Nashville Railroad employees and their pugnacious supporters.[13] But Brandeis felt no need to arm himself during his trip to northeastern Pennsylvania. In fact, he expressed sympathy with the region's working classes, and believed the protestors deserved improved conditions, increases in pay, and greater overall respect from the operators. Visiting the region in December, Brandeis pointed out that coal miners' work schedules were often irregular, complaining to Darrow that "one of the great evils from which the employees suffer is the lack of continuous occupation."[14] Brandeis insisted that the employers had the financial resources to employ workers for additional weeks at higher rates, but he stopped short of calling for them to officially recognize the UMWA as the exclusive bargaining unit. Yet Gray's commission refused to listen to Brandeis's suggestions, prompting him to leave northeastern Pennsylvania disappointed.[15]

The commission held a series of meetings and interviewed hundreds of strikers, strikebreakers, and witnesses. Commissioners also read reports, including Baker's sensational essay about the strikers' confrontational picket-line conduct. Gray was especially agitated by this particular article. After reading it and listening to testimony from over 100 nonunionists, Gray berated Mitchell for refusing to expel any of the "mob" participants, for failing to denounce "these evident misdeeds," and for Mitchell's unwillingness to promote "law and order."[16] Gray, selectively criticizing striker violence while ignoring the brutality of mine guards, told the *New York Times* five years after the conflict that he had truly wanted to "find an alternative to violence and the strong hand."[17]

Gray was not alone, and he and his colleagues participated in many contentious and polarizing gatherings throughout the winter months. The result of these meetings, according to most contemporary and historical accounts, was a genuinely fair resolution, which the commission issued on March 21, 1903. Both sides, not just Baer's, claimed victory—a noteworthy departure from previous labor-management conflicts. While workers won a 10 percent wage increase and a nine-hour day, operators were under no obligation to formally recognize the UMWA as the workers' exclusive bargaining agent—and they did not.[18] The commission, insisting that "the rights and privileges of non-union men are as sacred to them as the rights and privileges of unionists," framed its refusal to grant a closed shop in the language of America's virtuous presidential past: "Abraham Lincoln said, 'No man is good enough to govern another man without that other's consent.' This is as true in trade unions as elsewhere."[19] Roosevelt shared this sentiment and called the agreement the "Square Deal," proclaiming that it constituted a victory for everyone, including consumers, unionists, coal operators, nonunion workmen, and strikebreakers.[20] Nonunionists, the commissioners proudly declared, had "the right to remain at work where others have ceased to work, or to engage anew in work which others have abandoned."[21] This statement, legitimizing the democratic right of nonunionists to refuse to succumb to union pressure, was perfectly consistent with the position demanded by the owners, embraced by the nation's judiciary, and unreservedly championed by the planners of the budding open-shop drive. Importantly, Roosevelt had given his full blessings to the open-shop principle.

Employers in the vanguard of the emerging open-shop movement responded to Roosevelt's endorsement with undisguised enthusiasm. In 1905, emboldened employers began publishing a monthly magazine named after it, and intellectuals and activists from various employers' associations wrote articles for the *Square Deal*, "a magazine devoted to industrial peace," which was edited by novelist and Union-side Civil War veteran Wilson Vance. James Van Cleave, manager of St. Louis's Buck's Stove and Range Company and one time National Association of Manufacturers president, announced in 1907 that the settlement offered a clear template of how to properly settle "all future labor difficulties."[22] More than almost any other figure, Roosevelt, by agreeing that the open-shop principle was, above all, morally sound and impartial, rather than underlining its economic advantages for management, gave organized employers and their allies decades of powerful ammunition in their public relations campaigns against an increasingly embittered, closed shop-demanding labor movement.[23] Employers keenly embraced Roosevelt's Square Deal, and they invoked it repeatedly to build a highly inclusive, flexible, often liberal-sounding, and lasting open-shop movement publicly committed to safeguarding the rights of nonunion workers and business owners. Increasingly, organized employers and their allies distanced themselves publicly from the class-dominant ideas embedded in Social Darwinism while embracing the class-neutral-sounding Square Deal.

Roosevelt actually provided the public-relations-conscious employers' inspiration on more than one occasion. In late 1903, the president, building on the model created by the Gray-led commission, brought his open-shop advocacy to the public sector Government Printing Office, where he reinstated William A. Miller, a nonunion bookbinder who had lost his job in the face of union pressure.[24] Upholding a culture of solidarity, printers in this office practiced a "no union card, no work" rule. Roosevelt and his assistant in the Department of Labor and Commerce, George B. Cortelyou, an NCF member, apparently cared little about whether government printers held a union card, and decided to reinstate Miller over the union's strong objections. This act of rehiring, Roosevelt insisted, was fundamentally moral and just. In his autobiography, Roosevelt reflected on the controversy, insisting that "the non-unionist like the unionist, must be protected in all his legal rights by the full weight and power of the law."[25] His open-shop advocacy, framed in the language of inclusion and fairness, represented a blow to unionized printers and to the labor movement in general. And unionists, unsurprisingly, responded bitterly. The Cigar Makers' International Union's J. M. Barnes called the president's intervention a "slap in the face."[26]

While Roosevelt disillusioned and disappointed labor activists, organized employers were, unsurprisingly, elated by his actions. In October 1903, Ernest F. Du Brul, the energetic National Metal Trades Association organizer, responded to Roosevelt's involvement in the Miller controversy by campaigning for similar open-shop rules in Cincinnati, his hometown. Speaking about one of the chief goals of the recently formed Cincinnati Employers' Association, whose open-shop agenda mirrored that of the NMTA, the National Founders' Association, and the NAM, Du Brul announced, "The members [of the employers' association] are determined to wipe out the discrimination on public work in Cincinnati the same as President Roosevelt has done in Washington." Flying the flag of civic reform, Du Brul found organized labor's impact on public services as obnoxious as its involvement in impeding the productivity of factories and foundries: "we expect to put boycotting completely out of business, and see to it that public utilities are not tied up by strikes."[27] Here Du Brul, like Roosevelt, presented himself as a concerned, antidiscriminatory citizen, championing the interests of nonunionists and the larger public's rights over organized labor's supposedly selfish interests.

Others were equally inspired by Roosevelt's moral convictions in the face of labor union pressure. In nearby Dayton, the National Cash Register Company's John H. Patterson, an influential welfare capitalist and NCF member, noted in 1905 that Roosevelt's support "stamped him as a man and a courageous American citizen of the highest type." According to Patterson, Roosevelt's "sense of justice and his regard for the law have caused him to take a firm stand for the open-shop."[28] As Du Brul and Patterson presented matters, concerned employers' association activists and upstanding citizens leading the federal government, not labor unionists, were the nation's genuine reformers. Capitalizing on Roosevelt's policies and rhetoric, employers sought to illustrate that they were the foremost public-spirited men who selflessly attempted to implement the president's policies into their own communities and workplaces. The enthusiasm expressed by

Van Cleave, Du Brul, Patterson, and others underlines the importance of both the Square Deal and the Miller decision, which, according to a 1905 article in *North American Review*, gave "a strong impetus to the open-shop movement."[29]

Indeed, the industrial relations involvement of Roosevelt and the Gray commission, combined with Baker's journalistic contributions, helped align the open-shop system of management with traditions cherished by many Americans, including respect for individual rights, fairness, and policies designed to uphold law and order and peace. Moreover, the roles played by these and growing numbers of other high-profile academics, journalists, lawyers, clergymen, and politicians brought the controversy over open versus closed shops to larger audiences, giving renewed meaning to the labor question. Such figures effectively drew attention to, and helped build sympathy for, the plight of nonunionists, insisting that they, more than union members, constituted society's true underdogs.

Securing support from Roosevelt, Baker, Gray, and numerous other influential figures is precisely what open-shop employers desired. Employer activists aggressively sought allies from both within and outside industrial relations settings. Outside observers, after all, had the ability to reinforce the employers' position and thus provide this managerial system with a veneer of respectability. Improving public relations was critical, and employers embraced two basic strategies to win greater support for the open-shop philosophy in Roosevelt's America. The first approach was organizational. In addition to building associations made up exclusively of employers, they formed hundreds of reformist-sounding, inclusive, and supposedly class-neutral citizens' associations. Furthermore, employers helped promote the establishment of organizations of nonunion workers; such associations promoted the righteousness of the open-shop policy from below, demonstrating that the movement was not built or led exclusively by merchants, manufacturers, coal operators, or railroad owners.

Second, employers and their supporters ambitiously approached members from the general public, including distinguished figures, in an attempt to make this management system more palatable. Recognizing the importance of securing allies from politics, higher education, journalism, and the broad reform community, employers and their allies mailed millions of journals, pamphlets, and books about the moral superiority of the open-shop principle to journalists, academics, university presidents, teachers, clergymen, and fellow employers.[30] In some cases, their direct mail campaigns included reprinted articles, including Baker's "The Right to Work."[31] Additionally, employers invited community supporters to address meetings of open-shop activists. The results of the employers' multipronged public relations efforts were impressive. By the mid-1910s, numerous figures from across the political spectrum had concluded that the open-shop principle was fairer to workers than closed-shop unionism, the most efficient way to run businesses, and in many cases an expression of American patriotism. Moreover, influential public figures, as Roosevelt's Square Deal demonstrates, helped magnify the reformist, rather than the repressive, character of the open-shop principle. Together, employers and reformers used language and supported policies designed to promote workplace harmony in terms favorable to themselves and nonunion wage earners while proclaiming a desire to de-escalate class conflict. Some even denied the existence of class divisions. As a NAM member put it in 1914, "We have no classes in our country."[32]

Organized employers had reasons to cheer Roosevelt's involvement in both settling the anthracite coal strike and in reinstating Miller. Like Roosevelt, employers in the emerging open-shop movement spoke the language of reform. But they had much catching up to do in the early twentieth century, when organized labor, strengthened by the support of clusters of middle-class liberals, had long positioned itself as a leading carrier of the banner of progressivism.[33] Indeed, organized employers remained continuously fearful of the prospect of growing forces on their left, which found expression at the point of production, in voting booths, and in the press. Politically, they saw the nation threatened by pro-union activists who sought to move the country leftward. In fact, several politicians had proposed various forms of what open-shop supporters derided as "class legislation."[34] Some such legislation, typically advanced at the state level, was comparatively mild, designed to protect women and children from long hours and unsafe working conditions. Such reforms generally enjoyed support from both within and outside labor union circles. Other proposals called for fewer hours and an end to court injunctions against strikers.[35] Employers felt most uneasy by the threat of protests from below, fearing their economic and social impacts, especially the radical ideas that these movements helped generate. Could open-shop employers successfully compete with the cacophony of calls for working-class solidarity or the growing popularity of, say, socialism?[36] Could they offer attractive alternatives to organized labor's decades-old insistence, amplified persistently by the

Industrial Workers of the World, that "an injury to one is an injury to all"? They tried, and in the process found others willing to champion the virtues of individual hard work and labor-management harmony while criticizing instances of labor solidarity and outbreaks of working-class militancy. Open-shop proponents were clearly determined to play a meaningful role in shaping the very character of the era itself, in part by methodically steering public opinion against what the NAM's David M. Parry called in 1904 "the closed shop and other Socialistic schemes."[37]

Open-shop employers realized that effective framing and information dissemination were important years before Baker, Roosevelt, or the Gray commission defended nonunionists' "right to work" and therefore helped inspire the movement. Beginning in the late nineteenth century, they went to great lengths to illustrate that their managerial activities were not at all based on their narrow class interests as employers. Publicly, they seldom insisted that they wanted open shops because this management system was, say, the most cost-effective and profitable way to run businesses. Nor did they draw attention to their own power and privilege relative to the working classes. Instead, they sought to demonstrate that the critical divisions in society were not between hostile classes, but rather between individual employees and monopoly-imposing unionists and between law-abiding Americans and criminality. Simply put, the open-shop movement was not, they argued, against unions. Indeed, in 1901, the two-year-old NMTA passed a resolution prohibiting "the word 'non-union' in all official documents." Instead, the association's leadership required that rank-and-filers use the words "free men" and "free shops" when describing nonunionists and open-shop workplaces.[38] The underlying message was clear enough: open shops were nondiscriminatory, allowing both unionists and "free men" equal access to employment. According to this logic, open-shop workplaces protected workers' individualism, allowing them to refuse pressures to join monopoly-imposing labor unions.

The Citizens' Industrial Association of America

Acknowledging the need to tighten relationships between employers and nonemployers, as well as recognizing the importance of gaining greater respect for themselves and for "free workers," open-shop proponents formed new, reformist-sounding organizations, including city-based citizens' associations and the national Citizens' Industrial Association of America (CIAA), during the early twentieth century. Proposed by Kansas City employers in early 1903 and led by Parry—the Lincolnesque figure who helped transform the NAM into an open-shop-crusading powerhouse—the CIAA opened its membership to a multi-class and multi-occupational assortment of figures: doctors, professors, lawyers, judges, religious leaders, fellow employers, and even nonunion workers. "Let us not array class against class," remarked the Reverend William J. H. Boetcker, a Presbyterian minister and movement organizer from Shelbyville, Indiana, at the CIAA inaugural conference in Chicago.[39]

Yet the CIAA was not led by a cross-class partnership of employers and "free workers." Seasoned employer activists, a somewhat insular fraternity with shared managerial interests, served in most leadership positions, and the fourteen figures Parry tapped to help direct it included a number of the nation's most visible union fighters: Denver's J. C. Craig, Detroit's E. M. McCleary, Brooklyn's J. T. Hoile, Cincinnati's Du Brul, Dayton's John Kirby, Jr., Chicago's Frederick W. Job, Battle Creek, Michigan's Charles Post, New York's Berkley R. Merwin, Kansas City's Philip R. Toll, Minneapolis's J. L. Record, Wilkes-Barre, Pennsylvania's W. C. Shepherd, and Evansville, Indiana's Albert C. Rosencranz, a Civil War veteran who had fought in the famous battle of Chickamauga and for ten months languished in a Confederate prison.[40] The mostly northern and midwestern coalition also included two Confederate veterans, James Van Cleave of St. Louis and N. F. Thompson of Birmingham, who had battled under the command of Confederate general, former slave trader, and Ku Klux Klan leader Nathan Bedford Forrest.[41] As a Louisville member noted in 1904, "the South contended with the North to divide the nation, now it will fight with you side by side against the common foe to our industrial liberty!"[42] Decades after the Civil War, open-shop activists from both sides of the Mason-Dixon Line had mostly put their old partisan views aside, recognizing the importance of a new, though, in their collective view, equally momentous struggle. Under Parry's leadership, the old Confederates, by joining their one time foes, had begun to prioritize class and national, over regional, unity, echoing the decades-old Republican call for "free labor."

Parry's association was neither the first nor the last to use the word "citizen" in its title. The emergence and authority of various urban-based citizens' associations in places like Chicago, Denver, New York, Minneapolis, St. Louis, and Cincinnati, as well as in the coal regions of Colorado and northeastern Pennsylvania, were quite notable by the time of the inaugural CIAA conference in 1903.[43] Consisting of coal mine operators, merchants, manufacturers, bankers, and an assortment of mostly white, Protestant elites, these groups typically began during the second part of the nineteenth century in an effort to fight what members considered entrenched, urban-based political problems, including expressions of corruption emanating largely from machine politicians and the working class, the often property-less constituency that helped elect immigrant mayors. Traditionally, such organizations maintained rather strict membership requirements, partici-pated in various types of locally based lobbying activities, and often, though certainly not always, expressed themselves in nativist ways against the immigrant working classes. The membership of such groups, viewing them-selves as natural civic leaders, typically believed that municipal government must be run by professionals rather than by fortunate electoral victors. Some even called for suffrage restrictions, and many were deeply commit-ted to fighting what members of New York City's elite often referred to as "the dangerous classes." Some formed militias for this purpose.[44]

Members of Parry's association shared much with those active in earlier organizations, including anxiety related to the labor movement's tendency to engage in economically damaging, even riotous, activities. And the CIAA membership included business owners from these former campaigns. Yet the CIAA advertised itself as a respectable, inclusive, multi-class populist organization, rather than a refined and elitist group of snobbish business-men.[45] Parry and his colleagues wanted Americans to see them as authentic partners with the nation's workforce, not hostile rivals engaged in a class struggle for workplace or community control. The organization proclaimed its willingness to bridge class divisions, extending an open hand to the nation's millions of mostly nonunionists. Consider the CIAA's stationery letterhead: "For the protection of the common people." Rather than an anti-democratic organization, its stated purpose, printed on every official letter, was to safeguard the rights of ordinary people, including small shop owners and nonunion "free workers." Such language certainly represented a departure from the self-important and callous rhetoric articulated by cut-throat capitalists like Baer.[46] Publicly, these men had chosen benevolence over belligerency.

The close to 300 manufacturers, commercial club members, self-identified reformers, and citizens' alliance activists who arrived in Chicago in late October 1903 initially lacked a name. Wilbur F. Sanders, a Civil War veteran, Montana pioneer, former Republican senator, and leader of the recently formed Citizens' Alliance of Helena, proposed "Citizens' Industrial Association of America." Sanders, who had earned his reputation as a crusading vigilante lawyer against western gold thieves and murderers in the 1860s—Lew L. Callaway, a chronicler of these Wild West days, referred to him as the "chief counsel for the people"—won the delegates' unanimous approval: the name "was finally adopted without a dissenting vote."[47] Decades later, the sixty-nine-year-old veteran law-and-order campaigner and frontier savior sought to continue a struggle against opponents as equally menacing as the West's most notorious criminals. And the delegates clearly respected one of Montana's first two U.S. senators and likely appreciated his impressive background, which, in addition to helping tame parts of the Wild West, included extensive legal activities on behalf of the gigantic Northern Pacific Railroad between 1880 and 1890, and senatorial service alongside Democrat Gray (the two former railroad lawyers had served together on the seven-person Committee on Patents) in the early 1890s. Indeed, the famous Republican's participation in patriotic Civil War battles in Tennessee, his take-no-prisoners approach to western lawbreakers, and his criticisms of alleged acts of Democratic Party corruption in Montana during the 1890s suggested that he was fully prepared to help protect "the common people" in Roosevelt's America.[48]

Sanders was certainly no stranger to the labor question. Labor unrest repeatedly erupted in parts of Montana, and few of the region's residents could ignore the dramatic mine and railroad struggles that broke out in the 1890s.[49] Sanders, a staunch Republican intimately allied with the region's copper mining and railroad industries, predictably took the capitalists' side, and in 1897 he denounced union activists as "worthless characters."[50] In the face of repeated labor conflicts, he became a leading member of the open-shop Citizens' Alliance of Helena, which, according to its 1903 founding document, organized "in defense of Labor, from which it would remove all shackles." Helena's citizens' alliance, like similar associations, was "opposed to boycotts, to lockouts, to strikes, and to all conspiracies concocted with a view to invade the rights and privileges of American Citizens."[51] The organization, like the CIAA, presented itself as an undistorted patriotic outfit committed to assisting, not hurting, the rights of wage earners.

Sanders demonstrated a willingness to help a number of different underdogs. He served as a defense lawyer for a member of the Blackfoot Confederacy convicted of murder in 1879 and, in the 1890s, represented members of the Chinese community, a group that had repeatedly faced organized labor's wrath.[52] Growing numbers of western-based white unionists, arguing that Chinese residents were responsible for driving down wages, repeatedly lashed out at both Chinese laborers and small business owners in several Montana communities. In 1896 and 1897, an extensive coalition of Butte's unions, including locals representing brewers, carpenters, miners, and molders, organized a citywide boycott of Chinese and Japanese restaurants and laundries. Suffering financially as a result, dozens of these immigrants sought legal protections against the boycott and compensation for their financial losses—$500,000 in lost income in their estimation. In 1898, they secured Sanders's help, who represented them in the U.S. Ninth Circuit Court. Here the complainants discussed the boycott's crippling economic consequences, as well as the ways unionists mistreated both Asian business owners and their customers. Sanders reported that "three or four hundred" demonstrators, backed by walking delegates—the boycott enforcers—apparently stood in front of restaurants, harassing and discouraging potential customers from entering.[53] Speaking in court, Chinese-born Hum Fay, owner of the Palace Chop House, testified that union activists harassed his customers "day by day." As a result, business, he complained, "got so bad." Fay and members of his community desperately craved what he called "protection."[54] Sanders helped them win the case by securing an injunction against the protestors who, in his words, "willfully and maliciously combined, conspired, and confederated together" to destroy numerous businesses.[55]

Sanders was one of the numerous defenders of "free" workers, business owners, and, more generally, "the common people," who helped shape the CIAA's orientation. In order to respond properly and effectively to irksome and often destructive trade unionists, delegates at the CIAA's first conference took on a number of tasks. The most dedicated members joined committees, which focused on matters important to practically all voluntary organizations, including credentials, rules and orders of business, resolutions, constitution, dues, nominations, and the press. Most CIAA leaders served on at least one committee.

One of the CIAA's most noteworthy and influential subgroups was the three-member press committee, which included Chicago's Job, Parry's personal secretary John Maxwell, and a twenty-seven-year-old Kansas City newspaperman named George Creel. Creel first established a name for himself as a muckraker who had exposed a series of police scandals, first in

Figure 2. Wilbur F. Sanders in Butte, Montana (ca. 1890). Courtesy of the Montana Historical Society.

Kansas City and later in Denver. Given his background, it made sense that he served on the CIAA's press committee; Creel started his career as a newspaper reporter in 1894, and five years later purchased his own paper, the *(Kansas City) Independent*, which he owned and edited until 1908. Throughout the early twentieth century, Creel also served as Kansas City coal inspector, supported suffrage rights for women, advocated public ownership of utilities, and strongly opposed child labor, insisting that it, as he and his co-authors explained in 1914, is a "fundamental evil."[56] As a reporter, Creel had also criticized coal mine employers like Baer for stubbornly refusing to consider the larger public's interests during the 1902 coal strike. Given his moral sensitivity and muckraking zeal, Creel demonstrated that he certainly did not fit the image of the arrogant and pitiless labor-fighting capitalist. The tent the CIAA built was designed to be large enough to accommodate people like Creel, and by 1904, 247 employers' associations, impressed with the efforts of Sanders, Creel, Parry, and many others, had affiliated with the organization.[57]

In fact, one of the CIAA's central goals was to bring as many people as possible under this large, and expanding, tent—and to shape public opinion. As owner and editor of the *Independent*, Creel, like the handful of other newspaper-owning open-shop proponents, enjoyed certain advantages.[58] His newspaper routinely carried articles sympathetic to the struggles of employers, and from April 1903 to March 1904, it served as the official mouthpiece of the Kansas City Employers' Association, "Devoted to the Interest of Employer and Independent Employee." Using the *Independent* to disseminate its views, this CIAA-affiliated association promised to challenge those who sought to advance "the interests of any class against the other."[59]

National employers' association magazines occasionally reprinted and disseminated essays from Creel's paper. For example, in 1905, the *Open Shop* reprinted an essay by Hugh O'Neal about a successful union-cleansing campaign led by an Australian ship owner. O'Neal's story highlights the ways the owner, Malcolm Donald McEacharn, patiently waited out a strike of difficult unionists "led by," according to O'Neal, "asses." McEacharn had previously surrendered to union demands, but eventually decided the costs of negotiating exceeded the benefits of managing unilaterally. After ten weeks of picket line protests, "starvation," O'Neal reported, "won easily," and "the once great trades union [sic] of Australia were counted out." Many of the men eventually returned to work as individuals, leaving McEacharn unshackled by the bane of closed-shop unionism.[60] By printing this story, Creel and the open-shop leadership sought to demonstrate that American employers were not the only victims of nagging labor problems. Yet O'Neal's account was principally meant to inspire, illustrating an example of a distant "common" man's unmistakable triumph over union adversity.

Roughly a decade after he helped shape the CIAA's orientation, Creel became famous internationally as the primary architect of the Committee on Public Information, the name of President Woodrow Wilson's comprehensive propaganda campaign, which was designed to win public support for America's unprecedented military intervention in World War I. The wartime strategies that Creel employed were hardly new, and it is fair to say that his involvement in open-shop associations like the CIAA and the Kansas City Employers' Association helped him master propaganda disseminating techniques that Wilson later found useful as they both attempted to "make the world safe for democracy."[61]

Creel and his colleagues gathered in Chicago more than a decade before World War I partially because they wanted to build a sturdy organization that, according to the first of the CIAA's eight objectives, assisted, "by all lawful and practical means, the properly constituted authorities of the State and Nation in maintaining and defending the supremacy of the law and rights of the citizen." The men demanded "industrial peace" and sought to "create and direct a public sentiment in opposition to all forms of violence, coercion and intimidation." Unsurprisingly, the delegates proclaimed their support for "individual enterprise and freedom in management of industry, under which the people of the United States have made this the most successful and powerful nation of the world." In order to build and sustain such sentiment explicitly connecting the open-shop principle to American patriotism, the CIAA established a "Bureau of Education for the publication and distribution tending to foster the objects of the organization."[62] Reaching a broad public with messages that linked the open-shop system to justice, industrial efficiency, American patriotism, and protection of the underdog was critical in a context in which union activists challenged thousands of employers. Denver's Craig explained in 1904 that "It might almost be said that public sentiment is the most important factor in the settlement of all such [workplace] controversies."[63]

These activists, like NCF-affiliated businessmen, sought to demonstrate their progressive credentials by distinguishing themselves from the numerous cold-hearted employers who, over the years, had demonstrated little or no interest in the welfare of their wage earners. Such seemingly heartless figures ostensibly overworked their employees, cared about nothing but profit maximization, and frequently went into combat mode when confronted with shop floor grievances. Take, for instance, the words of Van Cleave, whose speech at the CIAA 1906 convention appeared Rooseveltian in its pledge to fairness: "As we all know, there are autocratic and oppressive employers. Judging by many of their acts they seem to believe that the relations between capital and labor are like those between belligerents in war." Though relatively small in number, in Van Cleave's estimation, this population was "numerous enough, however, to reflect discredit and to inflict injury on the entire guild of employers."[64] Though he refrained from identifying names, Van Cleave may have had in mind figures like Baer, individuals who, through their callous words, authoritarian actions, and managerial shortsightedness, created a poor image of businessmen as a whole. Whatever the case, Van Cleave sought to distance the CIAA from these "oppressive employers," believing that a small number of bad apples ultimately hurt the reputation of reasonable and magnanimous merchants and manufacturers. The CIAA, building on the open-shop movement's work generally, sought to chart a new course, one designed to establish trust with the general public and the working class by promoting what Van Cleave called "peaceable relations between employers and employed."[65] This was, quite clearly, the language of reform. After all, what forward-thinking social reformer or industrial modernizer was uninterested in establishing lasting "peaceable relations"?

The same year that Van Cleave called for establishing "peaceable relations" between employers and wage earners, the CIAA went on the record supporting laws and practices that reduced child labor "abuses." Its support appeared sincere and was hardly tepid; the membership announced approval for "every lawful and proper means for correcting these abuses either in the way of the education and enlightenment of public opinion, the enforcement of existing laws, or the passage and wise and humane enforcement of such additional laws as may be necessary and adequate to bring about a change in existing conditions." Finally, the organization called for punishing "the real offender, whoever he may be, employer or parent, or both."[66]

And on the question of organized labor, the CIAA, on paper, did not appear especially antiunion. It, like the NCF, as well as the NMTA and the NFA in their early years, defended responsible and lawful unionism, recognizing "the free right of workmen to combine." The CIAA's stated purpose was not to eliminate unions altogether. Workers nevertheless needed to understand, the organization held, that labor and management shared the same interests. Strikes, after all, had injurious impacts on employees, managers, and most of all, the general population. Unions had no reason to challenge employers because, as the CIAA put it in 1903, "our welfare is inseparable from theirs and theirs from ours; we are essentially interdependent, each is indispensably necessary to the other; and those who stir up strife between us are enemies of mankind."[67]

The CIAA's respect for, and willingness to unconditionally defend, mankind was on full display beginning in 1905 when the organization, showing its high regard for Roosevelt's famous involvement in settling the 1902 anthracite coal strike, began publishing the *Square Deal*, a monthly magazine that featured accounts of organized labor's excesses, fables and poems stressing the open-shop principle's moral soundness, and articles showcasing various court cases legitimizing the plight of "free" workers.[68] Contributors came from a wide-section of society. University-based economists offered hardheaded reasons why the open-shop system was the most rational, efficient and fair form of management while Protestant, Catholic, and Jewish spokespersons penned essays on the alleged impiety of closed shops.[69] Such impiety was rooted in the supposed corruption and brutal tendencies of union leaders, figures who went to great lengths, including using violence, to establish their supposedly selfish demands over the rights of nonunionists. The open-shop movement, the *Square Deal* habitually claimed, was concerned with tackling this problem from multiple angles. As J. Laurence Laughlin, the prominent University of Chicago economist, Roosevelt's former Harvard University professor, and one of the Federal Reserve Act's authors, explained in 1914, arguments against closed-shop unionism are "legally, economically, and morally overwhelming."[70]

In this spirit, the CIAA argued that closed shops resembled a new, and equally brutal form of slavery. The *Square Deal*'s pages contained numerous articles calculated to alarm readers about the supposedly deceitful, lawless, and thuggish labor leaders who frequently forced "free" men to join unions, pay dues, and follow their presumably loathsome and economically destructive dictates. And those who resisted were unfairly punished by these merciless and barbaric leaders. The cover page of the first issue of the *Square Deal* in 1905 set the tone; it featured a dramatic cartoon depicting a chained nonunion man receiving a whipping by an overbearing union business agent. The caption read, "Will the white slave have a Lincoln?"[71]

A Movement from Below?

There was hope. In fact, open-shop campaigners, unlike those active in earlier citizens' associations, sought to partner with ordinary, law-abiding Americans, including the "white slaves." These supposedly brutalized slaves had become active, paradoxically, in their own emancipatory, anti-union associations. In other words, independent workers, like late antebellum black slaves, had agency and were unafraid to actively champion the virtues of free labor in the face of hostile oppressors. Organized groups of "free workers" emerged in urban areas at roughly the same time that employers' associations began systematically cleansing their workplaces of union activists. In 1902, Albany's Rev. E. M. Fairchild, for example, proclaimed his commitment to helping closed-shop victims establish a "National League of Independent Workmen of America." The workers involved in the league would, in Fairchild's words, "demand that employers run their shops as 'open shops'."[72] Meanwhile, coercive labor activists in Dayton, home of open-shop leader Kirby, prompted nonunionists to form the Modern Order of Bees, a workingmen's group that challenged, according to a 1903 article in the NMTA's *Bulletin*, "the influence of the law-breakers and the intimidators."[73] And in early 1903, Elmira, New York, began hosting the first chapter of the Independent Labor League of America (ILLA), "organized by workingmen for the maintenance of their rights to personal liberty." These organizations, apparently built from below with management's enthusiastic approval, were chiefly concerned with promoting "good character" and showing, as Dayton's Modern Order of Bees put it in 1902, that "both employer and employee will recognize the fact that their interests are identical."[74] The underlying message was clear enough: the common people, both the employed and employers overseeing various-sized businesses, had shared interests and goals in promoting a more respectful and peaceful industrial relations system.

These organizations emerged with the assistance of open-shop employers and their middle-class allies. Consider the case of Fairchild, an Albany clergyman and published sociologist who first developed sympathy for nonunion workers during the course of an Albany streetcar strike in 1901.[75] He was appalled by the widespread violence that the strike generated, and afterward decided to deepen his knowledge of the causes, characteristics, and consequences of labor-management struggles. The next year, he, like Baker and Brandeis, visited northeastern Pennsylvania, where he spent ten days observing coercive tactics staged by UMWA members. He took his study seriously, reading books and articles about the labor question, conducting interviews with those embroiled in industrial unrest, and photographing strike scenes. He believed that his profession gave him a certain amount of credibility that employers simply lacked. "The very fact that I am a clergyman, and not an employer," he remarked in 1903, "has made it possible for me to get an understanding of this labor problem from the workman's point of view."[76]

While conducting fieldwork, the Oberlin College-educated Fairchild, like Baker, encountered numerous workers who rejected their union leaders' values and policies. Over the course of the century's first years, the clergyman talked with dozens of Pennsylvania coal miners, Albany streetcar workers, and southwestern New York machinists, who apparently valued hard work, appreciated their managers, respected the law, and sought a degree of upward mobility—values and goals often rejected by labor activists. Such individuals, he discovered, were often profoundly uncomfortable with some of the decisions of their union leaders. This was especially clear among ambitious and talented mechanics at Elmira's Payne Engineering and Foundry Company, a modest-sized manufacturer of iron and brass castings owned by N. B. Payne, an NMTA leader. Numerous mechanics here supported the company's premium system of payment—a system that rewarded individual workers with financial bonuses for increased productivity.[77] The International Association of Machinists, which had maintained a presence in the Payne Company, opposed this incentive plan, and called a strike shortly after management implemented it. But not all left their workstations: "Some twenty of Mr. Payne's best machinists refused to strike, and were immediately insulted as 'scabs'," Fairchild reported.[78] In the face of this struggle, which also involved union-initiated violence, these non-striking men demanded, and ultimately created, a new organization.

Fairchild and Elmira's "free men" celebrated the establishment of the ILLA on March 19, 1903. The organization's principal aim was perfectly consistent with the open-shop movement's goals: "To protect workmen in their independence."[79] The extent of Fairchild's involvement in the formation of this organization is difficult to measure, though we do know that the clergyman had established relationships with some of the antiunion workers before the strike. Whatever the case, union activists lampooned this organization and others like it. Writing in late 1903, a member of the Amalgamated Association of Iron and Steel Workers declared that "one can almost see the wage earners of this country falling over each other in an attempt to become members of this wonderful organization in order to obtain a reduction in wages or increased hours of labor."[80]

Despite sardonic comments from union activists, this supposedly bottom-up movement quickly gained momentum. Shortly after its formation in Elmira, "free workers" created other branches, and besieged employers approached these organizations during strikes for employment purposes. ILLA branches became highly useful to employers' associations embroiled in numerous workplace showdowns. For instance, during a Brooklyn shipyard strike in June 1903, Henry C. Hunter, secretary of New

York City's Metal Trades Association, was happy to employ league members as strikebreakers. Hunter, a talented strikebreaking architect, was enormously pleased that it "has a branch in New York and undertakes to supply competent men."[81] Some manufacturers contacted league chapters to obtain "free men" before launching new workplaces. Consider the words of an unnamed Ohio employer writing in 1903: "Our reason for writing to you is that we desire to employ members of the Independent Labor League of America in a large new foundry which we are ready to start."[82] The league essentially served as a reserve army of potential strikebreakers, delighting open-shop enthusiasts and labor-hungry supervisors alike. And this movement continued to grow after Roosevelt announced his Square Deal. By the end of 1903, six cities—Albany, Boston, Detroit, Elmira, New York City, and Sherman, Texas—hosted chapters. League branches reinforced the efforts of the CIAA, emboldened "free workers," and sent a powerful message demonstrating that the open-shop movement was more than a top-down campaign led exclusively by the moneyed elite.[83]

"Gratifying results of the employers' movement"

Clearly, by establishing the CIAA and collaborating with groups of non-union workers, organized employers demonstrated a willingness to confront the labor problem by aligning with wide sections of American society, including those who sought to play a central part in their own liberation from closed shops. Such an inclusive movement, they realized, needed to be class-neutral—or, at the very least, promote workplace harmony in the spirit of Roosevelt's Square Deal. Speaking at the CIAA's second annual conference in 1904, Kirby explained the logic:

> any movement which may be inaugurated by and confined within that class [of employers] will naturally be looked upon by the great public as a class movement in which outsiders have but little if any interest, and, therefore, public sentiment, the great factor, and the only factor, through which the evils can be entirely eradicated will be lacking.[84]

In other words, the CIAA set out to build the broadest coalition possible, one that secured the trust and backing of ordinary people, as well as leading thinkers and policy-makers.

The movement's broadness, involving management, employees, and members from the general public, led to a number of tangible successes. By the end of 1904, roughly 1,200 employers throughout the nation, encouraged by a liberating industrial relations climate in the wake of Roosevelt's Square Deal and in the context of the emergence of the CIAA and hundreds of local employers' associations, had proudly abandoned collective bargaining and had begun to manage unilaterally, rewarding hardworking individuals while punishing demanding unionists. "These results," according to a 1905 article about the CIAA's work by Edward H. Davis, "were largely brought about by the agitation incident to the Citizens' Industrial movement."[85] Speaking in late 1904, an upbeat Parry, extremely pleased with these victories, attributed the movement's effectiveness partly to the crucial roles played by those outside industrial relations settings:

> One of the most gratifying results of the employers' movement has been the remarkable change it has wrought in public opinion. In many parts of the country, several years ago, the employer was forced to surrender to all kinds of demands from the walking delegates or else incur the obloquy of the community. Not so now. He finds he receives a ready hearing, and if he is in the right he has but little trouble in obtaining the moral support of the public.[86]

According to this firebrand, public opinion, more than old-fashioned judicial intervention or police repression, was the most important factor that led to the emancipation of nonunionists, the growth of open-shop workplaces, and greater industrial peace. Parts of the general public in Roosevelt's America had apparently come to value the open-shop campaign's defense of individual rights for both management and workers. This public, consisting of individuals from all classes, favored moderation over the labor movement's call for working-class unity, militancy, and closed-shop exclusivity agreements.

The CIAA's reputation, built in the shadow of Roosevelt's open-shop advocacy, reached the attention of the most influential chroniclers of progressivism by decade's end. Take the role played by William Dwight Porter Bliss, a high-profile Christian socialist. Bliss's 1909 edition of *The New Encyclopedia of Social Reform*, the most authoritative account of the era's leading reformers and major social movements, contained an entirely uncritical write-up about the CIAA by Vance, *The Square Deal's* editor and thus far from an impartial figure.[87] Apparently, Bliss, who once held membership in the Knights of Labor, found nothing objectionable about the group's inclusion in his volume, which also contained a favorable entry on the open-shop principle itself. The CIAA, according to this source, had grown to include "between 400 and 500" separate employers' and citizens' associations and was responsible for reducing "the undesirable conditions established by the Labor Trust."[88] Bliss was apparently unconcerned that the CIAA and the open-shop movement generally valued individual rights over the labor movement's multi-decade calls for working-class solidarity. Open-shop employers certainly had reason to celebrate what appeared to be the triumph of individualism.

Intellectuals and the Open-Shop Question

Growing support for the open-shop principle found expression outside industrial relations and governmental settings with great frequency in Roosevelt's America. We can discern the ways in which certain open-shop arguments, articulated most pointedly by Roosevelt and organized employers, found supporters among those in the mainstream of reform movements. Some of these figures had ties to employers who were active in groups like the NCF and the CIAA. Others had no formal affiliation with employers' associations, though they nevertheless found the open-shop system morally, and occasionally economically, superior to closed shops. Whatever the case, it is clear that workplace management questions had begun to concern growing numbers of distinguished opinion makers outside workplaces.

Professors and university presidents, targets of employers' direct mail campaigns, played their own part in helping to legitimize the open-shop principle. Prominent individuals included Harvard University's Charles Eliot, Columbia University's Nicholas Murray Butler, Syracuse University's John Day, Worcester Polytechnic Institute's Ira N. Hollis, and Tuskegee Institute's Booker T. Washington. And in 1909, Princeton University's head and future president, Woodrow Wilson—who had served as one of Du Brul's political science professors at Johns Hopkins University seventeen years earlier—identified himself as "a fierce partisan of the Open Shop and everything that makes for individual liberty."[89] These figures, typically hailing from the same privileged-class positions as those in the open-shop movement's vanguard, denounced what they considered organized labor's excesses, addressed meetings hosted by employers' associations, and befriended union-fighting employers. Some held membership in open-shop organizations.[90]

Eliot, a higher education trendsetter whose administrative impact was felt on campuses throughout the nation, was especially critical.[91] An active NCF member, Eliot presumably felt an obligation to comment on, and influence, non-scholarly events outside Harvard's exclusive gates and to offer a platform within those gates to fellow open-shop proselytizers. And like Roosevelt, he gained national attention for his vocal support for the numerous emancipatory struggles waged by employers and "free workers" during labor conflicts, including some that predate the open-shop movement's formal emergence. In the midst of the 1877 railroad strike, for example, Eliot helped prepare the Harvard College riflemen for a possible confrontation with protestors, though that conflict did not spread to New England.[92] And in 1896, shortly before the open-shop movement's official launch, Eliot referred to "scabs" as a "good type of American hero." At the time, the Harvard president received little notice, but in 1902, when he repeated this claim before a gathering at the Boston Economic Club, labor leaders like the American Federation of Labor's Samuel Gompers took notice. So did the NAM, which republished his address in *American Industries* in late 1902.[93]

By calling strikebreakers "American heroes," Eliot sought to elevate the status of nonunionists, giving them an even more honorable identity than the labels "free men" or "common people," designated by organizations like the NMTA and the CIAA respectively. And while the Harvard president periodically addressed labor unions and talked to individual union leaders as an NCF member, he believed that closed shops were fundamentally regressive, places where unionists put their own interests ahead of those of the larger community. "The labor union monopolies," he stated in 1904, "are really much more threatening social and industrial evils than the capitalistic monopolies."[94]

Echoing his colleagues in the open-shop movement leadership, Eliot was no stranger to the language of reform. Employers were not, in Eliot's judgment, blameless in the context of labor-management disputes. Reiterating the CIAA's Van Cleave, he occasionally condemned what he believed were the supposed excesses of each side. Addressing a room full of veteran union fighters at the NFA's 1908 conference, he called for "a little more good will between the employer and the employe."[95] For Eliot, like Van

Cleave and the NFA's William H. Pfahler, changes in attitude, rather than structural modifications, were enough to reduce industrial strife and to reestablish kindness across classes. Like others, Eliot sounded moderate and sensible, believing that mutually satisfactory conditions would result from good-faith discussions between fair-minded employers and levelheaded, "free" workers.

During his presidency, Eliot welcomed to Harvard those on the front lines in the fight against the "social and industrial evils" caused by "labor union monopolies." For instance, in February 1905, Fairchild addressed the community with a lecture entitled "Photographic Studies of Riot and Violence During Strikes." The talk, open to the general public and presented by one of the nation's most visible champions of bottom-up open-shop organizing, illustrated the ways in which the "evils" of "labor monopolies" found expression in practice. Few individuals were better suited to reinforce Eliot's position that strikebreakers were, in fact, heroes than Fairchild, an educator who helped the public appreciate the common people's collective struggles against aggressive unionists.[96]

Some public intellectuals, reinforcing the language of Roosevelt, Baker, Fairchild, Eliot, and the CIAA, engaged with the open-shop question in their scholarship. Consider the case of pragmatist and reformer John Dewey. In an intellectually weighty 1908 book entitled *Ethics*, Dewey was to some extent undecided: "If a union is working for a morally valuable end, e.g., a certain standard of living which is morally desirable, and if this were threatened by the admission of non-union men, the closed shop would seem to be justified." But while he and his co-writer, philosopher James Tufts, imagined instances in which closed-shop conditions should prevail for moral reasons, he never ruled out scenarios in which open-shop policies may be preferable, particularly since he, like other reformers, held the view that unionists were often guilty of adopting "selfish" principles. These authors were clearly more ambivalent about this question than Baker, Roosevelt, and most employers.

Like all open-shop advocates, Dewey and Tufts were clearly sympathetic to the plight of peaceable nonunionists, "the common people." Their contribution to discussions about the labor problem was significant largely because they linked closed shops to religious bigotry and racial discrimination. In particular, they compared the discriminatory nature of closed shops to the religious intolerance of the Puritans and to the racism of anti-Chinese unionists and working-class rioters in the West: "The maxim 'This is a white man's country' is a similar 'closed shop' utterance."[97] According to this logic, unionists who demanded workplace-wide collective bargaining rights suffered from the same sort of narrow-mindedness that afflicted seventeenth-century Protestants and nineteenth-century nativists. And indeed, their defense of the Chinese placed them close to Sanders, the former Montana senator who, ten years earlier, had successfully defended this particular group of "common people."[98]

Louis D. Brandeis and "The Open-Shop with Honey"

One can identify additional echoes of Roosevelt's Square Deal and employers' defense of nonunionists by exploring the activities of Brandeis, who made a sincere attempt at workplace problem solving shortly after the conclusion of the great 1902 anthracite coal strike. Writing in 1905, Brandeis expressed appreciation for the UMWA's conduct during that conflict, maintaining that it was "so wisely led by John Mitchell"—the anti-socialist union leader who terminated the strike before the commission granted its award.[99] An iconic reformer, Brandeis had insisted that the coal executives needed to offer pay raises to coal miners in 1902. This son of a businessman, however, is perhaps best known for his critique of finance capital and for supporting reforms designed to ease the burdens on child and female laborers. He earned much attention as the architect behind the Supreme Court's famous 1908 *Muller v. Oregon* case. Here he helped popularize, though certainly not pioneer, the paternalistic view that women, unlike men, required special workplace protections, an analysis that had become widespread by the early part of the century.[100]

Moral sensitivity about supposed gender differences explains Brandeis's motivations with respect to *Muller v. Oregon*. That he received considerable sums of money from wealthy clients, including open-shop employers, helps us understand his motivations in other situations. According to historian Philippa Strum, Brandeis was "a master at impressing clients and making money."[101] In the years after Roosevelt announced his Square Deal, this meant securing injunctions for Boston-based employers' associations, including those with CIAA ties, faced with labor troubles. The *Boston Globe* reported in 1905 that Brandeis dutifully worked as "the attorney for employers or employers' associations in nearly all [of Boston's] big injunction and other legal proceedings against labor organizations."[102] By mid-decade, Brandeis, who offered legal representation to several open-shop groups, including the Boston Typothetae, the Boston Cloak Manufacturers' Association, the National Cigar Leaf Tobacco Association, and the Western Shoe Manufacturers' Alliance, helped arrange a number of meetings between striking union supporters and employers. His aim: that each side work out differences in a spirit of collegiality and respect. In essence, Brandeis helped get opposing sides to talk to one another in an effort to minimize the employers' financial and managerial hardships while restoring order.

For instance, during a weavers' strike at the Cochrane Manufacturing Company of Malden, Massachusetts, in summer 1906, Brandeis wrote to his friend J. Eugene Cochrane, the owner, proposing that he meet with his workforce, numbering about 80 spinners and weavers, to discuss ways of resolving their differences and ending the disturbance. While Brandeis appeared sincerely interested in helping the two sides, he stubbornly insisted that they do so "without reference to the question of union recognition."[103] A majority of protestors were union supporters, demanding that Cochrane recognize their organization and bargain collectively over issues like pay and hours. Yet Brandeis recommended that Cochrane essentially follow other employers, also "common people," by flatly refusing to accept a closed-shop agreement. Brandeis clearly remained unwilling to advocate a managerial position that fell outside the acceptable parameters outlined by Roosevelt's Square Deal and trumpeted loudly and recurrently by open-shop employers.

Half a decade and hundreds of strikes and lockouts later, Brandeis continued to express an unqualified faith in the open-shop principle. As late as 1909–10, during a series of massive, multi-workplace garment strikes in New York City staged by the International Ladies Garment Workers Union (ILGWU), Brandeis, who served as a high-profile mediator during the conflict, claimed that he "would have nothing to do with any settlement of the strike involving the closed shop. That I did not believe in it, and that I thought it was un-American and unfair to both sides."[104] Here his language differs little from that of organized employers, many of whom, including members of various citizens' alliances, flew the American flag high as they attacked protestors and denounced closed shops. Brandeis believed that open-shop conditions were entirely sound, protecting the liberties of employers and the rights of meritorious unionists and nonunionists alike. The closed shop, on the other hand, was wholly immoral, fundamentally incompatible with his vision of the country's allegedly glorious political traditions, which extended from the founders to the early twentieth century. This, of course, did not mean that employers could not sit down with members of organized labor to discuss issues of mutual concern. After all, Gray's coal strike commission demonstrated the viability of both meeting with union leaders and imposing open-shop conditions on those who demanded genuine collective bargaining rights.

While Brandeis, reiterating dozens of employers' and citizens' associations, unambiguously registered his disdain for closed shops, he eventually proposed a compromise, which he famously dubbed "the Preferential Shop." Under the preferential shop, the city's garment employers, overseeing roughly 400 workplaces, agreed to voluntarily hire and bargain with unions, but they were entirely free to hire nonunionists, as well. Responding to working-class protests, Brandeis pressured the garment employers, insisting that they give preference to unionized workers "where the union men were equal in efficiency to any non-union applicants."[105] The ILGWU pledged its willingness to provide the employers with efficient and subordinate workers. "The Preferential Shop," a patriotic Brandeis proclaimed in 1910, "seems to offer a solution consistent with American spirit and traditions as well as with justice and with the necessity of strengthening the Unions."[106]

Brandeis's preferential shop became a central component of the famous Protocol of Peace, a joint labor-management agreement that ended the nine-week strike by creating a system of conciliation and arbitration that was supposed to benefit both employers and workers. Employers profited in large part because the protocol, which historian Milton Derber called "a milestone" in industrial relations, outlawed strikes; workers in turn won pay increases and workplace improvements.[107] And both sides earned the opportunity to submit grievances to an ostensibly impartial board of arbitration. Yet sizable numbers of activists and their supporters, including socialists, were mostly unimpressed, condemning the preferential shop, as "the open-shop with honey."[108] Needless to say, they did not see it as "strengthening the unions."

In February 1911, shortly after helping to settle most of the strikes, Brandeis spoke at the National Cloak and Suit Buyers' Association's dinner at New York's prestigious Waldorf Hotel. During his presentation, the skilled lawyer, reinforcing the sentiment of open-shop advocates like Van Cleave and Eliot, criticized both labor and capital. "The Recent strike," he admitted, "was caused by grave abuses in many factories." At first, he reinforced many union activists as he listed the problems of "unsanitary conditions, excessive hours of work, low wages, and unfair treatment of the employes." Of course, he assured his audience, these acts of misconduct could be fixed without compromising the employers' authoritative position as managers. He concluded by offering comforting words to the "many" benevolent employers, mostly proprietary capitalists, who apparently suffered unfairly throughout the conflict: "there were many manufacturers who were absolutely innocent of the causes which led up to the strike. But what good did it do them? It rained alike on the just and the unjust."[109] In Brandeis's judgment, these manufacturers were not in the least bit exploitative or unfair, but irresponsible protesters nevertheless targeted them. In his view, these business owners were "common people" too, and they deserved the opportunity to run their businesses without confronting pressure from hordes of ill-mannered unionists. Yet Brandeis was mostly content: conditions had presumably improved, and the famous attorney and his friends from the garment industry looked forward to years of order and prosperity.

Brandeis's "preferential shop" represented a gain for union supporters. But in practice, it was only somewhat different from the classical open-shop method because employers remained in control of hiring, firing, and practically all areas of management. Unionists had a say in some matters, but employers could—and did—ignore them. The chief factor that employers had to consider when hiring employees was their level of "efficiency." Given that many employers believed that trade unionists were, by definition, less efficient than "free" workers, they continued to hire significant numbers of nonunionists.[110] And indeed, small numbers of wage earners and their middle-class supporters had established groups like the ILLA eight years earlier as a supposedly more proficient and loyal organization than traditional collective bargaining unions. Without closed-shop exclusivity agreements, employers were perfectly within their rights to fire or hire whomever they wanted, including strikebreakers on the payroll of employers' associations or independent strikebreaking agencies. Julius Henry Cohen, the lawyer who assisted the city's garment manufacturers during the strikes, later explained that managers were "free to discharge the incompetent, the insubordinate, the inefficient, those unsuited to the shop or those unfaithful to their obligations."[111] In fact, controversies over issues of hiring and firing sharply divided unions and management, ultimately resulting in the Protocol of Peace's collapse in mid-decade. Neither side could agree on precisely how to interpret Brandeis's preferential shop system. Tensions peaked in 1916 when a group of employers locked out over 20,000 workers, effectively abandoning their commitment to union-management cooperation. In response, tens of thousands of additional wage earners, valuing the principle of solidarity, left work and picketed on the streets.[112]

Like the vast majority of employers from different industries, the garment manufacturers wanted the complete flexibility to hire and fire unilaterally. The traditional open-shop system ultimately prevailed, which industry representative Henry Gordon called in 1915 the "natural and rational relationship between employer and employee."[113] These employers, claiming in 1916 "the right to be masters in our own business houses," followed the paths created by the NMTA and the NFA more than a decade earlier. Garment manufacturing employers, like those from the metal and foundry industries, were most content proclaiming their allegiance to the unvarnished open-shop system.[114]

If we take him at his word, Brandeis opposed closed shops because he, like the employers who paid him a handsome salary, apparently prioritized the interests of hardworking individuals over the union's demands. Basically, he used much of the same language that organized employers adopted when justifying the open-shop principle, claiming in 1904 to support a system in which "the powers of the individual employee may be developed to the utmost."[115] This is a rather standard comment made by various figures from at least the 1850s on: hard-working employees would apparently receive perks and promotions from their fair-minded employers. Who determined what constituted proficient workmanship? Answer: the employers. Like Roosevelt, an assortment of CIAA members, and most independent employers, Brandeis showed no tolerance for expressions of working-class militancy; he championed the rights of "responsible" trade unionists, but also thought that it was prudent to listen to, and protect, the "rights" of nonunionists, strikebreakers, and, of course, the "benevolent" manufacturers—in essence, a variety of "common people."

By the time World War I broke out, numerous figures, by embracing the open-shop principle, had helped give the employer-led struggle a progressive, class-blind identity. In a very short period, the open-shop movement had moved from the margins of the metal-working, foundry, construction, coal, and printing industries to the mainstream of the nation's reform community. The establishment of groups like the CIAA and the ILLA, combined with outside supporters in journalism, higher education, politics, religion, and law, showed that the movement was hardly a fringe campaign led by a handful of combative and dictatorial business-men simply interested in driving down wages to maximize their own power and profits. As I have illustrated, clusters of reformers played their own important roles in addressing the labor problem by helping to develop the creativity, flexibility, evenhandedness, and legality of the open-shop princi-ple while pointing out what they saw as the exclusivity, unjustness, and even slave-like conditions of closed shops. The development of the concepts of the Square Deal and the preferential shop, for example, reveal that lead-ing reformers like Roosevelt and Brandeis promoted the creation of open shops designed to appeal to employers, nonunionists, and even "responsi-ble" union members. Growing numbers of figures from across the political spectrum, including both members and nonmembers of employers' and citizens' associations, found little objectionable about the movement's con-cern with safeguarding the rights of business owners and nonunion, "free" workers while promoting law and order. Employers, by disseminating open-shop information, by invoking the ideas of politicians like Lincoln and Roosevelt, and by creating progressive-sounding organizations, includ-ing citizens' associations and "independent" labor leagues, had shown a desire to convince those outside the factory gates and coalfields to consider the ethical, social, and historical, not merely the industrial, dimensions of the open-shop question. The individuals behind these multidimensional crusades, backed by the federal government's power, repeatedly emphasized that they, unlike an earlier generation of employers, were motivated by a high standard of ethics, justice, and patriotism. They proclaimed a desire, in short, to protect the "common people." Open-shop proponents, not those favoring "class legislation" or closed shops, enjoyed rhetorical and organizational influence as they declared their preferences for fairness and inclusion, both on the shop floor and in society generally.

PART II

Region

Chapter 3

A Tale of Two Men: Class Traitors
and Strikebreaking in Cleveland

Which side are you on?

—Florence Reese, 1931

Many of the nation's business owners, labor activists, and students of the labor question generally had their eyes on Cleveland in 1900. Tensions had been mounting inside the city's foundries, climaxing in a workplace action that pitted hundreds of molders against their bosses. In July, workers at seventeen foundries struck because the employers declined to grant them a promised 10 percent wage increase and refused to reduce the workday by 10 percent. Six months later, members of the Iron Molders' Union (IMU) Local 218 remained on strike, demanding "living wages." The strike was a major test for both the IMU and the National Founders' Association (NFA), the two-and-a-half-year-old organization that represented most of the city's foundry operators. The NFA sent representatives, including John A. Penton, its Detroit-based secretary, to help the besieged industrialists. Penton spent months in Cleveland counseling employers about strategy as unionists demonstrated and attempted to prevent nonunionists from crossing picket lines.[1]

More than a dozen employers, representing modest-sized foundries, and hundreds of molders were impacted. Workers received help from the IMU leadership, and employers looked to each other for assistance. Penton and Jay P. Dawley, a Cleveland-based management-side labor lawyer, also assisted employers as they sought to resume production. Penton placed workmen willing to take the jobs of strikers in foundries; Dawley secured court injunctions against protesters. Penton was also the publisher of the *Foundry*, a nationally circulated trade journal, and he mentioned his involvement in the quarrel in its pages in September: "in the matter of procuring men, very satisfactory progress is being made; much more so, in fact, than was reasonably anticipated."[2] Penton and Dawley each worked with the NFA nationally and the Cleveland Employers' Association, a multi-industry organization formed in spring 1900, locally. Both were strong open-shop proponents, holding the legally accepted view that employers must enjoy the right to employ whomever they wanted irrespective of union status. As members of open-shop associations, they considered workers who sought to impose union restrictions on workplaces selfish, dangerous, lawless, un-American, a threat to industrial progress, and a menace to the rights of nonunionists.

This chapter investigates the lives of these two men, showing their decisive involvement in open-shop drives and exploring the ways they connected anti-union ideas to broader reform efforts. I explore their backgrounds both before and after the 1900–1901 strike. This chapter has two main purposes. First, it shows the key roles played by non-employers in the employer-led open-shop drive. National and local employers' associations' secretaries, including Penton, were critical in building and sustaining the movement: they recruited employers, kept scrupulous membership lists, and secured strikebreakers during emergencies. As a publisher, Penton wrote glowingly about employers' associations and their progress in campaigns against trade union "lawlessness." Lawyers, including Dawley, were also vital; they fought numerous courtroom battles, routinely invoking nineteenth-century laws to show the illegality of "combinations of labor." In courtrooms and print, they regularly stressed the importance of laws that protected private property and prohibited collective acts by workers that impeded interstate trade, management rights, and nonunionists' "right to work." Indeed, both argued passionately that wage earners had a lawful right to reject unionism and labor in peace in open shops.

My second purpose is to highlight expressions of apostasy. Ten years before the molders' strike, Penton was, by all appearances, a devoted labor unionist. He was president of the International Brotherhood of Machinery Molders, an IMU rival before the two groups merged in 1893. For several years, trade union politics were a central part of Penton's life. After breaking with the labor movement sometime in the 1890s, he became and remained a committed open-shop advocate, unnerved by the extent to which union activists challenged management rights and industrial stability. A decade after the NFA and the IMU settled the 1900–1901 strike, only Penton out of this pair, as opposed to Dawley, remained loyal to the employers. Penton had become a successful businessman himself, but was no longer employed by the NFA. Dawley, on the other hand, severed ties with the employers in 1911 when he very vocally offered his services to the International Ladies Garment Workers Union (ILGWU), a union that sought to represent most of Cleveland's garment employees. One of the union's lawyers during the massive 1911 strike, Dawley had come to sympathize with the plight of the mostly young, low-paid female garment workers. Evidence explaining precisely why, at these particular periods, each man broke ideologically with their earlier principles is unavailable. This should not be surprising since Cleveland Employers' Association members, like dues-payers of similar associations throughout the nation, conducted much of their work secretly.[3] Nevertheless, in 1911 the two men were, metaphorically speaking, on opposite sides of the picket line from their previous positions. Penton abandoned trade union solidarity in favor of promoting the open-shop principle, establishing his anti-union credentials during the 1900–1901 strike. He deserted working-class struggles gradually; Dawley severed ties with his bourgeois companions rather quickly. Although we cannot know with absolute certainty why Penton and Dawley switched sides, their evolutions provide valuable insights into their changing approaches to the labor question and to reform issues generally.

The city where Penton and Dawley resided was a major industrial center with a diverse economy and a growing population. Cleveland was home to dozens of heavy and light manufacturing establishments, including iron and steel producers, shipbuilding establishments, chemical manufacturers, and garment makers.[4] By the early twentieth century, Cleveland, thanks in large part to the mechanical abilities of engineer-entrepreneur Alexander E. Brown, was home to many hoisting plants. Such machinery, handling the loading and unloading of ore and coal, also played a vital part in the regional economy.[5] And the country's largest paint manufacturing plant, Sherwin-Williams, was in this lakefront community. Additionally, its proud spokespersons pointed out at the end of the first decade that Cleveland's manufacturers produced the second-largest number of automobiles in the nation.[6] The largest source of jobs at this time, the city's foundries and machine shops, together employed close to 12,000 Clevelanders, roughly twenty percent of all manufacturing employment in the community.[7]

Penton and Dawley's city was also home to much labor-management conflict, including the infamous 1899 streetcar strike, which pitted the privately run Cleveland Electric Railway against roughly 850 workers affiliated with the Amalgamated Association of Street Railway Employees of America. During the course of this violent affair, waged largely for union recognition and begun in June, strikers and their supporters staged a series of confrontational demonstrations involving thousands, which prevented numerous strikebreakers from running the cars. Some incensed protestors even chanted "kill the police" and "kill the scabs." The railway, seeking to maintain service in the face of these pugnacious challenges, provided a number of conductors with guns. It also enjoyed police and militia protection, and over the course of the summer months, these forces clubbed and arrested dozens of protestors.[8] "For a few days," a local clergyman noted in August, "the city had the appearance of an armed camp."[9]

Outside visitors, anti-union advocates, and local reformers said little about company or police violence, but much about the "lawless" conduct of the protestors. Birmingham's N. F. Thompson, the South's most influential and high-profile open-shop advocate, was in Cleveland during the episode and was taken aback by the protestors' use of dynamite, including an explosion that targeted a group of strikebreakers "about three blocks away" from his own car.[10] Hiram Haydn, a pastor, professor of biblical literature at Western Reserve University, and prominent reformer, was equally troubled and, like Thompson, silent on police and strikebreaker violence. He was especially bothered by those who sought to, as he put it in August 1899, force innocent "men into Union ranks."[11] This crisis was somewhat of an embarrassment to the city's boosterish elite. At the Cleveland-held annual meeting of the American Boiler Manufacturers Association, one Cleveland employer sought to calm delegates' fears by explaining, "I trust you will not get the impression that we are in a state of chronic strike, or that we always have a strike on in Cleveland, because we are a very peaceable, law-abiding and quiet sort of folk."[12]

During the strike, Dawley served as one of the two lawyers for the Cleveland Electric Railway. He spent much of his time in court representing nonunionists charged with violent offenses. Most dramatically, he served as the defense lawyer for Ralph P. Hawley, a nonunion conductor who had chased and killed eighteen-year-old Michael Cornzweit. Precisely why Hawley fatally shot Cornzweit remains a point of disagreement. Some sources suggest that the teenager threw rocks at the streetcar; other witnesses reported that he irresponsibly yelled "scab" and thus provoked Hawley. Others stated that he was simply minding his own business. Whatever the case, Dawley performed quite well in the courtroom: the jury acquitted Hawley in March 1900, months after the strike's conclusion.[13]

The strike impacted Clevelanders differently. In its aftermath, several members of the progressive-minded business community, uneasy about the negative attention, lobbied for an even bigger police force and for a new civic center because they did not want their city to have a reputation for "rioting, bloodshed, and anarchy."[14] And union supporters, frustrated by a political system that appeared to serve employers' interests, called for the development of a political environment more accountable to the working classes. Both labor and business communities won reforms.[15] Workers helped elect Democrat Tom L. Johnson to the position of mayor, partly because he had successfully tapped into growing anger at the power of streetcar monopolies.[16] Around the same time, Cleveland's elites celebrated the growth of the police force under Chief Frederick Kohler's leadership.[17]

In some ways, it seems somewhat strange that the city's workers regarded Johnson as an ally, since he was a former streetcar executive who lived in the same ritzy Euclid Avenue neighborhood—"Millionaires Row"—as the city's bankers and manufacturers. But his loyalties, he wrote in his autobiography, were with the "citizens" and the "people" of Cleveland. Johnson was himself somewhat of a class traitor, and generations of historians, including canonical writers of the period, have praised the mayor for his progressive governing style. As historian John D. Buenker has noted, Johnson's election in 1901 "heralded the beginning of progress in that city which was almost unequaled anywhere else in the nation."[18] And several Cleveland reformers, including some who gained useful experience in Johnson's administration, eventually served in state government, where they continued to promote the interests of consumers and workers. The city's prolabor policy-makers, Johnson's allies, fought for and won several pieces of legislation favorable to unions, including workmen's compensation laws and regulations protecting women and child laborers.[19]

Johnson's political rise coincided with the establishment of a strong open-shop movement. In the streetcar strike's aftermath, Cleveland's employers, following nationwide trends, organized local, and participated in national, union-breaking organizations. Cleveland hosted branches of the

National Metal Trades Association (NMTA) and the NFA, and numerous employers held membership in the National Association of Manufacturers and the Citizens' Industrial Association of America. In 1900, employers formed the inclusive Cleveland Manufacturers' Association. These organizations, like many others, worked closely with politicians, held meetings about managerial innovations, ran labor bureaus—that blacklisted union activists—pressured one another to ensure that no member accepted organized labor's demands for restrictive closed shops,[20] and disseminated open-shop pamphlets, including a monthly called *Facts*.[21] Like Johnson, they saw themselves as popular reformers, encouraging ordinary people, irrespective of class background, to develop their individual talents. As a Cleveland Employers' Association statement explained in 1909, "We believe, as has been advocated by President Roosevelt, that every man stand on his own base, and let him show the stuff that is in him. We believe in individual initiative. The Employers' Association of Cleveland stands for a square deal in labor as well as in law."[22]

The city's open-shop advocates demonstrated their support for the "square deal" in numerous ways. During Johnson's mayoral terms, a number were involved in various charitable activities, including efforts to protect children from industrial drudgery. On his Cleveland visit in November 1906, activist Owen R. Lovejoy of the National Child Labor Committee, for example, spoke to a small group of privileged Clevelanders in Howard P. Eells's home about the immorality of child labor. Eells was head of the Bucyrus Company, a prosperous manufacturer of dredging equipment, and held leadership positions in the NMTA. His wife organized Lovejoy's meeting.[23] Eells apparently saw nothing incompatible with stridently opposing closed-shop unionism on the one hand while offering a platform to a prominent liberal reformer on the other.[24] Lovejoy's visit to the home of one of the NMTA's most powerful members demonstrates that open-shop advocates were genuinely interested in listening to, not obstructing, the views of progressive reformers.

Yet upper-class support for laws protecting child laborers and the passage of pro-worker legislation had little impact on most labor-management conflicts in Cleveland. The community's wealthy residents tended to separate the two issues. As self-appointed guardians of Cleveland's working class, they naturally saw independent union organizing as a threat to order, to their own financial interests, and to the rights of nonunionists. Indeed, the most passionate struggles occurred between bosses and employees, not among politicians or policy-makers. The divisions between employers and labor organizations were impossible to ignore in strikebreaking campaigns. Both Penton and Dawley, as we will see, played major roles in these activities.

"The Dr. Jekyll and Mr. Hyde of the Labor Movement": John A. Penton

During the seven-month 1900–1901 conflict between the NFA and the IMU, striking molders—a somewhat ethnically diverse group of Poles, Bohemians, and native-born men—made the best of their situation. They set up camp in nearby Lorain on the banks of the Black River where they slept in tents, hunted, fished, and lived off their catches. "The game," one striker reported, "is secured in a way that would do no discredit to the chef of a fashionable restaurant." They boasted that they made "the best turtle soup in the country, and as for the catfish you must taste it to know how good it is." Spirits were high, but spokespersons did not believe the same could be said about the employers. "We are proud of our shop's crew," one striker explained, but "I doubt, if we could secure a photo of the Cleveland employers at this stage of the fight, if they would show up as good-humored and as well satisfied with the course of events."[25]

The campers were not, for the most part, angry at their employers. Rather, the strikers believed that the foundry managers acted unreasonably because they received poor advice: "We cannot but express some sympathy for our employers, for we feel sure they are victims of a bad advisor."[26] For decades, Cleveland's molders and foundry employers had resolved their differences locally through negotiations and trade agreements; now, the employers were part of a national organization, requiring that members stand together as a united front and take directives from NFA leaders. The NFA thereby changed the course of labor-management relations, insisting that Cleveland's industrialists refuse to capitulate to union demands. From the strikers' point of view, NFA representatives, especially Penton, were meddlesome outsiders who had no business interfering with local labor-management relations.

It is entirely understandable why they described Penton as "a bad advisor." During the course of the conflict, Penton, who at the time resided in Detroit, secured a room in Cleveland's extravagant Hollenden Hotel, where

he coordinated his nefarious strikebreaking activities. He was chief spokesperson for the employers and principally responsible for finding, vetting,
importing, and paying strikebreakers from distant cities. He placed advertisements in the nation's leading newspapers, promising job hunters high
wages and multiple years of guaranteed employment. According to Penton,
the NFA promised to give strikebreakers a "card which will always guarantee them permanent employment under the rules of the Association." "The
holder of these cards," Penton reported in the fall, "will possess a very
valuable document, one that will place him in a very unique position."[27]
Penton explained during the operation's beginning that the strikebreakers,
610 altogether, appreciated the cards more than the compensation.[28]

It was a difficult struggle for both sides. The strikebreakers, "the very
lowest and most degraded of scabs," according to the *Iron Molders' Journal*,
were often armed and unafraid to use their weapons. IMU members called
them all sorts of names, including "prostitutes" and "scum."[29] According
to unionists on the ground, "the dirtiest scum of the molding fraternity
have gravitated to Cleveland since the strike began."[30] They were apparently
rude and violent, "feeling that they have behind them powerful backing
and the power of the police."[31] And during the course of the conflict,
Charles Peck, a strikebreaker from "somewhere in Massachusetts," shot
and killed IMU member Henry Cronenberger. In other parts of the city,
furious gangs chased after and physically attacked nonunionists. Some violent strikebreakers, presumably holders of NFA employment cards, sought
solace in Penton's hotel room, where, on one occasion, police officers
arrested three men hiding.[32] The city police force, which generally sided
with employers in labor disputes, apparently had no qualms about arresting
these men. Whatever the case, protesters directed more rage at Penton than
any other figure, with the possible exception of Peck. According to the *Iron
Molders' Journal*, Penton's aggressive strikebreaking crusade was responsible for sowing "the seeds of dissension and distrust in our midst."[33]

Their anger should not be surprising in light of the strikebreaking architect's past: Penton was once a trade union leader committed to protecting
and advancing the collective interests of machinery molders. Born in Paris,
Ontario, in 1862, Penton began his career as a Detroit-based iron molder,
served as president of the International Brotherhood of Machinery Molders
from 1887 to 1892, and was founder and editor of the union's newspaper,
Machinery Molders' Journal. The brotherhood, like the IMU, fought for high
wages and workplace dignity by building shop floor solidarity, negotiating

with employers, and, when necessary, striking and picketing. Under Penton's editorship, the *Machinery Molders' Journal* covered a wide range of topics, including workplace conditions, strikes, molding techniques, and broad developments in the foundry industry. Penton was especially interested in adding members, insisting that fellow unionists help organize. "Let us," he wrote in 1888, "work together with energy and harmony until every one of the thousands of machinery molders of America who would make a good member is enrolled on our book."[34]

By most accounts, Penton was once a proud, politically moderate labor leader, praising the importance of both hard, skilled work and labor-management cooperation. He frequently wrote favorably about employee craftsmanship, applauding the contributions that molders made to industrial progress. Writing about a mammoth band wheel built by brotherhood members in Columbus, for instance, he noted in 1889 that "the wheel was not alone remarkable for its size or weight, but for the excellence of its workmanship, the joints in the mold being barely visible, and not a blemish of the most insignificant description could be found on its surface."[35] Penton's comments here, and elsewhere, demonstrate that he was, in many ways, the textbook example of a "responsible" labor chief, holding very little in common with disgruntled saboteurs or far-left activists, who, by participating in disorderly strikes and a handful of high-profile violent campaigns, helped to tar the image of labor unionism in general in the eyes of many economically privileged Americans.

But this does not mean that this trade unionist lived a conflict-free life. He felt somewhat threatened by, and strongly disliked, the IMU, a competitor organization with considerably more members. The two unions engaged in a number of jurisdictional conflicts during the late 1880s and early 1890s, and Penton periodically attacked the rival organization, claiming in 1889 that the writers of its newspaper, the *Iron Molders' Journal*, suffered from "illiteracy."[36] Molders had a choice of whether they wanted to join the IMU or the brotherhood, but one thing was certain, claimed Penton in 1890, "We have come to stay, and the puerile attempts of jealous and narrow-minded rivals to detract from our glorious record and stay our progress will only benefit ourselves."[37]

Tensions between the two labor organizations were particularly pronounced in Cleveland during the late nineteenth century. As Penton explained in 1890, "In no part of the country has the steady advance of the Brotherhood met with the amount of opposition that has been showered upon it by the Iron Molders Unions and their representatives in Cleveland." Penton helped launch Brotherhood Local No. 41 in Cleveland, and in response, he and fellow organizers were met with, as he explained, "abuse, threats, trickery and deception of the most contemptible nature." Some of the recruits belonged to both the IMU and the brotherhood, and the IMU leadership apparently sought to expel those with dual membership. Yet despite IMU challenges, the brotherhood's Cleveland chapter continued, he wrote in 1890, to grow "steadily and uninterruptedly."[38]

At the same time, the brotherhood had fewer members and thus was less powerful than the IMU, the nation's oldest continuously functioning labor organization. Formed in 1859 under William H. Sylvis's leadership, the IMU held regular meetings, elected officers, staged strikes for increases in wages, and created a modest-sized striker defense fund.[39] These organized molders, numbering roughly 10,000 immediately following the Civil War, typically enjoyed strong bargaining power, in large part because they, like those in the brotherhood, performed skilled jobs; they mastered their craft through years of hands-on experience and thus were not easily replaceable. Their skills, combined with traditions of working-class solidarity—plainly visible in the union press, at meetings, and on picket lines—helped them win pay increases, both in Cleveland and elsewhere.[40] The union's membership grew considerably, doubling during the twentieth century's first four years. It stood at 41,000 in 1900, and grew to 80,000 in 1904.[41]

Although Penton harshly criticized the IMU in Cleveland and elsewhere in the early 1890s, he genuinely wanted to improve the conditions of molders and took an uncompromising stand against the forces responsible for undermining the labor movement. Penton and his colleagues condemned "combinations of capital," stressing in 1892 that "they, and not the combinations of working men, form the real danger to the community."[42] Equally important, he denounced strikebreaking as "scabbing" as passionately as any union militant. The brotherhood regularly expelled members for crossing picket lines during work stoppages, and Penton accused strikebreakers in 1889 of having "so little sense of honor."[43] In 1891, he claimed that

Nothing is too vile for them to do; they are willing to put up with every indignity, to submit to any and all sorts of insults, to go to and from work under the guard of police protection, to be turned from every respectable boarding house, and after they have served their purpose to be turned adrift by those very employers whose degraded slaves they have been.[44]

Strikebreakers, he reasoned, threatened the livelihoods of skilled unionists, those who had spent years on the shop floor mastering their craft. They lacked dignity, experience, and training; they had little respect for sophisticated molding techniques and, most of all, did not understand the necessity of solidarity.

By the time of the 1900–1901 strike, the brotherhood was no more. Following Samuel Gompers's recommendation and a membership vote, it merged with the IMU in 1893, but it is almost certain that Penton did not support the majority's decision.[45] At this time, Penton, presumably disillusioned that he was on the losing side of the debate over the brotherhood's future, left trade union politics and embarked on a publishing career. In 1892, he launched *The Foundry*, "a trade journal devoted to the interests of the whole foundry business." Early issues covered a wide variety of foundry practices, developments in mechanical engineering, and even poems celebrating industriousness and skill:

The Molder
By Swab
What tradesman is there in this land
Who's skill is oftener in demand
Whose trade does date from ages back
The science of which many lack;
The Foundry's to be the unfolder,
The educator of the Molder.

Let every tradesman lend a hand
To forward on this movement grand.
Brush off the "beam dust" from our shelves.
And by aiding others help ourselves;
Hand to hand and shoulder to shoulder.
Exchange experience for the Molder.[46]

Here Penton, by providing space to this poem, continued to demonstrate his appreciation for the ways in which molders helped to improve American industrial life. Hundreds of foundry operators read the *Foundry*'s poems, viewed its advertisements, and learned from its articles about patents, foundry construction, and economic fluctuations. Yet, importantly, early issues do not reveal Penton as a promoter of anti-union causes.

However, he had certainly become one by 1900. At this time, he no longer thought that employers' associations or strikebreakers were dishonorable, and he apparently never got over his bitter frustration with the IMU. His anger at the rival union was clearly stronger than his commitment to working-class unity, and he believed that trade union solidarity and working-class activism hurt, rather than helped, industrial progress. In this later period, he made his living as an NFA organizer and publisher of trade journals. While the former labor leader impressed his employers, unionists certainly did not respect his newfound loyalties. One IMU member perceived him as a shameless betrayer of the working class, calling him "the Dr. Jekyll and Mr. Hyde of the labor movement." They cared little for him when he was a rival labor activist, but were especially disturbed by his willingness to do what they considered the employers' dirty work, strikebreaking coordination and propaganda dissemination. They were not the only trade unionists stunned by Penton's treasonous act; former members of the brotherhood were also upset by the jaw-dropping news of his activities. According to W. A. Perrine, an IMU member writing in late 1900, "every ex-officer and member of the Brotherhood whom I have met during the past three months, is mourning."[47]

In addition to publishing, Penton organized manufacturers into a number of trade associations. Most were nonconfrontational, mutually beneficial organizations formed in the 1890s for the purpose of helping American industries innovate and grow. The first was the American Malleable Castings Association (AMCA), which he helped launch in 1890 and where he served as secretary until 1901. The AMCA's purpose was to help manufacturers share technical information with one another in an effort to, as Penton himself explained in 1915, "make a good product better."[48] He also worked briefly as secretary for the American Foundrymen's Association, which, like the AMCA, brought manufacturers together to discuss developments in the foundry industry. Many were regular readers of Penton's *Foundry*.

Soon Penton began working for the emerging open-shop movement, serving as NFA secretary and commissioner between 1898 and 1903. His "indefatigable labors," *The Iron Trade Review* reported in 1900, were crucial in launching the NFA and bringing it to the attention of foundry operators in much of the nation.[49] In this capacity, Penton became acquainted with an even larger fraternity of industrialists, becoming friendly with the nation's most committed employer-activists and workplace reformers. Besides coordinating strikebreaking operations—which clearly proved that he had abandoned any commitment to the labor movement—Penton recruited dozens of foundry operators, organized meetings and "smokers" (evening receptions), and stressed the importance of cooperation and trust. Writing about the NFA's membership in 1904, William H. Pfahler, the organization's founder and Penton's supervisor, noted that foundry operators were initially suspicious of one another, but they gradually recognized their common interests in the face of repeated IMU demands and continual strikes: "now the members did trust each other, man to man." In essence, Penton helped the men, individuals representing different-sized foundries from mostly midwestern and northeastern cities, to see one another as part of a brotherhood with the same basic managerial goals.[50]

In 1901, Penton settled in Cleveland where he continued to promote the interests of this brotherhood while expanding his publishing business. Three years later, he took over the Iron and Steel Press Company and renamed it Penton Publishing Company (known today as Penton Media). Penton Publishing put out several directories of machinery products, books, and trade journals, including *Power Boating, Marine Review,* and *The Iron Trade Review. The Iron Trade Review,* like *Foundry* (which remained in circulation), was especially popular with intellectually engaged engineers, managers of all levels, and proprietary capitalists, including many who held membership in open-shop associations like the NFA and the NMTA. It was principally a dispassionate trade publication that contained information about the construction of new industrial workplaces, regional discoveries of raw materials, innovations in manufacturing techniques, and obituaries of well-known engineers and industrialists. It also included regular features on the activities of labor unions and employers' associations, including their involvement in the blossoming open-shop movement. Factory owners and engineers subscribed to, and put advertisements in, Penton's publications, further enhancing his reputation as a genuine promoter of manufacturing and manufacturers. There was a high demand for industrial news; Penton opened additional offices shortly after establishing operations in Cleveland. The central office remained on Lake Erie, but Penton coordinated with branch managers who administered offices in Boston, Chicago, Cincinnati, New York, and Pittsburgh. Each issue of his publications featured a masthead that read "printed in an open-shop."[51]

The employers demonstrated their appreciation for the onetime trade union leader on numerous occasions. This was especially evident in late 1903 when Penton, following numerous organizing trips and strikebreaking coordinating activities, decided to step down from his NFA position. At the NFA annual conference, the organization's leadership showered him with compliments and gifts, celebrating his "great personal sacrifice." The employers in attendance, beneficiaries of Penton's many promotional and organizational efforts, apparently respected him more "with each succeeding year."[52] They desperately wanted him to continue, but Penton sought to focus on his publishing business full time instead. He nevertheless remained ideologically committed to the open-shop philosophy and intimate with top members of union-fighting employers' associations, which was on full display at this meeting. Buffalo's Ogden P. Letchworth presented Penton with a three-stoned diamond ring and "a bound volume of letters from his friends." Ritualistic gift giving was followed by "feeling words of thanks, of regret, and of regard." All eyes, some of which were probably teary, were set on Penton.[53]

Although Penton was no longer employed by the NFA, he maintained close contact with his former colleagues. The ambitious publisher who introduced thousands of manufacturers to the latest developments in the marine, metal-working, and foundry industries hired two of his old bosses, NFA members Walter D. Sayle and John Howard Webster. All three had joined forces during the 1900–1901 molders' strike. Sayle's Cleveland Punch and Shear Works, a manufacturer of punches, shears, drills, and plate and rotary planers, and Webster's Variety Iron Works, which constructed boilers, tanks, pulleys, and hoisting machinery and employed roughly 1,000, were shut down briefly during that affair. Both men were indebted to Penton for his seemingly intrepid services at the time, and they showed their devotion by working for Penton Publishing Company. Sayle was secretary; Webster was vice president.

Fighting "Many Legal Battles in the Interests of the Open-Shop": Jay P. Dawley

Sayle and Webster were as appreciative to Dawley as they were to Penton. In 1906, Dawley demonstrated his movement loyalties by serving as president of the open-shop Cleveland Employers' Association. Additionally, he wrote for the organization's monthly magazine, *Facts*. He regularly secured injunctions against unions, and he defended nonunionists and employers in court. In essence, Sayle, Webster, and Penton all benefited from Dawley's legal expertise and steadfast commitment to the open-shop philosophy. The legal services were evidently one of the employers' association's strongest features: "the Association," *Facts* explained in 1909, "is in excellent shape to handle litigation growing out of labor troubles."[54]

Born near Cleveland in 1847, Dawley served as a Union soldier with the Eleventh Ohio Infantry during the Civil War and took part in Sherman's highly destructive Atlanta Campaign. During the course of it, he worked as an orderly and private, relaying information orally between military commanders on the battlefield.[55] Following the sectional conflict, Dawley returned to Ohio, where he studied law, passed the bar exam in 1872, and went into private practice. He served as a defense lawyer for both businesses and individuals, including murder suspects like Hawley. According to a history of Cleveland published in 1910, Dawley "has probably acted for the defense in more murder cases than any other lawyer of Cleveland and has been very successful in his practice."[56]

But the ambitious defense lawyer was not always successful. His most famous client was Cassie L. Chadwick, the Cleveland con-artist who for years posed as Andrew Carnegie's daughter. Using this false identity, Chadwick withdrew thousands of dollars from Cleveland banks before authorities discovered her schemes. Her 1905 case made it to the front pages of the nation's newspapers. Dawley was unable to persuade the jury that Chadwick was innocent—she was not. But Dawley appealed to the morality and gender assumptions of everyone in the courtroom during the trial: "A woman stands alone on one side and arrayed against her are all the forces of the great, the powerful, the magnificent United States government." Unpersuaded by Dawley's melodramatic theatrics, the jury found Chadwick guilty of fraud, and Judge Francis J. Wing, the same justice who had ordered injunctions against striking IMU members in 1901, punished her with a $70,000 fine and fourteen years in jail.[57]

Employers cared less about Dawley's involvement in the legendary Chadwick trial than they did about his wholehearted readiness to fight on behalf of the open-shop principle. The Cleveland Punch and Shear Works's Sayle was especially thankful for the lawyer's many years of assistance. When Sayle permanently fired almost all his unionized employees in June 1901, for example, Dawley secured a court injunction to prevent the angry men from interfering with the replacements. Sayle had rehired rebellious unionists in the past—including hundreds who participated in the seven-month 1900–1901 conflict—but he had become troubled that many of those same men had made additional demands for wage increases less than a year after the great molders' strike. These renewed demands compelled Sayle to reconsider his earlier decision to rehire the strikers. "The taking back of all the men was a mistake," he bluntly wrote in *Open-Shop* in 1905. He had demonstrated "leniency" in the past, but by mid-1901 was no longer willing to allow union agitators to hold his business hostage, believing that the large-scale firing was necessary: "It was time now for drastic action."[58]

At the time, the recipients of Sayle's termination notices were visibly irritated, and as they tried to return to the worksite and prevent nonunion-ists from entering the building, Sayle turned to Dawley for help. Both were naturally disturbed by the escalating tensions and expressions of violence that had erupted outside the factory's gates. The June 1901 injunction was necessary, Dawley believed, to stop what he called "bloodshed, rioting, and anarchy."[59] In the face of this legal pressure, the violent protesters, unable to regain their jobs, retreated, and Sayle expressed gratitude for his new, nonunion, trustworthy, and entirely lawful workforce. "My men," he reported to fellow activists in the open-shop movement in 1905, "are inter-ested, happy and contented in their work."[60] And business at Sayle's Cleve-land Punch and Shear Works had become, *The Iron Trade Review* reported in 1902, "excellent."[61] Sayle's assessment of the transformative development that occurred at his workplace illustrates that he cherished Dawley for both protecting his own management rights and for shielding his new, "happy and contented" labor force from riotous unionists. The effective marginali-zation of the demanding and dangerous unionists followed by the re-establishment of labor peace and productivity increases, was, from the standpoint of the local open-shop movement, the best possible outcome.

Others enjoyed similar outcomes. John Howard Webster, a fourth cousin of Whig leader Daniel Webster, was also a beneficiary of Dawley's legal proficiency and activism on behalf of the open-shop principle. John Howard Webster had his own employee-related difficulties throughout the early 1900s, which turned him into a stubborn opponent of union-imposed wage rates and a believer in his sense of shop floor meritocracy. "No intelli-gent workman," the Yale University-educated Webster argued in the pages of *The Iron Trade Review* in 1905, "will forever be content to put his supe-rior power to earn the highest wages upon a par with his lazy, inefficient brother."[62] Concerned with maintaining high productivity levels, he had no tolerance for what he called in 1907 "all this sentimental nonsense about the eight-hour or seven-hour day and the leisure of the workingman."[63] In light of these spiteful comments, we should hardly be surprised that Webster's Variety Iron Works continued employing nonunionists after the IMU and the NFA settled their differences following the 1900–1901 strike. IMU members were predictably enraged that Webster openly violated the joint labor-management agreement, which stated that the employers would rehire the strikers without pay increases and refrain from employing nonunionists.[64] IMU activists, annoyed by Webster's refusal to abide by the agreement, demonstrated their rage by attacking nonunionists in the months following the strike's official end. Well aware of their own vulnerability, several nonunionists armed themselves in response. On one occasion, in May 1901, a group of IMU demonstrators physically attacked two nonunionists, Ben Maylan and Edward Powers, which prompted the defensive men to draw guns. A police officer on the scene arrested the armed men.[65]

Deeply upset by the arrests, Webster solicited Dawley's legal expertise. In court, a well-prepared Dawley insisted that the two men were entirely innocent, arguing that they justifiably attempted to, in essence, defend themselves from a violent mob of intolerant radicals. These victims, Webster and Dawley believed, had a legal right to work—and to protect themselves against those who challenged that right. Judge Nicholas P. Whelan agreed, and issued his decision in late May 1901: "In discharging these defendants from the custody of the court I hold that they were perfectly justified in carrying the weapons they were said to have had in their possession, and others arrested in a like instance would be disposed of in the same manner."[66] This episode shows that Dawley had again proved himself as a faithful defender of the city's employers and nonunionists, including gunmen, against a labor movement fully intolerant of the rights of nonunionists and strikebreakers.

"Blustering Loudly about Law and Order": The Publisher and the Lawyer

In November 1906, Penton earned nationwide coverage just as Dawley received massive amounts of attention for his role in the Chadwick case. Faced with a labor disturbance provoked by members of the Typographical

Union, which sought recognition and shorter hours in workplaces in many of the nation's cities, including Cleveland, Penton took extreme action. The *New York Times* reported on the severity of this episode, noting that Penton "has declared war on the pickets of the Typographical Union who had been stationed near his establishment." The paper explained further that Penton had purchased dozens of .38-caliber revolvers for his nonunion men, "with instructions to use them if they were molested by the pickets."[67] In some ways, this conflict appeared even more dramatic than the much bigger 1900–1901 molders' strike.

Dawley had, of course, previously tested the legality of Penton's actions, and Penton, aware of these cases, defended his decision to arm 40 of his employees to every common pleas judge in Cleveland and to Johnson. Writing to the famous reform mayor, Penton, who also carried a revolver, explained himself:

> The courts of this city and state have invariably decided in accordance with the law when the issue was thoroughly tested, that any man whose life was in danger or threatened while in pursuit of his lawful calling was and would be perfectly justified in arming for self-protection. This being the case, we have decided to arm our employees fully hereafter and propose to see that the right of self-protection shall remain unquestioned.[68]

Penton saw his actions as entirely justified, unashamedly choosing to protect himself and his nonunion employees from what he called "A reign of terror."[69] Invoking the outcomes of previous court cases, he denied that he had violated any laws.

In a follow-up letter to Johnson, Penton reasserted the right of self-defense, arguing that his actions were reasonable because "the police" were "largely responsible for the non-enforcement of our laws."[70] This was an astonishing admission, especially since the city's bankers, merchants, and manufacturers, figures close to Penton, had lobbied successfully in the aftermath of the violent 1899 streetcar strike to increase the force's size and to improve the overall quality of its leadership.[71] In Penton's view, Cleveland's police were, in this particular context, an inadequate ally.[72]

Yet lack of police support represented only a minor setback. Penton reported that he had plenty of other allies, informing Johnson that he enjoyed "moral assistance" from his colleagues in the Cleveland Employers'

Association, including some of the mayor's well-to-do neighbors. By noting this support, Penton did not merely seek to remind Johnson of the legal justification of his actions; he also wanted his understanding and full sympathy.[73] Although Penton and Johnson were not close political allies, Penton was confident that further dialogue between the two would "result to the benefit of the entire community." By invoking the broad community's well-being, rather than the employers' association's more limited class interests, Penton basically held that Johnson—who had earned the backing of many trade unionists during previous electoral contests—needed to recognize that open-shop campaigns, including violent ones, were not designed to repress laborers, but instead to liberate large sections of the working-class from coercive agitators and from the brutal constraints of closed shops. Backed by "moral" forces, Penton clearly felt no need to apologize, noting to Johnson that he had witnessed a marked improvement in and around his workplace shortly after arming his loyal men: "for the past week business has been running along very smoothly with not a picket in sight, without anyone being slugged, and Erie Street seems to be about as safe as any other part of Cleveland." Penton wanted Johnson to join him in acknowledging—even celebrating—the end result: lasting neighborhood orderliness, combined with peaceful and productive labor relations based on the open-shop principle.[74]

Undoubtedly, Penton believed that his workplace battle was consistent with mainstream actions and ideas, which found expression nationally. By the time he armed his nonunionists, thousands of employers had established open-shop workplaces, hundreds of judges had issued injunctions against picketers, and growing numbers of high-profile reformers had helped legitimize the nonunionist's "right to work." Penton merely wanted to ensure that his own employees enjoyed this right, and by holding arms, they were in possession of the tools necessary to ensure their freedom to move. After all, Penton was part of a cohort of individuals—employers, judges, lawyers, newspapermen, and university administrators—who held that "there is no such thing as peaceful picketing." Workplace self-defense was, therefore, the natural response to this particular challenge.

Of course, not everyone, including Cleveland's United Trades and Labor Council, believed that Penton's actions were in any way acceptable. Instead, this umbrella association, consisting of a rich diversity of skilled and unskilled workers from many sectors of the economy, were shocked and outraged, pointing out the hypocrisy demonstrated by this so-called champion of "law and order." Its members characterized Penton as "an enemy of organized working people," complaining that he "is now making war on everything that looks like a union card." Unanimously, members adopted a resolution denouncing Penton and requesting that Johnson intervene to prevent bloodshed. If the mayor failed to take decisive action against Penton's men, then Cleveland's trade unionists demanded "the same right that the Penton company claims, namely, to arm the 25,000 union men of this city in order that they may protect themselves from assault at the hands of Penton's strikebreakers." Cleveland's labor activists, who undoubtedly enjoyed a numerical advantage over Penton and his forty nonunionists, also insisted that they were patriotic, acknowledging the right to bear arms "guaranteed by the United States Constitution."[75] Thousands of armed unionists, they insisted, constituted the best—and perhaps only— solution to what they called "the Penton threat."[76]

Labor activists complained about several instances of employer-backed violence, explaining in early November that "every act of slugging has come from the employer's side, and Penton knows it."[77] Some strikebreakers apparently shot their guns indiscriminately; others threatened to kill protesters. A few gunmen were arrested; others evaded police. Most drastically, Israel Whitworth, the owner of the building where Penton conducted his publishing business, drove a chisel into the back of protester Eli Black. Labor activists had witnessed examples of such brutality before, writing in December that all the acts of violence represented the methods "Penton popularized among the foundrymen," recognizing that the former trade union leader punished typographers as cruelly and uncompromisingly as he once challenged molders.[78] Penton's anti-union actions during his time in Cleveland reveal that he was less interested in drawing distinctions based on craft than he was in distinguishing between strikers and "free men." Unionists had reason to fear, believing that if Penton had his way, he would drive all workers "back to the stone age."[79]

Spokespersons from Cleveland's union community pointed out that Penton was wrong to characterize the city's printers as lawless troublemakers, since not one printer was serving time in Ohio's penitentiaries. Printers were ethical, law-abiding, and in their view "above the average man in intelligence." The jails were filled with individuals from virtually every other job: "Businessmen, farmers, mechanics and representatives of almost every other department of industrial activity are common there. But there is not one printer."[80] The "Penton way of blustering loudly about law and order" did not, in other words, resemble reality. Union supporters did not belong behind bars, but, in their view, Penton did. Penton was, as the socialist *Cleveland Citizen* explained in December, "a dangerous man outside of the penitentiary."[81]

Little came from the labor movement's call to arms against the so-called "Penton threat." Thousands of the city's working-class residents did not arm themselves in anticipation of a revolutionary-like confrontation with Penton and his strikebreakers, sparing the city's elite residents from dangerous and embarrassing riots of the sort that had broken out during the 1899 streetcar strike. And neither the belligerent threats nor the more level-headed arguments meant to highlight the fundamental wrongness of Penton's arguments and behavior appear to have had much influence on the city's law enforcement community. Simply put, the most class-conscious and militant sections of the labor movement were unable to convince authorities to charge Penton with breaking any laws.

But Whitworth, a "pupil of Penton," needed the best legal assistance available for nearly murdering Black. And like Sayle, Webster, and dozens of others, Whitworth sought help from the city's premier open shop–defending lawyer. Expectedly, Dawley did not disappoint. In an effort to minimize Whitworth's punishment, Dawley first insisted that his client should be tried for stabbing to injure, rather than charged with attempted murder.[82] Repeating earlier arguments, Dawley further maintained that Whitworth was innocent because he acted purely out of self-defense. The jury agreed, and Whitworth, Penton, and Dawley left the courtroom relieved that they had won another crucial battle, one that further legitimized the open-shop principle. Penton was the principal winner: he successfully defended his managerial policies at the point of production, in the streets, and, with help from Dawley, in the courtroom.[83]

Penton thanked Dawley publicly for his steadfast involvement in industrial reform efforts in the pages of *The Iron Trade Review*, observing in 1907 that he "fought many legal battles in the interests of the open-shop." Dawley did so, Penton explained, "not only for the right of employers to conduct their own business, but also for the uplifting of the workingmen."[84] Penton suggested, in essence, that a cross-class section of the city, not merely employers, were greatly fortunate to receive Dawley's aid. Importantly, this courtroom warrior was not motivated by any desire to defend the nonunionist's "right to work" as a permanent shop floor *worker*. He was instead, Penton informs us, committed to promoting upward mobility, implying that the "uplifting" process was only realizable under open-shop conditions, which, unlike closed shops, compensated examples of individual ambition and loyalty with bonuses and promotional opportunities. For workers seeking to rise in the ranks, it made perfect sense to identify with the interests of the city's employers and to view lawyers like Dawley as a source of seemingly unlimited assistance as they pursued their own workplace and career-oriented goals.

It all sounded very nice. Of course, missing from *The Iron Trade Review* pages was any mention of the messy, rather repressive reality on the ground. While mainstream and labor union sources had covered employer-backed violence in Cleveland somewhat extensively, Penton, understandably, did not. And readers of the journal learned nothing about Dawley's defense of Penton's colleague Whitworth. These omissions are unsurprising. Readers, a nationwide fraternity of backslapping metal-working and foundry operators, only needed to learn that Cleveland was home to a highly talented, diligent, and, above all, faithful open-shop attorney serving the community's interests as a whole, not merely the concerns of the employers.

But Dawley was well aware of who buttered his bread. And in the new decade, he continued to represent the city's elite residents, including manufacturers charged with violating the state's labor laws, which were designed to protect some workers. Such reforms, including laws banning the labor of children, created new challenges for manufacturers, and it was not uncommon for them to breach such rules. In May 1910, Sayle and Theodor Kundtz, a Hungarian immigrant and philanthropist who oversaw a workforce of 2,500 mostly skilled cabinetmakers, were each charged with two counts of violating the Reynolds Child Labor Law, a 1908 act initiated by Ohio legislator James A. Reynolds, a former International Association of Machinists (IAM) leader and onetime member of Johnson's administration. Despite Dawley's efforts on behalf of his clients, the judge fined each man twenty-five dollars and court costs. The city's working-class community, which generally supported child labor laws, denounced Dawley for his participation in the case. "Jay Pay Dawley defended the lawless child exploiters," commented the *Cleveland Citizen*.[85]

Indeed, class-conscious labor activists criticized Dawley as passionately as they condemned Penton, calling members of the Cleveland Employers' Association "Dawleyites."[86] Admitting that many once respected Dawley for his part in defending ordinary Clevelanders in criminal court, the *Cleveland Citizen* claimed he was now greedy, arrogant, and unethical. "Dawley has degenerated into a very tiresome little egotist who would defend the devil himself if he received his 30 pieces of silver every day," the *Cleveland Citizen* wrote in 1908. Dawley, who had also collaborated closely with many of the community's prosperous garment manufacturers, was ostensibly responsible for keeping "thousands of poor garment workers on the ragged edge of poverty."[87] The same source noted in 1910 that Dawley often worked deliberately slowly on legal cases: "The longer the delay, the fatter the rake-off for Jay Pee."[88]

Yet Dawley presented himself as someone concerned with matters more meaningful than money-making activities, declaring that he had routinely defended management during strikes because he disdained union-provoked violence, which routinely threatened both property rights and the non-unionist's "right to work." And like many open-shop proselytizers, he was obsessed about the supposedly nefarious activities of instigative radicals, rather than about the organically generated shop floor grievances plainly evident in hundreds of workplaces. Writing in 1909 in *Facts*, he maintained, "There isn't any trouble between labor and capital." The "trouble," he argued, "is between the agitators that want to make the unions subservient to their own selfish ends."[89] In his view, an opinion shared by almost all members of his class, including Penton, strikes and other forms of working-class protests resulted from intrusive outsiders, manipulative individuals who forced ordinary workers to join chaos-creating unions.

A short monthly edited by Dawley, *Facts* resembled company newspapers that circulated in nonunion workplaces. Like factory magazines and newspapers, it was propagandistic, containing repetitive essays about the moral bankruptcy of labor leaders, the inexcusability of union-provoked violence, the justness of the nonunionists' struggles, and the importance of respecting America's laws. It also broadcasted Cleveland's economic and managerial advantages over other medium and large cities. Ten years after the ferocious and embarrassing 1899 streetcar strike, *Facts* explained that the city had become a national center in the open-shop movement:

> we can invite outsiders within our gates and say to them, "Here we have no Chicago Teamsters' strike, no Toledo Labor Unrest, no New York Taxicab Disturbances, no Eastern Hat Workers' Difficulties, no May Day uneasiness. Come in, we are free from all this unrest, we are improving our harbor facilities to invite large industries to begin

operations here, come to us, we hope to have ideal industrial conditions."[90]

Needless to say, *Facts*, like Penton's *Iron Trade Review*, omitted much, including the palpable anger emanating from some working-class circles. It obviously chose not to remind readers—Cleveland's employers and outsiders considering investing in the lakefront city—that the city was actually home to a labor movement that had very publicly threatened to arm itself against violent nonunionists and Penton three years earlier. *Facts* was clearly uninterested in reporting the actual facts that challenged its hyperbolic narrative, one that stressed the pervasive presence of unequaled harmonious workstations, industrial prosperity, and community friendliness.

Unlike Penton's nationally distributed publications, the exaggeratedly titled *Facts* circulated locally, focusing almost exclusively on the ways in which Cleveland's allegedly fair-minded and forward-thinking employers confronted—and came close to solving—various labor problems. And in labor-management conflicts, the employers explained that their side was always reasonable and never wrong. The first issue, published in May 1909, was particularly self-righteous: "We know we are right in our contentions and in our work—we must, therefore, go forward, send the truth broadcast, disseminate knowledge."[91]

As editor, Dawley wrote more *Facts* columns than any other member of the city's employers' association. He mostly covered labor union unrest, which was, in his view, a pernicious symptom of anti-Americanism. Like others, he believed that the local employers' association was a fundamental force of respectability that had a singular role to play in aligning Cleveland with the country's most advanced political and industrial relations practices. Under his leadership, the association was determined to help ordinary workmen break from what he viewed as the lawlessness and suffocating constraints integral to trade unionism itself: "[the Cleveland Employers' Association] is one of the most potent factors in the community and that it can do much good, and is doing more good for all of the men engaged in labor than in any other organization in this city, and we are fighting for American rights, and for Americans only."[92] The self-congratulatory, flag-waving Dawley suggested that Cleveland's organized employers were engaged in a series of honorable, class-blind fights, which considered the interests of Americans as a whole—and those who subordinated individual freedoms to trade unionism threatened American values and the orderliness and prosperity of Cleveland's communities.

Like others, Dawley was especially sympathetic to the "free workers," "the common people" who had faced great personal risks in order to labor during strikes. He believed that union activists were responsible for unfairly targeting hardworking and honest men and women, and he recognized a pattern: "The history of nearly every strike discloses acts of violence and lawlessness committed against men whose sole offense is that, in the endeavor to earn a living, they seek employment in the places made vacant by strikers." Demonstrating sympathy for the abused "free workers," Dawley pointed out that the law repeatedly sided with those who chose to work during walkouts. "The Courts," he explained in September 1909, "have long ago announced that the capital of the laborer, is his labor, together with his skill, and he has the right to employ his talents and industry as he pleases, free from dictation of others."[93]

Seeing "new light": Jay P. Dawley and the 1911 Garment Strike

In late spring 1911, after years of publicizing the alleged evils of trade unionism and representing strikebreakers and employers in courtrooms, the well-known attorney had a major falling-out with his colleagues, renounced the open-shop philosophy, and began representing pro-union garment workers as they sought collective recognition from their employers. Dawley's dramatic turnabout shocked employers, thrilled union supporters, and astonished the general public. The news made it to the front page of the city's newspapers; Dawley earned almost as much press coverage for his repudiation of the open-shop movement as for representing fraudster Chadwick. According to the *Cleveland Plain Dealer*, "The announcement that Dawley has become the legal adviser of labor unions is one of the biggest surprises the city has had for many years."[94] The organized labor community was equally taken aback: "J. P. Dawley has seen new light, cut loose from the brethren with whom he was associated for many years." Unionists understood that "he startled Cleveland and probably a big part of the country by announcing his conversion to the labor side of the great social struggle that is now in progress."[95] In making the switch, Dawley had fundamentally changed his understanding of power relations, recognizing the unambiguous reality of class inequality found throughout Cleveland's workplaces and neighborhoods. The nonunion "free men," in his view, were no longer the primary underdogs in labor-management conflicts. He ceased to believe that the open-shop movement genuinely cared about their welfare, and now lent his support to a different group of underdogs: union supporters demanding contractually guaranteed rights and a genuine collective voice in their workplaces. As a result, union activists no longer referred to the city's organized employers as Dawleyites.

This unforeseen development was partially the result of lobbying by the garment workers' union and by one of their attorneys, socialist Louis A. Katz, but the press did not reveal the many details of these meetings. Following conversations with the New York City-based union and Katz, Dawley agreed to represent the workers on one major condition: that the strikers conduct their protests nonviolently. Dawley's discomfort with violence stemmed from years of exposure to it as a Cleveland Employers' Association leader, and he realized that picket-line scuffles exacerbated tensions, led to injuries and occasionally deaths, and alienated much of the general public. Dawley flatly refused to represent anyone accused of violence in court. Importantly, his endorsement of the strike nevertheless reveals an assumption almost universally rejected by his former colleagues in the open-shop movement: that unionists did have the ability to picket peacefully.[96]

Dawley saw nothing inconsistent with his decision to lend support to the labor movement, but he was clear-eyed enough to realize that he had burned "my bridges."[97] He had come to understand that employers were seldom innocent during labor conflicts, which often involved instances of manufacturer-provoked attacks on picketers. While he had proudly "defended the corporations in cases where violence was perpetrated by union men because of overzeal or frenzy," he also explained that he had "known as many dastardly assaults made by corporations-hired men as by union men." "While I have fought the battles of the dollar men," he continued, "I have never forgotten myself so far as to diminish in any way the God-given right of man to freedom."[98] Instead of championing the freedom of employers to run businesses without trade union interference or defending the freedom of employees to reject union membership offers, Dawley now believed that workers must be free to join with one another to advance their collective interests without confronting employer harassment.

Clearly, the sixty-four-year-old had reassessed questions of lawlessness and violence in the context of industrial conflicts, believing that he could no longer preach selectively against loathsome acts on picket lines or inside factories, since employers—many of whom had once profited handsomely from his assistance—were responsible for a disproportionate amount of them. Roughly two months after New York City's heart-wrenching fire at the open-shop Triangle Shirtwaist factory, which resulted in the deaths of 146 workers, he realized that employers, not only wage earners, regularly violated labor laws and ignored safety regulations. In light of this, he now refused to represent bourgeois lawbreakers, including Sayle and Kundtz, or to offer legal services to violent strikebreakers like Hawley and Whitworth. He also turned his back on the employers who condoned such acts of cruelty, including Penton. Penton reciprocated: he stopped praising Dawley in the pages of *The Iron Trade Review*.

Naturally, strikers and their supporters were joyful that their union secured legal counsel from one of their former opponents, a person who, like them, believed now that the numerous features of open-shop workplaces—low wages, long hours, dangerous conditions, and the "blacklist system"—hardly promoted feelings of "happiness" or encouraged economic "uplift." Even the *Cleveland Citizen*, a newspaper that for years contained articles highly critical of Dawley, reluctantly applauded his move in early June: "we welcome Dawley as a new recruit, pledging ourselves to forget the past, provided that he stalwartly strives to uphold the rights and dignity of labor." The paper reported that he had become "a square man."[99] As a "square man," Dawley had clearly come to reject Theodore Roosevelt's open-shop Square Deal.

In labor movement circles, Dawley attracted much attention. In one case, protesters arriving at a union meeting became somewhat suspicious, believing that Dawley's elegant car, audaciously parked outside the meeting hall, belonged to one of the garment manufacturers. Inside the meeting room, Dawley quickly reassured the skeptics by delivering a riveting speech, claiming that the fight was a virtuous one: "Wealth, property, and power all have their rights, but poverty and weakness also have rights, and I recognize the rights of all under the law." He continued, "I will devote the rest of my days to the cause of laboring manhood and womanhood. I will not rest happy until no workshop employs a girl younger than eighteen years old. The day when capital can grind labor at will has passed." After the conclusion of these Dickensian remarks, the crowd, numbering well over 1,000 men, women, and children, gave him a raucous, ten-minute standing ovation. The animated audience, consisting of strikers and their families, were overwhelmingly impressed, eager to watch his next moves as they prepared to mobilize against "the dollar men."[100] Unlike their opinion of Penton's earlier switch, unionists sincerely welcomed Dawley's change, viewing it as an act of redemption. While Dawley continued to drive expensive automobiles and in general live quite comfortably, he had clearly adopted new allegiances.

Dawley's gender assumptions, which were also held by other middle-class reformers in this era, certainly played an important part in his decision to support the largely female garment strikers. A growing number of reformers and policy-makers, including Ohio's Reynolds, had begun to support legislation protecting woman and child laborers from employer abuses, viewing these workers as more vulnerable than male wage earners. Dawley's thinking was likely influenced by the deaths of the young women from the Triangle Shirtwaist factory fire and by the Supreme Court's famous 1908 *Muller v. Oregon* ruling, which upheld Oregon's law restricting the number of hours females could work in industrial workplaces. The ruling legitimized such state laws for women, but not for men.[101] Like Louis D. Brandeis, the famous attorney and open-shop proponent who defended Oregon's law, Dawley believed that state and local governments were justified in passing protective regulations for female laborers. But Dawley, by adopting such a vocal and unyielding stand against "the dollar men" while proclaiming his desire to spend the remainder of his life supporting the labor movement, illustrated that he stood to the left of Brandeis. Above all, Dawley, unlike Brandeis and most of the era's reformers, held the view that labor was both entitled to state-backed protective regulations and that it must enjoy the freedom to form unions in closed shops.[102]

In Ohio, state legislators passed a number of laws intended to protect workers shortly after the *Muller* ruling. One of the most important was the 1911 voluntary Workmen's Compensation Act, which created a state fund requiring that all employers with at least five employees pay into it. The chief proponent of this bill, state senator William Green, a former leader of the United Mine Workers who in 1924 became head of the American Federation of Labor (AFL), also helped pass legislation restricting the number of hours to nine that factory-laboring women could work. Dawley changed sides at roughly the same time that trade union activists and pro-union politicians exercised greater legislative power. Ohio's political climate had become more favorable to some of organized labor's political goals.[103]

Of course, not everyone welcomed these developments or respected Dawley's dramatic change. Dawley's former companions, unsurprisingly, expressed disbelief and disappointment with his newfound faith in the righteousness of the trade union movement. Spokespersons for the Cleveland Employers' Association seemed more shocked and saddened than angry. A disconsolate Sayle, initially unwilling to believe the revelation, told a Cleveland newspaper, "I can hardly conceive the report is correct that Jay Dawley is the attorney for the strikers. That would be a change. I guess it's a mistake."[104]

We should not be surprised by Sayle's melancholic response, given their long history of comradeship together. They enjoyed membership in the same elite clubs, ate in the same swanky restaurants, and, most importantly, had struggled against the same enemies, including trade union militants, riotous protestors, factory inspectors, and pro-union politicians. Sayle had long depended on Dawley's loyalty, legal expertise, and editorials in the pages of *Facts*. Although Dawley had a falling-out with members of the employers' association, it is hardly likely that any of his former associates believed he would represent organized labor in such an unapologetically public and partisan way. Dawley's remarkable move was nothing short of treasonous. In their view, Dawley was now a pariah, indefinitely banned from the private meeting halls where Cleveland's "dollar men" schmoozed and planned their anti-union onslaughts.

Sayle must have been especially disappointed with the timing of Dawley's switch, since it happened just days before the Cleveland Employers' Association hosted a get-together with some of the biggest names in the national open-shop community, individuals who once enjoyed professional relationships with Dawley: the NAM's John Kirby, Jr., Walter Drew of the National Erectors' Association, and General Harrison Gray Otis, the West Coast's best-known open-shop advocate and owner of the *Los Angeles Times*. Surrounded by hanging American flags, the members of this distinguished group took turns denouncing unions for engaging in acts of thuggery and lawlessness while applauding the employers' alleged fairmindedness. Otis, "a veteran of three wars," spoke eight months after trade unionists had bombed the building that printed his newspaper. The crowd of about 150, which likely included Penton, heard the speakers address what the *Cleveland Plain Dealer* called "subjects of industrial betterment." Drew declared that the radicals responsible for the infamous Los Angeles bombing had also carried out acts of industrial sabotage in Cleveland.[105] Otis focused on "industrial freedom and said any invasion of that right was a menace to the whole country." Before he switched sides, Dawley was slated to serve as toastmaster at this important event.[106]

Shortly after the nation's leading open-shop promoters discussed "industrial betterment" activities while blasting trade unions, Dawley addressed the strikers:

> Cancel all Sunday gatherings; let there be no meetings of the strikers on the Sabbath; have them keep away from the vicinity of the factories; tell them to forget the strike and their troubles, take the kiddies and a basket of lunch, go to the park, spend the day there with the fresh air, the flowers, the sunshine, and come back on Monday, refreshed, invigorated and ready to continue the just and peaceful struggle for their rights.[107]

This recommendation reveals that Dawley clearly cared about the workers' well-being. He assumed that quality time spent at the park promised to reinvigorate the movement, providing the strikers with the renewed energy necessary to peacefully win. Of course, his insistence that they struggle peacefully suggests he was no radical, but there is no doubt he harbored a strong moral commitment, sincerely believing, as he put it, in "the cause of laboring manhood and womanhood."

And it was this strong sense of morality that helped to propel the roughly 4,000 strikers themselves over the course of the four-month dispute. Focused and confrontational, the protestors had demanded that Cleveland's garment manufacturers make significant improvements, including a fifty-hour workweek and union recognition. Conditions in Cleveland's garment factories, from the perspective of workers and union organizers, had been very poor for many years. In 1907, an out-of-state union organizer complained that "working conditions [in Cleveland] are even worse than in New York city if that can be possible."[108] Hundreds of men, women, and girls, fed up with low pay, long hours, and the "blacklist system," fought for improvements by organizing forceful marches and spirited meetings. Like the striking molders in 1900, these vigorous protestors confronted strikebreakers, defended themselves from police attacks, and organized meetings and fundraisers. The police made numerous arrests, but were unable to stop activists from marching and challenging strikebreakers.

Cleveland's socialists, led largely by a sizable minority of the city's Jewish population, were especially active in organizing militant gatherings and "monster" protests, including one that apparently involved close to 20,000 participants. Following such marches, strikers organized mass meetings where radicals of a variety of stripes gave talks about the importance of unity and the justness of their action. Leaders addressed the mainly immigrant crowds in multiple languages, including English, Yiddish, Hungarian, and Italian. As workers and union organizers strategized and protested, Dawley gave advice and raised money for the campaign.[109]

The garment manufacturers watched with frustration and dismay as strikers organized daily rallies in front of their mostly idled factories. They remained generally silent during the strike's first few days, but eventually "decided to make a concerted movement" against the protestors by forming the Cleveland Garment Manufacturers' Association, which functioned like comparable associations affiliated with other industries. Under the leadership of Morris A. Black—a Harvard graduate, civic reformer, and manufacturer who employed roughly 1,000 workers—they hired a full-time secretary and spokesperson, Philip Frankel, to coordinate strikebreaking activities. Frankel, who simultaneously worked for both the Cleveland Employers' Association and the NMTA's Cleveland branch, was an understandable choice. A salaried clerk at a printing establishment, Frankel had aspirations of becoming, in the words of one of his critics, a "union smasher."[110] To the delight of his superiors, Frankel imported strikebreakers and spies with the same high level of dedication Penton had shown when he oversaw strikebreaking operations eleven years earlier.[111] Backed by deep-pocketed employers like Black, Frankel apparently paid some strikebreakers as much as ten dollars a day—a considerably larger sum than the less-than-three dollars most garment workers earned.[112]

But the protesters pressed on, trusting that their militancy and solidarity would propel them to victory. Pauline Newman, the Russian-born union activist who had worked at New York City's Triangle Shirtwaist Company before the tragic fire in March 1911, noted, "This garment strike has aroused young and old among the workers. It has developed fighters among the girls. This is a class conscious fight. The ranks of the strikers are solid and we'll win." Cleveland's prolific socialist writer and activist, Max Hayes, explained in blunter terms, "we will whip them all."[113] Newman and Hayes clearly prioritized working-class unity, but they welcomed class traitors like Dawley.[114]

The "whipping" took different forms, though it was largely of a low-level type, directed against private guards, strikebreakers, and occasionally the husbands and wives of strikebreakers. Dawley's old companions remained physically unscathed. The press reported that riots broke out in some neighborhoods, causing hundreds of arrests. While some male strikers carried guns and used blunt objects in their confrontations against non-unionists and guards, women and girls preferred lighter, though no less damaging, weapons. Despite warnings from strike leaders and Dawley, many rebellious female strikers hurled eggs and rocks at their opponents.[115] Given the attacks, Drew called Cleveland "the hotbed of labor union thugs" in August.[116] Despite Dawley's repeated warnings, the strike was far from nonviolent, but it is doubtful that most of the city's residents saw Cleveland itself as a leading center of union thuggery. Nor was it a haven of industrial peace, as *Facts* had relentlessly propagandized. The truth lies somewhere in the middle.

Whatever the case, as the strike progressed, some supposedly impartial authorities attempted to bring the two sides together in an effort to end it. The Ohio State Board of Arbitration, for instance, proposed a conference between the employers and the strikers, but the manufacturers emphatically refused the request. Joseph Bishop of the board thought that the employers' refusal demonstrated their unreasonableness: "the attitude of the manufacturers is almost disgusting. There could be no harm in a conference, but they refused to see me."[117]

While state authorities criticized the manufacturers, the local police force protected their factories and guarded their strikebreakers. But it required some work on the part of the manufacturers to ensure such protection, since earlier conflicts indicated that the police were not always reliable. After all, employers like Penton had, five years earlier, complained about police ineffectiveness in the context of his dispute with the typographers' union. But this dispute was different, and three weeks after its start, union-breaking veteran Sayle visited city hall, where he met with Johnson's successor, Mayor Herman C. Baehr, about the necessity of defending the mobility of nonunionists under the banner of maintaining law and order. This was apparently a rather fruitful meeting for both men: Baehr, a former brewery owner, actually shared Sayle's concern about the presence of large, potentially dangerous gatherings of protestors near the factories and promised that the police would aggressively help the employers as they sought to resume production.[118]

The police proved their commitments to Sayle and his colleagues as they made many arrests throughout the summer months, jailing both weapon carriers and those who, following Dawley's advice, demonstrated peacefully. Both sides were guilty of violent acts, but in the words of a pro-union writer in September, "nine-tenths of the violence which is laid at the door of the strikers has been the result of aggression on the part of the so-called 'guards,' hired to create disturbances." The same writer commented sardonically, "Brave men, indeed, to ride roughshod among unarmed men and women who flee in terror and offer no resistance!"[119] Frankel denied that the employers' association or his strikebreaking operations generally were responsible for any of the clashes. "We are," he disingenuously maintained, "minding our own business."[120] Dawley found the large number of arrests, which exceeded 300, disturbing, noting that it "indicates a short-sighted policy on the part of the manufacturers and the police."[121] Dawley had once welcomed arrests of strikers; now he was dismayed by them.

He was also discouraged by the strike's outcome. He and his working-class allies were ultimately no match for Frankel's strikebreaking activities and the city's hostile police force. The signs of defeat were apparent in early fall: union resources were dwindling, expressions of solidarity were vanishing, and morale had reached a low point. Despite the leaders' early confidence, many strikers came to the realization that victory was unreachable, and they voted to return to work in mid-October. The garment employers had demonstrated, in essence, that they could resume production under open-shop conditions without receiving Dawley's help. They took back many, but not all—and they refused to increase wage rates, reduce hours, or recognize the union. The employers achieved victory because they were united, enjoyed superior financial resources and access to strikebreakers, and had won police and mayoral support. Dawley may have been an effective fundraiser, motivational speaker, and legal advisor, but, in the end, was unable to help defeat his powerful former associates.[122]

Dawley and Penton were, of course, no longer comrades in 1911. Dawley never reestablished professional dealings with his ex-colleagues and died in 1916. Obituary writers honored him for his many years of legal service. One writer called him "one of Cleveland's foremost criminal lawyers."[123] But his active involvement in the employers' and labor movements demonstrates that he was much more than a defense lawyer. Penton remained devoted to the employer side, continuing to churn out trade publications and collaborate with open-shop advocates. He retired in California, where he died in 1940. For more than a decade, the two men were passionate open-shop activists and spokespersons, gaining the respect of both local and national union-fighters. Their anti-labor union activism throughout the century's early years was vital, underlining the significance of non-employers in employers' associations. They were undoubtedly critical figures in Cleveland's major workplace conflicts and widely recognized for their efforts.

Penton and Dawley were clearly class traitors, disappointing their former companions for the sin of changing sides during bitter labor-management conflicts. An investigation into lives of these two enormously influential individuals helps us to better appreciate the open-shop movement's origins and limitations. Penton's career reveals that we must go back to the late 1880s and early 1890s, not to the turn-of-the century, to pinpoint the roots of his struggles with organized labor. As the leader of the International Brotherhood of Machinery Molders in these years, Penton, as we have seen, was involved in a number of brushes with the Iron Molders' Union. The following decade, as the secretary of the NFA, he had become one of the nation's most effective employer-organizers and strikebreaking planners, frustrating the IMU's efforts in Cleveland and elsewhere. Penton clearly remained committed to anti-union causes in the years after his NFA career; as an employer, he demonstrated a willingness to go to extremes, including arming nonunionists, to prevent organized labor from establishing a presence in his workplace. His former allies and rivals in the labor movement naturally found his confrontational behavior deeply troubling, but, like his allies in the open-shop movement, he defended his actions in the name of promoting community and industrial progress.

While Penton's life offers us new ways to consider the open-shop movement's origins, Dawley's career reveals fresh insights into its limitations. Indeed, labor activists gained an extraordinary recruit more than a decade after Penton's defection. Dawley—the one-time president of the Cleveland Employers' Association, passionate defense lawyer for nonunionists and employers, and *Facts* editor—spent his last years convinced that the labor movement consisted of men and women who were reasonable and moral, not lawless and detestable, as he had once thought. In 1911, he no longer believed that the open-shop movement's key planners and beneficiaries— "the dollar men"—were genuine agents of progress, sincere in their defense of "free workers," or honest proponents of a "square deal."

Yet Dawley's high-profile desertion, which happened in one of the nation's most renowned progressive cities, did nothing to change labor relations in its diverse workplaces, which, for the most part, remained profoundly inhospitable to unions. This chapter has also shown the dynamics of Cleveland's political economy in a new light, focusing on the ways in which the city's open-shop movement grew in the aftermath of the 1899 streetcar strike and remained a resilient force throughout Johnson's administration and beyond. Although the movement had lost a formidable organizer and skilled legal mind, the city's organized employers, united primarily by common class interests, continued to effectively challenge labor activists in workplaces and in courtrooms while presenting themselves as forward-thinking and class-neutral agents of "industrial betterment" activities. Of course, the many victims of Penton's strikebreaking endeavors, Cleveland's United Trades and Labor Council, low-wage garment workers, and Dawley himself found that their statements did not reflect the actual *facts*.

Chapter 4

Avenging McKinley: Organized Employers in Buffalo

I think I am just a little weary of manufacturing and manufacturing towns, however well I recognize and applaud their necessity. Some show a sense of harmony and joy in labor and enthusiasm for getting on and being happy; but others, such as Buffalo and Cleveland, seem to have fallen into that secondary or tertiary state in which all the enthusiasm of the original workers and seekers has passed, money and power and privileges have fallen into the hands of the few. There is nothing for the many save a kind of spiritless drudgery which no one appreciates and which gives a city a hard, unlovely and workaday air. I felt this to be so, keenly, in the cases of Buffalo and Cleveland, as of Manchester, Leeds and Liverpool.
—Theodore Dreiser, *A Hoosier Holiday*, 1916

Buffalo received international attention in 1901 for hosting the Pan-American Exposition, which is best remembered for its spectacular 400-foot electric tower, for exotic exhibits, and, most unforgettably, as the setting where anarchist Leon Czolgosz shot and killed president William McKinley. Like world's fairs before it, the exposition was supposed to symbolize modernization, progress, and prosperity,[1] but Czolgosz's unpardonable crime, which happened on September 6, a day after 116,660 spectators converged on the exposition grounds to watch and cheer the president as he delivered a speech celebrating America's global supremacy and national unity, overshadowed practically everything else, profoundly disheartening visitors, organizers, and Americans generally. The exposition's legacy would be forever associated with this high-profile murder.

Many called for swift punishment. Czolgosz, son of Polish immigrants and follower of well-known anarchist Emma Goldman, was quickly apprehended, sent to jail, interrogated by investigators, beaten by guards, and executed in the electric chair at Auburn Prison weeks later.[2] Aware of these developments, left-wing advocates and some trade unionists felt, at this time, a heightened sense of anxiety, believing they would likely encounter increased threats in the months and years ahead. The *International Socialist Review*, for example, predicted in October 1901 that the nation's employers and the state would use the assassination as an excuse to stage campaigns against what it called "all enemies of exploitation and oppression."[3]

In the meantime, Buffalo's business leaders and conference organizers were left deeply upset, and perhaps a bit embarrassed, that this beloved leader was murdered in their city. It is unlikely that they had contemplated such violent acts in the run-up to the exposition, but Czolgosz's brazen act showed what was possible. Nevertheless, members of this community, a forward-thinking group of manufacturers and merchants who had spent decades building and celebrating western New York's dynamic economy, were unwilling to allow McKinley's murder to define their city. In the years after the tragedy, they showed a continued readiness to boost Buffalo, attract investment, establish labor-management harmony, and grow. As the president of the city's Chamber of Commerce put it in 1905, "Buffalo hopes before very long to be the second[-biggest] city of the State."[4] Above all, they wanted to establish a business-friendly environment partially by preventing the spread of radicalism and its taint on their city. Manufacturers, especially those affiliated with the dozens of foundries that partially defined the region's eye-catching industrial landscape, sought to prove beyond any doubt that they were the city's uncontested industrial leaders, unwilling to let expressions of working-class radicalism go unchallenged. This chapter addresses the dilemmas of these men, exploring their efforts to advance the city's reputation and attract investment. It also documents the emergence of organizations of employers and workers, and the tensions and battles between them.

These tensions and battles were especially apparent in 1906, when foundry owners, representing workplaces of various sizes and holding membership in the National Founders' Association (NFA)-affiliated Buffalo Foundrymen's Association, faced off against roughly a thousand members of the Iron Molders' Union (IMU).[5] For the city's foundry operators, the months-long struggle, which featured the importation of many strikebreakers, episodes of picket-line violence, and court-issued injunctions, was a mixed blessing. While their workplaces suffered short-term disruptions in production, the strike gave them the chance to prove to the outside business community that they could effectively break the IMU's near-monopoly on molding jobs, restore "law-and-order," and demonstrate their commitment to employing workers based, according to John A. Penton's *Iron Trade Review*, "wholly on merit and efficiency"—the progressive virtues embedded within the open-shop principle.[6] They sought to show that neither radicalism nor closed-shop unionism were welcome in Buffalo's borders.

Building, Boosting, and Organizing

First, we must consider the city's early history. It is unsurprising that organizers picked Buffalo for the setting of the Pan-American Exposition. Incorporated as a city in 1832, this Lake Erie community was a highly significant and dynamic commercial center in part because of its strategic geographic position. Its businessmen enjoyed links to important waterways, including the Erie Canal and Lake Erie, which connected them to growing East Coast and Midwest markets: Rochester, Erie, Cleveland, Toledo, and Detroit. During McKinley's presidency, its harbor witnessed much commercial activity, becoming the nation's fourth busiest.[7] In 1905, the city's ports registered $11,574,171 worth of tonnage, a million more than Cleveland's ports.[8] And Buffalo became a leading center of land-based transportation. By 1903, twenty-eight railroads serviced it, making it second only to Chicago in traffic.[9] Nearby Niagara Falls helped generate the city's largest manufacturing establishments; in 1896, the city began using hydroelectric power, a relatively inexpensive energy source.[10] And between 1890 and 1906, investors established more than 400 factories within the city's boundaries.[11]

What explains Buffalo's economic growth? Ogden P. Letchworth, head of the giant Pratt and Letchworth Company, a major, nationally recognized manufacturer of malleable castings founded by his uncle William and Pascal and Samuel Pratt in 1848, offered one reason, explaining in 1902 that growing numbers of manufacturers "have been influenced in making this choice [to build in Buffalo] largely by the favorable impressions received while attending some one or another of the many conventions."[12] A regional philanthropist, socialite, and one of the original NFA officeholders, Letchworth had established close relationships with manufacturers through-out the nation partially as a result of organizing and attending confer-ences.[13] At these events, industrialists like Letchworth bragged about the city's industrial and infrastructural accomplishments. Additionally, outside observers, including professional engineers, reinforced the publicity gener-ated at conferences by underlining Buffalo's remarkable accomplishments, especially in the area of manufacturing. According to an American Society of Mechanical Engineers publication, Buffalo was home to some of the nation's most efficient and impressive American steam pumping engines.[14]

Buffalo's business leaders were especially active in trumpeting their city in the run-up to special occasions. One writer explained in 1909 that "from time to time special efforts have been made to advertise Buffalo. This was notably so just prior to the Pan-American Exposition."[15] Local businessmen made extensive preparations for the crowds and attention, and Letchworth, who at the time of the exposition served as the Buffalo Merchants' Exchange president, oversaw public relations activities.[16] Industrial leaders, collaborating with Letchworth, adopted several flattering names for the 250,000-person city in the months before the event: America's "best planned city," "the model convention city of America," the "Queen City of the Great Lakes," and "among the progressive cities of America."[17] Letchworth and his colleagues saw the occasion as an opportunity to lure additional investors to this "progressive" community. As a fellow Buffalo Merchants' Exchange member explained in 1900, "A very favorable oppor-tunity will be given to impress upon these people the desirability of Buffalo as a manufacturing point, and we think the exchange could do no better work during the coming year, then to arrange some systematic way of bringing the advantages of Buffalo to the attention of these people."[18]

Organizing coincided with boosting. Decades before Letchworth became a major figure in several exclusive businessmen's associations, Buf-falo's entrepreneurs launched a variety of collaborative activities in part to help make the city inviting to outsiders. The city's businessmen established the Chamber of Commerce, the nation's third, in 1844.[19] Under the leader-ship of attorney Russell H. Haywood, the organization was designed to, according to an early historian speaking in 1870, "cultivate friendship among the business men of Buffalo, to unite them in one general policy for the general benefit of trade and commerce of Buffalo, and to make it a market for western produce."[20] According to historian David A. Gerber, these early joiners adopted the belief "that cutthroat competition was ruinous to individual interests and debilitating to the morale of the trading community."[21]

Letchworth fully embraced the collaborative spirit first propagated by Haywood and his colleagues. In June 1901, he welcomed approximately 200 manufacturers to Buffalo for the annual meeting of the American Foundrymen's Association. The invitees were proprietors of medium-sized workplaces, producing machinery castings for steam locomotives, automobiles, turbines, power transmission equipment, pumps, and other heavy equipment sold on the local, national, and, in some cases, international markets. Letchworth, delighted by the opportunity to host the meeting on the Pan-American Exposition grounds—which, the *The Iron Trade Review* reported, "will be at its highest glory and brightness"—wanted the foundrymen, many of whom resided in places like Chicago, Cleveland, Milwaukee, Pittsburgh, and Philadelphia, to fully enjoy Buffalo and discover its many virtues.[22] The exposition offered plenty of opportunities for carefree fun and stimulation, and Letchworth attempted to charm the visitors, hoping that they would invest in the city, claiming at the time "that Buffalo's future greatness depends largely upon the establishing within our midst the greatest number of new manufacturing industries."[23]

Yet Letchworth identified one probable challenge to the city's "future greatness": labor unions. Indeed, labor-related problems were never far from the minds of employers in Buffalo or elsewhere; many were typically unable to run their manufacturing establishments without facing occasional challenges from below, a problem that seemed to weigh particularly heavy on Letchworth's mind at the time of the conference. According to *The Iron Trade Review*, Letchworth, after affectionately welcoming the AFA members to Buffalo, "touched upon the strained relations between capital and labor, in all sections of the country at the present time, and he deplored the stand taken by the labor leaders which he predicted, if persisted in, will result in the strangulation and destruction of the country's greatest interests."[24] Speaking only weeks after the International Association of Machinists (IAM) staged a highly disruptive multi-city strike against National Metal Trades Association (NMTA) members, Letchworth reminded the audience that the stakes were very high. Diverting attention from Buffalo, he emphasized that this was a *national* problem, noting that a significant number of union leaders, by calling strikes, halting production, and testing the patience of employers, threatened to derail the country's "greatest interests," which inevitably produced rising levels of nervousness in management circles. According to this view, the shortsightedness and irresponsibility of "the labor leaders," not structural inequality or simmering shop floor grievances, were the principal causes of this problem. His colleagues, certainly sharing an interest in maintaining uninterrupted production, lasting periods of control, and profits, most likely nodded their heads in agreement. According to a report of the meeting, at least one fellow union opponent "responded appropriately," and thanked "him on behalf of the association."[25]

Three months after Letchworth delivered his rather dismal remarks in front of a modest-sized number of foundry operators, McKinley gave an entirely optimistic address near the same spot on the exposition's grounds to a general audience of tens of thousands. The contrasts between the two talks are remarkable. "This country," McKinley cheered, "is in a state of unexampled prosperity." In order to protect the nation's affluence, he stressed the necessity of national unity: "our interest is in concord, not conflict." By following such advice, the president, employing the language of class neutrality, predicted a future of "greater commerce and trade for us all." As American businessmen continued to increase production and expand investment domestically and internationally, he anticipated "relations of mutual respect, confidence, and friendship which will deepen and endure."[26] While Buffalo's businessmen eagerly trumpeted their city even as they shed light on the seemingly insurmountable union-related problems, McKinley applauded the nation's economic health, predicting a harmonious future free of regional and class antagonisms.

"The Masters" Versus "the Boy in Buffalo"

McKinley's forecast was incorrect. The following day, he was shot twice by Czolgosz, the infamous working-class activist from Cleveland. Czolgosz failed to take McKinley's message to heart; he was unimpressed by the exposition's bright lights, glorious speeches, or the expansion of trade and economic development throughout the Americas. He appears to have acted out of genuine anger, which climaxed after years of performing mundane, unfulfilling labor in factories and following prolonged bouts of joblessness.

In his mind, the president was hopelessly disconnected from reality, claiming shortly after his arrest that "McKinley was going around the country shouting about prosperity when there was no prosperity for the poor man."[27]

In fact, Czolgosz had spent numerous years toiling in Cleveland, where he earned about ten dollars a week, a small sum. Hungry for ideas that offered an explanation for his financial misery, he also read left-wing literature and joined picket lines with co-workers, demanding higher wages. In 1893, managers at the Cleveland Rolling Mill Company fired and blacklisted Czolgosz in response to his participation in a strike there.[28] This event only added to his list of societal grievances. And in May 1901, the twenty-eight-year-old had heard anarchist Emma Goldman speak in Cleveland. She was a source of inspiration, helping to shape Czolgosz's worldview, one that questioned the legitimacy of capitalism itself. Czolgosz, radicalized by his experiences with workplace exploitation, joblessness, and Goldman's teachings, saw the nation's elites from both the private and public sectors not as agents of technological improvements or promoters of shared economic prosperity, but rather as oppressors of the working classes. He explained in rather stark terms, "I killed the president because of the working people. He belonged to a different class."[29]

It did not take long for authorities to discover the connections between Czolgosz and Goldman, which placed her at risk. Buffalo's police force wanted her for questioning, but Goldman, who sympathized with "the boy in Buffalo," maintained her freedom because the authorities were unable to prove that she had any direct involvement in the murder.[30] Indeed, she was innocent, but had little compassion for McKinley, asserting in her 1934 autobiography that the dead president "typified a hostile and reactionary attitude to labour: he had repeatedly sided with the masters by sending troops into strike regions."[31]

Members of this so-called "master" class were particularly distraught by the murder. McKinley had spent years cultivating relationships with bankers, merchants, and manufacturers prior to, and during, his presidency. In fact, he was present at some of the earliest manufacturers' association gatherings. In 1895, he spoke at the National Association of Manufacturers inaugural meeting, where, in his characteristically upbeat manner, he discussed ways of alleviating the period's economic crisis.[32] "We want our own markets for our manufactures and agricultural products; we want a tariff for our surplus products which will not surrender our markets and will not degrade our labor to hold our markets," the then Ohio governor announced to an enthusiastic crowd of business leaders and future open-shop activists.[33]

Attendees did not forget McKinley's collegiality and support, and one year after his famous speech at the NAM opening meeting, they engaged in a vigorous campaign to elect him to the presidency. During both the 1896 and 1900 presidential contests, businessmen, in Buffalo and elsewhere, were his most passionate backers.[34] Once elected, McKinley demonstrated his appreciation by endorsing several pro-business policies, including protective tariffs, and by continuing to present friendly talks at their gatherings.[35] In summer 1897, he visited Buffalo, where he delivered a presentation before the Buffalo Republican League, an organization Letchworth headed in the late 1880s. Here McKinley, an honorary member of the league, celebrated what he called "the spirit of comradeship" while applauding the enduring significance of national unity and the impressive growth and professionalism of the U.S. military. "Now," he pointed out with patriotic pride, "the army of Grant and the Army of Lee are together."[36]

Although McKinley promoted their financial interests, shared their values, and spoke at their exclusive gatherings, fellow Republicans and business leaders, following his death, believed he needed to be memorialized as a generous guardian of all Americans, not as a tool of the so-called "master" class. Some even suggested he was a sincere champion of the working class's financial interests. David M. Parry of the NAM, for instance, held an outlook wholly at odds with that of Czolgosz and Goldman. The Indianapolis carriage manufacturer found it truly preposterous that any working-class person would want to cause him harm: McKinley "certainly has given the poorer classes and the working classes the best that could be given to them; his fine administration has given the laborers all the work that they have been able to do."[37]

But Parry and his allies in the areas of business and politics had no tolerance for extremism done in the name of the working class, and in the days and weeks after the murder, a rising chorus of voices clamored for retribution against Czolgosz and the anarchist movement generally. George Creel's (Kansas City) Independent, for instance, argued that anarchists must be "gagged": "Had the Goldman woman been gagged long ago, the country would not now be in mourning, for did not Czolgosz expressly state that it was from her preachings that he gained his cursed inspiration."[38] Creel had essentially called for free speech restrictions in order to prevent further murderous attacks. Yet some drew distinctions between different forms of murder, and at least one prominent politician openly called for Czolgosz's death hours after the assassination. U.S. senator Thomas C. Platt of New York reasoned that "this is one of the instances where I think lynch law justifiable." Platt was not the only bigwig to clamor for such actions, but he certainly helped to legitimize an atmosphere thick with calls for vengeance.[39] In their collective view, business and political leaders, including McKinley himself, had done "right" by opening workplaces, creating jobs, and promoting economic development in Buffalo and throughout the nation. McKinley's murder, coinciding with the spread of left-wing ideas and the outbreaks of labor struggles, reminded them that they also needed to fight.

Shortly after McKinley's death, a handful of Buffalo's residents, responding to this climate, served on the jury to decide Czolgosz's fate. What, if any role, did the city's business community play in the trial? Answer: a very essential one. Significantly, one of Buffalo's leading manufacturers and National Founders' Association leader, Henry W. Wendt of the Buffalo Forge Company, was a central participant in the proceedings that decided its outcome.[40] Wendt, whose 11 fellow jurors chose him to serve as foreman, took his public service seriously: at 4:26 P.M. on September 23, after deliberating for eight hours, Wendt declared Czolgosz "Guilty of murder in the first degree."[41] A Republican with close ties to Letchworth, Wendt, whom a writer for the *Buffalo Express* identified as one of "the honest men, who believe in the laws and institutions of the United States," was entirely at ease with this decision.[42] Judge Truman C. White, himself a Buffalo booster, announced Czolgosz's punishment on September 26. A month later, Czolgosz, with the wholehearted approval of Wendt and White, became New York State's 50th person to perish in the electric chair.[43]

In the aftermath of these two murders, Buffalo's employers had become somewhat less publicly vocal and showy, but they still continued to organize, network, invest in the city, and prepare for the possibility of additional attacks by anarchists, socialists, or trade unionists. Like their counterparts in other cities, they joined local and national associations, which pledged to help them cope with labor-related difficulties.

Organized Labor

Buffalo established itself as a strong union town with a tradition of collective bargaining and periodic outbreaks of working-class combativeness at roughly the same time that manufacturers developed resilient partnerships with one another. And the city was home to numerous labor-management conflicts and unionization campaigns during the decades after the Civil War. The city's railroad workers participated in the greatly destructive 1877 strike, and two decades later, a grain shovelers' walkout resulted in a victory for the strikers.[44] About 1,000 Buffalo machinists participated in the IAM-sponsored national work stoppage in May 1901. Taken together, such strikes were staged by native-born Americans and recently arrived immigrants from Canada, England, Ireland, Italy, Hungary, Poland, and Russia.[45] And the city's craft workers formed the United Trades and Labor Council in the 1890s. Strikes, combined with aggressive organizing, demonstrated that the city had a strong labor movement. For many years, the city was, according to a 1906 article in the local newspaper, "a good union town."[46]

The IMU, which organized five locals in Buffalo during the second half of the nineteenth century, was one of the city's sturdiest, most powerful, and respectable labor associations. The IMU's first Buffalo local, No. 84, began representing molders in 1860, one year after the union emerged nationally. Throughout the 1890s, the molders, according to an 1897 trade union publication, were "on friendly terms with the employers of members with one exception, the Washington Iron Works on Broadway." Buffalo's Washington Iron Works apparently "discriminated against members of the union, and deterring its employees from joining, and so antagonized organized labor in general."[47] Most foundry owners recognized the union, negotiated with its leaders, and routinely agreed to minimum pay rates. During the second half of the nineteenth century, most, for purely pragmatic reasons, accepted closed shops provided that molders conducted their duties efficiently and skillfully, realizing that containment was more advantageous than confrontation. And the IMU, like most Buffalo unions, wanted to preserve its relationship with the employers; it was not especially radical.[48] Few union leaders, in other words, shared much in common politically with Goldman or Czolgosz.

Yet Buffalo's molders recurrently made requests for pay increases, and its members repeatedly demonstrated a willingness to shut down operations and join picket lines when employers failed to submit. In 1898, for instance, the IMU demanded a minimum pay rate of $2.25 a day. Fourteen employers granted this increase without protest, though a small number did not, resulting in a strike of 130 men from the Snow Steam Pump Works, Farrar and Trefts, the Fillmore Avenue Foundry Works, and the Buffalo Steam

Pump Works in nearby Tonawanda. This confrontation was ultimately effective: all employers, eager to resume production, increased the minimum pay rate.[49] At the time of this rather brief and unexceptional strike, the union leadership actually thought its demands were somewhat modest. According to IMU vice president Michael Keough, "We have had no desire to be arbitrary in asking an increase of pay, as shown by the fact that so low a rate was asked. No city in the United States pays such low wages as we have asked." He pointed out that molders in a number of western cities earned as much as $3.50 per day.[50] Nevertheless, this strike shows that unionists were perfectly comfortable leaving their workstations when they believed such actions produced meaningful results.

Almost immediately after these confrontations concluded, IMU members at the Buffalo Forge Company, which had been in operation since 1877, struck because their bosses, brothers William and Henry W. Wendt, demanded that they labor extra hours for the same daily pay rate, $2.25. Seeking sharp increases in efficiency, the Wendt brothers further insisted that employees begin to operate three machines instead of one. Viewing the new policy as deeply unreasonable, the molders' responded by leaving their stations, walking picket lines, and insisting that they should continue to receive the same rate while manning only one machine. The workers' solidarity and persistence, propelled by a commonsense belief in fairness, paid off: the employers withdrew their cost-saving proposal after a week of spirited demonstrations kept the workplace idle.[51] For protestors, the experience was certainly educational and empowering. By winning their strike, Buffalo's IMU members had become fully aware of their collective power.

The Employers' Response

But the employers sought to limit that power. Responding to this uptick in working-class combativeness, Buffalo's foundry operators joined national and local associations, organizations that helped them halt strikes at the point of production and articulate a common message of managerial and capitalist progressivism to the general public. Their interest in organizing became especially apparent after the IMU's multiple victories in 1898. In that year, a small number of employers, including Letchworth, helped build the NFA, a "defense association," for the explicit purpose of responding effectively to "demagogues, walking delegates, and agitators."[52] NFA organizers created several districts throughout the nation, and employers in New York and New Jersey constituted District 2. Letchworth was one of the early proponents of national employer unity, serving as the NFA's third president from 1899 to 1901, the association's formative years.

Locally, the foundry operators, organized in the NFA-affiliated Buffalo Foundrymen's Association, established a formal agreement with the Iron Molders Conference Board of Buffalo and Vicinity in 1902. Many of its terms appeared rather favorable to the union. For instance, molders received a minimum wage of $2.80 per day, as well as time-and-a-half pay for Sundays and holidays, which included the Fourth of July, Labor Day, Thanksgiving, and Christmas. Furthermore, they won the right to elect shop floor committees comprising three representatives in each foundry. In return for pay increases and representation improvements, IMU members agreed to honor employers' decision to introduce new molding machinery.[53] Union leaders had essentially traded a limited amount of control over the means of production for greater financial compensation. According to a 1905 article in the *Foundry*, the employers' association was "in a very healthy and prosperous condition."[54] Both sides seemed content.

Yet nationally, following the New York Agreement's collapse in 1904 in the midst of a violent molders' strike in Utica, the NFA leadership, viewing labor-management contacts as harmful to both nonunionists and to the long-term interests of employers, requested that the membership cease formal negotiations with the IMU. This was easier said than done. To the annoyance of NFA members, considerable numbers of unionized molders remained in foundries, where they continued to exert some control over the labor process while demanding collective bargaining rights. As a representative to the NFA national meeting in 1905 explained, "The more thoroughly a shop is unionized the greater the difficulty in educating apprentices. It matters little how much proprietors of any institution desire to accomplish in behalf of the apprentice boy; while the boy himself is surrounded by this union atmosphere it is an insurmountable barrier to his education."[55]

We should hardly be surprised by the delegate's criticism. By this time, foundrymen had become increasingly impatient with the IMU's near-monopoly on the labor supply in some regions, its persistent requests for wage increases, and its tendency to organize walkouts when it failed to get its way. In this context, employers felt a pressing need to protect "the apprentice boy." They urgently wanted this younger generation to focus its attention primarily on the work process itself rather than develop feelings of entitlement or become embroiled in labor conflicts due to the subversive influences of veteran IMU members—individuals who continued to demand that employers increase wages and run their foundries as closed shops. NFA members, in their quest to find ways of properly educating these boys and increasing their own positions of authority, had thus become convinced of the necessity of destroying this seemingly "insurmountable barrier."

"Practical Men" and the 1906 Strike

In early May 1906, Buffalo's NFA members believed that they could meet this goal. At that time, Buffalo's IMU leaders, speaking on behalf of hundreds of unionists, approached their employers and demanded that molders receive wage increases from $2.80 a day to $3.00, and that the somewhat less skilled coremakers earn $2.75 a day, up from $2.50. These demands seemed rather unremarkable and predictable given the local history of labor-management relations, but the employers' response represented a fundamental departure from past practices. Rather than immediately capitulate or battle for a short period before submitting, the employers—including Henry Wendt, Letchworth and thirty-two other foundry owners—refused to grant the request and instead declared their intention to enforce a new system of management, one that promoted and rewarded individual efficiency rather than one that functioned in response to union pressures. Following a common managerial practice, employers posted notices on their foundry gates, stating their unequivocal opposition to granting identical wage rates. As John Gorss, the city's principal strike-breaking architect and spokesperson for the Buffalo Foundrymen's Association, explained in late May, "What we object to is paying the men a uniform scale of wages. If a man is worth $5 a day, he will be paid it, and so with the individual who is worth $2 a day. We cannot see the justice of paying a poor, unskilled workman the same wages as the first class mechanic."[56]

Calls for rewarding efficiency and punishing incompetence reflected the wishes of both local employers and the NFA national leadership. Immediately prior to the strike, NFA leaders instructed members, both Buffalo's foundry owners and employers in other cities, to refuse to offer any across-the-board wage increases. NFA head Otis P. Briggs, following a resolution passed by the organization's administrative council declaring its nonnegotiable refusal to bargain, sent a directive to all local chapters in 1906. "The best plan to adopt [when hit by the strike]," Briggs declared, "is to keep your capable and fair-minded men well paid and satisfied but don't increase any minimum wage rate."[57] Briggs, who had succeeded Penton as chief NFA strategist in 1903, requested that foundry operators employ molders irrespective of union status, generously compensate loyal and skilled workmen, and stubbornly resist any temptation to negotiate with the workforce as a whole. The Minneapolis-based organizer assumed employers, cooperating closely with assistants like Gorss, could rely on enough skilled nonunionists to maintain production and in the process break the IMU near-monopoly on the labor supply.[58]

Buffalo's foundry operators participated in this campaign in part because they wanted to reduce labor costs. "With the constant demands of the unions for more money, Buffalo manufacturers cannot even compete with Erie and other cities where the open-shop prevails," Gorss explained in early May. "Year by year," he continued, "work is diverted from this city. As it is now, local firms are outbid on all classes of work."[59] Gorss's comments are revealing. Unlike many open-shop advocates, who tended to prioritize, at least publicly, organized labor's *moral* deficiencies in the context of workplace disputes, Gorss initially invoked an economic doctrine, explaining that manufacturers had serious problems with the IMU because of the profound threat it posed to the employers' financial interests. Of course, this view, the desire to increase regional competitiveness, had been a hallmark in the city for generations, especially during the McKinley years, but it took on a renewed urgency in 1906. To suitably compete with other cities and secure business contracts, employers understood that they needed to contain costs, which required drastic action: the removal of IMU-backed closed shops.

But the IMU was equally determined to win this contest, insisting that the foundrymen must continue to acknowledge their organization and increase their wages. This dramatic face-off was a national one, but the battle in Buffalo was, according to a report in the local press in June, a "hotbed of the strike."[60] The IMU, building on its long history of workplace activism and drawing on a $250,000 striker defense fund, was prepared for a protracted struggle. And the union's business agents, providing members

with a weekly allowance of $7, helped organize a series of angry and boister-
ous demonstrations.[61] "The quiet of the industrial situation at Buffalo,
N.Y.," the NFA's Briggs reported two years after the uprising, "was disturbed by the union of iron molders in May, 1906."[62] Briggs's report called
the rebellion, which also affected foundries in Chicago, Milwaukee, Kansas
City, and numerous smaller cities, "the most gigantic strike ever witnessed
in a mechanical line on this continent."[63]

Briggs overstated the strike's giganticness, but it certainly was an intense
confrontation that had a profoundly unsettling impact on the community.
Buffalo had become extremely polarized, tensions were pronounced, and
the streets showed signs of chaos as soon as the first strikebreakers, whom
the left-leaning *Cleveland Citizen* called "paid thugs and hirelings of the
National Foundrymen's Association," walked off their train cars.[64] Predictably, several unionists confronted the strikebreakers, tried to convince them
against taking the jobs, and, when persuasion and insults failed, used physical force. Violent attacks and counterattacks occurred well into the fall
months, resulting in dozens of injuries and at least one death, a nonunionist. Following the conflict, strikebreakers testified that they were routinely
harassed by protestors, who had issued threatening statements, such as
"When are you going to get out of town? If you don't we'll fix you so you
won't come back." Another reported that frightening demonstrators had
told him to "Go on about your business; we will give you your trimmings
to-night."[65] Strikebreakers were not the only targets of these attacks. Protestors also unleashed their collective fury on boarding house owners,
demanding that they refuse to rent to nonunionists.[66] *The Iron Trade Review*
noted that the "women, who took them as boarders had been subject to
vile language and threatened [with] bodily harm."[67] These sensational anecdotes, disseminated most powerfully by union critics, helped to underline
the message that picketers were notoriously brutish, hopelessly unable to
organize themselves in lawful or peaceful ways. Such critics highlighted
what they considered the moral deficiencies of union behavior, reinforcing
the widely held belief that "there is no such thing as peaceful picketing."

Yet the demonstrators actually succeeded in preventing at least some
men from entering the struck shops precisely *because they* adopted the very
strategies and tactics that their numerous critics deplored. For instance,
crowds of marauding strikers outside the Buffalo Foundry Company, a
leading builder of heavy castings,[68] frustrated Gorss's efforts by successfully
convincing twenty nonunionists to refrain from working; these men,

outnumbered by belligerents, complained to their supervisors that they were sick and therefore could not perform their jobs.[69] Perhaps out of embarrassment, the nonunionists chose to mask the true reasons for their reluctance to cross the picket line. It is fair to say that they made their decisions because they either sympathized with the union cause or because they feared the potentially violent consequences of working during the strike. It is doubtful that they were truly ill. Whatever the case, this episode illustrates that union members continued to recognize the power of collective protests. It also showed that Gorss and the Buffalo Foundry Company experienced a clear, though relatively minor, setback.[70]

In this context of mounting tensions, union leaders attempted to rebuild relationships with the employers, hoping to conclude the strike diplomatically and peacefully. In early June, Keough, who had attended numerous joint labor-management meetings during McKinley's presidency, visited with employers in a final attempt to convince them to recognize the union and to grant across-the-board raises. The Troy, New York–based IMU vice president, accustomed to give-and-take negotiations, appeared taken aback by the newfound stubbornness. "The foundrymen had never raised the open-shop issue before this strike," a dispirited Keough reported.[71] Keough had seen employers elsewhere become unyielding, cease negotiations with labor leaders, import strikebreakers, and ultimately bust unions while self-righteously waving the open-shop banner high, but this was the first time in his experience that Buffalo's foundry owners, speaking with one voice, refused to formally negotiate with, or even recognize, the union. Yet it is genuinely hard to believe that Keough was somehow startled by this turn of events. Any serious observer of labor relations, especially IMU leaders, must have certainly understood that the open-shop principle had begun to enjoy almost universal acceptance within management circles by this time. However, this does not mean that the employers' relinquishment of the earlier system was any less disappointing to Keough.

While Keough and the IMU leadership may have looked back nostalgically to a former period marked by a greater degree of labor-management cooperation, the foundry owners continuously looked forward, seeking new partners as they attempted to reward the "fair-minded" nonunionists and remove the troublemakers. Gorss, for example, collaborated thoroughly with law enforcement and nonunion men, figures who had little, if any, experience with collective bargaining activities, union affairs, labor protests, or radical politics. Of course, many of the foundries operated under capacity for a time as managers and engineers fended off attacks by protestors and taught the new men the dimensions of the molding process, including the importance of using good quality sand, the necessity of employing appropriate measurements, and the need to master the correct tools.[72] Gorss was largely impressed with the rapid pace of their progress and the general quality of their work, calling them "practical men." According to an interview with Gorss in the *Illustrated Buffalo Express*, "The output is even better. There is more tonnage than there was under the union rules."[73] The "practical men," in other words, were more reliable and productive than IMU members. The "practical men" were free to produce more precisely because they were unburdened by restrictive "union rules." They did not make unreasonable demands, stop or slow production, sabotage machinery, attack police officers, or spend time in socialist or anarchist meetings. In Gorss's mind, they were definitely not followers of Goldman or Czolgosz. The "practical men" were law-abiding, self-motivated, obedient, and conscientious learners, listening attentively to their instructors while ignoring the desperate pleas of union activists to join picket lines, leave western New York, or show any signs of company disloyalty. Above all, they played an indispensable part in the local industry's fast-moving transformation from an IMU stronghold to an open-shop citadel.

Yet given the IMU's traditions of picket-line militancy and overall mobilizing effectiveness, the "practical men" required security, and local law enforcement, numbering over 800 patrolmen, happily stepped up to look after their welfare. "Practically all of the work of replacing molders," Gorss admitted in August, "has been done under police protection."[74] Lyman P. Hubbell, the head of the Fillmore Avenue Foundry Works—a manufacturer of building castings that employed about seventy men—was especially thankful for their assistance, applauding them for protecting both nonunion workers and employers "from riot and mob rule."[75] By guarding workplaces and by arresting protestors during these unruly months, the police helped to ensure that nonunionists enjoyed the "right to work," that employers enjoyed greater workplace control, and that the city's citizens enjoyed protections from riotous demonstrators.[76]

Buffalo's police also sought to protect employers and the "practical men" from political radicals, especially anarchists. Most dramatically, in July, authorities succeeded in barring Goldman, who continued to agitate

against repression and inequality after Czolgosz's execution, from addressing a mostly working-class crowd in a meeting hall not far from the struck
workplaces. Hours before Goldman was scheduled to speak, a police official
told the event organizer, "a well-known Jew," that she was unwelcome in
Buffalo and that anarchists were prohibited from holding gatherings.[77] The
meeting's date, coinciding with the molders' strike, must have surely caused
additional concerns for the authorities; they most certainly wanted to prevent the tarnished rabble-rouser from offering sympathetic comments and
advice to an already incensed community of protesters. From the perspective of the employers and the police, nothing seemed more dangerous—or
aroused more disturbing memories—than the presence of an anarchist-
inspired labor movement. And nowhere was this truer than in Buffalo,
where, in Goldman's words, "The shadow of September 6 still haunts the
police of that city."[78]

The repressive actions of Buffalo's authorities—who had essentially
carried out Creel's earlier wishes by "gagging" Goldman—reflected the
broader, post-McKinley political climate. Shortly after assuming the presidency in September 1901, Theodore Roosevelt, determined to prevent
another attack like Czolgosz's, made his anti-anarchist views absolutely
explicit, insisting "that we should war with relentless efficiency not only
against anarchists, but against all active and passive sympathizers with anarchists."[79] Soon, numerous states, beginning with New York, passed a series
of stringent anti-anarchist laws, and Congress's Immigration Act of 1903
barred anarchists from entering the country. New York's law, passed by the
legislature in 1902, outlawed speeches and published statements advocating
the overthrow of the government "by force or violence, or by assassination."[80] It is hard to say whether Goldman would have advocated violence
had she been able to agitate in Buffalo. Whatever the case, by preventing her
from speaking, the city police had undoubtedly proved themselves faithful
followers of Roosevelt and loyal enforcers of New York State law.

Of course, the police were less influential than judges, who also played
a crucial part in helping employers marginalize strikers and resume production. Throughout the summer and fall months, they punished individual
labor activists with fines and jail time and, more meaningfully, issued a
number of solidarity-breaking injunctions. Indeed, foundry owners, like
many strike victims, desired injunctive relief against the disruptive, and
occasionally violent, molders. And perhaps no employer felt more vulnerable and thus in need of this assistance than Henry D. Miles, the head of the

Buffalo Foundry Company, a workplace repeatedly bedeviled by combative and effective picketers, who the trade press complained were "consistently stationed" near the foundry.[81] As we have seen, the molders here had successfully prevented, through force or persuasion, more than a dozen non-unionists from entering his shop. In response to months of physical and verbal abuse, Miles—who had become head of this medium and large castings manufacturing company in 1902 shortly after marrying the daughter of the company's founder—sought and received help from White, the same judge who had ordered Czolgosz to the electric chair five years earlier. White's comprehensive injunction, issued in October, declared it unlawful to force "any or all" workmen "to leave the employment of plaintiff" and prohibited "intimidating or threatening in any unlawful manner the relatives, wives and family of said employes at their homes or elsewhere."[82] *The Iron Trade Review* reported that this was, at the time, "one of the most sweeping injunctions" in the nation.[83]

Numerous employers enjoyed victories thanks to the efforts of judges, police forces, and Gorss's strikebreaking coordination. One of the early victors was Wendt. In late June, dozens of disheartened molders from his Buffalo Forge Company, one of the nation's longest-continuing manufacturers of forges, fans, and machine tools by the time of the protest, returned to work without winning any concessions. According to a July article in the *Buffalo Courier*, Wendt "has succeeded in whipping the men into line and on Monday they will return under the same terms existing before they struck. The molders will get $2.80 a day and the coremakers $2.50 with open-shop conditions." More importantly, the returners no longer enjoyed union benefits. A principled open-shop proponent, the forty-three-year-old Wendt, who at the time was a member of the NFA's nineteen-member administrative council, predictably elected to treat the men as individuals, rather than as IMU members. Those who continued to rebel, numbering about ninety, found themselves unwelcome in Wendt's foundry, or in any of the other NFA-affiliated workplaces.[84] Wendt had orders to fill, including shipping fanning systems, heating equipment, and other products to customers throughout the world, including in Australia and Japan. With help from Briggs, Gorss, the judiciary, and the police, he resumed production, no longer feeling any obligation to recognize the IMU.[85]

At this point, therefore, Wendt, like White, had become somewhat of a local hero, and his colleagues cheered the news of his victory. Hubbell was especially delighted with Wendt's achievement, believing it indicated a key

Figure 3. Henry W. Wendt (ca. 1920). Courtesy of the Buffalo Historical Museum.

blow against closed-shop unionism. This managerial triumph, according to Hubbell, enjoyed support from the molders and coremakers. It unequivocally showed, he wrote in the NFA's nationally circulated *Review*, that Buffalo's workers "are not in sympathy with the demands of the leaders for closed shops."[86] Wendt's decisive actions were clearly an inspiration to others, showing that it was needless to share power with, or make concessions to, organized labor. Wendt, like White, one of the men responsible for Czolgosz's death sentence, could now claim two critical victories for his class.[87]

Wendt was not the only nationally trumpeted open-shop activist to achieve industrial peace. Letchworth had reasons to be proud as well. While some IMU members struck the Pratt and Letchworth Company, there is little evidence of conflict here. Letchworth demonstrated his mastery of industrial diplomacy three months after the strike began by organizing a successful company-sponsored outing in August. Most workers here had not left their workstations during the strike. Roughly a thousand took an early evening trip to the city's Athletic Park, where they apparently relaxed, ate meals, and played music. Many watched the company band as it marched around the park in unison.[88] Letchworth's employees apparently preferred, to use the words of open-shop proponent Walter Gordon Merritt, "factory solidarity" over "class solidarity."

Yet not all Buffalo's employers were as uncompromising or managerially effective as Letchworth and Wendt. Some lacked the will or economic resources necessary to continue the fight beyond four or five weeks, surrendering to the union for purely pragmatic reasons. Despite boastful comments from other manufacturers and Gorss about the availability and productive capacity of the "practical men," some striking molders actually won pay increases because they withheld their labor power and successfully prevented strikebreakers from entering the shops, forcing concessions from foundry owners. In the beginning of June, several mostly small and medium-sized foundries, including the David Bell Engineering Works, Buffalo Pitts Company, Lake Erie Engineering Works, Frontier Iron Works Company, Lawler Iron Works, O'Brien's Foundry, John W. Pohlman, Standard Foundry Company, and the H. G. Trout Company, agreed to the $3.00 minimum daily rate for molders and the $2.75 for coremakers. Yet importantly, these employers did not present themselves as irredeemable losers overwhelmed by repellent demonstrators. Despite submitting to the striking workers' demands, employers from these workplaces, according to a report in the *Buffalo Evening News*, defensively insisted that they would continue to run their shops on the "'open-shop' principle."[89] Their compromise was undoubtedly a significant concession, but they spun it the best way they knew how. Their colleagues' peer pressure was almost as powerful as the stress from the strikers. They clearly responded to both.

Indeed, these employers, perhaps less financially able to withstand economic challenges than the other, more affluent owners like Wendt and Letchworth, lost this wage battle, but they refused to alter their identities as open-shop proponents. They publicly affirmed their solidarity with fellow employers while simultaneously practicing a type of managerial realism. Faced with pressures to conform from the national NFA leadership and from local foundry managers, they immediately understood that publicly embracing any managerial theory other than the principle of the open shop represented a clear sign of defeat and was thus unacceptable. Nevertheless, after spending several weeks observing protests while their workplaces remained mostly inactive, they realized that it was easier—and perhaps less expensive—to increase the wages of their tormentors than to continue to lose money by securing, feeding, and possibly even housing replacement workers. In many ways, they were also "practical men."[90]

Other employers had truly unambiguous reasons to celebrate. For Letchworth, Hubbell, Wendt, and close to two dozen other manufacturers, the men who constituted the vanguard of the city's open-shop campaign, the strike created somewhat of a temporary burden, but it offered them the opportunity to forcefully introduce *real* open-shop conditions, a fundamental rearrangement of their previous managerial practices. Like practically all of the foundry owners, they stood strong, refusing to sign closed-shop agreements with any union leaders. But unlike others, they refused to offer any across-the-board pay increases. Their victories were undeniable.

Spokespersons for the Buffalo Foundrymen's Association stressed victories, not defeats, appearing almost giddy as they observed the city's transformation. In one of the great understatements made at the time of the dispute, one employer stated in early July, "It looks as though the molders' union had lost its influence in Buffalo." He continued, "This has always been considered its stronghold."[91] The local labor union leadership had essentially surrendered in most workplaces as strikebreakers, judges, and police forces continued to help manufacturers resume production with a fragmented, ostensibly quiescent, and mostly nonunion labor force. In September, the NFA's *Review* gleefully noted that the strike committee "had simply laid down and died."[92] Under the enormous weight of the NFA campaign, most opted to return to work under pre-strike conditions, which, the *Review* noted in August, relieved "the drain on the strike payroll." Others left Buffalo altogether; their fates are unknowable.[93] Even sources sympathetic to the union, like the *International Socialist Review*, stressed the uneven power relations in the "hard fights against the open-shop bosses."[94] By late fall, it had become clear that the majority of foundry owners had achieved victory—and they were immensely excited about this new chapter in Buffalo's history.

After months of bitter conflict, Buffalo's employers, ideologically committed to the principle of the open shop, had mostly beaten the IMU and scored victories in most, though not all, of the city's foundries. And the IMU's membership continued to decline, both in Buffalo and nationally. Groups of molders continued to protest into the winter months of 1907, but their numbers gradually dwindled. By January 1907, 85 to 90 percent of the city's molders had lost their bargaining rights and therefore grudgingly agreed to work in open shops or leave the city.[95] A correspondent writing for *The Iron Trade Review*, reflecting on the strike in early 1907, noted that "The Buffalo foundrymen feel that a big victory has been gained in the cause of fairness."[96] Half a decade after the deaths of McKinley and Czolgosz, most of Buffalo's foundry operators had reason to be proud.

"Beyond all other places industrially": Buffalo After the 1906 Strike

The employers' victories over the IMU overlapped with renewed efforts to promote Buffalo. Leaders encouraged ordinary Buffalonians to boost for numerous reasons: organized labor and anarchists were in retreat, judges and police forces had successfully upheld "law-and-order" by protecting the non-unionist's "right to work," and the national antiunion community perceived Buffalo as a genuine open-shop city. Reflecting on the year's events, the 1906 Chamber of Commerce president, William H. Gatwick, praised the city's employers for a "very successful year." The open-shop triumph was a major part of the year's achievement, and Gatwick wanted its leading citizens, including the strike's heroic winners, to publicize the region. "Even if you start lukewarm," he announced to a meeting of businessmen in 1907, "talk Buffalo, and talk Buffalo steadily, and before you know it you will begin to believe, yourself, that Buffalo is beyond all other places industrially and from a manufacturing standpoint and as a home city."[97]

Gatwick was joined by other enthusiasts. As the strike entered its final stage, the Chamber of Commerce's F. Howard Mason, an industrial promoter and attorney who had worked alongside a number of national union-fighting figures—including the NMTA's Ernest F. Du Brul—engaged in what the local press called an "unremitting" effort "to boom Buffalo." Mason, who compiled extensive statistics on virtually all business activities in Buffalo from 1901 to 1908, sought to draw attention to the city's many cultural and industrial amenities by distributing buttons with pictures of buffalos that read "Boost for mine." The exercise appeared to be designed to forge cross-class unity under the banner of urban pride—clearly distinguishable from the "class politics" embraced by striking molders or anarchists. Mason's idea was actually unoriginal; as the press reported in August 1906, "The description of the buttons recall the old Pan American days when nearly every person in Buffalo wore buttons of an endless variety."[98] Exactly how the city's union supporters responded to Mason's tacky cheerleading campaign is impossible to know, but it is highly improbable that they were inspired by it. The Theodore Dreiser quotation that opened this chapter suggests that the atmosphere in the city was instead extremely gloomy.

Nationally, the pro-open shop community did their own boosting, noting the extraordinary work performed by Buffalo's "independent workmen," the "free" and "practical" men who had vehemently rejected unionism, helped employers restart production, and therefore set the stage for a new industrial chapter, one free of the burdens of inflexible union rules. These workmen, the NFA *Review* noted in May 1907, labored above and beyond the previously unionized workforce. Their achievements were outstanding, and they were reportedly responsible for constructing the "largest castings ever made in Buffalo."[99] Such examples of talented craftsmanship demonstrated to the NFA "that one does not necessarily need a union card to turn out good castings."[100] Bigger was better, and Buffalo's antiunion activists insisted that the nonunionized "practical men" were chiefly responsible for the impressive output. Briggs, speaking at the NFA 1906 convention, saluted the many workmen in Buffalo who had, in his words, joined "the ranks of the great unorganized."[101] Even a small number of formerly loyal IMU members, the *Review* noted in early 1907, eventually joined "the great unorganized."[102] As one of the nation's top union-busting directors, Briggs had seen this transformation take place in numerous cities, but was especially pleased to draw attention to its exceptional development in western New York. Briggs's nationally coordinated antiunion assaults, conducted in the name of "fairness," continued, resulting in significant IMU membership loss. Nationally, in 1908, the IMU lost 15,982 members.[103] Organized employers had sent a powerful message. A 1908 *Square Deal* article noted, "If ever the union molder is to profit by the experience of his brethren he should study the lesson of the great strike of 1906."[104]

According to the NFA, the "great unorganized" were independently minded "practical men," primarily dedicated to their trade, not to the union, and certainly not to any organization or ideology that promoted lawlessness, "class legislation," or closed shops. The antiunion press reported that such men were neither anarchists nor union sympathizers. Yet the same sources that touted them for their alleged independence omitted highly relevant information about the ways in which these men found their way to Buffalo's struck workplaces. Neither Briggs nor any NFA spokesperson explained publicly that the so-called "great unorganized" were in fact organized from above by a sophisticated national network of employers' associations, open-shop activists who carefully screened job hunters, secured help from judges and the police, and transported, fed, and housed nonunionists. Orchestrating such campaigns clearly required a considerable amount of organizational discipline.

Most of Buffalo's foundry owners were reliable team players who had followed the NFA leadership's instructions carefully and, as a result, created an industrial regime wholly uninviting to organized labor. They recognized that outside leadership played a critical role in their success. Letchworth expressed intense gratitude to Briggs at the NFA's national convention in November 1906. "By their works ye shall know them," a scripture-citing Letchworth announced, and "by this standard Mr. Briggs has measured up to a full stature of a man."[105]

Buffalo's foundry operators, many of whom were certainly latecomers to the open-shop movement, contributed few original ideas to the 1906 strikebreaking campaign, but originality had little to do with winning contests over workplace control or securing community legitimacy. Conformity, based chiefly on shared managerial goals, did. Successful open-shop advocates, in Buffalo and elsewhere, showed discipline, perseverance, patience, savvy public relations, and a willingness to sacrifice short-term financial losses for the promise of long-term power and prosperity. This employer-led movement had become contagious in Buffalo in 1906, and even those who had capitulated to the IMU by offering wage increases identified as open-shop supporters. Extolling the virtues of the open-shop philosophy was a critical part of union fighting, even though, in practical terms, some employers lost this particular battle. But most manufacturers enjoyed a newfound sense of freedom, unburdened by the rigidity of collective bargaining agreements, overt threats of disruptions, or troublemaking anarchists.

In 1907, members of Buffalo's diverse business community sought to properly honor McKinley's memory by hiring famous progressive architect Daniel H. Burnham to construct a monument dedicated to the late president. Manufacturers, including Letchworth, had spent years raising money for the memorial structure.[106] Burnham, one of the nation's premier urban planners who had played a leading part in designing Chicago's 1893 world's fair, did not disappoint them. The giant statue, situated downtown, became a permanent reminder of their late advocate and colleague.[107] Its construction marked a fitting end to their struggle, both ideological and at the point of production, against radicalism, labor unionism, and disorder. Outside dignitaries, including progressive New York governor Charles Evans Hughes, gave an impassioned speech at the dedication ceremony. Hughes, a reformer and friend of the city's open-shop proponents, reflected on the 1901 tragedy:

> At a time of rare prosperity, when American industry and commerce were celebrating their triumphs with every circumstance of proud display in a city of almost unprecedented progress, the powers of darkness moved to their attack and, in an infernal frenzy of hate, an abject creature struck down the foremost and best-loved of American citizens.[108]

For Hughes and the audience members, the murder was a heartbreaking tragedy forever associated with the great Pan-American Exposition. But Buffalo's industrial leaders had reaffirmed their commitment to the promotion of economic development and remained unfalteringly supportive of suppressing the forces—anarchists and trade union militants—who threatened to hinder the city's competitiveness and call into question its progressive identity. Above all, Buffalo's citizens had reason to celebrate what Hughes called "the lasting supremacy of law and order."[109]

Hughes's statement was certainly meaningful, and it is quite possible that the re-empowered businessmen in attendance thought back to the events of both 1901 and 1906 when he uttered them. These were trying times, but the employers largely prevailed in their struggles, and now they had their eyes on the future. As a result of winning approval and assistance from the national open-shop community and securing the support of judges and police forces—the principal agents responsible for coercively maintaining law and order, effectively "gagging" Goldman, and protecting private property—they had dealt a critical blow to the city's labor movement, frustrating the efforts of radical political activists and demanding trade unionists alike. In so doing, this private-public alliance had set the stage for future conventions, celebrations, economic prosperity, and greater peace of mind. McKinley would have certainly been proud. But the "enemies of exploitation and oppression," as the *International Socialist Review* wrote shortly after his death, had no reason to rejoice.

Chapter 5

Making the "City of Prosperity": The Poetry of Industrial Harmony in Worcester

> Employers in other cities may be stampeded into granting demands
> under pressure, but it ought to be plain enough now to the workmen
> of this city that Worcester employers are not in that class.
> —Donald Tulloch, quoted in the *Worcester Telegram*, October 30, 1915

This chapter explores the ways in which industrial employers in Worcester campaigned collectively to win open-shop conditions locally while promoting their Massachusetts city as exceptional nationally. The union-breaking process here, as elsewhere, involved manufacturer unity, coordination with national employers' associations, and unequivocal sympathy for the plight of nonunion strikebreakers during periods of industrial turmoil. "They should be defended at any cost," insisted Joseph H. Walker—longtime owner of boot, shoe, and leather manufacturing establishments, former Republican representative and chairman of the Committee on Banking and Currency, and Worcester Board of Trade member—during a lecture about the "labor question" in front of dozens of manufacturers, merchants, and bankers in 1903. Speaking "in memory of the great liberal minded men who preceded us," Walker called this "the greatest question of the age." This was a strong declaration, and Walker believed in action, requesting that the men in the room stand "in the very forefront" of the movement tasked with the aim of solving this thorny question.[1]

Truly effective union avoidance, Walker and his colleagues realized, also required that industrialists make a good-faith attempt to gain the undivided loyalty of their employees by developing benevolent workplace-based welfare programs. As an article in *Worcester Magazine*—the city's Board of Trade monthly publication—explained in early 1904, "It is a mistake to suppose that the only relation of the employed and the employing class is one simply of service on the one side and remuneration on the other. Such a view only emphasizes class distinction and widens a breach which should not exist."[2] The city's industrial employers, many of whom were accomplished engineers who saw themselves as diligent problem solvers and progressive managers, diverted attention away from the reality of class divisions as they attempted to create pleasant workplaces free of labor unions. This chapter notes the different ways in which these figures used both carrot and stick policies to reduce the power of organized labor and establish, by their own accounts, such conditions. In fact, Worcester's industrial employers were as comfortable employing strikebreaking and union-busting techniques as they were in offering what they considered attractive settings for their diverse workforce—mostly immigrants and their offspring with ties to Armenia, Canada, England, Ireland, Italy, Lithuania, Poland, Finland, and Sweden.[3]

They were also very boastful about their successes. In 1914, the city hosted the sixteenth annual National Metal Trades Association (NMTA) conference, which provided manufacturers and their spokespersons with an unequaled opportunity to show off Worcester's economic, technological, and managerial accomplishments to the open-shop movement's vanguard, figures who had spent years studying, confronting, and, in many cases, minimizing the labor problem. Worcester's NMTA members, a network of gregarious men, used the occasion of the conference to demonstrate their hiring, firing, and overall managerial accomplishments, immodestly claiming they had nearly perfected the craft of workplace supervision. They actively trumpeted their city, insisting that it was a leading open-shop center free of class conflict and led by entrepreneurial visionaries and managerial progressives.

Part of this narrative assumed that workers were sincerely uninterested in unions. But the truth was quite different. The city was undeniably one of the nation's premier open-shop communities, but not necessarily because its wage earners wanted it that way. This chapter, therefore, is intended to help us further recognize the tensions between rhetoric and reality in open-shop America. Indeed, Worcester is a perfect setting to investigate to better comprehend how a successful strikebreaking campaign in 1902, the subsequent establishment of powerful employers' associations, and the development of an effective union-busting labor bureau, followed by years of relative labor peace, led to the creation of an ostentatiously self-important ruling class, one that erroneously claimed that it could speak authoritatively on behalf of the community as a whole—including workers—not just itself.

First, we must consider the economic distinctiveness of this 160,000-person city. Unlike other New England communities like Fall River, Lowell, Lawrence, and New Bedford, Massachusetts, and Manchester, New Hampshire, places where one industry—textiles—dominated, Massachusetts's second-largest city was home to a diverse set of firms. Critical players in the Second Industrial Revolution, the industrialists made up an assorted group. They were involved in the manufacturing of abrasives, leather, looms, carpets, wire, shoes and boots, corsets, envelopes, firearms, sprinklers, and textiles. Many firms were family-owned and -operated, and several owners consolidated their businesses around the turn of the twentieth century, participating in what historians have called the "Great Merger Movement."[4]

Playing a critical part in sustaining Worcester's economic and industrial expansion was the symbiotic relationship between the city's manufacturers and one of the nation's premier technological and engineering schools, Worcester Polytechnic Institute (WPI). Originally named the Worcester Free Institute of Industrial Sciences, WPI had earned a national academic reputation by the end of the nineteenth century.[5] From its opening in 1865, pioneering industrialists, engineers, executives, and managers from Crompton and Knowles (looms), Heald Manufacturing (grinding machines), Norton (grinding machines and abrasives), Wyman-Gordon (fabrication tools), Morgan Construction (steelmaking equipment), Riley Stoker Company (fuel-burning and steam-generating equipment), Leland-Gifford (drilling equipment), Whitcomb-Blaisdell Machine Tool Company (envelope-making tools), Worcester Pressed Steel, Worcester Stamped Metal, and many others received their education at WPI, and in several cases served on the school's board of directors, funded scholarships, and occasionally taught classes. WPI offered diligent students a practical engineering and scientific education. With financial backing from industrialists and philanthropists, such as Ichabod Washburn and Stephen Salisbury, students often worked in the school's Washburn Shops, where they made lathes and other manufacturing articles.[6] "Many of the young men who received their first real training in shop practice," one Worcester promoter mentioned in 1914, "are now in charge of the great machine making factories of Worcester, and managing them with entire satisfaction and to the credit of their alma mater."[7] A sizable number of WPI graduates became members of what historian Monte A. Calvert has called "the mechanical engineering elite."[8]

This "mechanical engineering elite" had aspirations of shaping the local and, in some cases, national industrial landscape. They joined nationwide associations like the American Society of Mechanical Engineers, as well as local organizations of engineers, opened and managed factories in and outside Worcester, and in general sought to use their education to solve workplace problems, including the best ways to increase shop floor efficiency. The institute's graduates and instructors were, in the majority of cases, naturally attracted to the open-shop principle and eager to participate in the movement that brought it to the attention of fellow manufacturers and reformers. Many became active in the NMTA in its formative period.

The 1902 Strike and the "Non-Unionizing" Process

Before large numbers of Worcester's industrial employers became NMTA members, they were active in the Board of Trade, established in 1873, and the regional Worcester Metal Trades Association, which, according to the nationally circulated *Iron Age* in 1902, included "almost all the employers of machinists in Worcester."[9] The organization was initially led partly by Charles E. Hildreth, a former member of the Massachusetts state militia, son of one of Worcester's previous mayors, and one of the heads of P. Blaisdell and Company—later Whitcomb and Blaisdell Machine Tool Company—a manufacturing establishment that employed hundreds of machinists. A highly regarded specialty machine manufacturer that began operations in 1865, Blaisdell sold its tools, including the popular Blaisdell Drill, throughout the world.[10]

Neither Hildreth nor his fellow metal-working employers were immune from labor troubles, and in late spring 1902, roughly 350 workers, represented by the International Association of Machinists (IAM), launched strikes against four of the city's manufacturing establishments: the Prentice Brothers Company, the F. E. Reed Company, the H. C. Fish Machine Company, and Hildreth's P. Blaisdell and Company. Demanding a nine-hour day, pay raises, and union recognition, the men, seeking to highlight the justness of their cause, held a series of meetings and marches throughout the city.[11]

The employers, displaying extraordinary unity and determination, refused to give in to the demands, insisting that production would continue largely uninterrupted. The *Worcester Telegram* reported that "they are ready for whatever action their men may take."[12] They certainly were, and on the first day of the struggle, forty members of the Worcester Metal Trades Association met privately to give one another moral backing and to discuss strategies. Fortunately for them, they were joined by Cincinnati's William Lodge, an NMTA leader and a multi-patent-holding machine tool employer from the Lodge and Shipley Company. The experienced open-shop activist and rather famous lathe manufacturer offered words of encouragement and outlined a game plan. According to the press, he "told in detail of the strike of the machinists of Cincinnati, last spring." This was, he recalled, an intensely difficult struggle, but the southern Ohio employers, unwilling to submit to any form of "union dictation," eventually prevailed: "He told how the employers won the fight, which ended with the men going back to work without obtaining the concessions for which they struck, which were chiefly the recognition of the union and a nine hour day for 10 hours pay."[13] Under the leadership of Lodge, Cincinnati's employers helped frustrate IAM efforts in 1901 and thus played an indispensable part in transforming their city into a nationally recognized open-shop stronghold.[14]

Inspired by the Cincinnati lesson, Worcester's employers promised to follow a similar path. The *Iron Age* reported that the strike brought the men closer together, and as a result they pledged their unwillingness to "hire any machinist who has left the employ of other members under strike."[15] Meanwhile, they also sought to hire nonunion job hunters from outside the city. The men at the gathering, united principally by an increasing awareness of their shared managerial interests, were determined to, in the words of the city's major newspaper, "stand in every way possible by the Prentice Bros. Co., the F. E. Reed Co., and the H. C. Fish Machine Co," the initial three shops hampered by the work stoppage.[16] According to the local press, the city's employers, a majority of whom were not directly hurt by the strike, responded to the challenge with "great positiveness."[17]

The strikers appeared equally class-conscious and confident—and were initially somewhat effective. They received logistical support from IAM organizers, organized animated demonstrations near their workplaces, held "open air" meetings, and informed their union brothers in other cities about their campaign. They apparently received, according to witnesses, "moral support even inside the walls of the shops among the very men who have remained at their work."[18] And they received messages of solidarity and obtained financial assistance from fellow unionists, including carpenters and barbers.[19] Finally, aware of the employers' attempts to fill up the shops with nonunionists, protestors demanded that outside machinists stay out of Worcester. Overall, the protestors, according to the *Worcester Telegram*, were not especially rowdy or militant: "the behavior of the strikers was orderly in every respect."[20]

Orderly or not, the protestors put more than a modest dent into the production process, which in turn disrupted supply chains and hurt the employers' profits. For instance, in the strike's first days, only one of seven lathes at F. E. Reed remained in operation.[21] At this time, according to a union spokesperson, persuasive picketers had apparently turned back "two-thirds of the machinists" who had arrived from outside Worcester "to take their places."[22] According to a report filed by an IAM organizer, "the local is making rapid growth." He continued: "at the regular meeting there were several hundred men present and much interest shown. They were determined to procure the nine-hour day, and are satisfied it will not come till they go after it."[23]

The employers, hoping to resume production and impress their Cincinnatian instructor, were equally determined. Importantly, they enjoyed judicial and police backing, illustrating that the conflict was not merely one between private sector employers and union-building workers. A judge issued an injunction against picketers, and the city's police force assisted employers by physically shielding nonunionists, many of whom arrived from Springfield, from potential attacks. Police officers attempted to establish order as they escorted lines of strikebreakers "to an intelligence office" where the imported men received instructions from the Worcester Metal Trades Association about placement options.[24] Both the police and the employers were critical in ensuring that these nonunionists enjoyed their right to work.

At the time, Worcester's employers had developed a temporary system of centralized hiring, one meant to systematically undermine the IAM's collective strength by pitting nonunion job seekers against those who demanded bargaining rights. In essence, Hildreth vetted applicants and placed acceptable men, nonunionists, into one of the four struck workplaces. Exactly how many men he mobilized is difficult to know, but he appeared to have been effective, and by early June, momentum was clearly on the employers' side as growing numbers of outsiders crossed picket lines while union supporters looked on with disgust. Union members, typically upbeat, responded to Hildreth's system of hiring with a mix of alarm, frustration, and disorientation. The IAM's Hartford-based strike strategist, Maurice W. Landers, actually identified Worcester's employers as pioneers in the area of collective union breaking. Speaking in front of hundreds of protestors, Landers thundered, "Your board of trade here in Worcester is the first body of that kind I ever heard of in the United States which constituted itself into an employment bureau and sought to engage nonunion workmen to take away the living from its own citizens."[25] Landers, a veteran union activist, was clearly rattled, recognizing the manufacturers' willpower and impressive organizational unity. Their campaign, he believed, had damaging, far-reaching consequences for Worcester's residents and for the labor movement generally. The employers' activities had essentially sapped the union's confidence, signaling a critical moment in this confrontation.

The employers, on the other hand, seemed pleased with the imported nonunionists. Yet given the IAM's aggressive anti-strikebreaking activities, the employers could not rely exclusively on outsiders to help them with their labor needs. In light of this dilemma, they also took a gamble on the local labor market. But they were very clear about the terms, declaring in June that they would meet "their men as individuals, and not as members of the union."[26] This statement, as we have seen in other contexts, served both labor and public relations needs. The employers, increasingly confident in their ability to secure victory, wanted their workforce and the public to perceive them as fundamentally evenhanded. By proclaiming their readiness to meet with individual machinists about the prospects of returning to the shops, they sought to illustrate that they were compassionate and open to reconciling, not the coldhearted or selfish oppressors depicted by Landers. They conveyed a message that their managerial actions—the open-shop principle in practice—constituted an entirely enlightened, mutually beneficial solution to the reckless combativeness encouraged by the IAM.

By late June, the IAM was clearly losing its influence while the employers welcomed a steady stream of "individuals" back. The post-strike workforce, of course, lacked an effective collective voice or any meaningful bargaining power. Newcomers from outside the city's borders, outwardly uncorrupted by union influences, took positions next to former strikers who had reluctantly returned to their stations under prestrike conditions.

But the employers did not accept everyone. Speaking with one voice, they refused to reemploy any of the "ringleaders," placing them on a permanent blacklist, which ensured their separation from the mostly loyal, levelheaded men who were ostensibly uninterested in causing financial or managerial harm.[27] As the press explained, union leaders "will never be permitted to return to work again in their shops."[28] Worcester's employers had clearly shown their mastery of what the local paper referred to as the process of "non-unionizing."[29]

The nonunionizing process required perseverance, employer solidarity, leadership, and financial investments. After holding several meetings, screening job seekers, and paying $1,315 to cover legal expenses and procure "free men," the NMTA announced victory smugly: "the Machinists returned to work unconditionally." Unable to overcome employer-created obstacles and financially desperate, most, after seven weeks, chose exploitation over joblessness. Commissioner Ernest F. Du Brul, who had traveled to Worcester on a recruitment visit at the time of the uprising, applauded Worcester's employers for "handling the matter very well."[30] Nationally, *The Iron Trade Review* reported that "it is likely that unionism in Worcester and vicinity has learned a lesson it is not liable to forget."[31] In the face of this crushing defeat, the IAM's Landers observed rather unequivocally that "Worcester is a bad city for unions."[32] The lesson was undeniably clear to both sides.

Worcester's employers, having successfully followed Cincinnati's 1901 union-breaking template outlined by Lodge, were emboldened by their victory. The establishment of a nonunion workforce meant fewer shop floor disruptions, enabling employers to maintain production uninterruptedly and fill orders with ease. The manufacturers were, according to the press, "in a better position to handle contracts." This meant increased efficiency, fewer headaches, and future years shaped by prosperity and progress. According to the *Worcester Telegram*, "This year, for the first time, Worcester manufacturers of machine tools had to put a strike clause in their contracts, which in not a few instances caused orders to go to other cities. Hereafter such clause will be unnecessary." The victors felt, according to the local press, "jubilant."[33] The reasons for their jubilation are obvious.

The employers hardly perceived their dispute as a classic case of management versus union, since they had refused to recognize their workforce as a collective body. Instead, they saw the affair, in large part, as a fight between themselves and their loyal workmen on the one hand and the

IAM's Landers and a handful of "ringleaders" on the other. In the employers' minds, these opponents were guilty of disrupting the naturally harmonious relationship between themselves and the majority of the workmen, individuals who showed a temporary lapse of good judgment. They were, in other words, briefly poisoned by IAM agitation and misled by mischief makers, but they could now repent by distancing themselves from the labor movement. Of course, returners discovered that conditions and shop rules remained unchanged, but, unlike the "ringleaders," they had jobs.

By the time of the strike, only two Worcester workplaces, F. E. Reed and Prentice Brothers, were part of the NMTA. That soon changed, and by early 1903, thanks to the organizing work carried out by Lodge and Du Brul, the Worcester Metal Trades Association, numbering about fifty, became the NMTA Worcester branch. The merger was mutually valuable: Worcester's employers learned managerial techniques from national open-shop leaders, and the NMTA's mostly midwestern leadership had opportunities to draw lessons from the Worcester men.

Locally, Worcester's industrial employers, like those in other NMTA chapters, sought to effectively balance their own regional interests with the larger organization's concerns. Finding just the right balance was, Du Brul explained in a meeting in Cincinnati in early 1904, critical: "the local association without the national association, or the national without the local, is incomplete. For an employer to be a member of one and not of the other is about the same as a man standing on one leg when he could and should have two good sound legs to support him."[34] National affiliation carried responsibilities, and all NMTA members had to adhere to its rules in order to reap the full benefits. For instance, the NMTA leadership prohibited rank-and-file members from recognizing or bargaining with unions.[35] Of course, Worcester's members certainly did not see this, or most of the organization's policies, as unnecessary or burdensome. Instead, they demonstrated profound appreciation for its mission, activities, and resources, including its competent labor spies, growing blacklist of union supporters, and open-shop pamphlets, which, in many cases, were jointly published with the NFA.[36] They sincerely appreciated that the organization was well equipped to build and sustain open-shop conditions in Worcester and beyond. After all, it professed in 1904 that it was "always ready with a plan of action, a defense, a line of expert tactics."[37]

The NMTA did not restrict itself to direct union breaking at the point of production. Its members also gave "hearty approval" to industrial-based educational programs like those found at WPI. Furthermore, throughout the century's first two decades, it lobbied politicians against proposed eight-hour laws and it campaigned to keep explosives out of the hands of union activists.[38] The NMTA brought manufacturers from Worcester and other industrialized regions together in unprecedented ways, helping to create a common vision based on employer unity and power—a vision that differed considerably from "the old order of things." No longer would metal-working employers see themselves primarily as business competitors and, as the NMTA's Robert Wuest put it in 1912, "conjure up pictures of each other as the personification of all that is diabolical."[39] Worcester's members, appreciative to one another and indebted to their Cincinnatian trainers, followed the national organization's policies meticulously, claiming in 1904 to be "big-hearted men, ready at a moment's notice to give their time to anything that will further the interests of the National Metal Trades Association."[40] They were determined to play a critical role in helping it become one of the country's most effective open-shop organizations. By 1905, Worcester was one of thirty cities with an NMTA chapter.[41]

Yet not all Worcester's metal-working employers displayed an inclination to "give their time to anything that will further the interests" of the group. In fact, the membership initially lacked organizational discipline, which was especially apparent in the months immediately after winning the 1902 strike. Several employers became somewhat complacent, apparently believing that their struggles with the IAM were, in fact, a thing of the past. A series of poorly attended meetings discouraged leaders like Hildreth. Something, he believed, had to be done. In this context, he reasoned that if the branch offered complimentary food at meetings, interest would swell, attendance would improve, and discussions would become more dynamic, causing increases in morale and improved loyalty to the NMTA's local and national activities. He was absolutely correct. Indeed, when he built such an event, attendance climbed to over seventy people. "Wonder of wonders," Hildreth remarked, "every member was present." Hildreth was entirely pleased with the turnout, the discussion, "and a jolly good time was spent."[42]

Following the success of this gathering, recalled by Hildreth as "the turning point," the employers in attendance decided to spend more money on food, host more banquets, and continue discussing civic and managerial topics. At the next gathering, held in June 1903 "at one of our popular downtown restaurants," the men, following a suggestion by Hildreth, decided to develop a permanent labor bureau, one designed to prevent a repeat of the 1902 strike. The labor bureau, developed out of the 1903 meeting, would become central to their hiring and firing practices, both during periods of labor peace and in the context of strikes.[43]

How did it work? First, the NMTA placed job advertisements in newspapers. After responding to the job posts, applicants would then meet and interview with the bureau's secretary in the organization's downtown office. Meanwhile, the secretary assiduously collected information about the applicant's employment history, address, age, nationality, marital status, and moral character—information meant to protect members' "against unsteadiness, inefficiency and dishonesty." After the screening process, the bureau's secretary placed those without a record of union activism, "free men," in members' workplaces. Meanwhile, they added names to the blacklist. In essence, the system was a preventative measure, designed to keep pro-union, ostensibly lazy, inefficient, and incompetent men out of the shops, ultimately helping to, according to a 1904 edition of the NMTA *Bulletin*, ensure the "greater happiness and prosperity to a number of our fellow-men."[44] It enabled businesses to get in touch directly with those who had received favorable marks "for steadiness, sobriety and industry." The *Bulletin* asserted in 1904 that the service made sound business sense, since it saved "the employer far more than his yearly subscription in relieving him from the vexation and loss which is the result of hiring unsatisfactory and unreliable men."[45] Clarence W. Hobbs, another Worcester-based NMTA leader, explained that the exclusive role of the labor bureau was to provide needy employers with dependable hands; employers alone decided wage rates, hours, and the general organization of their workplaces.[46]

Worcester's labor bureau was initially headed by Herman S. Hastings, an attorney and the former secretary of the Worcester Republican Committee. Like Hildreth, Hastings—born in 1873 into a well-to-do family of large farmers and building contractors—became a prominent figure in the open-shop movement during its formative period.[47] In 1904, he began collaborating with other, nationally integrated union opponents as a member of the five-person Citizens' Industrial Association of America (CIAA) credentials committee. And in that same year, he wrote an instructive article about the benefits of labor bureaus in the *Bulletin*.[48] Presumably, NMTA secretaries in other cities found Hastings's advice useful, which they likely considered as they established their own union-avoidance employment bureaus.

Soon, other NMTA chapters established their own labor bureaus, and the trade press emphasized that this method of management was designed to help, rather than hinder, ordinary job seekers, law-abiding individuals who simply desired steady employment. According to an article in the *Iron Age* published in 1903, "many workmen have expressed themselves in sympathy" with labor bureaus.[49] An unnamed NMTA spokesperson, writing in *The Iron Trade Review* in 1905, insisted that the system was "invaluable to both sides"—employers and wage earners.[50] Precisely how most workers and job-hunters viewed NMTA-run labor bureaus is difficult to determine. Yet accepting declarations by the *Iron Age* and *The Iron Trade Review* at face value is rather unwise given that these sources remained consistent mouthpieces against the labor movement. It is certainly hard to imagine that pro-union workers saw labor bureaus as anything other than one of a number of managerial weapons in the NMTA arsenal. Anti-union job hunters were likely more supportive. Whatever the case, one thing is unmistakable: the national open-shop community wanted the public to think that "the common people," not just economically privileged managers, supported this system of centralized hiring.

Of course, many job seekers, particularly those denied employment opportunities by bureau secretaries, accurately viewed this managerial development as extremely unhelpful. Union supporters, as we will see below, bore the brunt of these exclusionary hiring policies. And under Hastings, Worcester maintained a lengthy blacklist of these "troublemakers," thereby distinguishing union activists from "good men." The trusty secretary covered much ground. The local chapter was active throughout Worcester County, stretching 20 miles north of Worcester into Fitchburg, an important hub of machine tool manufacturing and papermaking, and 15 miles south of the city into Whitinsville, named after the massive Whitin Mills, a textile machine manufacturing firm that employed roughly 1,700 workers.[51]

Naturally, plenty of managers were thankful for, and inspired by, the bureau's work. And Worcester's system of selective hiring received the attention of open-shop proponents well beyond Worcester County's borders.[52] Hastings also helped employers in other cities secure nonunionists from Worcester County in the context of industrial emergencies.[53] From the fall of 1903 to early 1904, employers from Vermont, Maine, New Jersey, and Pennsylvania corresponded with Hastings in an effort to recruit competent and loyal nonunionists—individuals who had successfully navigated their way through the thorough vetting process—to work in open shops outside Worcester County.[54] Word of Worcester's labor bureau even reached as far as Australia. In fact, in 1905, the Victoria Employers' Association secretary, seeking solutions to its own labor problems, wrote Worcester's NMTA branch requesting information about its hiring and firing techniques.[55] In the process of creating an effective labor bureau, Worcester's NMTA members, led by Hastings and Hildreth, helped put Worcester on the map internationally, ultimately demonstrating to large audiences that its leading citizens were fully committed to ensuring that the open-shop movement succeeded.

It must be clear that Worcester's NMTA branch had come a long way in a relatively short period. Its labor bureau had become a national model, and its members continued to hold well-attended and productive meetings. In the process, the membership became increasingly integrated into a national network of labor union opponents. The chapter's annual meeting in 1906, for example, had, according to *The Iron Trade Review*, "the largest attendance in the history of the association." Complimentary food could have been one reason for the high turnout, but the members may have also wanted to hear speeches by local leaders and James Emery, the National Association of Manufacturers and CIAA's chief lawyer and political lobbyist.[56] Hastings and Hildreth, close observers of the multidimensional labor problem, ensured that the city's membership got exposure to, and became inspired from, the movement's leading architects.

The Rise of Donald Tulloch

In 1906, Hastings left Worcester to help organized employers on the West Coast confront labor-related difficulties.[57] His replacement, Donald Tulloch, was especially impressive. Born in Scotland, Tulloch settled in Worcester near the end of the nineteenth century and started working as the personal secretary to James Logan, the owner of the Worcester-based U.S. Envelope Company and future mayor of the city. For a brief period, Tulloch worked as a reporter for the *Worcester Telegram*. An impeccably loyal assistant, Tulloch quickly earned the admiration of Logan and soon the appreciation of Worcester's employers. He was acutely impressed with the industrial expansion of his adopted home, opposing anything that interfered with the city's technological or financial growth, including, of

Table 2: NMTA Labor Bureau Activities in 1913

Bureau	Approximate number of applications in 1913	Approximate number of men placed in 1913	Approximate number of permanent records of workmen
Boston	3,600	561	23,454
Chicago	5,668	4,002	60,000
Cincinnati	8,000	N/A	38,000
Cleveland	4,500	1,700	42,000
Hartford	8,000	863	5,500
Indianapolis	8,250	5,174	77,000
New York and New Jersey	5,348	1,088	11,000
New Haven	314	200	4,900
Pittsburgh	1,000	500	3,000
Rhode Island	1,032	383	21,309
Saint Louis	1,376	574	18,920
Springfield	3,234	1,782	39,303
Tri-City	1,125	900	35,000
Worcester	14,643	1,435	25,000
Totals	**66,090**	**19,162**	**404,386**

Source: NMTA, *Synopsis of Proceedings of the Sixteenth Annual Convention*, 1914, 47–48.

course, labor unions. Under his careful watch, the employment bureau remained one of the key solutions to such potential threats. It was especially busy under his leadership. For example, in 1913, Worcester's bureau received over 14,000 applications, making it the NMTA's busiest in that year.[58]

Industry and technology were hardly Tulloch's only passions. As secretary for multiple organizations, including the city's Vacant Lot Cultivation Society, the Worcester County Football League, and the Anglo-Saxon Club, Tulloch demonstrated a highbrow interest in improving the aesthetic character of the city and an engagement with high-minded civic and cultural affairs.[59] A sensitive man, Tulloch was also an avid collector of poetry, editing and publishing a book of over 200 pro-British World War I poems in 1915.[60] His wide-ranging social interests and his active commitment to some of Worcester's exclusive community activities brought him into close contact with the city's wealthiest businessmen, patent holders, socialites, and reformers.

But nothing brought Tulloch closer to the city's notable employers and WPI alumni than his administrative involvement in the NMTA. He collected names of "troublemakers" and "good men" more energetically than he gathered works of poetry. Given Tulloch's effectiveness in denying employment opportunities to radicals and union "ringleaders," it is unsurprising that he made numerous enemies in the labor movement. The city's *Labor News* reported in late 1915 that Tulloch was largely responsible for undermining workers' struggles throughout Worcester County, using his NMTA contacts to import, house, and feed nonunionists during strikes.[61] Many of those who were active in the labor movement, went on strike, or otherwise challenged employer power made Tulloch's detailed blacklist, which permanently kept them out of the best-paying industrial jobs in Worcester County. According to a pro-union observer writing in 1931, "Tulloch blacklisted men all over the state so that they could not find employment and had to remove to the west."[62]

One of Tulloch's early union-breaking interventions occurred outside the city of Worcester. From May 1907 to early spring 1908, he worked closely with Fitchburg's machine tool manufacturers, men forced to confront more than 350 IAM members. Unionists at the Cowdrey Machine Works, the Fitchburg Steam Engine Company, the Fitchburg Machine Works, and the Simonds Manufacturing Company had demanded a five-cent-an-hour increase, a fifty-hour workweek, and exclusive recognition.[63] They craved, in the words of Washington-based IAM organizer Thomas Wilson, "a shorter work day, pay enough to purchase clothes and food with a chance to save a little for old age. This can't be done in this city at the present wage."[64] Exhausted from overwork and irritated by low wages, the workers from these small-to-medium-sized workplaces believed that united pressure constituted the most reasonable course of action. But they had little experience raising grievances or organizing protests. Their collective efforts, according to a *Machinists' Monthly Journal* August report, constituted "the first time that the machinists of Fitchburg have made an organized effort to improve their conditions."[65]

In response to the demands of these rookie activists, Tulloch set up secret meetings with the machine shop owners, all of whom gave their full blessings to the open-shop principle, held membership in the NMTA's Worcester branch, and pledged to stand united against the union just as Worcester's employers had stood in solidarity with one another against the same forces five years earlier. Tulloch, speaking on behalf of the city's employers, refused to give in: "Not one jot! Not one tittle."[66] The workers, meanwhile, prepared for combat.[67]

Tulloch's private, prestrike meetings with Fitchburg's proprietary capitalists constituted the beginning of what became a dramatic strikebreaking operation in Worcester County's second-largest city. In preparation for the walkout, Tulloch rented a room in downtown Fitchburg in June and invited the NMTA's Cincinnati-based commissioner, Wuest, to meet and discuss antiunion plans. A salaried NMTA employee since 1902, Wuest, like Du Brul and Lodge, regularly traveled the country, meeting with branch secretaries to plot strikebreaking activities.[68] A month after Wuest's visit, IAM members staged their action. Tulloch, collaborating with fellow employment bureau secretaries, succeeded in importing strikebreakers from Bridgeport, Cincinnati, New York City, Newark, Philadelphia, and Worcester. He initially housed and fed more than a hundred in the upper floors of his makeshift headquarters. According to the press, "others are coming in with such regularity that the association declares with confidence that the strike is broken." In the face of this aggressive mobilization, eventually involving more than 300 strikebreakers, many protestors—economically desperate and emotionally disheartened—chose to leave Worcester County for jobs elsewhere.[69] Deeply frustrated by the sequence of events, the IAM's Wilson reported in early 1908 that "everything that a mortal man could do to bring about an honorable adjustment has failed."[70] Yet Tulloch remained upbeat as he welcomed the newcomers, applauding their individualism and what he considered their heroism. Shortly after the first strikebreakers arrived, Tulloch proudly unfurled an American flag outside the office, which he claimed was "an emblem of liberty and an open-shop."[71]

By draping a flag over strikebreaking headquarters, Tulloch sought to illustrate that this was not a dispute between antagonistic classes, but was rather a noble, NMTA-led battle to protect the freedom of employers to peacefully manage open shops and a visible defense of the nonunionists' "right to work." And this command center, a space temporarily occupied by hundreds of allegedly lawful and honorable job seekers, was ground zero in this virtuous fight. Waving American flags in this context served as a blatant reminder that the individuals behind open-shop campaigns—manufacturers, nonunion "free men," and Tulloch himself—deeply treasured the nation's political traditions and employment laws, which in most cases protected individual rights over any form of "class rule." Such traditions and laws were, as Tulloch symbolically suggested, entirely incompatible with the IAM's activities, especially its demands for the creation of closed shops. The core message was unambiguous: the presence of open-shop workplaces helped to reinforce the spirit of American patriotism.

Welfare Capitalism and Worcester's Square Deal

At his Worcester Board of Trade meeting in 1903, Walker reminded audience members, including a number who had participated in the 1902 strike-breaking operation, that, as employers, they must "provide for their employees the most efficient machinery and most favorable working conditions known to them." In return, Walker expected that wage earners "must make the largest number of things and of the best quality that their utmost diligence and skill enable them to produce."[72] Mutual respect, in other words, was the key to increases in productivity, shop floor peace, and business success.

Throughout the early twentieth century, Worcester's open-shop advocates, including Walker, claimed publicly that they treated "honest," "loyal," and "industrious" workers with matchless warmth, which was ostensibly reciprocated. And one did not need to look far to identify meaningful, privately sponsored welfare activities. A number of employers, both NMTA members and nonmembers, oversaw athletic teams, organized company outings, and provided their employees with low-priced housing. By the second decade of the twentieth century, some started offering mutual savings plans and health benefits. Employer-administered welfare programs were typically designed to win the loyalty and trust of employees without compromising shop floor hierarchy or limiting industrial output. Moreover, such programs were meant, in part, to show that state intervention in this area of labor relations was unnecessary, though employers in Worcester and elsewhere had shown their appreciation for judicial and law enforcement support during strikes.[73] Some scholars have argued that welfare capitalism also served excellent public relations purposes, contending that the hype surrounding welfare benefits was to a large extent rosier than the reality of the programs themselves.[74] Worcester employers offered welfare programs to demonstrate to outsiders their benevolence, ensure greater productivity, and remain largely union-free.

They were not necessarily original; nationally, far-sighted employers had come to realize that successful strikebreaking campaigns, combined with detailed blacklists of militant agitators, had failed to solve the union threat. After all, strikes continued to break out in the months and years after the open-shop movement's multicity launch in 1903, compelling a few to look inward, engage in a bit of soul searching, and ask fundamental questions about their overall practices. Why did employees continue to join labor unions? Why did large numbers of wage earners continue to display signs of insubordination by staging strikes, organizing boycotts, and joining anarchist or socialist organizations? Speaking at the NAM annual conference in Pittsburgh in 1904, Du Brul offered a somewhat jarring proposition: "eighty per cent of the strikes in this country are the fault of the employer." Du Brul, who continued to collaborate with Worcester's organized employers, added, "it is the employer's fault if he has a foreman or superintendent who treats the men unfairly, thereby giving an excuse for the agitator to come in and work on the prejudices of the workmen, drawing away their loyalty from the employer to the organization."[75] This arresting statement, published in newspapers nationally, was an unambiguous call for employers to carefully consider the labor question holistically by taking the grievances of their employees seriously and by systematically exploring ways of improving factory conditions. Coercive management techniques, the country's leading open-shop activist contended, were often counterproductive and thus offered no long-term solution to the labor problem.

It is unlikely that Worcester's employers in the post-1902 strike period thought that Du Brul had them in mind when he made this statement. They saw themselves as considerably more enlightened than most. Worcester's spokespersons, believing it was of paramount importance to "maintain a shop atmosphere free from all harassing and hindering influences," did not publicly suggest that abusive foremen or supervisors constituted a significant local problem. "Hindering influences" like poor working conditions, according to an engineer writing in the *Journal of the Worcester Polytechnic Institute* in 1913, led to disorganized types of insubordination and strikes.[76] Unlike Du Brul, Worcester employers believed that outside labor agitators, not themselves or their workers, caused workplace conflicts.

Yet as managers and educators, they believed that they had an essential role to play in reducing the appeal of radical ideas. Consider the words of George I. Alden, NMTA leader, general manager of Norton Grinding Company, Cornell University graduate, and WPI professor of mechanical engineering. Alden was an advocate of social programs for Norton's workforce and for WPI students, emphasizing that employers must promote "a high code of business ethics" as a way to counter the popularity of socialism. According to Alden, "socialism" threatened "competition" and, more alarmingly, "the progress of civilization." In order to reduce the appeal of left-wing ideas and organizations, it was necessary that employers and entrepreneurs, Alden wrote in 1907, "follow the lead of men like Mr. [Andrew] Carnegie." Inspired by the great industrialist and philanthropist, Alden was hopeful that "we shall be able to run the tide of public sentiment into more healthful and hopeful channels." For Alden, it was not enough to reject closed shops and socialism; businessmen also had to, through their actions, convince employees of the supposed moral bankruptcy of these ideas and practices. A "true picture of social progress," Alden concluded, required that society's most economically fortunate stretch "out a hand of help" and thus promote "a square deal."[77]

Alden's colleague and WPI president, Ira N. Hollis—also appealing to the spirit of Theodore Roosevelt's 1903 Square Deal—contended that both representatives of business and labor must put aside differences and cooperate with one another for the sake of industrial harmony and technological progress. While Alden denounced socialism as a moral evil that Americans must condemn unapologetically, Hollis—who had previously served under open-shop enthusiast Charles Eliot as the chairman of Harvard University's engineering department—deplored workplace conflict as outright counterproductive. Speaking passionately at WPI's 1913 commencement, Hollis posed a series of forceful questions: "who is to get the benefit of the energy made available by the steam engine and other prime movers, the laboring man or his employer?" He went on:

> What is the value of the mechanical age to us if it produces only surfeit and strife? Can the capitalist not interest himself in his employee and limit his own profit? Can a member of a trades union not think of his employer as a human being with the same motives, desires and rights as he has himself? If the answer to these two questions is "no," we might better go back to the tallow candle and the stage coach of our ancestors.[78]

Hollis held that the true benefits of technology had disappointingly not been fully realized. For the profits of technology to reach all "men," it was necessary for members of both labor and capital to reestablish mutual respect and understanding for the sake of "progress." Like Roosevelt and the employers active in the open-shop movement, Hollis employed the language of reform. The city's top engineer reasoned that welfare capitalism and friendly atmospheres in Worcester's shops—in contrast to the wide-spread problem of mismanagement identified by Du Brul in 1904—would bring the capitalist and employee together, thereby reducing distrust and thus preventing labor unrest.

Left-wing organizations, strikes, and other forms of class conflict that impeded "progress" and thus created consternation for Alden and Hollis seemed less apparent in Worcester than elsewhere. And Worcester's engineers, employers, and other promoters of the open-shop principle had the finest opportunity to show the country's most active union fighters their creative strategies for dealing with the labor question in a broad sense in April 1914, when the national body of the NMTA held its sixteenth annual convention at Worcester's fancy Bancroft Hotel. Attendees of this extravagant event—"the most successful of these meetings ever held"—received copies of Tulloch's *Worcester: City of Prosperity*, a 300-plus-page celebratory book dedicated "to the Employers and Employees of Worcester."[79] The book describes Worcester's welcoming institutions and its political and industrial evolution, paying close attention to its innovative firms and to its dazzling transition from a tranquil New England town in the colonial years to a diverse manufacturing hub in the decades after the Civil War.[80] This exciting, progressive development was only possible because of the deep-rooted goodness of the city's workers and employers, to whom Tulloch paid homage poetically:

> Worcester is the City of my Adoption,
> Coming here an Entire Stranger,
> Like Thousands of other Strangers,
> From "Auld Scotia's Shores."—
> Land of the Free and the Brave,
> To the Land of Democracy and Opportunity.
>
> A Quarter of a Century's residence
> Within its inviting Borders,
> Has taught me that,
> For the Worker,
> For the Employer,
> For every one from every Clime,
> There is not a more attractive place than
> Worcester, "Heart of the Commonwealth."[81]

A quixotic Tulloch distributed 430 copies of *City of Prosperity*, providing open-shop campaigners from throughout the United States and Canada with a valuable and seemingly touching souvenir, one that celebrated the ways both employers and workers contributed to the city's managerial accomplishments.[82]

Coincidentally, the NMTA convention began on the same day as the infamous Ludlow massacre, a massacre sparked by the Colorado National Guard that resulted in the deaths of several striking workers and their families, including women and children, in a mining camp in Ludlow, Colorado.[83] While the bloody Ludlow slaughter was a public relations debacle for the Rockefellers, the well-organized NMTA convention was, according to the local press, a public relations triumph. The Ludlow tragedy represented the era's sharpest, most graphic example of class conflict and state repression; the NMTA convention was a celebration of community harmony and success, featuring the "who's who" of the open-shop movement. Buffalo's William H. Barr, president of the NFA, was in attendance, as was George S. Boudinote, secretary of the NAM. Henry Morgan and Justus H. Schwacke, prominent figures from Philadelphia's industrial battlefield, hobnobbed with likeminded men from across New England and Ohio, including Cleveland's leading strikebreaking practitioner, Philip Frankel. Manufacturers from nearby Fitchburg, veterans of the 1907 strike, roamed the hotel's halls and schmoozed with employers from the Midwest. Well-known University of Chicago economist J. Laurence Laughlin and Walter Gordon Merritt, the American Anti-Boycott Association's high-profile lawyer, delivered well-received speeches on the importance of defending capitalism against various forms of government regulation. Several of the NMTA's original members, including Brooklyn's Henry N. Covell and Cincinnati's Lodge, were also present. Lodge, who had served as an invaluable consultant to Worcester's nascent open-shop campaign twelve years earlier, must have been especially impressed with the chapter's sophistication, successes, and enormous growth. Hundreds of others, including publishers, university professors, and politicians, attended sessions on labor, domestic affairs, and international relations, particularly in connection with escalating tensions between the United States and Mexico.[84] Patriotic excitement permeated the evening's reception as news spread about the U.S. military's occupation of Veracruz: "the whole audience of men and women arose in a body and sang with considerable vim, 'The Star Spangled Banner,' to the accompaniment of an orchestra." Following this song, NMTA leaders John

D. Hibbard of Chicago, W. A. Layman of St. Louis, and Worcester's own Hildreth and Tulloch held up a gigantic American flag in front of the gathering, which sang "America." The banquet room audience, according to an eyewitness account, carried on with "enthusiastic patriotic pride."[85]

The convention, partly stage-managed by Tulloch, consisted of much more than traditional seminars on the dimensions of industrial relations. Part of it took place in a fair-like atmosphere, as delegates from around the country went on walking tours of several "modern" factories, where they learned clever ways to confront the perennial labor problem and discover, as Tulloch advertised, how Worcester, unlike other cities, had maintained labor peace for over a decade. Lengthy periods of industrial harmony, Tulloch held, translated into greater output, which set Worcester apart. "The industrial supremacy of Worcester," he asserted with Henry Grady-like vigor, "is due to the combined efforts of the employers and the employees."[86]

Worcester's upbeat factory owners and their sycophantic assistants celebrated the city's recent past. But they also had their minds on the future, a time, they anticipated, that would be characterized by even more labor-management harmony and uninterrupted production in the spirit of Roosevelt's Square Deal. Tulloch used the occasion to declare the formation of another, more inclusive open-shop group, the Employers' Association of Worcester County, an organization with the goal of achieving a "strikeless Worcester."[87] Tulloch served as secretary; Alden was president. Now the county's non-metal working industrialists could follow the NMTA's central mission, which Tulloch believed would assist everyone in preventing unnecessary "industrial strife" and further promote "the principle of the 'Open Shop'."[88] Tulloch explained that the new association's headquarters, which shared space with the NMTA's chapter, was "a place where workers may discuss complaints or suggestions for their betterment with the Secretary." Tulloch promised that he would "endeavor to correct abuses and eliminate trouble wherever found."[89] In essence, *Worcester: City of Prosperity* describes the activities and goals of imaginative and compassionate social engineers, figures who had constructed this open-shop city without resorting to any sort of conflict-ridden Social Darwinistic tactics that were commonplace in the later part of the previous century. Unsurprisingly, examples of vulgar union busting, strikebreaking, and other expressions of struggle were entirely missing from Tulloch's overweening narrative. Tulloch and the city's diverse coalition of employers were unwaveringly immodest, shamelessly flaunting their overall managerial effectiveness and technical innovations, and thus demonstrating a sense of regional superiority. While manufacturers in other cities faced the burdens of collective bargaining and episodic outbreaks of labor unrest, Tulloch and the people he worked for had helped foster, in his words, "a spirit of co-operation, friendliness and progressiveness."[90]

By the time of the 1914 gathering, most firms had established at least some welfare benefits for their employees. However, implementing welfare programs was more complex and financially expensive than maintaining a thorough blacklist of disloyal workers, and not all capitalists had the resources to afford substantial benefits, which resulted in much unevenness. Nevertheless, Tulloch made some generalizations about industrialists as a whole, asserting that welfare programs and employer benevolence were the norm in Worcester, rather than the exception. Ten years after Du Brul issued his provocative statement essentially blaming insensitive and short-sighted managers for causing most strikes, Tulloch noted that Worcester members of the NMTA "are to be found in the vanguard of those endeavoring to lighten the burden of daily toil among their employees." "For more than a decade," he wrote, "there has been industrial peace in this city in metal trades lines."[91] He explained that magnanimous employers were committed to the welfare of their employees throughout the seasons, giving "the wherewithal to furnish an enjoyable day's outing in summer" and inviting "employees to a sleigh ride and supper in the winter."[92] Above all, "employers have done their part in bringing about the principle of the square deal."[93]

Conference delegates discovered that some workplaces were genuinely special. For example, the large Norton Grinding Company provided numerous tangible benefits, establishing itself as one of the nation's great leaders of welfare capitalism. Anchored on the city's northern edge, Norton prided itself on its safety record and even ran its own hospital. It also sponsored athletic teams, a drama club, outings, and company parties.[94] Norton presented its employees with an impressive array of programs, but it was hardly alone. Norton and its next-door neighbor Heald Manufacturing Company established employee savings plans, while Rice, Barton, and Fales, a long-running papermaking machinery company, had an extensive group insurance plan. This family-owned open shop was, according to a 1937 company publication, "the first, and for a number of years the only industry to invite its employees to suggest possible improvements in the production methods and plant upkeep."[95] Tulloch called Rice, Barton, and Fales—which actually employed a minority of union molders—"one of

Worcester's best firms."[96] Visitors also surveyed the immense, eye-catching industrial establishment on the south end, Whittall Carpet Company. Beginning in the late nineteenth century, Matthew Whittall, founder of the mill and an active member of the exclusive Anglo-Saxon Club, built an Episcopal church and a park, and regularly sponsored games of cricket for his largely English-immigrant workforce.[97]

Guests also witnessed a variety of other benefit-granting workplaces between Norton in the north and Whittall in the south. Wives of conference delegates visited the Royal Worcester Corset Company, a company whose workforce was 90 percent female.[98] David Hale Fanning, its paternalistic owner from 1861 until his death in 1926, had constructed a number of noteworthy facilities in his factory, including a sparkling cafeteria, an elegant dining hall, a hospital, a library, and a stage and auditorium where managers encouraged employees to give shows.[99] Tulloch recalled fondly that deferential employees presented this noble patriarch with a silver cup for his eightieth birthday.[100] Some concluded their visit with a tour of WPI's immaculately groomed and scientifically equipped campus. The city's open-shop designers sought to illustrate that Worcester was a prosperous city because it contained numerous technologically diverse, financially successful, and progressive workplaces—and because relentlessly ingenious employers and well-behaved, highly appreciative, and productive workers had taken the advice of figures like Walker, Alden, Hollis, and Tulloch and moved beyond industrial conflict. The city's employers and workers had presumably achieved what Merritt later called "factory solidarity"— smooth-operating workplaces based on mutual admiration, understanding, and peace.[101] In Tulloch's imagination, this was all poetry in motion.

"The strike fever" Affects Worcester

Yet polished dining rooms, employer-organized sleigh rides, and even group insurance plans could not keep the city's working classes fully satisfied and deferential. A massive, multi-workplace strike hit the city a year after the NMTA's landmark meeting, stopping production in a few renowned firms and shattering the Employers' Association of Worcester County's prediction of a "strikeless Worcester." In June 1915, molders launched a walkout at Rice, Barton, and Fales because management had fired union leaders and refused to bargain with workers.[102] Months later, in September, Washington-based IAM organizer Joseph H. Gilmour (aka "Eight-Hour Gil"), who had established contact with pro-unionists from virtually all of Worcester's metal-working plants, helped mobilize hundreds of machinists from several specialized manufacturing firms, including Crompton and Knowles, Hobbs Manufacturing Company, Heald Machine, Leland-Gifford, Whitcomb-Blaisdell Machine Tool Company, the recently consolidated Reed-Prentice Company, and the world's leading manufacturer of abrasives, Norton Grinding Company. This was the first major work stoppage to hit the city in more than a decade, and the protestors were confident. *Labor News* reported that rebellious strikers, expressing numerous pent-up grievances, marched and chanted throughout the city, demanding an eight-hour day and union recognition, and hundreds joined the IAM. Many protested what they called the "speed-up system," and others expressed annoyance with the "bonus system"—which rewarded a minority of the most productive workers with increases in pay and thus undercut union solidarity.[103] The marchers, an assorted group of American and foreign-born non-English-speakers from Armenia, Finland, Quebec, and Sweden, received tremendous support, especially on the south end, where "several hundred young women in the windows of the Whittall Carpet mills cheered the strikers." Resentful protestors also marched in front of the Whitcomb-Blaisdell Machine Tool Company and the Reed-Prentice Company, where, according to the local press, they "shouted eight hours and sang eight-hour songs."[104]

The defiant actions of machinists and molders, numbering roughly 3,000 by the end of the fall, attested to the shortsightedness and naiveté of the poet's hyper-cheerful and self-serving rhetoric. We do not know if any of these protestors had previously attempted to resolve their problems by approaching Tulloch or his assistants with what he had called "complaints or suggestions for their betterment." Whatever the case, they clearly chose to express their complaints outside the channels deemed appropriate by the employers. And by staging a strike against multiple welfare capitalist workplaces, they helped demonstrate what historian Brian Kelly has called "the limits of reform from above."[105]

Thoroughly prepared, employers reacted swiftly to this outpouring of militancy and solidarity, revealing marvelous unity and perfect obedience to the NMTA's policies. With assistance from industrious foremen, some simply fired the demonstrators. Managers at the Norton Grinding Company pressured employees to sign "yellow dog" contracts, ensuring that they would refrain from joining independent labor organizations.[106] Less than half the company's 570 machinists signed these contracts, prompting seventy-one-year-old Alden to terminate and blacklist more than 300 workers.[107] Works manager of Reed-Prentice, Albert E. Newton, agreed to talk to the picketers, but only as individuals, not as union members. Newton, the recent inventor of Reed-Prentice's automatic lathe, announced that the strike resulted from the dishonorable work of outside agitators, people who, he asserted, had little understanding of the distinctiveness of Worcester industries or of the mutually respectful conditions that existed within them.[108] Newton sought and secured help from Mayor George M. Wright, who had offered welcoming remarks to the delegates at the 1914 NMTA conference. Wright did not hesitate in dispatching "five special officers for duty at the plant."[109] Whitcomb-Blaisdell's Hildreth, the highly respected union-fighting veteran, also took a predictably hard line against the combatants, refusing to acknowledge their collective organization or to reduce hours. He spoke rather matter-of-factly: "It simply can't be done."[110] Meanwhile, the IAM offered its own critique, insisting that organized employers were responsible for ensuring that Worcester remained a "cesspool of industrial serfdom."[111] The sequence of events should be all too familiar to us by now.

In any event, concerned about keeping the workplaces running and pleasing his superiors, the trustworthy Tulloch oversaw the hiring and transportation of hundreds of strikebreakers, many of whom traveled from Boston, Springfield, and Portland, Maine.[112] Some of the would-be strikebreakers were uninformed about their expected duties, unpleasantly surprised when they arrived in the conflict-torn city, and others were simply outraged that they "were taken to a lodging house which undoubtedly has escaped the attention of the Worcester board of health."[113] Meanwhile, Tulloch, representing the interests of more than 100 manufacturing establishments at this time, related the work stoppage to an unfortunate illness, declaring that the protesting men had lamentably "caught the strike fever." "Like any other fever," Tulloch maintained, "it has to run its course." But Tulloch remained characteristically optimistic, believing that the employers could fix the troubles: "The medicine will have to be taken before conditions improve."[114]

As the strike progressed, state authorities took notice. In October, Massachusetts's Board of Conciliation and Arbitration investigated the conflict. Commissioners criticized the NMTA's hiring, firing, blacklisting practices, and overall stubbornness, but they ultimately lacked the legal authority to prevent the NMTA from engaging in its tactics. Speaking to the board's commissioners, Alden remained adamant that the city's employers would neither accept closed shops nor reduce hours given their economic interests: "The question of an eight-hour day, when there is so much production needed, does not seem to be reasonable."[115] NMTA members, following their time-honored strategy, insisted that no outside force should interfere with their personnel matters.[116]

Labor leaders realized this clearly, singling the city out for its exceptionalness: "Worcester Firms Stand Alone in Refusal to Recognize Employees."[117] IAM spokespersons maintained that the protestors and the commissioners were, in fact, "reasonable," but that "abuse has taken the place of argument with the N. M. T. officials."[118] Obviously, employers from outside the city were not the only class of figures to identify the managerial effectiveness of the NMTA's Worcester chapter. Worcester's employers continued to send the message, both individually and through Tulloch, that they were the city's uncontested leaders, accountable to no one but themselves. Newton explained candidly, "we maintain the right to maintain our own business without interference."[119]

Yet Tulloch and his pigheaded colleagues were unable to win all of their struggles. The machinists certainly faced what seemed like impenetrable, NMTA-constructed barriers, but protesting molders ultimately succeeded in forcing the Rice, Barton, and Fales Company—which Tulloch once called "one of Worcester's best firms"—to improve conditions in early 1916. According to the settlement reported in the union press, "all strikebreakers will be dismissed, and working conditions improved."[120] This victory, achieved after several months of confrontational protests, indicates that employer unity was not entirely shatterproof.

The molders' triumph, however, was radically overshadowed by numerous NMTA victories. The employers clearly failed to prevent work stoppages as the publicly optimistic and frequently sentimental Tulloch predicted but, enjoying help from the police, strikebreakers, and each other, they succeeded in stopping the IAM from obtaining any significant numerical gains and from forcing the employers to bargain collectively. In response, many demonstrators simply left the city shortly after the strike began. Recognizing the difficulty of gaining recognition from the city's employers, about 150 pro-union workers chose to depart Worcester as early as late September, according to the *Worcester Telegram*, for "positions in shops in Springfield, Bridgeport, and other cities where union conditions obtain."[121] The numbers continued to rise sharply as the months progressed. By the end of the battle in early winter, almost two-thirds of the strikers had departed the city for employment elsewhere.[122] These workers had come to realize that conditions were better, wages were higher, and hours were less outside Worcester County. They obviously showed no interest in taking Tulloch's medicine.

Again, the open-shop system of management, uncompromisingly defended by Worcester's employers, prevailed. We must not be surprised by their raw power or inflexibility; they naturally understood that unions challenged their interests as capitalists, managers, and boosters while threatening the nonunionists' "right to work"—a right embedded in Roosevelt's Square Deal and, in their view, a right consistent with the spirit of Americanism itself. In the context of this and earlier conflicts, they revealed their loyalty to Walker's 1903 directive by defending this right "at any cost." In the "City of Prosperity," no cost seemed too high.

This was one of a number of reasons why spokespersons like Tulloch believed that Worcester was extraordinary. Tulloch aggressively presented its industrial leaders as highly effective agents of managerial and technological progress leading a remarkably prosperous city that provided workers with "a square deal." Employers had reasons to be proud, and one can certainly measure their successes by pointing to their effective 1902 union-breaking effort, their internationally recognized labor bureau, their welfare capitalist programs, and their commitment to the NMTA's overall well-being. An almost obsessive advocate of his adopted home's people and institutions, Tulloch helped to ensure that the nation's most influential union adversaries understood the city's many contributions to the cause.

Yet the 1915 citywide uprising reveals that Worcester's employers and their assistants were unable to prevent thousands of intensely dissatisfied workers from organizing collectively against even the most generous welfare capitalists. The employers reacted differently to this IAM-generated uprising than they did to the more modest-sized 1902 disturbance. In 1902, just as the open-shop movement came to fruition in both Worcester and nationally, the struck employers essentially fixated on the disruptive role played by "ringleaders," effectively driving a wedge between labor activists and the majority of machinists, men who had—in the employers' collective interpretation—mistakenly followed the lead of nefarious union leaders. In a sign of mercy, the Worcester Metal Trades Association indicated a willingness to forgive most participants by reemploying them after the strike's conclusion. Thirteen years later, neither Tulloch nor the veterans of the 1902 conflict, including Hildreth, saw this second battle as simply a struggle against a minority of dissenting outsiders. Given the insurgency's sheer size, the city's employers could not simply isolate and punish a handful of "ringleaders."

But this certainly does not mean that the manufacturers or Tulloch used the later strike's occasion as an opportunity to look inward and contemplate their own shortcomings as managers. They displayed no visible humility, and certainly did not abandon their support of the open-shop principle. Reducing hours, increasing wages across the board, or recognizing unions remained, in essence, out of the question. In the face of the protest, they felt that they had no other option but to contain the damage, refusing to allow their city to lose its reputation as a nationally recognized open-shop stronghold led by generous and reasonable managers. Like thousands of other employers, they fought, drawing on their own resources and networks—each other and law enforcement authorities. Enjoying police protections and access to a steady stream of strikebreakers, they succeeded in crushing the demonstration while adding names to the NMTA's growing blacklist. They retained Tulloch as secretary for both the NMTA and the Worcester County Employers' Association, continued to fly the open-shop banner high, and continued to assert that they, rather than outside union organizers, slogan-chanting protestors, or state commissioners, understood what was best for the city's workers. In their collective minds, they had commendably followed one of the national open-shop movement's mottos: "Do Right—Then Fight."

Chapter 6

"A Solid South for the Open-Shop": N. F. Thompson and the Labor Solution

I am not an enemy to the Negro.
> —Nathan Bedford Forrest, *(Shelbyville) Republican*,
> September 11, 1868

No one questions the right of labor to organize for any legitimate purpose.
> —N. F. Thompson, *Report of the US Industrial Commission on
> the Relations and Conditions of Capital and Labor*, 1900

According to N. F. Thompson, labor unions constituted "the greatest menace to this Government." Speaking before the Congressmen-led United States Industrial Commission in June 1900, Thompson—secretary of the Huntsville, Alabama, Chamber of Commerce, a commercial real estate investor, industrial promoter, former Confederate soldier and Klansman, and leading temperance advocate—explained that "their influence for the disruption and disorganization of society is far more dangerous to the perpetuation of our Government in its purity and power than would be the hostile array on our borders of the army of the entire world combined."[1] Thompson outlined numerous reasons he believed labor unions were extraordinarily menacing. Many, he grumbled, were led by socialists, weaken "the ties of citizenship among thousands of our people," show no "respect for law and authority," demand "class legislation," and "are educating the laboring classes against the employing classes." In the face of this growing problem, Thompson proposed a number of remedies. First, believing that public authorities had a role to play, he advocated the establishment of "State and national boards of compulsory arbitration," which would, he predicted, "disseminate the widest possible education among the laboring classes as to the correct relation between labor and capital."[2] He also recommended the development of employers' associations "in all lines of business," "public sentiment" that promotes industrial peace, and, most radically, the creation of a law "that would make it justifiable homicide for any killing that occurred in defense of any lawful occupation."[3] He explained, "If I could make this statement any stronger or clearer I would gladly do so."[4] His central message was unmistakable: labor unionism posed the single leading threat to America's most sacrosanct institutions and conscientious citizens, and government officials needed to stop this danger.

This was obviously a strongly worded speech, but it was hardly a spontaneous, ill-controlled rant. Instead, Thompson made his statements and developed, more generally, a hard-hitting critique of organized labor, "after years of close study."[5] He had been pondering the labor question's dimensions for several decades before delivering this attention-grabbing presentation. He had closely observed the labor movement's coercive activities, was well aware of the numerous boycotts and strikes staged by working-class activists, and remained troubled that labor leaders had often pressured workers to join unions while demanding that employers fire those who refused. At some point in the mid-1870s in Louisville, Thompson himself was victimized, informing the Industrial Commission that one of his most efficient printing shop employees was unfairly pressured by the Typographical Union: "That young man had been raised with me; he was loyal to my interests; he had proven himself proficient; he was thoroughly acquainted with my work." Focused exclusively on building the labor organization, the union's business agent had demanded that the printer sign a membership card or Thompson would fire him. Thompson flatly refused: "I would not, under any circumstances, discharge him."[6] But the intimidation continued, resulting in a disruptive job action: "That whole office went on a strike, and caused a considerable loss to the publishers of my paper." Finally, "in order to harmonize the matter," Thompson reluctantly "advised my young man to become a member of the typographical union."[7] His own intensely unpleasant experience with organized labor, combined with repeated nationwide outbreaks of strikes and boycott campaigns, turned him into a

Figure 4. N. F. Thompson. Courtesy of the Huntsville-Madison County Public Library.

diehard defender of "free labor" and proponent of "justifiable homicide" laws against coercive unionists. By 1900, he had already played a part in both chronicling, and working against, organized labor's activities. He had become the South's most ambitious and visible opponent of closed-shop unionism.

Thompson earned a reputation as an open-shop enthusiast beyond the South's borders in part because of his blistering statements in 1900. National publications took immediate notice of his troubling history and provocative recommendations. The *New York Times* gave him coverage, and the *Nation* seemed especially awestruck, noting, "There may have been others, before Mr. Thompson came forward, who have applied the scalpel with equal thoroughness and intrepidity, but we have not happened to hear of them."[8] Others, especially labor movement campaigners, were predictably bothered by this pioneer's attacks, and Thompson complained of receiving much hate mail, including letters from unionists threatening to tie a rope around his neck. But a writer from one union, the International Association of Machinists (IAM), actually welcomed Thompson's remarks: "It is pretty generally known that the class represented by Mr. Thompson has very little, if any, sympathy with organized labor, but it is very much out of the common for that want of sympathy to be publicly expressed. Mr. Thompson told the truth, and he deserves the thanks of organized labor for doing so."[9]

A strong-minded New South booster and union opponent, Thompson worked on behalf of numerous employers' and commercial organizations during the late nineteenth and early twentieth centuries. He gained widespread respect, including from the nation's leading anti-union activists. In 1903, the National Association of Manufacturers' David M. Parry appointed the Alabamian to serve on the Citizens' Industrial Association of America's 14-person leadership committee. Thompson was the sole figure from the Deep South to serve in this capacity, though Van Cleave's involvement indicates that Thompson was not the only Confederate veteran to play a leadership role in an organization designed to protect employers and ordinary workers from what many considered the bane of labor violence and closed shops. The IAM spokesperson was absolutely correct that Thompson represented the interests of a certain "class."

Yet Thompson was considerably more interested in defending the welfare of southern businessmen and investors in the name of progress and modernity than in championing the concerns of employers nationally. "I am first, last, and all the time, for the industrial upbuilding of the South," he professed in July 1900.[10] He often articulated an underlying belief that a manufacturing loss for the North was a gain for the South, repeatedly spotlighting examples of southern prosperity and industrial harmony while drawing attention to labor-caused chaos, corruption, bloodshed, and class politics in the North. The South, in his view, offered a lasting solution to such problems. Writing about the outbreak of violent strikes and the emergence of pro-union politicians in places like Cleveland, Chicago, and Philadelphia shortly after delivering his Industrial Commission presentation, he declared, "The North cannot remedy this evil as it exists throughout that section, because labor unionism absolutely dominates political parties and the press there, but the South can handle this question and on the grounds of absolute fairness to both [labor and capital]."[11] Combining the language of New South boosterism with Rooseveltian reform, Thompson bragged that the South "should be honest with herself by proclaiming the superior rights of the public, so that neither capital nor labor can 'run' our government affairs." "The South," he insisted, "has the opportunity of the century to place herself in the forefront of industrial life and progress."[12] These and plenty of other statements illustrate his near-obsession with ensuring regional economic development based largely on the open-shop principle.

We should not be surprised by Thompson's often inflammatory comments in light of his military experiences, class background, and financial interests. The owner of the Huntsville-based Thompson Land and Investment Company, an industrial real estate concern, essentially offered besieged northern manufacturers an unambiguous option in the face of continuous labor unrest: fight or flight. By investigating the activism and career of Thompson, this chapter sheds new light on the links between the New South's rise and the open-shop movement's emergence, insisting on the necessity of acknowledging meaningful regional distinctions and taking a long view of southern antiunionism.[13] Attention to Thompson's regionally focused antiunion agitation provides us with a fresh perspective to understand the connections between a mostly northern labor problem and southern economic development. Thompson actively reminded audiences about the stark labor-related differences between these two areas.

Birth of a Union Fighter

To properly understand the evolution of his antiunion ideas and activism, we must first explore his early life. Born into a prosperous slaveholding family in Shelbyville, Tennessee, on Christmas day in 1844, Newcomb Frierson Thompson observed the dynamics of coerced labor at an early age. Located roughly 60 miles south of Nashville, the landlocked town, Bedford County's largest, was established in 1810 and incorporated nine years later. Several of the town's earliest settlers, including Thompson's father, Joseph (b. 1807), arrived from North Carolina. Shelbyville's wealthiest residents typically owned slaves, and slavery was more extensive in Middle Tennessee than in any other area of the state. Bedford County had a slave population of somewhere between 30 and 40 percent.[14]

As a boy, N. F. Thompson marveled at the ways the black laborers on his father's plantation conducted their multiple tasks. Joseph Thompson, the Bedford County sheriff, wholesale grocer, and friend of future president Andrew Johnson, ostensibly oversaw a sophisticated and harmonious operation, one in which the labor force apparently took tremendous pride in their toil. "My father's plantation," Thompson nostalgically recalled in 1900, "was absolutely self-supporting in every department—blacksmiths, machinists, carpenters, bricklayers, seamstresses." He insisted that the slaves—a sizable number—were enormously resourceful, dexterous, and obedient as they allegedly labored ceaselessly under a comprehensive system of benign paternalism: "They took the wool from the sheep's back, carded it, spun it, dyed it, wove it into cloth, made it themselves. They took the wood from trees in the forest, took it to their workshops, and made whatever the farmer required in every line."[15]

This system collapsed dramatically in the beginning of the 1860s, forcing Thompson to come to terms with the labor problem a decade before large numbers of social scientists, journalists, union activists, and employers began debating the causes and character of industrial unrest.[16] At this point, roughly four million slaves staged, as W. E. B. Du Bois famously put it in 1935, a "general strike."[17] This vast, multistage labor action was, by any measure, more politically significant, bloody, far-reaching, and revolutionary than any other strike or uprising in all of U.S. history. In Thompson's mind, these laborers were supposed to toil subordinately and selflessly and appreciate the generosity of their masters, benevolent individuals who provided the slave with, as he put it in 1899, "his meat and bread."[18] But this was clearly not the case, and the workforce, clamoring for freedom, profoundly destabilized the method of political economy that Thompson and his class of allies cherished.[19]

Large numbers of Middle Tennesseans responded to northern aggression and slave insubordination militarily. In order to lure men into fighting for the Confederacy, several military recruiters visited Shelbyville, where they delivered speeches about the need to defend the rebel cause and the dominant managerial system that had existed from the state's beginning.[20] At age sixteen, Thompson, attracted to these arguments, began serving under the command of Colonel George C. Maney, a military leader who had fought in the Mexican-American War. Thompson served for a short period until he was discharged in Tupelo, Mississippi, because of his young age. He soon reenlisted, serving directly under Nathan Bedford Forrest, the semiliterate, skillful, gallant general and wealthy former slave trader. Reports of Thompson's wartime activities indicate that he was fearless, engaging in several epic battles, including an especially dramatic one in Selma, Alabama. Here he lost five horses and apparently suffered "fourteen bullet holes through his clothing, yet he escaped unhurt."[21] With mounting casualties and victory clearly unreachable, Forrest's cavalry ultimately surrendered to the mightier Union forces in Gainesville, Alabama, in April 1865.

Thompson's community had changed considerably, but he remained relatively comfortable financially in Shelbyville. He pressed on, studying law in 1866 under the direction of Judge Henry Cooper, a Middle Tennessee native and future U.S. senator. A Whig turned Democrat, Cooper enjoyed a reputation as a prominent lawyer and community leader, and offered Thompson a rigorous one-on-one legal education.[22]

In Middle Tennessee, Thompson was concerned by what he and his fellow Confederate veterans perceived as a breakdown in law and order, the sight of disobedient free blacks, and the presence of intrusive northern "carpetbaggers." Fistfights occasionally broke out in Shelbyville between New England educators and, as a *New York Times* reporter put it in September 1865, "gentlemen sons of wealthy negro owners."[23] In this violent atmosphere, Thompson became a leader of the original Ku Klux Klan, which emerged to protect as much of the Old South-style white supremacy, political order, and planter power as possible. The organization, led in part by his old commander Forrest, employed terror against African Americans, Republican politicians, and northern educators and, according to an 1868 report in a Shelbyville newspaper, "coerced many into voting the rebel ticket."[24] The precise role that Thompson and his colleagues played in this secretive vigilante organization is unclear, but we know that others in his situation attempted to restore what the historian Eric Foner has called "labor discipline on white-owned farms and plantations."[25]

The available evidence suggests that Foner is certainly correct. Forrest, for example, insisted that former slaves remained absolutely necessary to the region's postbellum economy, defensively claiming in 1868 that he was "not an enemy to the negro": "We want him here among us; he is the only laboring class we have, and more than that, I would sooner trust him than the white scalawag or carpetbagger."[26] In an effort to achieve this management goal, hundreds of Klansmen like Forrest, Thompson, and other members of the agricultural elite felt a duty to severely curb the political activities of the mostly white proponents of Reconstruction reforms. Precisely how to restore managerial control, both electorally and on worksites, remained the central, enduring question confronting the South's ruling class. Klan activities, including violent raids intended to intimidate pro-Reconstruction proponents, northern teachers, and Republican Party members, was a common response to this dilemma. In essence, Forrest, Thompson, and Klan leaders throughout the region sought to protect what they believed were their fundamental rights: their unrestricted ability to manage their land, labor, and local politics.

Klan undertakings, Thompson wrote in a Baltimore newspaper nearly half a century after the original organization's rise and fall, were carried out in a spirit of camaraderie. He explained in 1924 that the organization was fundamentally righteous and inclusive, involving "Jew and Gentile, Catholic and Protestant, alien and native born." All, he insisted, had mobilized energetically against "carpet-bag rule in the South."[27] In a 1921 interview about the differences between the first and second Klan organizations, Thompson explained that "I became a member of the Klan in 1866 as did nearly every Confederate soldier." He noted further, "We accomplished our work in the next five years and disbanded in 1871."[28] Exactly what he meant by "our work" is not entirely clear. The organization's history is difficult to assess, chiefly because of its underlying secretiveness.[29]

Yet we can draw some important conclusions. Above all, while most accounts of the Klan show, correctly, that it was a notoriously brutal organization that disgracefully terrorized large numbers, Thompson did not perceive the group in this light. Instead, he regarded the organization as having played a defensive and noble role, one designed to protect a traditional way of life that he and his southern comrades valued. Klan members saw themselves as promoting law and order, defending class and racial hierarchies, encouraging regional camaraderie against outside influences, and restoring dignity to a class of individuals permanently scarred by a destructive war and a massive—and ultimately successful—labor rebellion. In essence, during and immediately after the war, privileged white men like Thompson organized in regions throughout the South to limit the achievements of that rebellion.

Business, Catholicism, and Temperance

Thompson left Shelbyville and the Klan sometime in the early 1870s. He spent a short period practicing law in Dallas before moving to Louisville, where he became intensely active in the growing temperance movement. He served as secretary and treasurer of his local temperance lodge and became a delegate to the Kentucky order of the Good Templars, a highly influential organization that explicitly condemned what it considered the evils of the liquor trade and the damaging practices of alcohol consumption. To obtain membership, one needed to believe in God and maintain a lifelong commitment to sobriety.[30]

The Templars were, as historian David M. Fahey explains, "the world's most numerous and most militant" temperance organization.[31] Kentucky's chapter emerged in 1854 and grew to 33,000 members by the mid-1870s, a period when large numbers of middle-class men and women reformers became active in anti-alcohol campaigns.[32] Thompson served as state secretary, as well as editor and proprietor of one of the organization's publications, the Louisville-based *Riverside Weekly*, a newspaper "devoted to literature, agriculture, news, morality, and temperance." Thompson's involvement in this cause was undoubtedly important. He was a passionate campaigner and, according to an 1872 article in the *Nashville Union and American*, "is said to be one of the best temperance orators in Kentucky."[33] And his influential newspaper regularly featured fables and nonfiction pieces, all of which reflected Thompson's moral values. As editor, his objective was, as he explained in 1875, to develop the "higher cultivation of [man's] moral and mental faculties."[34] He set a rather high, almost immodest goal. Under his editorship, the *Riverside Weekly* would become, he hoped, "the most popular and widely known family and temperance journal in America."[35] By 1876, a year after Thompson left the northern Kentucky city, it had a circulation of 2,534.[36]

After leaving Louisville, Thompson lived in Wilmington, North Carolina, for a brief period before moving to Savannah, Georgia. In Wilmington, Thompson worked for the Standard Oil Company. In Savannah, he was the southern agent of the United Gas Improvement Company, a Philadelphia-based firm formed in 1882, which by 1904 had operations in forty cities.[37] He then became a manager of the Mutual Gas Light Company, which, according to the rather boosterish press, helped Savannah become "the best lighted city in the South."[38] Thompson's collaborator and boss was J. H.

Estill, a fellow Confederate veteran who also owned the *Savannah Morning News* and the Morning News Steam Printing House.

Thompson had his mind on more than moneymaking and career-building activities while residing in Savannah. Raised a Methodist, he converted to Catholicism in 1883 because his wife, Julia Queen, was a Catholic. His conversion had no impact on his passionate dislike of whisky, beer, and wine, or the drinkers of these intoxicating beverages. He often tied his strong religious beliefs to the prohibition cause, continually writing in nationally circulated publications, including the well-regarded *Catholic World*, about what he saw as the immorality of alcohol consumption: "We are persuaded that a true knowledge of Catholic morality might strengthen the cause of prohibition in some localities."[39] At a time when many working-class Catholics, especially northerners, routinely consumed alcohol, the article apparently had the effect of, as a short biography of Thompson explained in 1887, removing "from the mind of the general public the idea that the Catholic Church opposed prohibition."[40] Thompson insisted that abstinence was consistent with the teachings of "the best theologians."[41]

In light of this comment, we should not be surprised that Thompson continued to organize and agitate, serving as president of St. John the Baptist Total Abstinence and Beneficial Society, which held regular meetings at Savannah's Catholic Library Hall. Here he continued to preach against what he called "the fatal poison." According to an 1884 *Savannah Morning News* article, "Mr. Thompson is an earnest and devoted advocate of temperance, and his efforts in behalf of the cause, have accomplished a great deal in promoting the welfare of the people among whom he has labored."[42] Outside speakers active in the temperance movement, inspired by Thompson's steady moral leadership, regularly visited the hall and discussed the increasingly popular campaign against the liquor trade's power. According to an 1884 report, "they are doing good work, and their influence is being felt throughout the entire community."[43] Thompson clearly saw himself as an influential urban reformer, encouraging his community to practice sobriety as a necessary solution to what he viewed as a pressing social problem.

While residing in the Georgia city, Thompson also learned about New South boosterism. A decade before Thompson helped to lure northern businessmen to Alabama with assurances of industrial harmony and prosperity, Estill had advertised the attractiveness of Savannah with a 77-page publication titled *A Guide to Strangers Visiting Savannah for Business,*

Health, or Pleasure. The seaside city, Thompson's business partner announced in this 1881 publication, was "the most important seaport between the capes of the Chesapeake and New Orleans."[44] Estill's pamphlet featured much information about Savannah's rich history, attractive location, efficient utilities, and impressive architecture, including statues memorializing the bravery and decency of Confederate soldiers.

Thompson certainly respected this history and culture while he sought business opportunities and fought to reform the South morally. In Louisville, Wilmington, and Savannah, he enjoyed prosperity in his business pursuits and respect in reform circles for his uncompromising temperance advocacy. His conversion to Catholicism ostensibly had no effect on his rising influence in the urban South's elite circles. He certainly enjoyed many connections with influential individuals and became a respected leader in his communities, unafraid to challenge disobedient African Americans, the liquor trade, and consumers of alcohol.

The South and the "Disintegration of the North"

In the nineteenth century's final years, Thompson added labor unions to his list of problems that threatened American—or, more specifically, southern—society. He expressed strong antiunion ideas as a leader of numerous powerful, urban-based organizations. From the 1880s to the 1910s, Thompson developed an impressive résumé that included service on behalf of Birmingham's Commercial Club, the Johnstown, Pennsylvania, Board of Trade, the Huntsville Chamber of Commerce, and the Southern Industrial Convention. In 1905, he moved to eastern Tennessee, where he took over editorial responsibilities for the *Tradesman*, which, following Theodore Roosevelt's open-shop advocacy in response to the 1902 anthracite coal strike, proudly "stood for a 'square deal' alike to both capital and labor throughout the south."[45] While residing in cities like Birmingham, Huntsville, and Chattanooga, Thompson aggressively promoted the South by advertising its natural resources, low labor costs, lack of workplace regulations, and, most importantly, its supposedly quiescent and racially fragmented workforce.[46] In particular, he emphasized the region's wholehearted commitment to the open-shop principle. In his quest to help industrialize, enrich, and ultimately modernize the South, he hobnobbed with prominent figures, including mayors, governors, congressmen, and factory managers.

He collaborated with newspaper owners like Birmingham's Rufus N. Rhodes, Savannah's Estill, and the *New York Times* Adolph Ochs. And he established relationships with college presidents, including prominent black administrators like Tuskegee Institute's Booker T. Washington and Alabama Agricultural and Mechanical College's William H. Councill.

Perhaps influenced by Estill's promotional activities, Thompson proved to be an especially impressive industrial recruiter. In the 1880s and 1890s, he helped Birmingham become a national center of, in his words, "iron supremacy."[47] As secretary of that city's Commercial Club in the mid-1890s, Thompson regularly met with representatives from, according to an 1894 report in the *Birmingham Age-Herald*, "very large and important industries."[48] Years later, he helped recruit northern-based textile capitalists to northern Alabama, overseeing the construction of half a dozen, mostly medium-sized firms in Huntsville while he was chamber of commerce secretary and head of the Thompson Land and Investment Company. This company prided itself, in part, on mobilizing "extensive advertisers in the north and west."[49] Thompson was, the *Weekly Mercury* reported in 1900, "actively engaged in building up Huntsville."[50] Partially because of Thompson's actions, Huntsville, by 1899, had become, according to the *American Wool and Cotton Reporter*, "the Manchester of the South."[51] Businessmen from nearby communities appeared jealous of the cities that profited from Thompson's promotional advocacy and recruitment successes. Realizing his influence on the economic development of Birmingham and Huntsville, an unnamed spokesperson from the modest-sized northern Alabama town of Florence enviously pointed out in 1901 that his own community lacked an effective representative. "We have the advantages of location and cheap water and railway shipping rates," the individual announced. "All we lack," the person continued, are "a few Col. N. F. Thompsons."[52]

Investors and promoters like Thompson came to hold the view that the principal forces with the power to potentially destabilize industrial progress were "the labor agitators," which, he argued in 1906, "bodes no good for either labor or capital."[53] And as organized labor continued to bedevil communities throughout much of the nation, Thompson took notice, holding that the labor movement—which he insisted was concentrated mostly in northern cities—was out of control, economically dangerous, and deeply immoral because it denied "free workers" the "right to work." In numerous speeches and newspaper editorials, he denounced organized labor for its communitywide destructiveness, inefficiency, insobriety, and even silliness.

The devout Catholic sometimes invoked religious language, describing labor disturbances as constituting a moral and spiritual, as well as a profound economic, problem. In 1900, at the second Southern Industrial Convention in Chattanooga, which Thompson helped organize, he complained about union efforts in Chicago's coffin and cradle factories. "If the coming generation must be rocked in union cradles or not at all," he asserted, "why not be married by a union priest with a union-labeled license." Shameless unionists would demand even more, he warned:

> Having "unionized" us from the cradle to the grave, would they stop there? Will they not try to extend their authority over the resurrection, and refuse to rise until Gabriel uses a union-labeled trumpet? Or will they decline to enjoy the delights of Paradise until the angels use union-labeled harps?[54]

Thompson warned that strikes, union-organizing campaigns, and wage earners' outrageous demands in cities like Chicago marked the beginning of what he called in 1900 "the disintegration of the North."[55] While he had zero patience for union activism, as a southern booster with a passion for the former Confederate states and a material stake in the South's financial growth, he actually welcomed this development.

Thompson was by far one of the most expressive, forceful, and visible southern antiunion activists, but he was not the first. He followed a tradition that emerged in the nineteenth century's final decades, when regional industrialists and their spokespersons distinguished themselves from those in the North by insisting they faced very few union-related troubles.[56] Of course, the region was far from free of labor unrest or union organizing in the late nineteenth and early twentieth centuries. The eruption of railroad protests in numerous communities, the militant mining strikes that broke out around Birmingham, and the wave of waterfront workers' demonstrations in New Orleans proved the existence of a confrontational labor movement, which episodically involved instances of black-white solidarity.[57] And powerful unions like the IAM emerged in Atlanta in the late 1880s. Yet most of the South was, comparatively speaking, calm with respect to labor-management relations. This was especially true in the textile industry, though it too experienced periodic occurrences of labor conflict.[58] Southern investors and managers nevertheless forcefully promoted, and wanted to uphold, a North-South differential.

Spokespersons offered at least two reasons for this differential. First, they claimed that they had become exceptionally proficient in mastering the art of industrial diplomacy, presenting themselves and their workforces as friendlier than those residing outside the region. According to an 1892 essay in the *Tradesman*, southern "labor is generally on very friendly terms, with the employer, and the strikes and difficulties that so often interfere with the Northern mills and which keep them closed for so large a portion of the year are almost unknown in the South."[59] The Baltimore-based *Manufacturers' Record* reinforced this message four years later:

> labor agitators and organizers are not wanted in the South, because the relations of the mill hands with their employers are harmonious, and their condition is entirely different from the hardship and suffering which attend the life in many of the New England mill towns. There is no necessity for them to part with 5 or 10 or 20 percent of their wages weekly because they belong to some labor union, and are forced, whether they desire or not, to help support others who are on a strike.[60]

Southern publications like the *Tradesman* and the *Manufacturers' Record* had long helped perpetuate the notion that southern factory owners and supervisors, mostly unharmed by the massive labor battles in East Coast and midwestern cities, were enormously shrewd problem solvers and thus managerially more sophisticated than their northern brethren. Additionally, the southern workforce, these sources explained, showed an exceedingly high level of company faithfulness and common sense, unwilling to part with their personal earnings to pay dues to "some labor union."

Second, some employers used racism effectively to divide the working classes. Of course, southern employers were hardly the only figures to harbor white supremacist ideas and articulate racist statements, but they benefited from racial divisions in ways that white workers did not. An unidentified foundry operator, writing in John A. Penton's *Foundry* in 1901, explained the rationale of pitting blacks against whites: "We employ as you see, negroes enough to occupy about half our floors. This is not because they are good molders, for not one of them has ever attained the average standard of the white molder, or ever will." Then why, readers must have wondered, did he hire them in the first place? He went on: "This is an open shop, and some of our people think it good policy to keep enough negroes to show that, if necessary, we could fill up with them. If a white man gets 'cocky,' it does him good to ask him how he would like to see a nigger get his job." "If I had my way," he continued, "I would not have one of them around the place, but under the circumstances it may be good policy to keep a few of them simply to keep the union from attempting to get control of the shop." The writer was confident that black workers, if asked, would reject unionization: "the highest function of the negro is found in the fact that he will not join the union."[61]

This unnamed foundry owner expressed a general view that was somewhat consistent with the managerial logic put forward by Klan leader Forrest. Thirty-three years earlier, following the Civil War, Forrest had explicitly called for black laborers to stay in the South, remarking that this exploitable, largely rural workforce remained essential to the welfare of the section's economy. The *Foundry* article, illustrating how one employer benefited from the divide-and-rule style of racism that partly defined the emerging Jim Crow regime, demonstrated that blacks continued to serve valuable economic roles decades later. After all, wage earners tended to uncomfortably view one another as adversaries, rather than as potential allies, in these contexts; this general shop floor climate of distrust prevented acts of biracial collaboration and thus protected employers from class-based demands from below. In essence, a disorganized workforce, employers realized, was unthreatening and therefore good for business. For this reason, industrial strategists like Thompson, intellectually and strategically indebted to both generations of management educators, viewed the South's long history of racism and class rule as regionally advantageous.

The Johnstown Board of Trade

Thompson took a noticeable geographical detour in 1896 when he left Birmingham for western Pennsylvania, where he began working as the secretary for the Johnstown Board of Trade, a businessmen's organization founded in 1890, one year after a massive flood destroyed large parts of the city. Johnstown's business leaders, financially hurt by the flood, recruited Thompson to help them revive their community.

While residing in Johnstown, Thompson engaged in energetic community and public relations work, differing little from his activities on behalf of the Birmingham Commercial Club. He served, for example, as the general manager of the Pennsylvania State Fair, held in Johnstown in 1896.[62] And during these years, labor matters became especially central to his activities. In his first year on the job, he wrote glowingly in the journal *Public Opinion* about the city's largest employer and one of the nation's most productive iron and steel manufacturers, the Cambria Iron Company. Thompson praised the company's long-lasting prosperity and labor peace, explaining that its absence of dangerous "walking delegates" and unions was a crucial factor in its success: "It has run almost continuously ever since its formation, and practically without a shut-down or a lock-out. Through all the panics that have occurred it has still paid a dividend, and through all the labor troubles elsewhere it has been without a strike." Why had this particular workplace been at peace at a time when other industries faced so much labor unrest? The reason was straightforward: "no labor union has ever been permitted among its employes."[63]

Yet employer-backed anti-unionism alone, Thompson maintained, did not explain close to fifty years of uninterrupted production, labor-management tranquility, and shared prosperity. He insisted that one also needed to understand the company's benevolence and values, which, in Thompson's words, "fostered the spirit" of home buying. Company managers helped to make "the terms [involving home purchasing] as easy as possible with their men." Such investments apparently served the interests of both managers and managed. Homeownership, as another western Pennsylvania transplant, Andrew Carnegie, had long believed, served as a barrier to socialism, ensuring that workers had a material stake in capitalism.[64] Thompson thought that industrial and living conditions in Johnstown were markedly better than circumstances elsewhere, and widespread homeownership helped ensure stability and lawfulness in his adopted city. While Chicago, New York, and Philadelphia suffered from the ills of "pauperism and crime," more Johnstown residents, Thompson emphasized proudly, "own their own homes." Furthermore, Thompson insisted that Johnstown suffered from less crime than anywhere else "on this continent."[65] These examples, he sought to demonstrate, were clear signs of progress.

More important than homeownership and low crime rates was Johnstown's lack of a strong labor movement, which he related to patriotism:

What is more un-American than the doctrine that labor shall not have employment unless it belongs to some "union"? The constitution of our country gives to every citizen the right to earn an honest living, and whatever agency tends to impair that right is against the principles and policy of good government under the form we now enjoy.[66]

Here, in 1896, he swathed himself in the American flag and articulated the open-shop principle's virtues before the phrase became popular and organizations like the National Founders' Association, the National Metal Trades Association (NMTA), the NAM, and the CIAA launched a multi-community movement. The salaried agent of Johnstown's business community presented readers here with a class-blind analysis, noting that, above all, closed-shop contracts constituted a genuine menace to "the principles and policy of good government," not simply to the obvious financial interests of businessmen. In the following decade, members of open-shop organizations, seeking public acceptance for their campaigns, were equally selective in how they presented themselves. Like Thompson, they routinely drew attention away from their own class interests as they commended nonunionists for their patriotism and insisted that labor activists threatened "good government" policies.

While residing in western Pennsylvania, the South was never far from Thompson's mind. Although he publicly praised Johnstown for its supposed labor peace and overall prosperity, he continued to enthusiastically promote southern economic development. He wrote a number of letters to northern newspapers about the South's attractive investment opportunities, and in 1898, one year before moving to Huntsville, expressed his true commitments in a note to fellow Confederate veteran and Southern Railroad Company head Samuel Spencer: "I have worked continuously since coming here for the welfare of Alabama and the South."[67]

Industrial Development and Biracial Anti-Unionism

Thompson left Johnstown for Huntsville a year after insisting to Spencer that he was no carpetbagger in reverse. He clearly felt more at home in post-Reconstruction Huntsville than in post-flood Johnstown. Growing numbers of northern businessmen also felt the region's magnetic pull; indeed, numerous New England-based textile manufacturers decided to reduce production, or shut it down altogether, in the North as they looked to invest in and around Huntsville. Thompson, as secretary of the city's

Chamber of Commerce, part developer of the Huntsville Railway, Light, and Power Company, and owner of the Thompson Land and Investment Company—which purchased 600 acres of land with $50,000 in capital stock in early 1899—played an indispensable part in helping investors relocate.[68] Writers throughout the South took note of Huntsville's transformation under Thompson's leadership. A Texas newspaper reported in August 1900, for instance, that "Col. Thompson believes that within the next twelve months more northeastern mills will move to the south than ever before."[69] The report was correct.

But "the selling of the South," as historian James Cobb put it with respect to a later period, had its challenges.[70] Northerners, including potential investors, hardly perceived the region as perfectly welcoming or strife-free. Most bruising, from the viewpoint of developers like Thompson, were widely circulated reports of gruesome deaths caused by white supremacist lynch mobs, which terrorized African Americans in communities throughout the region.[71] In response to examples of racist violence, some liberal northerners joined anti-lynching leagues, denounced white-instigated violence, and, in extreme cases, threatened to invade the area in order to protect the victims. The negative publicity made the investment-conscious Thompson feel vulnerable and defensive. This was especially clear during one of Thompson's business trips to Boston in the summer of 1899 when he stumbled into a "big mass meeting" hosted by the Anti-Lynching League. The participants had gathered to discuss the high-profile case of Lillian Clayton Jewett, a white activist who had helped South Carolina's Baker family escape to the North after a mob lynched the family's father.[72]

Deeply annoyed, the former Klan leader responded to these activists by writing an editorial in a Huntsville newspaper contextualizing lynchings and pointing out what he considered the hypocrisy of northern do-gooders: "prior to the [Civil] war the crime of assault by a negro on a white woman was unknown in the south." Painfully recalling the Reconstruction years, he explained that the average African American "was made to believe by his fool friends that the southern people were entitled to no respect at his hands, that freedom meant privilege to pilfer and loaf at will, that his vote must always be cast against the southern whites, though he got his meat and bread from them as well as schooling for his children."[73] In his interpretation, lynchings and, more notably, the conditions that led to them became common only in the wake of Reconstruction Era benevolent programs, which, he held, created a generation of discourteous and seemingly unmanageable African Americans scattered throughout the former Confederacy. Northern, Republican Party-dictated developments, Thompson complained, led to a multi-decade African American crime wave and thus profoundly destabilized social and economic conditions. In Thompson's mind, organized lynchers, beginning with the Klan, constituted the sole entity standing between chaos and rebellion on the one hand and a well-ordered, hierarchical, and increasingly market-friendly society on the other. Thompson viewed lynch mobs as a form of, in historian Christopher Waldrop's words, "neighborhood crime fighting."[74]

After justifying lynchings, Thompson shifted attention away from the southern race problem to the northern labor problem. Writing shortly after the violent 1899 Cleveland streetcar strike, which he had personally witnessed, Thompson noted that he would never imagine organizing a comparable "rescue league" in the South to save Clevelanders from what he labeled the tyranny of organized labor:

> Suppose that I should go home and call a public meeting in Huntsville, and organize a "council" that should have as its object the suppression of the boycott and strike spirit in the North. Suppose that meeting should declare the scenes enacted in Cleveland last week—the jeopardizing of human life through the blowing up of a street car with innocent passengers aboard—as "inhuman," "beated," etc, and that civilization demanded the prompt punishment of the wretches who perpetrated that crime. Suppose, further, that I should attempt to organize similar councils throughout the South to save the North from these crimes and the growing tyranny and danger to American liberty from labor unionism. Does anyone suppose that I could safely go to Cleveland or other northern cities on such a mission? But Miss Lillian Clayton Jewett can seek cheap notoriety in Boston by going South to correct "southern outrages," about the origin and causes of which she knows absolutely nothing, and yet she can go with perfect safety, for no one will harm or molest her.[75]

Sections of the North, Thompson explained, were overwhelmed by union-generated mob violence far more damaging and frightening than what he considered southern law-and-order efforts. Thompson certainly hoped that potential investors soberly assessed these meaningful regional differences.

They needed, Thompson believed, a much fuller and, in his view, more accurate picture of southern race relations than what was presented by agitators like Jewett and her supporters. He sincerely hoped that hardheaded businessmen, concerned above all about production and profits, understood that organized labor represented a far greater hazard to their basic interests than the forces of law and order that sought to reestablish long-term African American subordination.

While Thompson raised no moral or legal problems with lynchings against "lawbreakers," he saw little reason to support such forms of repression against the majority of African Americans, most of whom were presumably nonthreatening to the interests of the southern ruling class. In fact, in the context of potential struggles with organized labor, Thompson believed, like others before him, that large segments of the black working class constituted a financial asset chiefly because many remained unwilling to join labor organizations, arguing before the U.S. Industrial Commission that they constituted "the reserved productive capital of the South."[76] By pointing out that the post-Reconstruction generation of southern blacks had a singular economic role to play, Thompson had become a practitioner of what historians Elizabeth Esch and David Roediger have called "race-management."[77]

But what if blacks opted not to work as strikebreakers, union-busters, or, more generally, for employers simply facing labor shortages? Like other southern spokespersons, Thompson periodically complained about "idleness." One solution to the presence of unproductive African Americans on city streets, Thompson suggested to Roosevelt in 1906, was the expansion of vagrancy laws: "the enforcement of the vagrancy laws uniformly all over the South will tend largely to the elimination of the idle negro." Violators of such stringent laws in cities like Birmingham were normally captured by authorities and forced to build roads, harvest crops, or shovel coal. But Thompson also thought that groups of "idle negroes" could be used outside the country, recommending to Roosevelt that they "dig the Panama Canal"—an especially draconian punishment for vagrancy.[78]

Of course, Thompson did not see the African American community monolithically, distinguishing the African Americans masses, including vagrants, from the small number of elite "race leaders." And in an effort to shape race and class relations in ways compatible with his vision of southern economic development, he established durable relationships with some of these elites, including Washington and Councill, the president of the

Alabama Agricultural and Mechanical College who the late historian Louis R. Harlan claims "could out-Booker Booker, and he frequently did."[79] Both men served important functions. As top level educational administrators, they enjoyed positions of authority, which they used as they attempted to delegitimize independent working-class activism while condemning those who stayed out of the labor force. In the process, they signaled to business owners and prospective investors that growing numbers of southern African Americans respected private property and laws, refrained from drinking and electoral politics, and promised to show unreserved deference to their employers. Thompson admitted in his essay in response to Jewett's actions that sizable minorities of African Americans were, regrettably, part of what he called "the criminal class." Yet he held out hope that the new generation would, under Washington and Councill's tutelage, learn what he called in 1899, "the rights and obligations of citizenship."[80]

In many ways, Councill's views closely mirrored Thompson's, and most likely appealed to prospective investors in search of a low-wage, nonunionized, and submissive workforce. In 1887, the former slave published *The Negro Laborer: A Word to Him*. Writing a year after a major labor uprising crippled part of the nation's railroad system, Councill instructed the African American community on values that were near and dear to Thompson. Like Thompson, Councill, four years younger than the former Klansman, was a temperance proponent: "Avoid intoxicants, especially while you are at work, for as your time belongs to your employer, you should strive to render faithful, intelligent service, which can not be done under the influence of liquor."[81] On questions of the labor movement, Councill offered explicit reassurance to employers and those seeking industrial stability: "Strikes are not the means by which wrongs may be set right." And "the appeal to strikes," Councill wrote, "is an appeal from reason to error, from justice to injustice, from order to disorder, from law to riot, from morality to immorality, from virtue to sin, from innocence to murder."[82] The unions, the college president complained, jeopardized industrial prosperity by threatening managerial and societal harmony. Above all, the labor movement severely endangered the interests of free labor, and Councill cautioned that ordinary wage earners "are threatened with great danger growing out of the slavery entailed by labor organizations."[83] Councill clearly painted trade unions in the worst possible light, and insisted that the answers to achieving black progress, racial harmony, and southern prosperity were found in a commitment to sobriety, enduring respect for employers, individual hard work, and an uncompromising rejection of a movement that sought to confine workers, both blacks and whites, to a new, equally restrictive type of bondage. Councill's words may help explain why Thompson was so fond of the former slave. The two men started their lives on opposite sides of the color and class lines, but both, in their late middle age, embraced mutually complementary and almost identical philosophies with respect to economic development and the management of labor.

Thompson certainly found use for Councill at several southern industrial conferences, which the former Klansman organized. One of the first sessions of the six-day Southern Industrial Convention, which was held in Huntsville in fall 1899, focused in part on the "race question." William Henry Baldwin, Jr.—railroad tycoon and financial benefactor to the Tuskegee Institute—and former West Virginia governor William MacCorkle spoke as representatives of the white race. Washington and Councill presented the southern black view. Writing to President William McKinley in the weeks before the conference, Thompson explained his reasons for picking these four individuals to address what he called "the race problem." This problem, he announced, will "be presented by the two broadest, most enlightened, practical and conservative representatives of the negro race." And "on behalf of the Southern white man's view," Thompson concluded, "two gentlemen equally capable in their special capacity" promised to explain the problem from their community's vantage point.[84] According to a report in a Huntsville paper just days before the event, these presentations promised to mark "a new era of progress in the industrial development of the South."[85]

Thompson, viewing himself as a crucial agent of this progressive evolution, played a central role in inviting the guests and, in some cases, explaining to them what to say. For instance, Thompson had something to do with the content of Washington's remarks; at a minimum, he explained to Washington what he wanted the famous black leader to convey to the distinguished audience. Washington happily agreed: "I am glad to say that I feel quite sure that I now have matters so arranged that I can attend the Industrial Convention and will try to treat the subject in the manner suggested by you as far as possible."[86]

While serving as Birmingham Commercial Club secretary, Thompson had witnessed Washington deliver his famous "compromise" talk in Atlanta in 1895, and requested the Tuskegee leader deliver a similar message in Huntsville. In Atlanta, Washington, underlining the core ideas in Councill's 1887 booklet, recommended that the sons of slave masters "Cast down your bucket among these people who have, without strikes and labour wars, tilled your fields, cleared your forests, builded your railroads and cities, and brought forth treasures from the bowels of the earth, and helped make possible this magnificent representation of the progress of the South."[87]

Four years later, Thompson wanted the Wizard of Tuskegee to make a similar appeal in Huntsville. Washington had a mind of his own, of course, but nevertheless showed a sincere willingness to please Thompson and the other businessmen in attendance, including both members of the southern ruling class and investment-hunting northerners. Consistent with his Atlanta presentation, Washington promised to continue to teach African Americans the necessity of respecting authority and obeying laws, assuring audience members that "capital and lawlessness will not dwell together." At the same time, the white employing class must recognize

> the black man for furnishing you with labor that is almost a stranger to strikes, lock-outs and labor wars; labor that is law-abiding, peaceful, teachable; labor that is one with you in language, sympathy, religion and patriotism; labor that has never been tempted to follow the red flag of anarchy, but always the safe flag of his country and the spotless banner of the cross.[88]

The black working classes, Washington reassured his illustrious audience, were fundamentally lawful, patriotic, and Christian, wisely rejecting anarchism and distancing themselves from those who sought industrial harm by staging strikes, organizing boycotts, or otherwise challenging the shrewd judgment and wishes of their bosses.

Next up was Councill, who lashed out against the "criminal class"—that is, in his view, jobless men from both races. The most appropriate response to the presence of such "criminals," Councill declared, was the establishment of impartial and comprehensive laws across racial lines: "We want less public criticism and more prompt enforcement of the law among all classes—less slander and abuse and more wisely constructed and rigidly enforced vagrant laws until idlers shall be whipped from among us and the crimes which shock us cease."[89] The former slave, proving his ability to "out-Booker Booker," had essentially recommended that authorities impose swift and draconian actions against the South's poorest residents. By articulating this message, Councill, like Washington, helped Thompson make the case that southern public policies were mainly intended to serve the business community's labor and safety needs, signaling that the region was entirely ripe for further investment.

Of course, it is easy to identify at least one glaring contradiction in Councill and Thompson's managerial views with respect to jobless African Americans. The solution, in their view, was clear: ensure that African Americans labored willingly under the direction of private sector employers or forcibly under the discipline of chain gang bosses. After all, violators of "rigidly enforced vagrant laws"—laws upheld by public authorities who ensured that the jobless did not congregate on urban streets—were often forced into bondage-like arrangement where they labored for long hours constructing roads, cutting timber, digging coal, or harvesting crops. This method of involuntary labor, of course, resembled slavery more than it did the "free labor" system relentlessly touted by open-shop advocates.[90] Neither addressed this rather blatant inconsistency.

Race relations and issues of law and order were not the only subjects that delegates covered at the Huntsville meeting. Most offered race-neutral presentations on various aspects of the region's economic development. H. H. Hargrove of Shreveport, Louisiana, presented a speech titled "Why Cotton Mills Should Be Built in the South," Erwin Craighead, the prominent Mobile-based journalist, discussed "The Timber and Lumber Interests of the South," the Honorable V. W. Grubbs of Greenville, Texas, reported on "The need for Industrial Education for the South," and the incredibly affluent Stuyvesant Fish of the Illinois Central Railroad spoke about "The Railroads of the South and Their Relation to its Development." Longtime U.S. senator and former Klansman, Alabama's John Tyler Morgan, discussed the ways southern industries would benefit from the creation of a Central American canal. Baltimore's Richard Edmonds, editor of the widely circulated and influential *Manufacturers' Record*, gave a presentation entitled "The Press of the South and its Relationship to the Industrial Development of the South." Altogether, over twenty papers were read by economically privileged and politically influential participants representing all southern states.[91] The number and diversity of contributors at the conference reflected Thompson's desire to present the South as a coherent and vibrant region, home to farsighted leaders united, above all, by a thirst for economic growth and managerial stability.

Indeed, the conference's central message, picked up by national newspapers and covered widely in trade publications, was clear enough: the South's infrastructure was impressive, its leadership unwavering in its commitment to economic progress, its workforce fully obedient and capable, and its race and class relations more harmonious than in any other part of the country. Thompson had essentially put the call out for a very specific type of Yankee invader: northern capitalists prepared to turn their backs on the places of their birth and assist the South in fulfilling its celebrated move forward.

"A Solid South for the Open-Shop"

Thompson's reputation rested in large part on his support for southern industrial development and on his unwavering opposition to labor unionism. His conference organizing, newspaper editorial writing, and high-profile presentations—especially his 1900 comments before Congress—brought him national recognition. For these reasons, Parry appointed the former Klansman to the CIAA's 14-member executive committee in October 1903. The Lincolnesque Parry must have certainly approved of Thompson's unequivocal position that collective action was necessary to protect what the Confederate veteran called in 1900 the "free American citizen" from becoming "a slave to some labor organization."[92]

How did Thompson, who had recently relocated to Birmingham where he helped organize and run the city's Citizens' Alliance, interact with his mostly northern peers? Did he abandon his southern identity for the sake of the broader, national movement against the labor problem? In a word: no. Evidence suggests that he certainly shared the fundamental managerial positions adopted of his largely northern colleagues. However, Thompson's regional partisanship remained basically unaffected. Rather than helping to advance the CIAA's goals—national unity against closed-shop-demanding unionists and against outbreaks of working-class lawlessness—Thompson continued to promote the narrower interests of the South's economic elite.

Yet Thompson's address at the second annual CIAA convention, which was held in New York City in 1904, demonstrates his collegiality and overall commitment to the open-shop movement. Like others at the gathering, he lamented the ways in which the labor problem found expression throughout the nation. He highlighted the near-civil war conditions in the coalfields of Colorado and discussed his own personal experiences in Cleveland, where he witnessed the destructive bombings of streetcars during the notorious 1899 strike. Profoundly disturbed by the viciousness in Cleveland, Thompson remarked that "my southern blood was beginning to get up."[93] And he raised the issue of the dramatic St. Louis streetcar strike in 1900, when, as he put it, "women were stripped naked on the street by the strikers and men were afraid to protect them." These horrific scenes could not reoccur in 1904, Thompson smugly reported, because "you have Mr. Van Cleave," the fellow Confederate veteran who led St. Louis's open-shop movement.[94] The conference proceedings indicate that Thompson received much applause during the course of his colorful and passionate speech. Clearly, CIAA members, including many on the front lines against organized labor's demands for "class legislation" and closed shops, found Thompson's words praiseworthy.

While Thompson shared an ideological commitment with his mostly northern associates, he continued to demonstrate a not so subtle belief in southern superiority. Indeed, more than half of his address concerned the accomplishments of the South's many union-avoiding employers. Importantly, few of these union-free managers and owners held membership in national employers' associations, but they remained unburdened by serious labor troubles or collective bargaining arrangements. Thompson boasted that "a movement was started in the South to save that section from the possibility of such conditions as have prevailed elsewhere."[95] In what appears to have been an egotistical game of one-upmanship, he mentioned the presence of "a solid South for the open shop." He maintained that cities throughout the region, including Mobile, Knoxville, and Nashville, enjoyed unparalleled industrial productivity and long-lasting managerial accord precisely because employers and employees valued one another and rejected closed shops. Nashville contained "only one or two closed shops," but the most remarkable city, in his view, was Chattanooga, which was home to "285 manufacturing establishments—all open-shops."[96] The applauding delegates, many of whom personally experienced the financially bruising and emotionally humiliating experiences caused by labor unrest, apparently found inspiration from these accomplishments.

Thompson concluded his address by offering advice to the dozens of mostly non-southerners. In his words, "Now, we come to you a solid South, and I would beg of you to make this a solid North, a solid East, a solid West, on this grand principle of American labor and American freedom."

Flying the flag high, he believed that the CIAA, which he called "the most patriotic association that this country produces," had the capacity to "protect our country" from the many dangers associated with demanding union activists. But the South remained the indisputable leader of this patriotic movement: "if you will just watch the South in the next few years you will realize that they, like the stone which was rejected by the builders, will become the keystone in the arch of our nation's progress and prosperity."[97]

Did southern open-shop proponents see themselves as part of a national movement? Given his membership in the CIAA and the NAM, Thompson did to some extent. Yet conference attendance records indicate the presence of very few southerners. Thompson mentioned employers' successes in Mobile, Knoxville, Nashville, and Chattanooga, but, tellingly, not one of the hundreds of delegates in attendance at the first or second CIAA meetings hailed from these cities. At the first convention, Birmingham sent two, Thompson and J. C. King. The Louisville employers' association sent four. A total of four also attended from St. Louis, including Van Cleave. One delegate represented New Orleans, the city that hosted the NAM's breakthrough 1903 meeting. No attendees represented Atlanta, Charleston, Charlotte, Dallas, Jacksonville, Little Rock, Memphis, or Shreveport.

Why? Perhaps southern employers realized that they had no need to hold membership in the CIAA—or any employers' association for that matter—to impose open-shop conditions on workers, to combat intrusive walking delegates, to ensure industrial tranquility, and to maintain managerial power. Merchants, manufacturers, and coal operators from the "solid South" apparently saw little reason to pay dues to, and take directions from, a national organization led by "the Abraham Lincoln of the twentieth century" in order to protect the rights of themselves and nonunionists. In his speech, Thompson invited open-shop proponents outside the South to, in essence, follow the lead of thousands of mostly non-affiliated employers.[98]

Such figures, the businessmen and investors responsible for launching and sustaining southern industrialization, clearly inspired Thompson and the mostly northern employer class active in the CIAA. But what explains their accomplishments? How did they help solve, or at least contain, the labor problem in their communities? Thompson did not specify, but we know southern employers formed their own local manufacturers' associations and chamber of commerce groups, and usually received state support for their managerial practices. Many certainly read the trade and open-shop literature, which was published and distributed throughout the country.

Whatever the case, Thompson showed little interest in trumpeting national employer unity in the name of patriotism once back in the South. His speeches, editorials in newspapers, and personal correspondence following appearances at CIAA-sponsored meetings indicate that he continued to promote southern growth, prosperity, and managerial harmony at the North's expense. His actions carried out in the decade's second half suggest that he was hardly motivated to truly bridge the regional divide between southern and northern interests. He certainly wanted to maintain a "solid" open shop throughout the South, but it is highly doubtful that, despite his words suggesting otherwise, he genuinely desired to see the creation of a "solid" network of open-shop workplaces throughout the country as a whole. In many ways, he remained a strategic scaremonger, distinguishing the supposedly harmonious South from what he identified as the scourge of northern-based union dictation.

Thompson had reasons to celebrate his home team, and non-southern CIAA members had good cause to envy the efforts of his Birmingham Citizens' Alliance. Just months before the CIAA's emergence, Thompson's organization successfully lobbied the Alabama Legislature to pass the "Individual Rights Bill." Vigorously opposed by organized labor, the bill, also endorsed by Governor William D. Jelks and the state senate, was rather broad, "punishing by a fine of not less than $50 nor more than $500, or by imprisonment at hard labor for not more than sixty days, persons convicted of boycotting, blacklisting, picketing and such assaults upon the rights of individuals."[99] The 1903 law explicitly sought to protect business owners and nonunionists by preventing boycotts and picketing:

> That it shall be unlawful for any person or persons to go near to or loiter about the premises or place of business of any person, firm, or corporation engaged in a lawful business for the purpose of influencing or inducing others not to trade with, buy from, sell to or have business dealing with such person, firm or corporation, or to picket the works or place of business of such other person, firm or corporation, for the purpose of interfering with or injuring any lawful business or enterprise.[100]

By prioritizing the rights of individual economic actors over the collective actions of protestors, the bill was fully consistent with the spirit of Roosevelt's recently declared Square Deal. According to the *Corporations Auxiliary Bulletin*, a journal that trumpeted the open-shop theory, it was entirely impartial, "applicable alike to employers and employes."[101] Despite such class-neutral language, its most enthusiastic supporters were the mostly northern employers embedded in the open-shop building community. In late 1903, the NMTA called the law "more advanced towards what such laws should be than any we know of."[102] The union opponents in this organization undoubtedly viewed Alabamians as clearheaded citizens unafraid to forcefully confront the "labor trust" in the area of official politics. Of course, Alabama's policy was not as drastic as the justifiable homicide law that Thompson had proposed three years earlier, but it certainly was a gain for the state's ruling class and it served as an inspiration to union fighters based outside the state.

In 1905, shortly after helping to transform Alabama into one of the nation's foremost open-shop states, Thompson moved to Chattanooga, where he began editing the *Tradesman*. Under his editorship, which lasted four years, the *Tradesman* churned out many articles that explicitly promoted the South's pro-business advantages over the North's. In its pages, Thompson, articulating long-simmering grievances, continued to define the North as a place habitually tormented by a hopelessly out-of-control, immigrant-led labor movement, one that created discord and innumerable headaches for factory owners, investors, innocent bystanders, and even employees—in essence, what the CIAA called "the common people." Attitudes and views in the rapidly industrializing South, in his mind, differed markedly from sentiment in the North. "Public sentiment" in the South, unlike that in the North, Thompson proclaimed in 1907, supported "the open shop."[103] One should not be surprised by his use of the term "public," rather than the words "manufacturers," "employers," or "bosses." Use of this word in this context was perfectly consistent with the language employed by his mostly northern colleagues. The open-shop movement, as employers presented it, constituted a series of class-neutral campaigns designed to protect employers, employees, and the public in general.

But Thompson did not avoid the topic of class altogether. Propertyless northern immigrants remained one of his favorite targets. In his view, these groups, especially those from eastern and southern Europe, were routinely involved in high-profile cases of political corruption and thus threatened the virtues of government institutions. "I gave close study to those classes [in numerous cities]," he wrote in 1906. Working-class immigrants, he warned in the pages of the *Tradesman*, "were becoming voters and politically debauching those cities. I have seen these classes at elections in Pittsburg, Johnstown and Philadelphia openly purchased at so much a head."[104]

The former Johnstown resident feared the electoral clout of ordinary people in densely populated urban centers, believing that they had the capacity to pass pro-union laws and decisively shift power away from respectable businessmen. But this problem was, as he told it, almost exclusively concentrated outside the South. Writing in the *New York Times* in 1906, Thompson—no longer financially obligated to defend the reputation of Johnstown's economy—reminded readers about the blatant differences between the regions: "there does not exist in the South any problem that begins to compare in seriousness with that which springs from the slums in New York, the Anarchists in Chicago, the race prejudice in San Francisco, and the 'mob spirit' found practically in all the labor centres of the North and East."[105] The South as a whole, he argued, was mostly free of these seemingly unsolvable labor-related evils. He sought to illustrate that southerners, irrespective of race or class, had mostly distanced themselves from labor activists, a morally impoverished and brutish force that promoted anti-Chinese racism in the Far West, radical anti-American ideologies in the Midwest, and riotous activities throughout the industrial North. The South, he maintained, was largely free of these "dangerous classes."

Yet despite their best efforts, southern employers and activists like Thompson were unable to eradicate the labor threat altogether. Machinists, miners, mill hands, telegraphers, and streetcar workers continued to organize, stage strikes, and demand closed shops. Some protests became violent, which certainly complicated Thompson's narrative depicting a glorious harmony of interests. But he tended to downplay their effects, insisting they constituted an anomaly, though a few eruptions were far too destabilizing to ignore. Writing about a violent Montgomery, Alabama, streetcar strike in 1907, for example, he argued stridently that these "crimes would have been a disgrace to Chicago and San Francisco, which are the hot-beds of unionism in America." "It is about time," he declared, "that the South in turn should declare its opposition to any such unionism."[106] Unable to shake the painful memories of the immediate post-Civil War period, Thompson, writing a year later, held that southern working-class agitators were "as much traitors and enemies to this section" as "the carpetbaggers in reconstruction days."[107] Rather than joining his mostly northern colleagues in calling, patriotically, for the nation as a whole to denounce and combat labor unions, Thompson focused narrowly on the need to mobilize a regional, business-led coalition against this problem. He was most comfortable pointing out the ways in which labor activists severely threatened the model that he and his fellow southern developers sought to establish.

Violators of this model—one based on labor-management peace in open shops that safeguarded the rights of nonunionists—were essentially hot-headed outsiders and destructive criminals responsible for impeding southern progress and prosperity.

But the region's elites—coal mine owners, college presidents, industrialists, large landholders, newspaper editors, judges, lawyers, politicians, and real estate investors—were far from powerless. And they could surely draw inspiration from history. Forty years earlier, the Klan, led by former slave masters, had mobilized energetically and, in many cases, successfully against this first generation of "traitors and enemies." Thompson, a battle-hardened veteran from these early scuffles, was hopeful that his colleagues would assist him in confronting the equally threatening second set of agitators.

Remarkably, the angry editor was not satisfied with merely challenging working-class protestors, walking delegates, left-wing activists, immigrant-led political machines, jobless African Americans in the South, or northern liberals. His personal correspondence also demonstrates his displeasure with those from his own class, especially northern-based capitalists active in the National Civic Federation (NCF), the businessmen-led organization that opened its membership to politically moderate union leaders and powerful members of the general public. The NCF had organized a series of conferences broadly related to economic development and social reform, and most of its meetings were held in northern cities. The regionally conscious Thompson actively discouraged others, especially southern business owners and politicians, from attending these gatherings. Writing in 1905 to Tennessee governor John Cox about an NCF-sponsored conference in New York City about transportation matters, Thompson insisted that southerners must not attend because the conference is "held mostly in the interest of the transportation companies with a view to make it appear that the South is so badly off for labor that it will take any they can bring." He noted further, "I have been against that meeting all along and hope that the South will have a slim representation there, for the reason that we are able to take care of our own interests down here, and prefer doing it our own way, especially when other suggestions are in the line of selfish interests."[108] His sectionalism, even jealousy, is very clear in this context. As a southern booster, Thompson saw himself and his regional organizations in direct competition with a mostly northern-based NCF membership. And, of course, he had no respect for the northerners who belittled the South's industrial progress or practices. A financial gain for the North, Thompson continued to believe, was a loss for the South. Sectionalism continued to trump both American patriotism and national class unity.

This was not the last time that Thompson criticized the NCF or northern business interests. The *Tradesman* editor also expressed annoyance with some of the NCF's labor reform efforts. He remained particularly irritated that the organization had planned to send "investigators" to the South to observe instances of child labor in cotton mills. The question of child labor sharply divided the business community, but Thompson believed that southern manufacturers, including NCF members, must enjoy the unquestioned authority to decide whether to employ this workforce, asserting that factory inspectors deserved no say in the matter. Writing to Daniel A. Tompkins—a Charlotte-based industrialist, newspaper owner, and member of both the NCF and the NAM—Thompson asked in 1907 whether "this continued effort, originating in Northern Sources, to 'investigate' Southern Cotton Mills spring more from enmity than real interest in them?" He continued: "Is it not time for Southern Mill owners through official channels to put an end to this kind of intermeddling with their affairs?"[109] Thompson held that southern textile mill owners had clear financial interests in opposing such interference. After all, the widespread presence of easily exploitable children, like the existence of racially segregated open-shop workplaces and vagrancy laws, helped give the South a competitive advantage over the considerably more regulated and union-dense northern states. From a strictly business perspective, the benefits seemed obvious.

Yet Thompson expressed impatience that, in his opinion, too few investors had acknowledged these and other financial advantages. Writing in the *Tradesman* in 1907, he admitted the region "has shown remarkable percentages of increases each year," but, he declared, "we should" not "be satisfied with it." Pointing to 1905 figures, Thompson noted that out of 216,262 manufacturing establishments in the U.S. as a whole, only 32,001 were southern-based. For Thompson, this was simply unacceptable: "the South should hold the leading position in these industries instead of the one it now occupies." Despite his earnest efforts and earlier predictions, the South had not developed as quickly as he would have preferred. Why? We can certainly speculate. Perhaps the region was unable to entirely overcome the negative publicity generated by northern anti-racists or by snobbish northeastern businessmen associated with groups like the NCF. Whatever the case, Thompson did not allow any of his antagonists to

Table 3: The South's Manufacturing Status

State	Capital invested by end of 1905
Louisiana	$150,810,608
Virginia	147,987,182
North Carolina	147,282,475
Georgia	141,000,339
Texas	135,211,551
South Carolina	113,422,224
Alabama	105,382,859
Tennessee	102,439,481

Source: "The South's Manufacturing Status," *Tradesman* 57 (May 15, 1907): 43. The table is incomplete: Thompson did not offer investment numbers for West Virginia, Mississippi, or Florida. He did note that Arkansas, the South's least economically developed state, had "only $25,384,636 invested in manufacturing enterprises."

weaken his resolve; he remained hopeful, believing that growing recognition of the area's multiple economic virtues—availability of raw materials, a generally low cost of living, and, above all, the widespread presence of open-shop workplaces—constituted "evidence of what it is destined to achieve in the future."[110]

Thompson served the interests of southern capitalism well into his 70s. He expanded his real estate interests following his tenure at the *Tradesman*, and divided his time between Birmingham and Mobile in the 1910s. In this decade, he headed the North Mobile Development Company, which, according to an article in a 1911 issue of the *National Magazine*, was "one of the important factors in the industrial development of Mobile."[111] He remained a devoted Catholic, a prosperous investor, a proud southerner, and a clear-eyed union opponent. He spent his final years with one of his sons in Baltimore, where he died in February 1929. He is buried in Bardstown, Kentucky, his wife's birthplace.

Thompson's life is important for several reasons. Above all, his long career offers insights into the links between sobriety and morality, between race and management, and between region and identity. He never abandoned his identity as a Confederate veteran and southerner, even though many in the open-shop movement's leadership called for national, rather than sectional, unity against the labor problem. Rather than merely underline the South's supposed assets—a low-wage region home to a largely unorganized workforce of blacks and whites—he actually took pleasure in pointing out what he considered the North's countless economic and moral failings, which, in his view, were caused by repeated eruptions of labor unrest, the spread of discriminatory closed shops, and the presence of obnoxious, pro-union politicians. Despite establishing relationships with businessmen in Johnstown and collaborating with the mostly northern employers in the CIAA, Thompson continued to fight regional, not only class, conflicts. He remained intolerant of labor unions wherever they existed, but continuously pointed out that the South, under the leadership of a biracial alliance of industrialists, promoters, politicians, and educators, was home to the nation's highest density of open-shop workplaces and thus offered a genuine alternative to those looking to escape what he relentlessly characterized as an incurable dystopia. Finally, we must realize that Thompson established a legacy that we can clearly identify today. More than a century after he delivered his provocative speech before the Industrial Commission, the South remains a marvelously attractive region for businesspeople seeking to avoid unions while maximizing profits under open-shop conditions.

Conclusion. Creating the "Common Good": Individual Rights, Industrial Progress, and Virtuous Citizenship

> Whether a solution is "progressive" or not depends on who is "reforming" whom.
> —Glenda Gilmore, 2002

In considering the ways historian Glenda Gilmore's astute observation applies to the many individuals and associations responsible for shaping the character of the turn-of-the-century open-shop movement, we must ask some fundamental questions: Was this multilocation movement truly consistent with, or even part of, the period's great reform efforts? Or, using current meanings of these words, was it a reactionary response to the assortment of liberal individuals and groups that, taken together, profoundly shaped this dynamic time? Were open-shop proponents progressive reformers? Given the diverse set of organizations and people who helped to define this period, combined with the hotly contested meanings of the terms "progressive" and "reform," it is impossible to provide entirely satisfactory answers.[1]

Yet most historians have put forward reasonable interpretations, typically categorizing the activities of employers and their associations as constituting one of a number of antiprogressive movements that had mobilized on numerous occasions to halt social justice campaigns.[2] Conservative forces, they have told us, organized formidable challenges to the liberal march forward, one energetically driven by a varied set of participants promoting greater rights and dignity for women, African Americans, immigrants, farmers, and workers. According to the usual narratives, an array of anti-suffragists, white supremacists, nativists, and anti-populists staged their own, often successful counter-activities—which found expression on both the grassroots and institutional levels—in response to such progressive campaigns.[3]

But, as we have seen, open-shop proponents, including both employers and those outside workplace settings, certainly did not perceive themselves as part of a counterreformist crusade standing in the way of human progress. Instead, they saw themselves following a noble tradition stretching back to the mid-nineteenth century, one fashioned by an assortment of abolitionists, antimonopolists, and promoters of peace. Employers, the most passionate and outspoken open-shop organizers, presented themselves as patriotic and class-neutral proponents of industrial fairness and guardians of ambitious, honest, and law-abiding underdogs, individuals who rejected what open-shop proponents considered the stifling constraints of union rules and the supposed violence inherent in the labor movement. Together, organized employers held the view that they alone— merchants, manufacturers, managers of construction sites, operators of coal mines, and railroad leaders—must enjoy the right to hire, fire, promote, or demote. In the process of establishing open-shop workplaces, employers aligned their efforts with the political mainstream, including, most of all, that represented by Theodore Roosevelt's 1903 Square Deal, a labor-management agreement that the president and his commission insisted offered genuine justice to coal operators, consumers, former strikers, and nonunionists. Open-shop campaigners repeatedly proclaimed a desire to protect, rather than punish, ordinary people. By invoking the Square Deal, they publicly championed the rights of a heterogeneous group of Americans—no one narrow category or class.

Moreover, numerous employers' and citizens' association members were also welfare capitalists, demonstrating another way their reformism found expression.[4] Welfare capitalist workplaces, open-shop proponents contended, constituted a significant improvement over antagonistic industrial relations systems based on the closed shop, which, in their collective interpretations, suppressed the talents and ambitions of individuals and thus forced unwilling employees to participate in coercive, and often unlawful, activities, including violent strikes. Employers sincerely believed that they had the ability to halt such developments by treating their workers fairly. Workplaces led by caring and respectful managers, John Kirby, Jr., of the National Association of Manufacturers and the Dayton Employers'

Association argued in 1906, constituted "the strongest defense of all against the tyranny of the labor trust."[5] Rather than tolerate closed shops and eruptions of class conflict, the movement's true believers saw themselves promoting what David M. Parry called in 1904 "the common good."[6]

In their shared view, the "common good" meant a properly arranged society, one that valued the law, rewarded individual hard work, promoted workplace harmony, and honored America's political history and institutions. By equating the open-shop principle with American patriotism and by forming hundreds of citizens' associations, advocates of this managerial system hoped to draw attention away from the country's hardening class divisions. They relentlessly stigmatized unionists and leftist activists who organized around class lines, insisting, as N. F. Thompson claimed in 1900, that such individuals threatened "God, country, civilization, and humanity."[7] And they repeatedly invoked the American flag, proudly distancing themselves from those who waved the black flag of anarchy or the red flag of revolutionary socialism. Movement agitators also denounced and challenged pro-union liberals and moderates like Samuel Gompers, figures who campaigned for various forms of what open-shop activists insultingly called "class legislation." Calls for closed shops, "class legislation," and class struggle remained, from their standpoint, un-American, well into the 1910s and beyond. Erasing class from the consciousness of ordinary people was one of the movement's central, long-term goals. As one NAM member bluntly insisted to his colleagues—individuals who controlled the means of production, resided in opulent homes, attended meetings in extravagant hotels like the Waldorf-Astoria, held membership in exclusive urban-based gentlemen's clubs, and routinely vacationed in Europe and sunny California—in 1914, "Let not the word class or classes pass our lips. We have no classes in our country."[8]

This statement, like many others, demonstrates that these well-organized union opponents employed public relations as shamelessly as they sought injunctions, recruited strikebreakers during industrial conflicts, and hired non-unionists during periods of industrial calm. A variety of publications—the NAM's *American Industries*, the CIAA's *Square Deal*, the NFA and NMTA's jointly published *Open Shop*, the Cleveland Employers' Association's *Facts*, George Creel's *(Kansas City) Independent*, John A. Penton's *Iron Trade Review*, Thompson's *Tradesman*, and Donald Tulloch's *City of Prosperity*—contained many tiresome accounts about the fairness of open shops and the importance of protecting nonunionists'—the "free men's"—"right to work" against what Kirby called in 1910 "mob law and violence."[9] These and other sources also habitually saluted the day-to-day managerial policies of "benevolent" employers, as well as the successful campaigns led by patriotic cross sections of society over union-imposed closed shops. By establishing employer unity regionally and nationally, effectively securing injunctions and armed enforcement against thousands of unionists during strikes, winning support from wide-ranging sections of society, and saturating the public with reformist-sounding language in publications and speeches, the open-shop movement unarguably left an enduring mark on this period.

The fraternity that propelled this multifaceted movement had their sights on the future, a time that they hoped would be characterized by honest government, municipal efficiency and order, industrial progress, and further modernization and professionalization—themes that we have come to associate with the period. They did much more than fight unions. Many were philanthropists, held membership in good government organizations, contributed to the temperance movement, and endorsed urban beautification endeavors. The National Cash Register Company's John H. Patterson, for instance, was one of the nation's earliest and most outspoken advocates of the development of the city commission and manager plan of urban governance; such plans were intended to replace elected mayors with what this well-known welfare capitalist called in 1896 "men who are skilled in business management and social science."[10] And William H. Pfahler, widely heralded as the "father of defense organizations," was one of the eight original founders of the Committee of Seventy, a Philadelphia civic organization founded in 1904 that campaigned against the city's Republican machine, which had earned a notorious reputation for vote buying. Tulloch sought to eradicate areas of urban blight as a member of Worcester's Vacant Lot Cultivation Society. And beginning in the late nineteenth century, between his stints as a Klansman and union fighter, Thompson edited a prohibition publication and toured parts of the country, speaking about what he viewed as the immorality of alcohol consumption. These and many other open-shop campaigners thought of themselves as forward-thinking reformers and honorable stewards of American society.

Their reform activities were generally consistent with the agendas of the period's most celebrated progressive campaigners, individuals who also promoted industrial changes, individual rights, and efficiency while honoring the spirit of visionaries like Abraham Lincoln. Many others voiced

unease with manifestations of managerial exploitation and industrial bigness in the same way that employers and their allies bemoaned the power
and activities of organized labor. The antimonopoly ethos that motivated
numerous activists, policy-makers, judges, lawyers, and muckrakers to critique the great trusts in the late nineteenth and early twentieth centuries
was essentially compatible with the growing chorus of voices demanding
that job seekers compete equally with one another, rather than receive special treatment simply by possessing union membership cards. Political leaders like Theodore Roosevelt, for example, demonstrated consistency as an
opponent of both the concentrated economic power of J. P. Morgan's railroad business, the Northern Securities Company, on the one hand, and the
United Mine Workers of America and the government printers' union that
demanded closed shops in their industries, on the other.[11] And in 1910,
while out of office, Roosevelt delivered a series of speeches calling for higher
taxes on what he called "swollen fortunes."[12] We can say much of the same
about Louis D. Brandeis. The well-known lawyer, concerned about the
overpowering economic control of major banks, railroad corporations, and
dominant companies like Standard Oil, worried in 1911 that many business
leaders "wanted to go the limit" instead of going "safely."[13] As we have
seen, in that same year, Brandeis made similar arguments about organized
labor, contending that its members needed to respect the wishes of nonmembers and acknowledge the managerial rights of proprietary capitalists.
Brandeis's statements, like the arguments of others, suggest that his discomfort with industrial bigness and closed shops stemmed from a general desire
to promote greater economic democracy while opposing expressions of
exclusivity within the framework of capitalism.[14]

Many of the same individuals who championed the rights of "free"
workers as part of a wider effort against monopolies were also proponents
of some forms of protective legislation, especially laws designed to protect
consumer health, as well as measures meant to restrict the labor of females
and children—reforms we also associate with this era. Additionally, by the
end of the twentieth century's first decade, growing numbers of employers
began making meaningful improvements in the area of workplace safety.[15]
There was considerable overlap; one does not need to search far to find
reformers—both in and outside industrial relations settings—who criticized both "unfair" employers and "lawless" workers. Employers' association members also backed, and in some cases participated in, organizations
designed to address the needs of industrial society's most vulnerable

members, not only nonunionists. In late 1906, two years after the National Child Labor Committee's formation, the CIAA went on record supporting restrictive child labor laws. Also, some prominent manufacturers' association members even participated in state agencies tasked with the responsibility of improving workplace safety.[16] Bear in mind, there was nothing inconsistent with experimenting with industrial welfare work, supporting workplace safety measures, recognizing the need for income taxes, acknowledging the necessity of food safety agencies, and championing laws prohibiting the labor of children while insisting that America's economic institutions performed best as open shops. Plenty of reformers viewed all of these developments as complementary signs of modernization and progress.

This was true nationally and at the local level, and the places we have explored demonstrate the various, regionally distinctive ways in which self-identified reformers endorsed campaigns to weaken unions while promoting what they perceived as civic and industrial progress. As we have seen, an effective way of understanding how the open-shop movement took on a progressive and boosterish coloration while often overlapping with other civic reform efforts is to focus on regions like Cleveland, Buffalo, Worcester, and parts of the U.S. South. Cleveland's open-shop movement thrived at the same time that one of the nation's most famous reform mayors, Tom L. Johnson, occupied city hall; Johnson did nothing meaningful to challenge the system of labor relations practiced by the city's employers. In western New York, a joint public-private partnership of employers, judges, police officers, and strikebreakers collaborated to defeat strikers and leftist activists, illustrating to the nation that Buffalo's leading residents valued the rule of law. In a symbolic gesture, members of Buffalo's business community hired famed architect Daniel Burnham to construct a memorial honoring William McKinley in 1907, shortly after employers crushed most of the Iron Molders' Union-sponsored strikes. Worcester's employers, led by savvy engineers and an optimistic poet, saw themselves in the forefront of solving the labor problem, believing that a combination of selective hiring practices and welfare capitalist programs was enough to ensure what Tulloch called in 1914 a "strikeless" future shaped by shared prosperity. Speaking for the South, Thompson relentlessly bragged that the region would lead the nation industrially because it, unlike the North, was led by enlightened businessmen and educators, including former slaves, who had succeeded in teaching southerners the values of citizenship—and such values were irreconcilable with closed-shop unionism and leftist ideolo-gies.[17] The open-shop principle profoundly influenced the actions of some of the era's most influential industrial and urban developers.

While open-shop proponents often anchored their activities in Ameri-ca's far-reaching reform traditions and ideals, we must recognize that their actions were hardly progressive from the standpoint of union activists and their supporters. From the collective perspectives of labor unionists, open-shop campaigns were primarily designed to discipline, not reward, the working class. As targets, union members had endured numerous indignit-ies: firings, blacklistings, long periods of joblessness, and occasionally police repression, fines, and jail time. Union-breaking campaigns sent an unam-biguous message to the working class as a whole: those who challenged employers' management rights to employ non-unionists and strikebreakers would likely confront disciplinary clampdowns waged by both private and public forces. Overwhelmed by these forces, protestors in many places had the option, in essence, of submitting to management or leaving their com-munities. Union activists did not accept as true that employers welcomed them in what Pfahler famously called in 1903 "Free Shops for Free Men."[18] This catchphrase made no sense to the wageless sufferers of employer-generated blacklists, including the thousands of rebellious machinists, molders, printers, and high-profile anarchists like Leon Czolgosz—who had experienced a prolonged period of unemployment because of his participa-tion in an 1893 strike.[19] We have learned that union supporters holding a range of political perspectives hardly enjoyed the freedom to join with one another and participate in collective activities from below.

Trade union publications and workers' cooperative actions in the face of open-shop campaigns provide us with many clues about how large sec-tions of the working class regarded employers' associations, the language of open-shop activists, and workplace management issues generally. Despite employers' persistent public relations efforts throughout the country, labor activists frequently revealed an unflinching disdain for the open-shop prin-ciple and deeply held frustrations with the figures responsible for upholding it. Yet some expressed annoyance at the open-shop movement's rhetorical achievements. An unnamed writer for the *Official Journal of the Brotherhood of Painters, Decorators and Paperhangers of America* conveyed irritation in 1905 that many ordinary people failed to acknowledge "that behind all the palaver about the heroism of the scab, the boosting of the so-called 'independent' workmen, and the opposition to the 'closed shop' is the desire to coin more money out of wage earners."[20] Reinforcing this message in that same year, Victor Yarros, writing in the AFL's *American Federationist*, called on union supporters to relentlessly challenge "the rant of the Parry employers about 'Americanism' and 'individual liberty'."[21] Working-class activists continued to demonstrate that they valued solidarity and bargaining rights over "individual liberty."

Furthermore, we must acknowledge that not all upper-middle-class, self-identified reformers trumpeted the open-shop principle and cheered on the activities of its practitioners. Settlement house activist Jane Addams, prominent economist Richard T. Ely, influential lawyer Clarence Darrow, and Cleveland attorney Jay P. Dawley—after he dramatically abandoned his allies in the open-shop movement at the time of the city's 1911 garment strike—argued that working men and women needed to enjoy the right to bargain collectively in order to achieve a higher standard of living and greater dignity.[22] These reformers, like workplace victims of open-shop campaigns, identified an overwhelming gap between what employers and their allies said publicly and the reality of open-shop conditions on the ground. As Darrow put it in 1920, employers had repeatedly defended the open-shop principle with "all sorts of statements and arguments."[23] By the century's second decade, union activists and their supporters rejected the notion that the individuals behind the movement harbored a sincere desire to actually protect "the common people" or to provide them with a "Square Deal."[24] Moreover, unlike many middle-class commentators who championed the open-shop principle, these figures were unwilling to deny the reality of America's deepening class divisions or the ways in which such divisions helped inspire resentment, workplace conflicts, and, in many cases, an abhorrence of capitalism itself.

Even Ray Stannard Baker, the prolific muckraker who borrowed the slogan "right to work" from late nineteenth-century union critics and helped popularize it in 1903, expressed skepticism about the open-shop movement's supposed progressiveness at the end of 1904, a year when employers successfully broke the back of unions in hundreds of workplaces. In "The Rise of the Tailors," Baker acknowledged that forceful labor unions were actually necessary to combat the agendas of greedy, cost-cutting employers. "Without [workplace] resistance," Baker explained in this 1904 *McClure's* article about New York City's garment industry, "employers will gradually fill up their shops with non-union men—because non-union men, unprotected by organizations, will work cheaper."[25] This analysis certainly suggests that Baker's thinking had evolved somewhat from the previous year, when the same magazine published "The Right to Work." Rather than singling out and denouncing intolerant union supporters for involvement in heavy-handed recruitment practices or picket-line scuffles, as he had in 1903, Baker instead turned his attention to unchecked garment manufacturers, recognizing that they established open shops for self-interested reasons, not because they cared about their workers' welfare.

Baker's analysis describes the managerial tendencies of the nation's organized employers in general, not just the activities of New York City's garment manufacturers. With indispensable assistance from mainstream reformers and authoritarian arms of the state, open-shop employers largely succeeded in weakening their working-class opponents while legitimizing an economic system that empowered and enriched the few at the expense of the many. Despite their often high-minded, patriotic, and class-blind rhetoric about fairness and freedom, they were fundamentally self-interested, concerned above all about profits and power. Their actions in the face of labor activism spoke much louder than their words. By breaking strikes, busting unions, blacklisting working-class activists, and broadcasting propaganda, they ultimately played a dominant role in undermining rather than advancing "the common good."

More than eleven decades after the open-shop movement burst into the nation's workplaces and communities, employers and their allies continue to challenge the activities of an increasingly ineffective labor movement while diverting attention away from growing class divisions and from communities struggling with high levels of poverty and workplace exploitation.[26] In this so-called "second Gilded Age," employers, human resource managers, and union-avoidance lawyers still warn employees in captive audience meetings that unions undermine productivity, are run by greedy dues-collecting outsiders, represent an intrusive third party and relic of the past, establish unnecessary divisions between employees and management, and seek to force workers to strike against their will while preventing motivated individuals from enjoying their "right to work." Like earlier generations, a number of employers in union-free workplaces also support merit pay schemes, which are intended to stimulate productivity increases and promote individual competitiveness. Establishing labor solidarity is rather difficult in these environments. Above all, employers and their allies continue to maintain that organized labor constitutes a societal threat even as low-wage jobs, workplace insecurity, and class inequality continue to grow at alarming rates. Clearly, today's aggressive union opponents owe an intellectual and strategic debt to the diverse figures—conservative and liberal academics, attorneys, bankers, clergymen, engineers, journalists, judges, non-union wage earners, and employers representing workplaces of all sizes—who shaped the character of the nation's first open-shop campaigns.

Notes

Introduction. Reformers and Fighters: Employers and the Labor Problem

Epigraph: David M. Parry, "President's Address," *Proceedings of the Second Annual Convention of the Citizens' Industrial Association of America, November 29 and 30, 1904* (Indianapolis: CIA Publication Department, 1904), 8.

1. Richard Hofstadter, *The Age of Reform* (New York: Vintage, 1955); and Beverly Gage, *The Day Wall Street Exploded: A Story of America in Its First Age of Terror* (Oxford: Oxford University Press, 2009).

2. According to industrial relations scholar Bruce E. Kaufman, "Many Americans at the turn of the twentieth century regarded the Labor Problem as the most serious of all domestic problems facing the United States." See Kaufman, *Managing the Human Factor: The Early Years of Human Resource Management in American Industry* (Ithaca, N.Y.: Cornell University Press, 2008), 93. Writers often use the phrase "labor question" interchangeably with the term "labor problem." See Rosanne Currarino, *The Labor Question in America: Economic Democracy in the Gilded Age* (Urbana: University of Illinois Press, 2011); and Jean-Christian Venel, *The Employee: A Political History* (Philadelphia: University of Pennsylvania Press, 2013), 31.

3. Critics did not always use the term "closed shop." They also employed the phrase "compulsory unionism." For uses of this term, see Rev. Frank Foster, "The Street Car Strike at St. Louis," *Independent* 52 (July 26, 1900): 1784; "John Mitchell's Book," *Public Policy* 9 (December 19, 1903): 298; and "Unionism and the Steel Trade," *Review* (September 1912): 17. For a history of the closed shop, see Frank Tenney Stockton, "The Closed Shop in American Trade Unions" (Ph.D. dissertation, Johns Hopkins University, 1910).

4. George B. Hugo, *Socialism, "the Creed of Despair": Joint Debate in Faneuil Hall, March 22, 1909* (Boston: n.p., 1909), 11. This was a debate between Hugo and socialist James F. Carey. Roughly two years before this encounter, unionists had sought to organize Hugo's workplace. See "New England Notes," *American Bottler* 27 (June 15, 1907): 70.

5. Historian Sanford M. Jacoby has argued that American employers were exceptional in their resistance to unionization. See Jacoby, "American Exceptionalism Revisited: The Importance of Management," in *Masters to Managers: Historical and Comparative Perspectives on American Employers*, ed. Jacoby (New York: Columbia University Press, 1991), 173–200.

6. The open-shop philosophy appears largely consistent with nineteenth-century Republican Party ideas. For now-classic statements on this, see David Montgomery, *Beyond Equality: Labor and the Radical Republicans, 1862–1872* (1967; Urbana: University of Illinois Press, 1981), 14, 26, 30–31; Eric Foner, *Free Soil, Free Labor, Free Men: The Ideology of the Republican*

Party Before the Civil War (Oxford: Oxford University Press, 1970), 11–39; Daniel T. Rodgers, *The Work Ethic in Industrial America, 1850–1920* (Chicago: University of Chicago Press, 1978), 35; and Heather Cox Richardson, *The Death of Reconstruction: Race, Labor, and Politics in the Post-Civil War North, 1865–1901* (Cambridge, Mass.: Harvard University Press, 2001). For an important discussion of "free labor ideology" in the 1880s, see Theresa A. Case, *The Great Southwest Railroad Strike and Free Labor* (College Station: Texas A&M University Press, 2010). For an analysis of the fluidity of "free labor," see Robert J. Steinfeld, *Coercion, Contract, and Free Labor in the Nineteenth Century* (Cambridge: Cambridge University Press, 2001).

7. American employers were hardly unique in this regard. Most members of the bourgeoisie throughout the industrialized world embraced, in the words of historian Marc Mulholland, "a belief in the free market *in employment.*" See Mulholland, *Bourgeois Liberty and the Politics of Fear: From Absolutism to Neo-Conservatism* (Oxford: Oxford University Press, 2012), 5.

8. A. J. Hain, "Nation Swinging to the Open-Shop," *The Iron Trade Review* 67 (September 23, 1920): 846–52.

9. My organizational approach differs from others. Earlier studies of organized employers, including those by William C. Pratt, Thomas Klug, Howell Harris, William Millikan, and Jeffrey Haydu, have focused principally on particular communities or industries, richly detailing the ways largely proprietary capitalists built city-based open-shop associations and battled—and in some cases negotiated with—unions in mostly northern, midwestern, and western cities. Pratt, "The Omaha Businessmen's Association and the Open Shop, 1903–1909," *Nebraska History* 70 (1989): 172–83; Klug, "The Roots of the Open-Shop: Employers, Trade Unions, and Craft Labor Markets in Detroit, 1859–1907" (Ph.D. dissertation, Wayne State University, 1993); Harris, *Bloodless Victories: The Rise and Fall of the Open-shop in the Philadelphia Metal Trades, 1890–1940* (Cambridge: Cambridge University Press, 2000); Millikan, *A Union Against Unions: The Minneapolis Citizens Alliance and Its Fight Against Organized Labor, 1903–1947* (St. Paul: Minnesota Historical Society Press, 2001); and Haydu, *Citizen Employers: Business Communities and Labor in Cincinnati and San Francisco, 1870–1916* (Ithaca, N.Y.: Cornell University Press, 2008). Haydu focuses on two cities. Others including Robert Wiebe, Daniel R. Ernst, Sidney Fine, and Vilja Hulden have explored the dynamics of national struggles, highlighting the roles played by certain organizations, such as the NAM, the American Anti-Boycott Association, the National Erectors' Association, and the National Civic Federation. Fine, *"Without Blare of Trumpets": Walter Drew, the National Erectors' Association, and the Open-Shop Movement, 1903–57* (Ann Arbor: University of Michigan Press, 1995); Ernst, *Lawyers Against Labor: From Individual Rights to Corporate Liberalism* (Urbana: University of Illinois Press, 1995); and Hulden, "Employers, Unite!: Organized Employer Reactions to the Labor Union Challenge in the Progressive Era" (Ph.D. dissertation, University of Arizona, 2011). This study's organizational structure follows models offered by Leon Fink (Knights of Labor) and Jacoby (Welfare Capitalism). Both wrote two chapters outlining their respective subject's relationship to national contexts followed by a series of case studies. See Fink, *Workingmen's Democracy: The Knights of Labor and American Politics* (Urbana: University of Illinois Press, 1983); and Jacoby, *Modern Manors: Welfare Capitalism Since the New Deal* (Princeton, N.J.: Princeton University Press, 1997).

10. By highlighting the ways open-shop businessmen connected their management methods to progress in general, my analysis complement's one of Pamela Walker Laird's

central points. As she has explained, "businesspeople, especially industrialists, projected them-
selves as agents of change—as the engines of material and, therefore, cultural progress." See
Laird, *Advertising Progress: American Business and the Rise of Consumer Marketing* (Baltimore:
Johns Hopkins University Press, 1998), 102. Also see Joshua B. Freeman, "Giant Factories,"
Labour/Le Travail 72 (Fall 2013): 190.

11. Quoted in James Livingston, "The Social Analysis of Economic History and Theory:
Conjectures on Late Nineteenth-Century American Development," *American Historical
Review* 92 (February 1987): 86.

12. "Employers Propose to Combine," *Omaha Daily Bee*, March 31, 1903, 3.

13. Quoted in "Industrial Alliance to Take Strong Stand Against 8-Hour Bill," *Indianapolis Journal*, February 22, 1904, 4.

14. George Creel, "A Mighty Organization's Birth: The New 'Citizens' Industrial Association of America," *(Kansas City) Independent*, November 7, 1903, 4.

15. Quoted in "Violent Attack on Labor Unions," *(Richmond) Times*, June 13, 1900, 2.

16. Quoted in "Industrial Congress," *Evening Star*, December 3, 1906, 14.

17. "Combining Foundries," *St. Paul Globe*, August 24, 1902, 1.

18. "New Leaders," *(Kansas City) Independent*, August 15, 1903, 4.

19. "The Perverted Union Label," *Tradesman* 37 (July 1, 1907): 46.

20. Ferd C. Schwedtman quoted in David Moss, *Socializing Security: Progressive Era Economists and the Origins of American Social Policy* (Cambridge, Mass.: Harvard University Press,
1996), 28.

21. "The Employers' Association," *(Kansas City) Independent*, July 4, 1903, 11.

22. "The Foundry Trade School," *Foundry* 20 (May 1902): 88.

23. William H. Pfahler, "Free Shops for Free Men," *Publications of the American Economic Association* 4 (February 1903): 184. Open-shop activists applied the concept of what
historians have called "antimonopolism" to the labor market. "At its heart," Richard White
has explained, "antimonopolism was a belief that the economic system of a democracy had
itself to be democratic, and that the goal of a republican economy was to produce republican
citizens." White, *Railroaded: The Transcontinentals and the Making of Modern America* (New
York: Norton, 2011), 513. Complementing White, Richard R. John has noted that a wide
variety of Americans, including some late nineteenth century businessmen, embraced "antimonopolism" because they shared the view that "the citizenry had an obligation to hold
the powerful accountable for their conduct and performance." John, "Robber Baron Redux:
Antimonopoly Reconsidered," *Enterprise and Society* 13 (March 2012): 6. Also, see Case, *The
Great Southwest Railroad Strike*, 32; Joshua D. Wolff, *Western Union and the Creation of the
American Corporate Order, 1845–1893* (Cambridge: Cambridge University Press, 2013), 2; and
Robert MacDougall, *The People's Network: The Political Economy of the Telephone in the Gilded
Age* (Philadelphia: University of Pennsylvania Press, 2014), 10. On efficiency, see Daniel T.
Rodgers, "In Search of Progressivism," *Reviews in American History* 10 (December 1982):
113–32; and James Kloppenberg, *Uncertain Victory: Social Democracy and Progressivism in
European and American Thought, 1870–1920* (Oxford: Oxford University Press, 1986). For
centuries, members of the bourgeoisie on both sides of the Atlantic have stressed the supposed
virtues of "efficiency" in industrial workplaces. See Franco Moretti, *The Bourgeois: Between
History and Literature* (London: Verso, 2013), 39–44.

24. "Regarding Labor," *(Kansas City) Independent*, November 16, 1901, 1.

25. "The Foundry Labor Problem," *Iron Age* 77 (May 31, 1906): 1764.

26. "A Notable Case of the Open Shop's Success," *Square Deal* 3 (July 1908): 80.

27. Quoted in Henry M. McKiven, *Iron and Steel: Class, Race, and Community in Birmingham, Alabama, 1875–1920* (Chapel Hill: University of North Carolina Press, 1995), 100.

28. Class divisions grew widely during the twentieth century's first decade. According to Willford Isbell King, the cost of living increased from 1899 to 1909 "faster than the money earnings of labor and, hence, the real annual returns for labor showed a slight decline in the case of manufacturing and a decided decrease in the case of railway employees." King, *The Wealth and Income of the People of the United States* (New York: Macmillan, 1915), 179.

29. "Employers Must Organize," *Bulletin of the National Metal Trades Association* 2 (May 1903): 283. This article was first published in the *New York Commercial*.

30. "Do Right—Then Fight," *Review* 3 (Spring 1906): 45. The Dayton Employers' Association first used this phrase in 1900.

31. In the conclusion to their edited book about American elites, Steve Fraser and Gary Gerstle make a similar point, noting that the nation's upper classes increasingly "have adopted a democratic demeanor and portrayed their motivations, purposes, and policy as grounded in the principle of popular sovereignty." See "Coda: Democracy in America," in *Ruling America: A History of Wealth and Power in a Democracy*, ed. Steve Fraser and Gary Gerstle (Cambridge, Mass.: Harvard University Press, 2005), 289.

32. Quoted in Fine, *"Without Blare of Trumpets"*, 3.

33. Walter Gordon Merritt, "New Ideas in Industrial Organization," *Iron Age* 103 (June 19, 1919): 1627. Merritt was a management-side labor lawyer and leader of the American Anti-Boycott Association.

34. "The Square Deal," *Exponent* 4 (May 1907): 6.

35. Historians are in disagreement about the nature and success of welfare capitalism. We know welfare capitalist programs were uneven across businesses and regions. The most generous employers implemented profit sharing programs, provided health insurance, and offered subsidized housing. Others oversaw the development of athletic teams and drama clubs. Some offered more modest benefits, including providing employees with free turkeys at Christmas time. Here the distinction between small and large workplaces really mattered. The most benevolent firms were rather large, while smaller and mid-sized workplaces simply did not have the resources to match the services offered by the larger firms. As this study will show, a number of sizable workplaces with generous programs were unable to avoid labor troubles. Several critical historians have explored the tensions between what employers said about their programs and the reality of the programs themselves. See Howard Gitelman, "Welfare Capitalism Reconsidered," *Labor History* 33 (Winter 1992): 5–31; William Littmann, "Designing Obedience: The Architecture and landscape of Welfare Capitalism, 1880–1930," *International Labor and Working Class History* 53 (Spring 1998): 88–112; Brian Kelly, *Race, Class, and Power in the Alabama Coalfields, 1908–1921* (Urbana: University of Illinois Press, 2001), 60–64; Howell J. Harris, "Industrial Paternalism and Welfare Capitalism: 'Where's the Beef?' or 'Show Me the Money!'" in *Public and Private in American History: State, Family, Subjectivity in the Twentieth Century*, ed. Raffaella Baritono, Daria Frezza, Alessandra Lorini, Maurizio Vaudagna and Elisabetta Vezzosi (Turin: Otto, 2003), 459–82. My understanding of workers' response to welfare capitalism comes chiefly from Gerald Zahavi. See Gerald Zahavi, "Negotiated Loyalty: Welfare Capitalism and the Shoeworkers of Endicott Johnson, 1920–1940," *Journal of American History* 70 (December 1983): 602–20.

36. Quoted in Albion Guilford Taylor, *Labor Policies of the National Association of Manufacturers* (Urbana: University of Illinois Press, 1927), 96.

37. "The Open-Shop Movement," *New York Times*, April 29, 1904, 8.

38. See "Some Shops Open on 'Open Shop' Principle," *Buffalo Evening Times*, June 12, 1906, 4. Andrew Wender Cohen has used the phrase "union governance" to describe scenarios in which workers forced reluctant employers to bargain. According to Cohen, "many cities" were home to a variety of workplaces—brick building, construction, retail, and manufacturing—where unionized workers defied the wishes of their employers and enjoyed a degree of shop floor control. See Cohen, "Resisting Judgment," *Labor: Studies in Working-Class History of the Americas* 10 (Winter 2013): 98.

39. For a fine treatment of this tendency, see Shelton Stromquist, *Re-Inventing "The People": The Progressive Movement, the Class Problem, and the Origins of Modern Liberalism* (Urbana: University of Illinois Press, 2006); and Stromquist, "Response: Re-Class-Ifying the Progressive Movement," *Journal of the Gilded Age and Progressive Era* 6 (October 2007): 467–71. Stromquist is not alone in this view. See Robert Justin Goldstein, *Political Repression in Modern America: From 1870 to the Present* (Cambridge, Mass: Schenkman, 1978), 65; Alan Dawley, *Struggles for Justice: Social Responsibility and the Liberal State* (Cambridge, Mass.: Harvard University Press, 1991), 136; Christopher Tomlins, "Necessities of State: Police, Sovereignty, and the Constitution," *Journal of Policy History* 20 (Winter 2008): 60; Jeffrey Haydu, *Citizen Employers: Business Communities and Labor in Cincinnati and San Francisco, 1870–1916* (Ithaca, N.Y.: Cornell University Press, 2008), 121; Christopher W. Shaw, "'No Place for Class Politics': The Country Life Commission and Immigration," *Agricultural History* 85 (Fall 2011): 520–39; Venel, *The Employee*, 25–28; and Joseph J. Varga, *Hell's Kitchen and the Battle for Urban Space: Class Struggle and Progressive Reform in New York City, 1894–1914* (New York: Monthly Review Press, 2013). And Nancy Cohen argues that liberals played a significant role in defending corporate capitalism; see Cohen, *The Reconstruction of American Liberalism, 1865–1914* (Chapel Hill: University of North Carolina Press, 2002).

40. In their respective case studies of Chicago, Los Angeles, and Michigan's northern copper district, historians Andrew Wender Cohen, John H. M. Laslett, and Gary Kaunonen and Aaron Goings make similar points, noting that progressives often sided with management rather than with labor during industrial disputes. See Cohen, *The Racketeer's Progress: Chicago and the Struggle for the Modern American Economy, 1900–1940* (Cambridge: Cambridge University Press, 2004), 122–38; Laslett, *Sunshine Was Never Enough: Los Angeles Workers, 1880–2010* (Berkeley: University of California Press, 2012), 49; and Kaunonen and Goings, *Community in Conflict: A Working-Class History of the 1913–14 Michigan Copper Strike and the Italian Hall Tragedy* (Lansing: Michigan State University Press, 2013), 18–19.

41. "When They Will Be Wiped Off the Face of It," *American Industries* 3 (August 15, 1904): 15. Social Gospelers like Gladden were liberal Protestant reformers who condemned economic inequality, poverty, crime, child labor, and war. Ken Fones-Wolf offers a thoughtful analysis of their approach to class issues, noting that its advocates expressed both "moral indignation at inequality and the fear that organized labor might acquire radical characteristics." See Fones-Wolf, *Trade Union Gospel: Christianity and Labor in Industrial Philadelphia, 1865–1915* (Philadelphia: Temple University Press, 1989), 96. Also see Jacob Henry Dorn, *Washington Gladden: Prophet of the Social Gospel* (Columbus: Ohio State University Press, 1968), 215.

42. "No More Closed Shops in the N.C.R.: Last Straws That Didn't Break Its Back," *American Industries* 3 (October 16, 1905): 1.

43. Gustavus A. Weber, "Open Shop," in *The New Encyclopedia of Social Reform*, ed. William D. P. Bliss (New York: Funk and Wagnall, 1908), 853.

44. "The Situation at St. Louis," *New York Times*, July 28, 1877, 1.

45. Quoted in Paul Avrich, *The Haymarket Tragedy* (Princeton, N.J.: Princeton University Press, 1982), 216.

46. "The Peace That Debs Gives," *Richmond Dispatch*, July 10, 1894, 2.

47. According to legal historian William E. Forbath, "In their attitude toward strike-breakers, pickets were often ambivalent: sometimes they tried to persuade, exhort, cajole, or shame; at other times they tried to menace and intimidate. The courts, however, recognized no such distinctions." See Forbath, *Law and the Shaping of the American Labor Movement* (Cambridge, Mass.: Harvard University Press, 1989), 109.

48. Eliot quoted in Marcus O'Brien, "Reply to President Eliot," *Railway Conductor* 21 (July 1904): 484. A year later, Iowa judge Smith McPherson made the same comment. For McPherson's comment, see Sidney Fine, "Frank Murphy, the Thornhill Decision, and Picketing as Free Speech," in *The Labor History Reader*, ed. Daniel J. Leab (Urbana: University of Illinois Press, 1985), 362. Organized employers were sincerely thankful for judicial backing. According to an article in *Open Shop*, "The veiled threats of peaceful picketing and persuasion have been very efficacious in driving such from the field of competition, but it is refreshing to observe that the courts, in recent decisions, have torn the mask from these hypocritical pretenses, and have shown them in their true character." See Azel F. Hatch, "The Rights of the Scab," *Open Shop* 4 (October 1905): 449–50.

49. William J. Novak, "The Myth of the 'Weak' American State," *American Historical Review* 113 (June 2008): 758–59; Richard White, *Railroaded: The Transcontinentals and the Making of Modern America* (New York: Norton, 2011). Also see Richard R. John, "Business Historians and the Challenge of Innovation," *Business History Review* 85 (Spring 2011): 185–201; and Leo Panitch and Sam Gindin, *The Making of Global Capitalism: The Political Economy of American Empire* (London: Verso, 2012).

50. Julie Greene, *Pure and Simple Politics: The American Federation of Labor and Political Activism, 1881–1917* (Cambridge: Cambridge University Press, 1998), 84.

51. "The 'Blacklist' Upheld," *New York Times*, November 25, 1896, 1; "Can Discharge Man for Joining Union," *New York Times*, January 28, 1908, 1; and Victor S. Yarros, "The Labor Question and the Social Problem," *American Journal of Sociology* 9 (May 1904): 776–77. Passed by Congress in 1890, the Sherman Act was initially meant to prohibit practices that harmed business competition, but authorities began using it against "combinations of labor" in 1893. In that year, a federal district court targeted general strikers in New Orleans. See Elizabeth Sanders, *Roots of Reform: Farmers, Workers, and the American State, 1877–1917* (Chicago: University of Chicago Press, 1999), 93–100.

52. For more on the state and labor, see Edwin E. Witte, *The Government in Labor Disputes* (New York: McGraw-Hill, 1932); Morton Keller, *In Defense of Yesterday: James M. Beck and the Politics of Conservatism, 1861–1936* (New York: Coward-McCann, 1958), 73–75; Forbath, *Law and the Shaping of the American Labor Movement*; Gerald Friedman, *State-Making and Labor Movements: France and the United States, 1876–1914* (Ithaca, N.Y.: Cornell University Press, 1998); Venel, *The Employee*, 34–45.

53. On the contested meanings and thus pitfalls of using these terms, see Julie Greene, "Not So Simple: Reassessing the Politics of the Progressive Era AFL," *Labor: Studies in Working-Class History of the Americas* 10 (Winter 2013): 105–10.

54. Upton Sinclair, *I, Candidate for Governor: And How I Got Licked* (1934; Berkeley: University of California Press, 1994), 109.

55. Harris, *Bloodless Victories*, 2.

56. On the South, see C. Vann Woodward, *The Origins of the New South, 1877–1913* (Baton Rouge: University of Louisiana Press, 1951); Paul M. Gaston, *The New South Creed: A Study in Southern Mythmaking* (New York: Knopf, 1970); Don H. Doyle, *New Men, New Cities, New South: Atlanta, Nashville, Charleston, Mobile, 1860–1910* (Chapel Hill: University of North Carolina Press, 1990); and John F. Kvach, *De Bow's Review: The Antebellum Vision of a New South* (Lexington: University Press of Kentucky, 2013). For a sampling of this trend in the West, note Carl Abbott, *Boosters and Businessmen: Popular Economic Thought and Urban Growth in the Antebellum Middle West* (Westport, Conn.: Greenwood Press, 1981); William Cronon, *Nature's Metropolis: Chicago and the Great West* (New York: Norton, 1991), 31–46; Jocelyn Wills, *Boosters, Hustlers, and Speculators: Entrepreneurial Culture and the Rise of Minneapolis and St. Paul, 1849–1883* (St. Paul: Minnesota Historical Society Press, 2005); and Eric J. Morser, *Hinterland Dreams: The Political Economy of a Midwestern City* (Philadelphia: University of Pennsylvania Press, 2011), 77–105.

57. Quoted in Jon C. Teaford, *Cities of the Heartland: The Rise and Fall of the Industrial Midwest* (Bloomington: Indiana University Press, 1993), 116.

58. "Mayor Issues Proclamation," *Cleveland Plain Dealer*, May 17, 1908, 1. For a fine analysis of the strike, see Arthur Edward DeMatteo, "The Downfall of a Progressive: Mayor Tom L. Johnson and the Cleveland Streetcar Strike of 1908," *Ohio History* 104 (Winter–Spring 1995): 24–41; DeMatteo, "Urban Reform, Politics, and the Working Class: Detroit, Toledo, and Cleveland, 1890–1922" (Ph.D. dissertation, University of Akron, 1999), 198–205; and Robert Bionaz, "Streetcar Politics and Reform Government in Cleveland, 1880–1909," *Ohio History* 119 (2012): 27–28.

Chapter 1. Fighting "Union Dictation": Birth of the Open-Shop Movement

Epigraph: William H. Pfahler, "Free Shops for Free Men," *Publications of the American Economic Association* 4 (February 1903): 186.

1. Rosanne Currarino, *The Labor Question in America: Economic Democracy in the Gilded Age* (Urbana: University of Illinois Press, 2011).

2. "Event of the Year," *Foundry* 10 (April 1897): 80.

3. "The Foundry Movement Gaining," *The Iron Trade Review* 31 (June 16, 1898): 6.

4. "Event of the Year," 79–80.

5. On the SFNDA, see Howell Harris, "Coping with Competition: Cooperation and Collusion in the US Stove Industry, c. 1870–1930," *Business History Review* 86 (December 2012): 671–75.

6. "American Foundrymen's Association," *Railway Age and Northwestern Railroader* 23 (April 16, 1897): 327.

7. P. D. Wanner, *Proceedings of the Philadelphia Foundrymen's Association* (January 1898): 86.

8. This was not the only model. Groups like the General Managers' Association, which earned a reputation for repression in the context of the 1894 Pullman strike, demonstrated

234 Notes to Pages 26–30

another way of approaching the labor question. On this group, see Donald L. McMurry, "Labor Policies of the General Managers'Association of Chicago, 1886–1896," *Journal of Economic History* 13 (Spring 1953): 160–78.

9. "American Foundrymen's Association," *Foundry* 10 (June 1897): 161.

10. "Secretary's Report," *The Iron Trade Review* 31 (June 16, 1898): 13.

11. "The Abram Cox Stove Company," *Manufacturer and Builder* 22 (July 1890): 157.

12. "The Blake Rock and Ore Crusher," *Brick and Clay Record* 22 (January 1905): 70. Yagle had faced labor difficulties at his workplace close to a decade before he helped establish the NFA. See "Molders Mean Business," *Pittsburg Dispatch*, October 19, 1889, 2; and "Yielding, But Doing So Slowly," *Pittsburg Dispatch*, October 26, 1889, 2.

13. Will Thomas Hale and Dixon Lanier Merritt, *A History of Tennessee and Tennesseans* (Chicago: Lewis, 1913), 2049–50. On Chattanooga's industry generally, see "Tennessee Iron," *Review of Reviews* 11 (March 1895): 339. Molders at this workplace engaged in an unsuccessful strike in 1888, which received the notice of Great Britain's Board of Trade. See "Labour Correspondent to Great Britain Board of Trade," *Report on Strikes and Lock-Outs in the United Kingdom* (London: n.p., 1889), 229.

14. On Yagle's involvement in the Board of Education, see "Local Items, Limited," *Pittsburg Dispatch*, February 8, 1889, 2. On his involvement in the local foundrymen group, see "Another Foundrymen's Association," *Foundry* 9 (September 1896): 21.

15. "The Tradesman's 18th Annual," *[Chattanooga] Daily Times*, January 5, 1897, 6.

16. Quoted in Evelyn Bodek Rosen, *The Philadelphia Fels, 1880–1920* (Cranbury, N.J.: Associated University Presses, 2000), 119.

17. Reprinted in "Female Drudgery," *Brotherhood of Locomotive Firemen and Enginemen's Magazine* 26 (1899): 519.

18. Ibid.

19. "Death of Ex-President Pfahler," *The Review* 5 (April 1908): 1.

20. "Ways of Gauging Success," *The Iron Trade Review* 14 (May 19, 1898): 6.

21. On the ways in which changes in the economy forced many to come to terms with the labor question, see Currarino, *The Labor Question in America*.

22. "Ways of Gauging Success," 6. For more on free labor ideology, see Eric Foner, *Free Soil, Free Labor, Free Men: The Ideology of the Republican Party Before the Civil War* (Oxford: Oxford University Press, 1970), 11–39; John Ashworth, *Slavery, Capitalism, and Politics in the Antebellum Republic*, vol. 2, *The Coming of the Civil War, 1850–1861* (Cambridge: Cambridge University Press, 2007), 267, 275–78; and Eric Foner, *The Fiery Trial: Abraham Lincoln and American Slavery* (New York: Norton, 2010), 112–17. For a useful analysis of the debates surrounding the different ways of defining success in the late nineteenth and early twentieth centuries, see Claire Goldstene, *The Struggle for America's Promise: Equal Opportunity at the Dawn of Corporate Capital* (Jackson: University of Mississippi Press, 2014).

23. For a useful analysis of Social Darwinism and the ways in which reformers reacted to it, see Richard Hofstadter, *Social Darwinism in American Thought* (1944; Boston: Beacon, 1992); and Arthur Mann, "British Social Thought and American Reformers of the Progressive Era," *Mississippi Valley Historical Review* 42 (March 1956): 672–92. Historians have disagreed about the extent to which Herbert Spencer's views influenced late nineteenth- and early twentieth-century businessmen. For a stimulating exchange, see the roundtable in a mid-1970s edition of *Annals of Science*. "Harold Issadore Sarlin, "Herbert Spencer and Scientism,"

457–80; Joseph Frazier Wall, "Social Darwinism and Constitutional Law with Special Reference to *Lochner v. New York*," 465–76; and David A. Hollinger, "Comments on Papers by Sharlin and Wall," 476–80, all *Annals of Science* 33 (1976).

24. The average number of molders employed by NFA members was 50. See Howell Harris, "The Rocky Road to Mass Production: Change and Continuity in the U.S. Foundry Industry, 1890–1940," *Enterprise and Society* 1 (June 2000): 401.

25. On elites' fears of the working-class masses and their attempts at suffrage restrictions, see Sven Beckert, *The Monied Metropolis: New York City and the Consolidation of the American Bourgeoisie, 1850–1896* (Cambridge: Cambridge University Press, 2001), 211; Sven Beckert, "Democracy and Its Discontents: Contesting Suffrage Rights in Gilded Age New York," *Past and Present* 174 (February 2002), 156; and Patrick G. Williams, "Suffrage Restriction in Post-Reconstruction Texas: Urban Politics and the Specter of the Commune," *Journal of Southern History* 68 (February 2002): 31–64. My assessment of the elites in the emerging open-shop movement is incompatible with Herbert Gutman's more general views of privileged Americans. He maintained that elites from the late antebellum years to the early twentieth century essentially perceived those below them as lawless and unruly: "the rhetoric of influential nineteenth and early twentieth-century elite observers remained consistent." See Gutman, *Work, Culture and Society in Industrializing America* (New York: Vintage, 1977), 71.

26. E. F. Du Brul, "An Open Letter," *Monthly Review of the National Civic Federation* 1 (June 1903): 13.

27. William H. Pfahler, "Co-Operation of Labor and Capital," in *The Making of America: Labor*, ed. Robert Marion La Follette (New York: Arno, 1969), 92.

28. "A Rift in the Clouds," *Locomotive Firemen's Magazine* 30 (1901): 973.

29. "An Important Movement," *Iron Molders Journal* 34 (January 1898): 24.

30. See National Founders' Association, *Synopsis of Proceedings of the National Founders Association*, Iroquois Hotel, Buffalo, N.Y., February 1, 1899, 5.

31. Margaret Loomis Stecker, "The National Founders' Association," *Quarterly Journal of Economics* 30 (February 1916): 373.

32. "Foundrymen's Defense Association" *The Iron Trade Review* 31 (February 3, 1898): 8; "Death of W. H. Pfahler," *The Iron Trade Review* 42 (April 2, 1908): 621.

33. Penton served as president of the International Brotherhood of Machinery Molders Union from 1886 to 1892. As editor of *Machinery Molders Journal*, he celebrated improvements in the foundry industry and stressed the importance of labor-management harmony. Note the favorable comments employers made to him. See George Imlay to John A. Penton and John E. Sweet to John A. Penton, both in *Machinery Molders' Journal* 3 (June 1890): 5, 6. Penton abandoned trade unionism in 1892 or 1893.

34. J. C. B., "Harmony Between Capital and Labor Promoted by Union of Manufacturers," *New York Times*, December 7, 1902, 26. I would like to thank Howell Harris for bringing this source to my attention.

35. "Retirement of Commissioner Penton," *The Iron Trade Review* 36 (November 19, 1903): 49.

36. "Important Meetings of Foundrymen," *Iron Molders' Journal* 33 (June 1897): 263.

37. National Founders' Association, *Synopsis of Proceedings*, 13.

38. "The Labor Situation," *The Iron Trade Review* 38 (January 12, 1905): 46; and "Metal Trades Association Notes," *The Iron Trade Review* 38 (January 26, 1905): 47.

39. For an analysis of "walking delegates," see "Effects of the Walking Delegate," *Bulletin of the National Metal Trades Association* 3 (October 1904): 465–66; and Timothy John Houlihan, "The New York City Building Trades, 1890–1910" (Ph.D, dissertation, SUNY Binghamton, 1993), 107–79.

40. "National Founders' Association," *The Iron Trade Review* 32 (February 9, 1899): 6. Gates's father, P. W. Gates, Sr., was, according to *Iron and Machinery World*, "the pioneer manufacturer of Chicago and the region west of the Alleghenies." The patriarch had run the Eagle Works Manufacturing Company, a major machine and foundry shop that employed roughly a thousand workers from 1861 to 1871. See "Personal," *Iron and Machinery World* 95 (March 19, 1904): 28.

41. On Frank see Corinne Azen Krause, *Isaac W. Frank: Industrial and Civic Leader, 1855–1930* (Pittsburgh: Pittsburgh Historical Society Press, 1984). According to his *New York Times* obituary, Frank claimed "philanthropy was his hobby." See "Isaac W. Frank Dies," *New York Times*, December 2, 1930, 25.

42. On the Pratt and Letchworth company, see John Theodore Horton, Edward T. Williams, and Harry S. Douglas, *History of Northwestern New York: Erie, Niagara, Wyoming, Genesee and Orleans Counties*, vol. 1 (New York: Lewis Historical Publishing, 1947), 356; "The Pratt and Letchworth Company," *Buffalo Illustrated Times*, March 3, 1907, 53; "The President of the National Founders' Association," *The Iron Trade Review* 33 (March 1, 1900): 10; and "The Pratt and Letchworth Co.," *The Iron Trade Review* 36 (April 2, 1903): 94–95.

43. "National Founders' Association," *The Iron Trade Review* 32 (February 9, 1899): 6.

44. "National Founders' Association," *The Iron Trade Review* 33 (February 8, 1900): 12.

45. National Founders' Association, *Synopsis of Proceedings*, 5.

46. "Secretary's Report," *Open-Shop* 4 (May 1905): 219. Ernest F. Du Brul offered a somewhat more detailed account in the NAM's newspaper. See Du Brul, "The National Metal Trades Association," *American Industries* 2 (April 1, 1903): 13.

47. See "Metal Firms Combine to End Labor Troubles," *Brooklyn Eagle*, September 21, 1902, 1.

48. Devens quoted in "Metal Trades' Defiance," *New York Times*, June 2, 1901, 10. On the Murray Hill Agreement, see Marguerite Greene, *The National Civic Federation and the American Labor Movement, 1900–1925* (Washington, D.C.: Catholic University of America Press, 1956), 21; Bruno Ramirez, *When Workers Fight: The Politics of Industrial Relations in the Progressive Era, 1898–1916* (Westport, Conn.: Greenwood, 1978), 106; and David Montgomery, *Workers' Control in America: Studies in the History of Work, Technology, and Labor Struggles* (Cambridge: Cambridge University Press, 1979), 48–82.

49. The Utica molders' strike was indeed violent. According to the press, it "has been marked by many murderous assaults on non-union molders." See "The Molders' Strike in Utica," *The Sun*, July 26, 1904, 2.

50. Quoted in "The National Founders' Association," *Iron Age* 80 (November 26, 1908): 1509. For a thorough analysis of the rise and fall of the New York Agreement, see Margaret Loomis Stecker, "The National Founders' Association," *Quarterly Journal of Economics* 30 (February 1916): 352–86; and Howell Harris, "Following the Pattern—the National Founders' Association and the New York Agreement" (unpublished paper in author's possession). Thanks to Howell Harris for providing me with a copy of this essay.

51. Clarence E. Bonnett, *Employers' Associations in the United States: A Study of Typical Associations* (New York: Macmillan, 1922), 128.

52. John Kirby, Jr., "The Disadvantages of Labor Unionism," *Square Deal* 6 (March 1910): 118.

53. "National Metal Trades Association Meeting," *The Iron Trade Review* 40 (March 22, 1906): 13. On the size of the NFA, see "Secretary's Report," *The Iron Trade Review* 36 (November 12, 1903): 42.

54. Reynolds began his career as an apprentice in Connecticut in the 1840s. In the 1850s, he served as a superintendent of the Aurora, Indiana-based Stedman and Company, which made engines, saw mills, and drainage pumps for plantations in Mississippi. "This business was seriously crippled by the Civil War cutting off the market," *The Iron Trade Review* noted in 1909. In 1867, following the Civil War, Reynolds returned East, where he began managing Providence, Rhode Island's Corliss Steam Engine Company. Four years later, Reynolds became head engineer of Milwaukee's Allis-Chalmers Company, which at the turn of the century employed roughly 2,500 men. He astonished fellow manufacturers with his long resume of patents, which numbered over forty. His innovations catapulted him to the presidency of the American Society of Mechanical Engineers in 1902. On his life and accomplishments, see "Death of Edwin Reynolds," *The Iron Trade Review* 43 (February 25, 1909): 404. Also, see "To Build Powerful Engine," *New York Times*, August 23, 1902, 2; "The Opportunity and the Man," *Minneapolis Journal*, May 20, 1901, 4; and Walter F. Peterson, *An Industrial Heritage: Allis-Chalmers Corporation* (Milwaukee: Milwaukee County Historical Society Press, 1978), 41–66.

55. John A. Laird, "Test of Two Ten-Million-Gallon Pumping Engines at the Baden Pumping Station, St. Louis Water Works, June 1899," *Transactions of the American Society of Mechanical Engineers* 21 (1900): 327.

56. Historian Stephen Meyer mentions Reynolds' role as NMTA leader and head of Allis-Chalmers. See Meyer, *"Stalin over Wisconsin": The Making and Unmaking of Militant Unionism* (New Brunswick, N.J.: Rutgers University Press, 1992), 18–19, 27–29.

57. On Sweet, see "Sweet's Measuring Machine," *The Iron Trade Review* 32 (March 23, 1899): 7; Monte A. Colvert, *The Mechanical Engineer in America, 1830–1910: Professional Cultures in Conflict* (Baltimore: Johns Hopkins University Press, 1967), 110–12; "The Fiftieth Anniversary of the American Society of Mechanical Engineers," *Science* 70 (November 29, 1929): 532–33; Paul Uselding, "Measuring Techniques and Manufacturing Practice," in *Yankee Enterprise: The Rise of the American System of Manufacturers*, ed. Otto Mayr and Robert C. Post (Washington D.C.: Smithsonian Institution Press, 1981), 119–20. For his own comments on engineering, see John E. Sweet, *Things That Are Usually Wrong* (New York: Hill, 1906). For a brief description of Sweet at Cornell, see Morris Bishop, *A History of Cornell* (Ithaca, N.Y.: Cornell University Press, 1962), 169. On the Straight Line Engine Company's award in Atlanta, see "Prizes Given at Atlanta," *New York Times*, November 22, 1895, 2. Reynolds and Sweet fit the definition provided by historian Kenneth Lipartito: they perceived themselves as promoting "science, efficiency, and reason." Lipartito, "The Utopian Corporation," in *Constructing Corporate America: History, Politics, Culture*, ed. Kenneth Lipartito and David B. Sicilia (Oxford: Oxford University Press, 2004), 95.

58. On Covell, see "New Officers of the N.M.T.A.," *The Iron Trade Review* 36 (April 16, 1903): 52. On his involvement in the Brooklyn Engineers Club, see *Brooklyn Engineers Club Proceedings for 1898, Constitution and By-laws with List of Members and Catalogue of Reference Works in the Library* (January 1899), 141. On Covell's participation in other Brooklyn-based

activities, see "Bygone College Days," *Brooklyn Eagle*, April 12, 1893, 8; "Yale Alumni Reunion," *Brooklyn Eagle*, January 16, 1894, 9; "The Hamilton Club," *Brooklyn Eagle*, April 15, 1896, 5; "Hamilton Bank Directors," *Brooklyn Eagle*, April 11, 1899, 16; "Yale Alumni at Dinner," *Brooklyn Eagle*, February 7, 1900, 13; "Midwood Club Committees," *Brooklyn Eagle*, November 18, 1901, 10; "Midwood Club Dinner," *Brooklyn Eagle*, February 7, 1902, 9; and "Vestryman at St. Paul's Church," *Brooklyn Eagle*, March 9, 1902, 7. Covell participated in the National Guard at a time when Guard officers were drawn exclusively from the middle and upper classes. See Nell Irvin Painter, *Standing at Armageddon: The United States, 1877–1919* (New York: Norton, 1987), 22.

59. William Lodge, "Nominating Committee's Report," *Bulletin of the National Metal Trades Association* 2 (July 1903), 597. Lodge established himself as a well-known lathe manufacturer. See "Improvement in Taber Lathes," *The Iron Trade Review* 31 (January 20, 1898): 15. Lodge outlined his managerial philosophy in print. See Lodge, *Rules of Management: With Practical Instructions on Machine Building* (New York: McGraw-Hill, 1913). For more on Lodge and his workplace innovations, see "William Lodge: An Appreciation," *Industrial Management* 53 (December 1917): 433–41; Thomas J. Misa, *A Nation of Steel: The Making of Modern America, 1865–1925* (Baltimore: Johns Hopkins University Press, 1995), 200–201; and Philip Scranton, *Endless Novelty: Specialty Production and American Industrialization, 1865–1925* (Princeton, N.J.: Princeton University Press, 1997), 35, 42, 137–39, 145, 159, 193, 209–13, 217, 300.

60. "Employers Must Organize," *Bulletin of the National Metal Trades Association* 2 (May 1903): 283. For more on the ways in which social bonds and friendship mattered in business, see Pamela Walker Laird, *Pull: Networking and Success since Benjamin Franklin* (Cambridge, Mass.: Harvard University Press, 2006); Richard White, *Railroaded: The Transcontinentals and the Making of Modern America* (New York: Norton, 2011), 93; and Francesca Carnevali, "Social Capital and Trade Associations in America, c. 1860–1914: A Microhistory Approach," *Economic History Review* 64 (August 2011): 905–28.

61. "Trades Unions and New Shop Methods," *The Iron Trade Review* 36 (July 2, 1903): 104.

62. Pfahler, "Free Shops for Free Men," 183.

63. E. F. Du Brul, "Shop Management Discussion," *Transactions of the American Society of Mechanical Engineers* 24 (1903): 1457–60. In the late nineteenth century, England's employers formed their own "free labour congresses" in an effort to combat unionism. See William Edward Hartpole Lecky, *Democracy and Liberty*, vol. 2 (New York: Longmans, Green, 1899), 453; John Saville, "Trade Unions and Free Labour: The Background to the Taff Vale Decision," in *Essays in Labour History*, ed. Asa Briggs and John Saville (London: Macmillan, 1960), 319; James Hinton, *Labour and Socialism: A History of the British Labour Movement, 1867–1974* (Amherst: University of Massachusetts Press, 1983), 51; and Arthur J. McIvor, "Employers' Organization and Strikebreaking in Britain, 1880–1914," *International Review of Social History* 29 (December 1984): 1–33.

64. "Trades Unions and New Shop Methods," 104. David Montgomery suggests Du Brul got more attention than Taylor. See Montgomery, *The Fall of the House of Labor: The Workplace, the State, and American Labor Activism* (Cambridge: Cambridge University Press, 1987), 253.

65. Hugh G. J. Aitken, *Taylorism at Watertown Arsenal: Scientific Management in Action, 1908–1915* (Cambridge, Mass.: Harvard University Press, 1960), 19.

66. "New Officers of the N.M.T.A.," *The Iron Trade Review* 36 (April 16, 1903): 52; and "His First Strike Settling Job," *Building Trades Employers' Association Bulletin* 3 (October 1902): 188.

67. Du Brul attended Johns Hopkins as a graduate student from 1894 to 1896, but left before earning his degree. I would like to thank Johns Hopkins University archivist Jim Stimpert for providing me with this information.

68. Du Brul remained director and vice president of Miller, Du Brul and Peters while working full time for the NMTA. See "Personal," *The Iron Trade Review* 35 (August 28, 1902): 42. For more on the company, see Patricia A. Cooper, *Once a Cigar Maker: Men, Women, and Work Culture in American Cigar Factories, 1900–1919* (Urbana: University of Illinois Press, 1987), 170–73.

69. Thomas J. Misa, *A Nation of Steel: The Making of Modern America, 1865–1925* (Baltimore: Johns Hopkins University Press, 1995), 200. Also see Victor S. Clark, *History of Manufacturers in the United States*, vol. 3 (New York: McGraw-Hill, 1929), 153–55.

70. According to Samuel Haber, "Cincinnatians rushed to form these associations." Samuel Haber, *The Quest for Authority and Honor in the American Professions, 1750–1900* (Chicago: University of Chicago Press, 1991), 158.

71. Historian Zane L. Miller makes brief mention of Du Brul's Catholicism. See Miller, *Boss Cox's Cincinnati: Urban Politics in the Progressive Era* (Chicago: University of Chicago Press, 1968), 139. For a fine analysis of late antebellum elites' suspicion of Catholicism, see Bruce Levine, "Conservatism, Nativism, and Slavery: Thomas R. Whitney and the Origins of the Know-Nothing Party," *Journal of American History* 88 (September 2001): 467–68. Indeed, organized nativism, which found expression in political formations like the Know-Nothing Party, attracted, in the words of one scholar, "a disproportionately high number of merchants and manufacturers (primarily the former)." See Tyler Anbinder, *Nativism and Slavery: The Northern Know Nothings and the Politics of the 1850s* (Oxford: Oxford University Press, 1992), 36. On late antebellum elite anti-Semitism, see David A. Gerber, "Cutting Out Shylock: Elite Anti-Semitism and the Quest for Moral Order in the Mid-Nineteenth Century American Market Place," *Journal of American History* 69 (December 1982): 615–37. Frank was hardly the only Jew to participate in the movement. Clifford M. Kuhn highlights the struggles of Oscar Elsas, president of Atlanta's Fulton Bag and Cotton Mills and NAM leader. See Kuhn, *Contesting the New South Order: The 1914–1915 Strike at Atlanta's Fulton Mills* (Chapel Hill: University of North Carolina Press, 2001). For more on the somewhat ethnic and religious diversity of elites, see Sven Beckert and Julia B. Rosenbaum, eds., *The American Bourgeoisie: Distinction and Identity in the Nineteenth Century* (New York: Palgrave Macmillan, 2010).

72. "National Metal Trades Association Officers," *The Iron Trade Review* 35 (May 1, 1902): 42.

73. Ernest F. Du Brul, "The National Metal Trades Association," *American Industries* 2 (April 1, 1903): 13.

74. "The Metal Trades Convention," *Iron Age* 73 (March 24, 1904): 39.

75. "Report of the Seventeenth District," *Bulletin of the National Metal Trades Association* 2 (July 1903): 520. Historians have noted the ways business and political leaders downplayed damages immediately following urban disasters, including the Chicago fire of 1871, the Galveston, Texas, hurricane of 1900, the great Baltimore fire of 1904, and most important, the San Francisco earthquake of 1906. On post-disaster civic boosters, see Christine Meisner

Rosen, *The Limits of Power: Great Fires and the Process of City Growth in America* (Cambridge: Cambridge University Press, 1986), 317; and Philip L. Fradkin, *The Great Earthquake and Firestorms of 1906: How San Francisco Nearly Destroyed Itself* (Berkeley: University of California Press, 2005), 13, 18–19, 200. Open-shop proponents also conducted damage control. See Upton Sinclair, *The Industrial Republic: A Study of the America of Ten Years Hence* (New York: Doubleday, Page, 1907), 114–15.

76. "National Metal Trades Association," *Iron Age* 73 (April 14, 1904): 27. The success of Bates over the IAM during this conflict may have also been due partly to the injunction a Joliet judge granted. See "Sues Union for $200,000," *New York Times*, March 20, 1904, 3.

77. On the 1901 strike at Bates, see "Courts Tie-Up Machinists," *Brooklyn Eagle*, July 7, 1901, 8; and "Nine-Hour Strike May Soon End," *New York Times*, July 7, 1901, 3.

78. "Joliet," *Bulletin of the National Metal Trades Association* 3 (December 1904): 559.

79. "Address by Mr. J. W. Glover," *Open Shop* 5 (June 1906): 258–59.

80. Hunter played an important role in breaking the six-month-long waterfront strike involving International Association of Machinists and Iron Shipbuilders Union members in New York and New Jersey in 1903. The strikers eventually returned to work without winning wage increases. See "Refuse Machinists' Demands," *New York Times*, June 9, 1903, 3; "Indicted Strikers Arrested," *Newark Evening News*, June 16, 1903, 3; "Strikers Appeal," *Elizabeth Daily Journal*, July 20, 1903, 1; "Still No Settlement," *Elizabeth Daily Journal*, July 28, 1903, 1; "Tie-Up May Be Avoided," *Elizabeth Daily Journal*, August 19, 1903, 1; "Big Strike Is Likely," *Elizabeth Daily Journal*, August 20, 1903, 1; "No Shipyard Concession," *New York Times*, August 22, 1903, 5; "Employers Stand Firm," *New York Times*, August 29, 1903, 5; "Metal Trades' Statement," *New York Times*, August 30, 1903, 12; and "Shipyards' Strike Ended," *New York Times*, November 4, 1903, 16.

81. "Address by Mr. J. W. Glover," *Open Shop* 5 (June 1906): 258–59.

82. Du Brul stepped down as NMTA commissioner in 1904, though he remained active in the association. On Du Brul's resignation, see "President's Report," *Open Shop* 4 (May 1905): 209. In Cincinnati, Du Brul helped create an industrial education system for boys. Many graduates secured jobs in the city's factories. On industrial education in Cincinnati, see "Supplemental Report on Industrial Education," *American Industries* 7 (June 1, 1908): 37–38; and Jeffery Haydu, "Business Citizenship at Work: Cultural Transposition and Class Formation in Cincinnati, 1870–1910," *American Journal of Sociology* 107 (May 2002): 1456.

83. "Splendid Showing," *The Iron Trade Review* 42 (March 26, 1908): 576.

84. Robert Wuest, "The Metal Trades Strike Situation," *Iron Age* 80 (July 11, 1907): 125. Du Brul recruited Wuest in 1902. By 1910, Wuest had gained a reputation as one of the nation's most successful strikebreaking coordinators. According to a 1910 report, Wuest "handled more strikes than any other single man in the United States. He has had charge for the employers of no less than 368 strikes and is credited with winning 366 of them." See "Robert Wuest," *Salt Lake Tribune*, May 22, 1910, 3. For more on Wuest, see "New Officers of the N.M.T.A.," *The Iron Trade Review* 36 (April 16, 1903): 52. Across industries, employers won 53.7 percent of strikes between 1906 and 1908. See P. K. Edwards, *Strikes in the United States, 1881–1974* (Oxford: Blackwell, 1981), 42.

85. Walter D. Sayle, "President's Annual Report," *Open-Shop* 6 (May 1907): 212.

86. Clarence E. Bonnett, *Employers' Associations in the United States* (New York: Macmillan, 1922), 108. On the use of the word "art," see Craig Heron and Bryan D. Palmer,

"Through the Prism of the Strike: Industrial Conflict in Southern Ontario, 1901–14," *Canadian Historical Review* 13 (December 1977): 447.

87. For more on these organizations, see Sidney Fine, *"Without Blare of Trumpets": Walter Drew, the National Erectors Association and the Open-Shop Movement, 1903–1957* (Ann Arbor: University of Michigan Press, 1995); and Daniel R. Ernst, *Lawyers Against Labor: From Individual Rights to Corporate Liberalism* (Urbana: University of Illinois Press, 1995). Some employer-led organizations, including the United Typothatae of America, the master printers' association that emerged in 1887, did not demand members run open shops until after World War II. Yet many members vehemently supported the open-shop principle. See "Employers Favor the Open Shop," *Los Angeles Herald*, June 24, 1904, 5. For more on this organization, see Howard R. Stanger, "From a 'Negotiatory' to a 'Belligerent' Employers' Association: Organized Master Printers of Columbus, Ohio, 1887–1987," *Advances in Industrial and Labor Relations* 17 (2010): 69–125. Other employers unaffiliated with union-fighting organizations, especially in the extractive industries, also supported the open-shop principle. See Jerry Calvert, "The Rise and Fall of Socialism in a Company Town, 1902–1905," *Montana: The Magazine of Western History* 36 (Autumn, 1986): 2–13; and Greg Gordon, *When Money Grew on Trees: A. B. Hammond and the Age of the Timber Baron* (Norman: University of Oklahoma Press, 2014), 295–334.

88. "Address of Daniel Davenport," *Proceedings of the Second Annual Convention of the Citizens' Industrial Association of America, November 29 and 30, 1904* (Indianapolis: CIA Publication Department, 1904), 88. On Davenport's support for women's suffrage, see "Connecticut Topics," *New York Tribune*, January 12, 1902, 9.

89. "Employers' Union Launched," *Building Trades Association Bulletin* 4 (June 1903): 89.

90. Ibid., 88. Yet members of this organization continued to negotiate with union craftsmen, principally because of shortages of comparably skilled nonunionists. At the same time, they repeatedly clashed with unions and frequently declared support for the open-shop movement. See "Big Iron Trade War On: Open Shop the Issue," *New York Tribune*, November 26, 1905, 4.

91. The movement was hardly restricted to the U.S. A number of Canadian employers formed union-breaking organizations as well at this time. See Desmond Morton, *Working People: An Illustrated History of the Canadian Labor Movement* (1980; Montreal: McGill-Queens University Press, 2007), 83; and Andrew Yarmie, "The State and Employers' Associations in British Columbia: 1900–1932," *Labour/Le Travail* 45 (Spring 2000): 53–101.

92. Quoted in Isaac F. Marcosson, "Labor Met by Its Own Methods," *World's Work* 7 (January 1904): 4310. Decades earlier, in the mid-1880s, Marshall Field himself joined with other prominent Chicagoans in a fundraising campaign designed to strengthen the city's police department, which was involved in numerous scuffles with anarchists and socialists. See Painter, *Standing at Armageddon*, 48. For a thorough analysis of the origins of Chicago's police department and the ways it served the elite's interests, see Sam Mitrani, *The Rise of the Chicago Police Department: Class and Conflict, 1850–1894* (Urbana: University of Illinois Press, 2013).

93. Marcosson, "Labor Met By Its Own Methods," 4310–11, 4313. Labor activists were hardly passive victims of the city's employers' association. They continued to fight aggressively. See "Labor Notes," *Iron Age* 71 (April 7, 1904): 31. For more on Chicago, see Andrew

Wender Cohen, *The Racketeer's Progress: Chicago and the Struggle for the Modern American Economy, 1900–1940* (Cambridge: Cambridge University Press, 2004).

94. On the NAM's formative period, see Sarah Lyons Watts, *Order Against Chaos: Business Culture and Labor Ideology in America, 1880–1915* (Westport, Conn.: Greenwood, 1991), 144; and Cathie Jo Martin and Duane Swank, *The Political Construction of Business Interests* (Cambridge: Cambridge University Press, 2012), 89–108.

95. John Bartlow Martin, *Indiana, an Interpretation* (1947; New York: Knopf, 1972), 123; and "Big Increase in Stock," *Indianapolis Journal*, February 21, 1901, 8.

96. Quoted in "Assailed by Parry," *Indianapolis Journal*, November 26, 1902, 1. For more on the political conflicts between the AFL and the NAM, see Julie Greene, *Pure and Simple Politics: The American Federation of Labor and Political Activism, 1881–1917* (Cambridge: Cambridge University Press, 1998), 93–97.

97. Quoted in "D. M. Parry and Union," *Indianapolis Journal*, August 15, 1901, 10; and "Conference with Parry Men," *Indianapolis Journal*, August 30, 1901, 3.

98. Quoted in "D. M. Parry and Union," 10. Parry provides a colorful glimpse of what such a disquieting scenario might resemble in his *The Scarlet Empire*, an anti-socialist and dystopian novel that explores the soul-crushing fictionalized society of Atlantis. Parry, *The Scarlet Empire* (New York: Grosset and Dunlap, 1906).

99. On the NAM's evolution, see Albion Guilford Taylor, *Labor Policies of the National Association of Manufacturers* (Urbana: University of Illinois Press, 1928), 12–13; and Richard W. Gable, "Birth of an Employers' Association," *Business History Review* 33 (Winter 1959): 535–45.

100. "President Parry's New Orleans Address," *The Iron Trade Review* 36 (April 16, 1903): 56.

101. Max S. Hayes, "The World of Labor," *International Socialist Review* 4 (July 1903): 51.

102. Gable, "Birth of an Employers' Association," 545.

103. Quoted in Mary Wood Simons, "Employers' Associations," *The International Socialist Review* 5 (October 1904): 201. For more on Parry, see Linda B. Weintraut, "The Limits of 'Enlightened Self-Interest': Business Power in Indianapolis, 1900–1977" (Ph.D. dissertation, Indiana University, 2001), 93. For more on Kirby, see Carl M. Becker, "Mill, Shop, and Factory: The Industrial Life of Dayton, Ohio, 1830–1900" (Ph.D. dissertation, University of Cincinnati, 1971), 328.

104. Barry Schwartz, *Abraham Lincoln and the Forge of National Memory* (Chicago: University of Chicago Press, 2000), 128; also see Jason R. Juriden, *Claiming Lincoln: Progressivism, Equality and the Battle for Lincoln's Legacy in Presidential Rhetoric* (DeKalb: Northern Illinois University Press, 2011), 33–63; and Jean M. Yarbrough, *Theodore Roosevelt and the American Political Tradition* (Lawrence: University Press of Kansas, 2012), 198.

105. "Event of the Year," *Foundry* 10 (April 1897): 80.

106. C. W. Post, "Employer and Employees Union," *Bulletin of the National Metal Trades Association* 2 (July 1903): 390. For more on Post, see Peyton Paxson, "Charles William Post: The Mass Marketing of Health and Welfare" (Ph.D. dissertation, Boston University, 1993).

107. Ernest F. Du Brul, "Approval of National Association of Manufacturers," *Bulletin of the National Metal Trades Association* 2 (July 1903): 593.

108. David M. Parry, "President's Address," *Proceedings of the Second Annual Convention of the Citizens' Industrial Association of America, November 29 and 30, 1904* (Indianapolis: CIA Publication Department, 1904): 12.

109. "Change in the Relations of Employers and Employes in 1904," *The Iron Trade Review* 38 (January 19, 1905): 49.

110. Historians have had much to say about this organization. Half a century ago, new left scholars explored the ways in which the group ostensibly consisted of supposedly pro-union corporate heads. Such historians have insisted that these figures had succeeded in co-opting labor leaders in an effort to reduce workplace conflicts. More recently, scholars like Christopher Cyphers, rejecting this rather old interpretation, have argued that the NCF promoted a spirit of genuine liberalism. For assessments of the NCF, see Robert H. Wiebe, *Businessmen and Reform: A Study of the Progressive Movement* (1962; Chicago: Quadrangle, 1968), 20; James Weinstein, *The Corporate Ideal of the Liberal State, 1900–1918* (Boston: Beacon, 1968); and Martin J. Sklar, *The Corporate Reconstruction of American Capitalism, 1890–1916: The Market, the Law, and Politics* (Cambridge: Cambridge University Press, 1988), 16. For the anti-new left view, see Christopher J. Cyphers, *The National Civic Federation and the Making of a New Liberalism, 1900–1915* (Westport, Conn.: Praeger, 2002).

111. For overlapping membership, see Larry J. Griffin, Michael E. Wallace, and Beth A. Rubin, "Capitalist Resistance to the Organization of Labor before the New Deal: Why? How? Success," *American Sociological Review* 51 (April 1986): 156.

112. "To Have Charge of Strikes," *New York Times*, August 24, 1902, 3. Also, see E. F. Du Brul to Ralph Easley, January 2, 1903, Folder 2, Box 5, National Civic Federation Papers, New York Public Library. I would like to thank Vilja Hulden for providing me with a copy of this document.

113. I am not suggesting that there were no tensions between the NCF and others. For instance, the NMTA discussed the NCF at its 1903 conference, posing the question: "National Civic Federation: Is it an honest effort to reconcile capital and labor, or is it a trick to ensnare capital and pull the wool over the eyes of the public?" See "The National Metal Trades Association," *Iron Age* 71 (March 26, 1903): 45. We must, however, recognize that the similar ities between NCF employers and those in groups like the NFA, the NMTA, and the NAM outweighed the differences. Employers in all of these organizations opposed anarchism, socialism, expressions of working-class militancy like strikes, and closed shops.

114. William English Walling, "Can Unions Be Destroyed," *World's Work* 8 (May 1904): 4758.

115. "Civic Federation Dinner," *Building Trades Employers' Association Bulletin* 5 (January 1904): 2–3.

Chapter 2. "For the Protection of the Common People": Citizens, Progressives, and Free Workers

Epigraph: "Address of J. C. Craig," *Proceedings of the Second Annual Convention of the Citizens' Industrial Association of America, November 29 and 30, 1904* (Indianapolis: CIA Publication Department, 1904), 77

1. Clarence Darrow, "Strike, Arbitration," in *Attorney for the Damned: Clarence Darrow in the Courtroom*, ed. Arthur Weinberg (Chicago: University of Chicago Press, 1989), 358.

2. Quoted in Perry K. Blatz, *Democratic Miners: Work and Labor Relations in the Anthracite Coal Industry, 1875–1925* (Albany: State University of New York Press, 1994), 120. On Social Darwinism, see Richard Hofstadter, *Social Darwinism in American Thought* (1944; Boston: Beacon Press, 1992). Historians have insisted Social Darwinism was in decline by the 1890s. For a statement on its fading influence, see Louis Menand, *The Metaphysical Club: A*

Story of Ideas in America (New York: Farrar, Straus, and Giroux, 2001), 301–5. Not all writers have identified tensions between Social Darwinism and liberalism. See Domenico Losurdo, *Liberalism: A Counter-History* (London: Verso, 2011), 213–17. On earlier strikes in Pennsylvania, see Andrew B. Arnold, *Fueling the Gilded Age: Railroads, Miners, and Disorder in Pennsylvania Coal Country* (New York: New York University Press, 2014).

3. Quoted in Walter Gordon Merritt, *Destination Unknown: Fifty Years of Labor Relations* (New York: Prentice-Hall, 1951), 186. The letter, written to a clergyman, was leaked to the press, which published it. The result was a serious public relations problem for Baer. Edmund Morris, *The Rise of Theodore Roosevelt* (New York: Random House, 2010), 137.

4. "The Coal Strike," *(Kansas City) Independent*, July 19, 1902, 1.

5. "Roosevelt's Submission," *Independent*, October 18, 1902, 1.

6. Ray Stannard Baker, "The Right to Work: The Story of the Non-Striking Miners," *McClure's Magazine* 20 (January 1903): 323–36. The owner of *McClure's*, S. S. McClure, enjoyed a close relationship with James Emery, NAM attorney. For more on this relationship, see Vilja Hulden, "Employers, Unite! Organized Employer Reactions to the Labor Union Challenge in the Progressive Era" (Ph.D. dissertation, University of Arizona, 2011), 290. Employers and legal authorities had used the phrase "right to work" on a number of occasions throughout the second part of the nineteenth century. See "The Labor Question," *New York Times*, April 29, 1866, 4; "The Master Masons and the Bricklayers, *New York Times*, August 18, 1868, 5; "Another Lesson of the Strikes," *New York Times*, June 25, 1872, 4; Henry George, *The Condition of Labor: An Open Letter to Pope Leo XIII* (New York: Charles L. Webster, 1893), 90; and "The Right to Work," *The Public: A Journal of Democracy* 3 (1900): 244–45.

7. Baker, "The Right to Work," 336.

8. Ibid., 334.

9. The governor did in fact dispatch National Guardsmen to the strike areas in early October. Roosevelt believed the move was ineffective, failing "to bring about more than a trifling increase in the number of miners who returned to work." Quoted in Robert J. Cornell, *The Anthracite Coal Strike of 1902* (Washington, D.C.: Catholic University of America Press, 1957), 194.

10. For an analysis of Baer, see Blatz, *Democratic Miners*, 118–20.

11. Ibid., 121.

12. For more on Mitchell, see Craig Phelan, *Divided Loyalties: The Public and Private Life of Labor Leader John Mitchell* (Albany: State University of New York Press, 1994).

13. The precise role Brandeis played is unclear, but he did join the city's "influential and wealthy citizens" who, in the words of historian Bill L. Weaver, "expressed fear of a revolution triggered by 'communist orators'." See Weaver, "Louisville's Labor Disturbance, July 1877," *Filson Club Historical Quarterly* 48 (1974): 178. In late July that year, roughly 700 mostly financially privileged militia men reinforced the work of 175 policemen. The protestors, a multiracial mobilization of railroad workers and laborers from the city's factories, destroyed much property, including every window in the home of Dr. E. D. Standiford, the Louisville and Nashville Railroad president. Brandeis joined the businessmen-led militia after rioters smashed the front window of his family's home. Alfred Lief, *Brandeis: The Personal History of an American Ideal* (Harrisburg, Pa.: Telegraph Press, 1936), 15; Alpheus Thomas Mason, *Brandeis: A Free Life* (New York: Viking, 1946), 47–48; and Philip S. Foner, *The Great Labor Uprising of 1877* (New York: Monad, 1977), 127. Louisville's most privileged citizens were

hardly the only group to form such organizations. According to Theresa A. Case, "six hundred 'citizen militia' quickly defeated the largely unarmed strikers." See Case, *The Great Southwest Railroad Strike and Free Labor* (College Station: Texas A&M University Press, 2010), 34. For a good account of the strike in Louisville, see Steve J. Hoffman, "Looking North: A Mid-South Perspective on the Great Strike," in *The Great Strikes of 1877*, ed. David O. Stowell (Urbana: University of Illinois Press, 2008), 117–20. For more on elite militias, see Larry Isaac, "To Counter 'The Very Devil' and More: The Making of Independent Capitalist Militia in the Gilded Age," *American Journal of Sociology* 108 (September 2002): 353–405.

14. Quoted in Melvin I. Urofsky, *Louis D. Brandeis: A Life* (New York: Pantheon, 2009), 232.

15. Ibid.

16. Quoted in "A Warning to Unions," *The (Kansas City) Independent*, January 24, 1903, 1.

17. Quoted in "George Gray—Of Delaware—And His Democracy," *New York Times*, December 1, 1907, 5. It is doubtful that Gray was unaware of the violent acts, including two murders, committed by members of the coal and iron police, since numerous regional newspapers reported on these events. See Robert J. Cornell, *The Anthracite Coal Strike of 1902* (Washington, D.C.: Catholic University of America Press, 1957), 151–161.

18. Not all historians or contemporary observers believed the settlement was a good one for labor. According to historian Joe Gowaskle, many rank-and-file unionists, unlike Mitchell, saw the strike as a failure. See Gowaskle, "John Mitchell and the Anthracite Mine Workers: Leadership Conservatism and Rank-and-File Militancy," *Labor History* 27 (Winter 1985–6): 54–83. Also see Clarence E. Wunderlin, Jr., *Visions of a New Industrial Order: Social Science, and Labor Theory in America's Progressive Era* (New York: Columbia University Press, 1992), 73–94; and Andrew E. Kersten, *Clarence Darrow: American Iconoclast* (New York: Hill and Wang, 2009), 111–12.

19. Anthracite Coal Strike Commission, *Report to the President on the Anthracite Coal Strike of May–October, 1902* (Washington, D.C.: Government Printing Office, 1903), 64–65.

20. See Irving Greenberg, *Theodore Roosevelt and Labor, 1900–1918* (New York: Garland, 1988), 91–182; and James R. Holmes, *Theodore Roosevelt and World Order: Police Power in International Relations* (Washington, D.C.: Potomac, 2006), 45–51.

21. Quoted in William Millikan, *A Union Against Unions: The Minneapolis Citizens Alliance and Its Fight Against Organized Labor, 1903–1947* (St. Paul: Minnesota Historical Society Press, 2001), 13. This evenhanded language in 1903 closely resembled the comments of some earlier industrial relations thinkers. Take, for instance, the words of Abram Hewitt, an iron manufacturer, lawyer, and philanthropist who won election to mayor of New York City in 1886. In 1890, he said that "no one has the right to compel any other workman to cease from labor, nor has the employer any right to lock out his workmen in order to compel submission to obnoxious rules." Quoted in Howell Harris, "Between Convergence and Exceptionalism: Americans and the British Model of Labor Relations, c. 1867–1920," *Labor History* 48 (May 2007): 149. Harris reminds us that scholars have treated Hewitt as a liberal, yet, in Harris's words, "Hewitt's kind of liberalism was perfectly compatible with anti-unionism" (166).

22. James W. Van Cleave, "Collective Bargaining if Right; Industrial Peace if Right and Honorable," *American Industries* 5 (April 1, 1907): 5. For more on Van Cleave, see Daniel R.

Ernst, *Lawyers Against Labor: From Individual Rights to Corporate Liberalism* (Urbana: University of Illinois Press, 1995), 7, 125–30, 145; and Rosemary Feurer, *Radical Unionism in the Midwest, 1900–1950* (Urbana: University of Illinois Press, 2006), 8.

23. According to Howell Harris, "union recognition and collective bargaining remained firmly at the top" of organized labor's agenda. See Harris, "Industrial Democracy and Liberal Capitalism, 1890–1925," in *Industrial Democracy in America: The Ambiguous Promise,* ed. Nelson Lichtenstein and Howell Harris (Cambridge: Cambridge University Press, 1993), 55.

24. Writing to Gray after issuing the Miller decision, Roosevelt stated that "I take it for granted you approve my action in the Miller case in Washington. You may have noticed that I quoted a part of your admirable report in dealing with the matter. I am more and more convinced that that report will be the guide post for all our future actions as regards labor and capital." *Letter from Theodore Roosevelt to George Gray,* July 28, 1903, Theodore Roosevelt Papers, Manuscripts Division, Library of Congress, http://www.theodorerooseveltcenter.org/en/Research/Digital-Library/Record.aspx?libID=o185495, Theodore Roosevelt Digital Library, Dickinson State University. See also "Unions and Public Service," *New York Times,* September 29, 1903, 9; and Michael McGerr, *A Fierce Discontent: The Rise and Fall of the Progressive Movement in America, 1870–1920* (New York: Free Press, 2003), 126.

25. Theodore Roosevelt, *The Rough Riders: An Autobiography* (New York: Library of America, 2004), 737.

26. "Criticized the President," *New York Times,* November 13, 1903, 2.

27. Quoted in "Organize Against Boycott," *New York Times,* October 10, 1903, 6. An IAM member believed Du Brul regularly turned reality upside down: "Facts are ignored by Mr. Du Brul, but in their place he conjures up romance, calls it reality and makes it do duty for the facts he ignores. Evidently the Du Brulian imagination is independent of fact and loves to roam untrammeled in the regions of exaggeration," *Machinists' Monthly Journal* 15 (December 1903): 1028.

28. "No More Closed Shops in the N. C. R. Last Straws That Didn't Break Its Back," *American Industries* 3 (October 16, 1905): 1. On NCR's welfare capitalism, see Paul Monroe, "Possibilities of the Present Industrial System," *American Journal of Sociology* 3 (May 1898): 731, 749, 750; and Nikki Mandell, *The Corporation as Family: The Gendering of Corporate Welfare, 1890–1930* (Chapel Hill: University of North Carolina Press, 2002), 51, 54–55, 98, 117.

29. Henry White, "The Issue of the Open and Closed Shop," *North American Review* 180 (January 1905): 30. At a National Founders' Association conference in 1905, Rabbi J. Leonard Levy talked favorably about Roosevelt, which "was received with loud applause." See "Founders in Session," *New York Times,* November 16, 1905, 4. For a critical examination of Roosevelt's open-shop advocacy, see Max S. Hayes, "The World of Labor," *The International Socialist Review* 5 (July 1904): 115. After leaving office, Roosevelt continued to demonstrate loyalty to employers by criticizing workers who engaged in protests. Writing to essayist Walter E. Weyl a few months after the Colorado National Guard killed a number of individuals in Ludlow in April 1914, Roosevelt argued that too many workers, not just those in the mine fields, were unreasonable radicals and that "the bulk of the labor men sided with the McNamaras" following the 1910 *Los Angeles Times* building bombing. John and James McNamara, members of the International Association of Bridge and Structural Iron Workers union, were found guilty of bombing the building. Roosevelt was, his letter to Weyl indicates, apparently

more outraged by examples of working-class lawlessness than by state or business repression. See Theodore Roosevelt to Walter Weyl, August 6, 1914, Folder 5, Box 2, Weyl papers, Alexander Library, Rutgers University.

30. The NAM and its affiliate employers' associations claimed to have disseminated over 150 million pieces of literature between 1903 and 1906. See Sidney Fine, *"Without Blare of Trumpets": Walter Drew, the National Erectors' Association, and the Open-Shop Movement, 1903–57* (Ann Arbor: University of Michigan Press, 1995), 7; Sarah Lyons Watts, *Order Against Chaos: Business Culture and Labor Ideology in America, 1880–1915* (Westport, Conn.: Greenwood, 1991), 146; and Andrew Edward Neather, "Popular Republicanism, Americanism, and the Roots of Anti-Communism, 1890–1925" (Ph.D. dissertation, Duke University, 1994), 312–13.

31. Baker's essay was featured in the NAM's monthly journal in early 1903. Ray Stannard Baker, "The Right to Work," *American Industries* 2 (January 15, 1903): 9–12.

32. Quoted in Millikan, *Union Against Unions,* 32.

33. Many historians have written about the establishment of labor-liberal coalitions in the decades after the Civil War. See John D. Buenker, *Urban Liberalism and Progressive Reform* (New York: Scribner's, 1973), 80–117; Sarah Deutsch, "Learning to Talk More like a Man: Boston Women's Class-Bridging Organizations, 1870–1940," *American Historical Journal* 97 (April 1992): 379–404; Leon Fink, *Progressive Intellectuals and the Dilemmas of Democratic Commitment* (Cambridge, Mass.: Harvard University Press, 1997); Richard Schneirov, *Labor and Urban Politics: Class Conflict and the Origins of Modern Liberalism in Chicago, 1864–97* (Urbana: University of Illinois Press, 1998); Kevin Boyle, ed., *Organized Labor and American Politics: The Liberal-Labor Alliance* (Albany: State University of New York Press, 1998); Robert D. Johnston, *The Radical Middle Class: Populist Democracy and the Question of Capitalism in Progressive Era Portland, Oregon* (Princeton, N.J.: Princeton University Press, 2003); Georg Leidenberger, *Chicago's Progressive Alliance: Labor and the Bid for Public Streetcars* (DeKalb: Northern Illinois University Press, 2006); Doug Rossinow, *Visions of Progress: The Left-Liberal Tradition in America* (Philadelphia: University of Pennsylvania Press, 2008); John P. Enyeart, *The Quest for "Just and Pure Law": Rocky Mountain Workers and American Social Democracy, 1870–1924* (Stanford, Calif.: Stanford University Press, 2009); and David A. Zonderman, *Uneasy Allies: Working for Labor Reform in Nineteenth-Century Boston* (Amherst: University of Massachusetts Press, 2011).

34. According to Allison L. Hurst, "class language" employed by political parties, especially socialist organizations, increased during the century's first decade. See Hurst, "Language of Class in U.S. Party Platforms, 1880–1936," *Journal of Historical Sociology* 23 (December 2010): 544, 546.

35. On state-based labor reforms, see David Brian Robertson, *Capital, Labor, and the State: The Battle for American Labor Markets from the Civil War to the New Deal* (Lanham, Md.: Rowman and Littlefield, 2000), 37–64.

36. Groups like the Socialist Party grew considerably at roughly the same time that the open-shop movement experienced growth. See Nell Irvin Painter, *Standing at Armageddon: The United States, 1877–1919* (New York: Norton, 1987), 193.

37. Quoted in "To Fight 'Closed Shops'," *New York Times,* January 24, 1904, 9.

38. "Attitude of Machinery Manufacturers," *The Iron Trade Review* 31 (June 20, 1901): 18. For an elaboration of this view, see William H. Pfahler, "Free Shops for Free Men," *Publications of the American Economic Association* 4 (February 1903): 183.

39. Quoted in "Banded to Resist Unions," *Chicago Daily Tribune*, October 30, 1903, 3.

40. Frank M. Gilbert, *History of the City of Evansville and Vanderburg County* (Chicago: Pioneering Publishing, 1910), 414.

41. "Parry Is the President," *Chicago Daily Tribune*, October 31, 1903, 2; and "Parry Names Assistants," *American Manufacturer and Iron World* 73 (November 1903): 763.

42. "Address of F. C. Nunemacher," *Proceedings of the Second Annual Convention of the Citizens' Industrial Association of America, November 29 and 30, 1904* (Indianapolis: CIA Publication Department, 1904), 71.

43. See Louis G. Silverberg, "Citizens' Committees: Their Role in Industrial Conflict," *The Public Opinion Quarterly* 5 (March 1941): 17–37; Cornell, *The Anthracite Coal Strike of 1902*, 146–50; Melvyn Dubofsky, *We Shall Be All: A History of the Industrial Workers of the World* (New York: Quadrangle, 1969), 47–50; George G. Suggs, Jr., *Colorado's War on Militant Unionism: James H. Peabody and the Western Federation of Miners* (1972; Norman: University of Oklahoma Press, 1991), 68–72, 75, 77, 109, 146, 151–52, 184; Elizabeth Jameson, *All That Glitters: Class, Conflict, and Community in Cripple Creek* (Urbana: University of Illinois Press, 1998), 201–25; Richard Schneirov, *Labor and Urban Politics: Class Conflict and the Origins of Modern Liberalism in Chicago, 1864–97* (Urbana: University of Illinois Press, 1998), 58–63, 87, 142, 163–67, 204, 334; Sven Beckert, *The Monied Metropolis: New York City and the Consolidation of the American Bourgeoisie, 1850–1896* (Cambridge: Cambridge University Press, 2001), 318; Millikan, *Union Against Unions*; and John B. Jentz and Richard Schneirov, *Chicago in the Age of Capital: Class, Politics, and Democracy During the Civil War and Reconstruction* (Urbana: University of Illinois Press, 2012), 133, 179–86. Canadian employers also formed "Citizens' Committees." See Reinhold Kramer and Tom Mitchell, *When the State Trembled: How A. J. Andrews and the Citizens' Committee Broke the Winnipeg General Strike* (Toronto: University of Toronto Press, 2010).

44. Sven Beckert, "Democracy and Its Discontents: Contesting Suffrage Rights in Gilded Age New York," *Past and Present* 174 (February 2002): 156; Patrick G. Williams, "Suffrage Restriction in Post-Reconstruction Texas: Urban Politics and the Specter of the Commune," *Journal of Southern History* 68 (February 2002): 31–64; Painter, *Standing at Armageddon*, xxix; and Sam Mitrani, *The Rise of the Chicago Police Department: Class and Conflict, 1850–1894* (Urbana: University of Illinois Press, 2013), 118–19.

45. Rosemary Feurer, *Radical Unionism in the Midwest, 1900–1950* (Urbana: University of Illinois Press, 2006), 8. Of course, as Charles Postel notes, there was nothing incompatible between capitalism and populism. Postel, *The Populist Vision* (Oxford: Oxford University Press, 2007).

46. Baer's disregard for the working class masses was far from unique. As David Huyssen reminds us, late nineteenth century magnates like William Vanderbilt and J. P. Morgan made equally insensitive comments about workers. See David Huyssen, *Progressive Inequality: Rich and Poor in New York, 1890–1920* (Cambridge, Mass.: Harvard University Press, 2014), 246.

47. *Proceedings of the Preliminary Convention of the Citizens' Industrial Association of America* (Indianapolis: Levey Publishing, 1903). 14. On Callaway's account of Sanders, see Lew L. Callaway, *Montana's Righteous Hangmen: The Vigilantes in Action* (Norman: University of Oklahoma Press, 1982), 31.

48. For more on Sanders, see C. C. Goodwin, *As I Remember Them* (Salt Lake: Salt Lake Commercial Club, 1913), 326. According to Richard Maxwell Brown, the high-profile vigilante movement Sanders helped lead from 1863 to 1865 was responsible for popularizing "the

term 'vigilante' in American English." See Brown, "The History of Vigilantism in America," in *Vigilante Politics*, ed. H. Jon Rosenbaum and Peter C. Sederberg (Philadelphia: University of Pennsylvania Press, 1976), 85. For more on Sanders's vigilante activities, see Thomas J. Dimsdale, *The Vigilantes of Montana or Popular Justice in the Rocky Mountains* (1866; Norman: University of Oklahoma Press, 1988); and Frederick Allen, *A Decent, Orderly Lynching: The Montana Vigilantes* (Norman: University of Oklahoma Press, 2004), 126, 129, 153–55, 164, 168, 184, 198, 347. For a discussion of Sanders's criticisms of members of Montana's Democratic Party, see Michael P. Malone, *The Battle for Butte: Mining and Politics on the Northern Frontier, 1864–1906* (Seattle: University of Washington Press, 1981), 155.

49. Numerous strikes erupted in Montana. American Railway Union members, for example, temporarily shut down the Northern Pacific Railroad in 1894. See Dennis L. Swibold, *Copper Chorus: Mining, Politics, and the Montana Press, 1889–1959* (Helena: Montana Historical Society Press, 2006), 51.

50. Quoted in Stacy A. Flaherty, "Boycott in Butte: Organized Labor and the Chinese Community, 1896–1897," *Montana: The Magazine of Western History* 37 (Winter 1987): 47.

51. W. M. Muth and Sherwood Wheaton, *Address by the Citizens' Alliance Explaining the Purpose of the Organization* (Helena, Mont.: n.p., 1903), 3.

52. Sanders served as a defense lawyer for Spopee, also known as Turtle, who in 1879 shot a white man to death. For more on Spopee's case, see William E. Farr, *Blackfoot Redemption: A Blood Indian's Story of Murder, Confinement, and Imperfect Justice* (Norman: University of Oklahoma Press, 2012), 74–76. As Andrew R. Graybill says, "Though renowned for his combativeness and obstinacy, Sanders had a softer side." Graybill, *The Red and the White: A Family Sage of the American West* (New York: W. W. Norton and Company, 2013), 159. For a classic account of anti-Chinese racism, see Alexander Saxton, *The Indispensable Enemy: Labor and the Anti-Chinese Movement in California* (Berkeley: University of California Press, 1971). Also see Chang Kornel, "Circulating Race and Empire: Transnational Labor Activism and the Politics of Anti-Asian Agitation in the Anglo-American Pacific World, 1880–1910," *Journal of American History* 96 (December 2009): 678–701; Enyeart, *The Quest for "Just and Pure Law"*, 60–64; Richard White, *Railroaded: The Transcontinentals and the Making of Modern America* (New York: Norton, 2011), 293–305; and David R. Roediger and Elizabeth Esch, *The Production of Difference: Race and the Management of Labor in U.S. History* (Oxford: Oxford University Press, 2012), 70–86.

53. W. F. Sanders, "Bill of Complaint," *Papers Relating to the Foreign Relations of the United States with the Annual Message of the President* (Washington, D.C.: GPO, 1902), 107. Judge Hiram Knowles, who issued his decision in 1900, also awarded the victims $1,750.05 for legal expenses, but the boycotters did not have the money to pay. For more on the case, see Flaherty, "Boycott in Butte," 34–47.

54. Legal transcript page 247, Folder 3, Box 1, Hum Fay, et al. vs. Baldwin, et al. records, Montana Historical Society Archives, Helena, Mont.; W. F. Sanders, II, and Robert T. Taylor, *Biscuits and Badmen: The Sanders Story in Their Own Words* (Butte, Mont.: Editorial Review Press, 1983), 58. The Chinese, according to historian Liping Zhu, made up 90 percent of the construction jobs of the Central Pacific, Southern Pacific, Great Northern, and Northern Pacific Railroads. See Zhu, "Chinese Inclusion in the History of the American West," *Journal of the West* 45 (Winter 2006): 3. Sanders must have appreciated Montana's Chinese laborers, since thousands had conducted the backbreaking labor of laying tracks for the Northern

Pacific Railroad. In return, employers generally provided these wage earners with considerably less compensation than they offered white workers. Whatever the case, one thing is clear: the Chinese, widely stigmatized, denied membership in labor unions, and periodically attacked by white mobs, were unquestionably underdogs throughout the West. As a big business representative, Sanders was hardly unusual in his defense of Chinese laborers. Jeffrey Haydu notes that large businesses in San Francisco also exploited Chinese workers. See Haydu, *Citizen Employers: Business Communities and Labor in Cincinnati and San Francisco, 1870–1916* (Ithaca, N.Y.: Cornell University Press, 2008), 61–82.

55. Sanders, "Bill of Complaint," 108.

56. Leonard Ray Teel, *The Public Press, 1900–1945: The History of American Journalism* (Westport, Conn.: Praeger, 2006), 75. On Creel's opposition to child labor, see Edwin Markham, Benjamin B. Lindsay, and George Creel, *Children of Bondage: A Complete and Careful Presentation of the Anxious Problem of Child Labor—Its Causes, Its Crimes, and Its Cure* (New York: Hearst's International Library, 1914), 18.

57. This number comes from Marguerite Greene, *The National Civic Federation and the American Labor Movement, 1900–1925* (Washington, D.C.: Catholic University of America Press, 1956), 102.

58. Indeed, several prominent newspaper owners were open-shop partisans, and some played leadership roles in employers' associations. In North Carolina, Daniel Augustus Tompkins, a board of directors' member of the NAM, owned several newspapers, including the *Daily Charlotte Observer, Charlotte Evening Chronicle,* and *Greenville News.* Perhaps the highest-profile anti-union newspaper owner was the *Los Angeles Times*'s Harrison Gray Otis. For more on the relationship between the press and open-shop employers, see Vilja Hulden, "Employer Organizations' Influence on the Progressive-Era Press," *Journalism History* 38 (Spring 2012): 43–54. Otis's conflicts with unions began in 1890, when he refused to sign a contract with International Typographical Union Local 174. Twenty years later, union activists bombed the *Los Angeles Times* building. See John H. M. Laslett, *Sunshine Was Never Enough: Los Angeles Workers, 1880–2010* (Berkeley: University of California Press, 2012), 25–28, 39–46.

59. "New Leaders," *(Kansas City) Independent,* August 15, 1903, 1.

60. Hugh O'Neal, "Practical Socialism: The Story of the Victorious Struggle in Australia," *Open Shop* 4 (October 1905): 467.

61. For more on Creel during World War I, see Alan Axelrod, *Selling the Great War: The Making of American Propaganda* (New York: Palgrave Macmillan, 2009); and Susan A. Brewer, *Why America Fights: Patriotism and War Propaganda from the Philippines to Iraq* (Oxford: Oxford University Press, 2009), 55.

62. *Proceedings of the Preliminary Convention of the Citizens' Industrial Association of America* (Indianapolis: Levey Publishing, 1903), 12.

63. "Address of J. C. Craig," *Proceedings of the Second Annual Convention of the Citizens' Industrial Association of America, November 29 and 30, 1904* (Indianapolis: CIA Publication Department, 1904): 75. Craig certainly had reasons to worry about the image of employers, especially in Colorado. Here mine owners had recently led a spectacularly violent, months-long campaign against striking Western Federation of Miners' members, known as the 1903–4 "mine wars." During these conflicts, employers were backed by sheriff deputies, national guardsmen, and most important, governor and Citizens' Alliance member James Peabody.

Together, these forces unleashed a successful campaign of repression. Suggs, *Colorado's War on Militant Unionism*; and Jameson, *All That Glitters*, 201–25.

64. James W. Van Cleave quoting himself from his 1906 speech. See Van Cleave, "The Work of Employers' Associations in the Settlement of Labor Disputes," *American Academy of Political and Social Science* 36 (September 1910): 120.

65. Ibid., 124.

66. "The Chicago Convention," *Exponent* 4 (January 1907): 17.

67. "Resolutions Adopted," *Proceedings of the Preliminary Convention of the Citizens' Industrial Association of America* (Indianapolis: Levey Publishing, 1903): 15. CIAA members were hardly unique. Numerous employers publicly expressed support for unions despite fighting them. See, for example, Gary Kaunonen and Aaron Goings, *Community in Conflict: A Working-Class History of the 1913–14 Michigan Copper Strike and the Italian Hall Tragedy* (Lansing: Michigan State University Press, 2013), 40–41.

68. According to William J. H. Boetcker, a CIAA organizer and clergyman, the *Square Deal* was the third name of the CIAA's official publication. The first, *The Alliance*, was published in Shelbyville, Indiana, under Boetcker's editorial direction. According to Boetcker, it "carried the picture of an Employer and Employee shaking hands and the motto was: 'United we Stand, Divided we Fall.'" David M. Parry took over editorial duties of *The Alliance* after Boetcker's brief tenure and changed its name to *Industrial Independent*. Boetcker's 1946 recollections are imprecise on the timeline of these changes. See "Background of CIA (Citizens Industrial Alliance) and Kimball Hall," typescript undated, Series 11: Early Life, 1873–1919, Subseries 3: Toledo, Ohio, 1905–1913, Folder 15, Box 1, William J. H. Boetcker Manuscript Collection, Special Collections, Princeton Theological Seminary.

69. For example, see Walter J. Shanley, "A Catholic Priest on Labor Agitators," *Square Deal* 4 (July 1909): 49–50. *The Square Deal* was not the only publication that carried the views of open-shop religious figures. Also, see Rev. Albert Bushnell, "The Open-Shop; a Clergyman's View," *American Industries* 2 (December 15, 1903): 6; John A. Ryan, "The Morality of the Aims and Methods of the Labor Union," *American Catholic Quarterly Review* 29 (April 1904): 326–55; "Suggestive Themes and Texts," *Homiletic Review* 46 (December 1903): 443; Rabbi J. Leonard Levy, "The Rule of Right vs. the Rule of Might," *Review* 3 (January 1906): 13; "Cardinal Gibbons Denounces the Boycott," *American Industries* 6 (October 15, 1907): 5; and "Curbs on Labor Unions Proposed by Church," *American Industries* 13 (October 1912): 27.

70. Quoted in George Pope, "The New Unionism," *Square Deal* 15 (August 1914): 39. Organized employers were highly supportive of Laughlin's scholarly contributions. According to the chief NAM lawyer, he was "practical," unlike other economists who were "influenced by an amount of sentimental twaddle in theory that finds no concrete reality." See James Emery to James R. Day, February 21, 1907, RG/01, Box 5, James R. Day Papers, E. S. Bird Library, Syracuse University, Syracuse, New York. On the mentorship relationship between Laughlin and Roosevelt at Harvard, see Jean M. Yarbrough, *Theodore Roosevelt and the American Political Tradition* (Lawrence: University Press of Kansas, 2012), 31–33. For the best introduction to Laughlin's anti-union writings, see J. Laurence Laughlin, *Industrial America: Berlin Lectures of 1906* (New York: Scribner's, 1906). Numerous scholars have written about Laughlin's larger role in debates over the direction of the nation's political economy. See Wesley C. Mitchell, "J. Laurence Laughlin," *Journal of Political Economy* 49 (December 1941): 875–81; A. W. Coats, "The Origins of the 'Chicago School'," *Journal of Political Economy* 71

(October 1963): 487–93; Gabriel Kolko, *The Triumph of Conservatism: A Reinterpretation of American History, 1900–1916* (Chicago: Quadrangle, 1967), 148, 156, 188, 218–25, 227, 236–37, 242–47; Lawrence Goodwin, *A Short History of the Agrarian Revolt in America* (Oxford: Oxford University Press, 1978), 266–67; and James Livingston, *Origins of the Federal Reserve System: Money, Class, and Corporate Capitalism, 1890–1913* (Ithaca, N.Y.: Cornell University Press, 1986), 91, 106–107, 113, 121, 144, 146–148, 204, 209, 211. At least one historian, Ellen Fitzpatrick, has praised Laughlin for his involvement in mentoring female college students. Laughlin was, as Fitzpatrick puts it, "extremely sympathetic to women students." See Fitzpatrick, *Endless Crusade: Women Social Scientists and Progressive Reform* (Oxford: Oxford University Press, 1990), 49.

71. *Square Deal* 1 (August 1905). The *Square Deal* was not the first publication to feature a cartoon comparing unions to slavery. In 1886, *Harper's Weekly* employed cartoonist Thomas Nast who drew a similar connection between unions and slavery during the Southwest railroad strike. In Nast's picture, a former black slave stands beside a chained white Knights of Labor member. The caption reads: "Willful Slavery Makes Woeful Suffering. Colored Labor to White Labor: 'No sooner am I really set free than you enslave yourselves, and at the expense of your families, too.'" The cartoon is reproduced in the frontispiece in Theresa A. Case, *The Great Southwest Railroad Strike and Free Labor*. Nast was, as historian Fiona Deans Halloran puts it, "The Father of Modern Political Cartoons." See Halloran, *Thomas Nast: The Father of Modern Political Cartoons* (Chapel Hill: University of North Carolina Press, 2012).

72. "For Independent Labor," *New York Times*, January 1, 1903, 3.

73. "Organization of Employers," *Bulletin of the National Metal Trades Association* 2 (July 1903): 553.

74. Quoted in F. W. Hilbert, "Employers' Associations in the United States," in *Studies in American Trade Unionism*, ed., Jacob H. Hollander and George E. Barnett (New York: Henry Holt, 1912), 209; and "A Non-Union Union," *(Kansas City) Independent*, June 13, 1903, 8.

75. For Fairchild's scholarly contribution, see E. M. Fairchild, "The Function of the Church," *American Journal of Sociology* 11 (September 1896): 220–33.

76. E. M. Fairchild, "Independent Labor League of America," *Corporations Auxiliary Bulletin* 2 (April 1903): 81.

77. Payne was not the first to experiment with this method of management. R. H. Thurston credits F. A. Halsey, a high-level manager with the Canadian Rand Drill Company, for introducing the "Premium Plan of Paying Labor" at some point in the 1890s. See Thurston, "Economics in Manufactures," *Science* 9 (April 21, 1899): 583.

78. Fairchild, "Independent Labor League of America," 83.

79. Ibid., 84; and *Constitution and Bylaws of Grand Lodge of the Independent Labor League of America* (N.P: 1903), 3–4.

80. "Parry Scab Trust Launched," *Amalgamated Journal* 5 (December 31, 1903): 8.

81. "Refuses Machinists' Demands," *New York Times*, June 9, 1903, 3.

82. Quoted in Fairchild, 83.

83. Emmett Hildebrant, "Independent Labor League of America," *Bulletin of the National Metal Trades Association* 3 (January 1904): 30.

84. "Address of John Kirby, Jr.," *Proceedings of the Second Annual Convention of the Citizens' Industrial Association of America, November 29 and 30, 1904* (Indianapolis: CIA Publication Department, 1904), 141. The language of CIAA members resembled the words used

by Cincinnati's organized employers. As Jeffry Haydu has noted, "Cincinnati's business leaders defined themselves as representatives of the general community and rejected suggestions that they acted on behalf of any class interest." See Haydu, *Citizen Employers*, 108.

85. Edward H. Davis, "The Citizens' Industrial Association," in *Social Progress*, ed. Josiah Strong (New York: Baker and Taylor, 1905), 288.

86. David M. Parry, "President's Address," *Proceedings of the Second Annual Convention of the Citizens' Industrial Association of America* (Indianapolis: CIA Publication Department, 1904): 13.

87. See Wilson Vance, "Citizens' Industrial Association of America," in *The New Encyclopedia of Social Reform*, ed. William D. P. Bliss (New York: Funk and Wagnalls, 1909), 237–38. It is unlikely Bliss was unaware of Vance's CIAA involvement. Historian David Burns has called Bliss "the most prominent Christian Socialist of the 1890s." See David Burns, *The Life and Death of the Radical Historical Jesus* (Oxford: Oxford University Press, 2013), 63; and Zonderman, *Uneasy Allies*, 195–202.

88. Gustavus A. Weber, "Open Shop," in *New Encyclopedia of Social Reform*, ed. William D. P. Bliss (New York: Funk and Wagnalls, 1909), 853–54.

89. Quoted in James D. Startt, *Woodrow Wilson and the Press: Prelude to the Presidency* (New York: Palgrave Macmillan, 2004), 63.

90. Philip S. Foner, *History of the Labor Movement in the United States*, vol. 3, *The Policies and Practices of the American Federation of Labor, 1900–1909* (1964; New York: International, 1981), 50. Of course, the Ivory Tower has enjoyed a long history of housing scholars and administrators who have offered intellectual support to the powerful and the privileged. In the late nineteenth century, Yale University's William Graham Sumner famously wrote *What Social Classes Owe Each Other*. In Sumner's words, "We shall find that every effort to realize equality necessitates a sacrifice of liberty." See Sumner, *What Social Classes Owe Each Other* (1883; Auburn, Ala.: Ludwig van Mises Institute, 2007), 15. Richard Hofstadter has maintained that Sumner was "the most vigorous and influential social Darwinist in America." See Hofstadter, *Social Darwinism in American Thought* (1944; Boston: Beacon, 1992), 51.

91. According to Louis Menand, Eliot was "the most important figure in the history of American higher education." See Menand, *The Metaphysical Club*, 117.

92. On Eliot's involvement with the Harvard riflemen's club, see Robert M. Fogelson, *America's Armories: Architecture, Society, and Public Order* (Cambridge, Mass.: Harvard University Press, 1989), 27–28.

93. For a discussion of the different times Eliot called strikebreakers "heroes," see Charles J. Bonaparte, "President Eliot and the American University," *Boston Evening Transcript*, March 19, 1904, 2. Also, see the NAM publication: "President Eliot on Violence and Folly Among the Unions," *American Industries* 1 (November 15, 1902): 10. Eliot was not the first to call strikebreakers heroic. According to a trade union source, the first person to use the word "hero" to describe strikebreakers was a Florida publisher in 1886. See "The Non-Unionists—Individualist," *Amalgamated Journal* 4 (March 19, 1903): 8. For more on Eliot's anti-unionism, see Mark Koerner, "The Menace of Labor: Anti-Union Thought in the Progressive Era, 1901–1917" (Ph.D. dissertation, University of Wisconsin, Madison, 1995), 75–124.

94. Quoted in Hugh Hawkins, *Between Harvard and America: The Educational Leadership of Charles W. Eliot* (Oxford: Oxford University Press, 1972), 151. Eliot was hardly the first to

denounce organized labor as a trust. John W. Faxon, the Chattanooga-based vice president of the American Bankers' Association, made a similar statement in 1900. In his words, labor unions constituted "one of the greatest combinations in the world." Manufacturers, Faxon believed, needed protection from the "unworthy members of these [labor] societies." See Faxon, "Trusts and Labor," *Manufacturers' Record* 45 (March 29, 1900): 157–58.

95. Quoted in "Quiet Year for the National Founders' Association," *The Iron Trade Review* 43 (November 26, 1908): 883.

96. "Mr. Fairchild on Crowd Photography," *Harvard Crimson*, February 20, 1905.

97. John Dewey and James H. Tufts, *Ethics* (New York: Henry Holt, 1908), 560–61. Robert B. Westbrook maintains that this book is "an interesting document in progressive social thought." Here, Westbrook continues, "Dewey outlined the moral underpinnings of the positions he took a few years later as he launched his career as a public intellectual." See Westbrook, *John Dewey and American Democracy* (Ithaca, N.Y.: Cornell University Press, 1991), 152. Alan Ryan states that *Ethics* "was a staple of university courses for four decades after its publication." See Ryan, *John Dewey and the High Tide of American Liberalism* (New York: Norton, 1995), 79.

98. Dewey was far less important to the open-shop movement than Baker or Roosevelt. He is particularly known for his work in the area of public education and, more generally, in the words of biographer Westbrook, as someone tightly anchored "in the radical wing of progressivism." He was, according to scholarly opinion, a friend, rather than an opponent, of the labor movement, which he witnessed closely during the 1894 Pullman strike while living in Chicago. Nevertheless, his brief, though critical, attention to closed-shop unionism puts him, essentially, on the side of open-shop employers. Like other liberal thinkers, writers, progressive activists, and even employers' association leaders, Dewey did not denounce trade unions altogether, but was distressed about the extent to which they carried out their solidarity-building campaigns. For more on Dewey, see Westbrook, *John Dewey and American Democracy*, 189; and James T. Kloppenberg, "Pragmatism: An old Name for Some New Ways of Thinking," *Journal of American History* 83 (June 1996): 100–138.

99. Louis D. Brandeis, "An Economic Exhortation to Organized Labor," *Conductor and Brakeman* 22 (June 1905): 402.

100. As the late Sidney Fine pointed out, "the economists approved of labor legislation for children and, perhaps, women, since these groups could not take care of themselves; but they proclaimed their opposition to legislative aid for adult male laborers." Fine, *Laissez Faire and the General-Welfare State: A Study of Conflict in American Thought, 1865–1901* (Ann Arbor: University of Michigan Press, 1956), 60.

101. Philippa Strum, "The Legacy of Louis Dembitz Brandeis, People's Attorney," *American Jewish History* 81 (Spring/Summer 1994): 407. Brandeis made an early fortune representing a paper manufacturing company. See Thomas K. McCraw, *Prophets of Regulation: Charles Francis Adams, Louis D. Brandeis, James M. Landis, Alfred E. Kahn* (Cambridge, Mass.: Harvard University Press, 1984), 84–87. On his early management-side law career, see Urofsky, *Louis D. Brandeis*, 46–74.

102. "A Friendly Critic," *Official Journal of the Amalgamated Meat Cutters and Butcher Workmen of North America* 6 (April 1905): 1.

103. Louis D. Brandeis to J. Eugene Cochrane, July 8, 1906 in *Letters of Louis D. Brandeis*, vol. 1, *1870–1907*, ed. Melvin I. Urofsky and David W. Levy (Albany: State University of New

York Press, 1971), 450; also, see Brandeis to Lewis Flanders and Company et al., May 14, 1907 (572–73).

104. Quoted in Richard A. Greenwald, *The Triangle Fire, the Protocols of Peace, and Industrial Democracy* (Philadelphia: Temple University Press, 2005), 59. On class tensions in New York City's garment industry, see Daniel Soyer, "Cockroach Capitalists: Jewish Contractors at the Turn of the Twentieth Century," in *A Coat of Many Colors: Immigration, Globalism, and Reform in the New York City Garment Industry*, ed. Daniel Soyer (New York: Fordham University Press, 2005), 91–113.

105. Quoted in John Bruce McPherson, "The New York Cloakmakers' Strike," *Journal of Political Economy* 19 (March 1911): 175.

106. Brandeis to Lawrence Fraser Abbott, September 6, 1910 in *Letters of Louis D. Brandeis*, vol. 2, *1907–1912: People's Attorney*, ed. Melvin I. Urofsky and David W. Levy (Albany: State University of New York Press, 1972), 371–372. Also, see Louis D. Brandeis, "The Preferential Shop," *Human Engineering* 2 (April 1912): 179–81; "Conference in Cloak Strike; Union Waives Demand for a Closed Shop and Submits Grievances," *New York Times*, July 26, 1910, 4; and Hadassa Kosak, "Taylors and Troublemakers: Jewish Militancy in the New York Garment Industry, 1889–1910," in *A Coat of Many Colors*, ed. Soyer, 137–38. For more on the "Protocol of Peace" see Greenwald, *Triangle Fire*.

107. Milton Derber, *The American Idea of Industrial Democracy, 1865–1965* (Urbana: University of Illinois Press, 1970), 135. Chicago's garment manufacturers' also adopted the preferential shop. Youngsoo Bae, *Class and Community Among Men's Clothing Workers of Chicago, 1871–1929* (Albany: State University of New York Press, 2001). Labor activists in Chicago identified the shortcomings and possibilities of this system in 1910, noting that a "preferential shop is far from being a closed shop, but can be made almost as effective by clever manipulation and tactics." "Garment Workers May Settle on Preferential Plan," *The Labor World*, November 26, 1910, 1.

108. Quoted in Graham Adams, Jr., *Age of Industrial Violence, 1910–15: The Activities and Findings of the United State Commission on Industrial Relations* (New York: Columbia University Press, 1966), 117. Urofsky cites a somewhat different statement: "the scab shop with honey and a sugar-coated poison pill." See Urofsky, *Louis D. Brandeis*, 249.

109. "Brandeis for Co-Operation," *New York Times*, February 15, 1911, 3.

110. William English Walling, "Open-shop Means Destruction of the Unions," in *Selected Articles on the Open Versus Closed Shop*, ed. E. Clyde Robbins (Minneapolis: Wilson, 1912), 66; and "Union Labor Prevents Higher Efficiency," *Manufacturers' Record* 51 (June 28, 1906): 665. To its credit, the union succeeded in representing roughly 90 percent of the industry's cloakmakers by 1912. Greenwald, *The Triangle Fire*, 75. Importantly, the New York Clothiers' Association, which represented the city's large tailoring trade establishments, remained unwilling to accept the preferential shop. "Will There Be More Protocols," *The Survey* 29 (January 18, 1913): 492–93.

111. Julius Henry Cohen, *An American Labor Policy* (New York: Macmillan, 1919), 52.

112. Meanwhile, Woodrow Wilson nominated Brandeis to the Supreme Court. One of his vocal backers was fellow open-shop proponent Charles Eliot. See "Eliot Lauds Brandeis as 'Learned Jurist'," *New York Times*, May 23, 1916, 1. Brandeis also admired Fredrick Winslow Taylor's system of scientific management. See Christopher D. McKenna, *The World's Newest Profession: Management Consulting in the Twentieth Century* (Cambridge: Cambridge University Press, 2006), 35.

113. Quoted in Greenwald, *Triangle Fire*, 120. Also see Will Herberg, "Jewish Labor Movements in the United States: Early Years to World War I," *Industrial and Labor Relations Review* 5 (July 1952): 501–23.

114. E. J. Wile, Manufacturers' Protective Association president, quoted in "Policemen Stoned in Garment Strike," *New York Times*, June 11, 1916, 11.

115. Quoted in Philippa Strum, *Louis D. Brandeis: Justice for the People* (Cambridge, Mass.: Harvard University Press, 1984), 108.

Chapter 3. A Tale of Two Men: Class Traitors and Strikebreaking in Cleveland

1. On the strike, see "Lorain and the Molders Camp," *Iron Molders' Journal* 36 (September 1900): 507.

2. "The Cleveland Molders Strike," *Foundry* 9 (September 1900): 33.

3. As one critical source explained, members "meet in secret, exchange secret circulators, are in collusion with spying agencies, and in every manner are committed to the dark-lantern methods of the ku klux klan." See "Trend of Events," *Cleveland Citizen* August 7, 1909, 1.

4. For a general account of the city's late nineteenth-century economy, see Harold C. Livesay, "From Steeples to Smokestacks: The Birth of the Modern Corporation in Cleveland," in *The Birth of Modern Cleveland, 1865–1930*, ed. Thomas F. Campbell and Edward M. Miggins (Cleveland: Western Reserve Historical Society, 1988), 24–53; Darwin H. Stapleton, "The City Industrious: How Technology Transformed Cleveland," 54–70; Leslie Seldon Hough, "The Turbulent Spirit: Violence and Coaction Among Cleveland Workers, 1877–1899" (Ph.D. dissertation, University of Virginia, 1977), 19; and Philip Scranton, *Endless Novelty: Specialty Production and American Industrialization, 1865–1925* (Princeton, N.J.: Princeton University Press, 1997), 48, 95, 133, 140, 159, 198, 201, 211, 227, 309.

5. Alexander E. Brown erected the first hoisting plant in Cleveland in 1886. See "Cleveland Leads in Hoisting Machinery," *Cleveland Plain Dealer*, June 7, 1909, 6.

6. "Good Citizens Have Made Cleveland a Great City," *Cleveland Plain Dealer*, June 7, 1909, 2; and Helen M. Strong, "Cleveland: A City of Contacts," *Economic Geography* 1 (July 1925): 198–205.

7. Naphtali Hoffman, "The Process of Economic Development in Cleveland, 1825–1920" (Ph.D. dissertation, Case Western Reserve University, 1981), 180–81.

8. Robert Emery Bionaz, "Streetcar City: Popular Politics and the Shaping of Urban Progressivism in Cleveland, 1880–1910" (Ph.D. dissertation, University of Iowa, 2002), 134.

9. Hiram C. Haydn, "The Cleveland Strike," *Independent* 51 (August 31, 1899): 2336.

10. "Address of N. F. Thompson," *Proceedings of the Second Annual Convention of the Citizens' Industrial Association of America, November 29 and 30, 1904* (Indianapolis: CIA Publication Department, 1904): 150. According to Stephen H. Norwood, private strikebreaking agencies planted at least some of these explosives. See Norwood, *Strikebreaking and Intimidation: Mercenaries and Masculinity in Twentieth-Century America* (Chapel Hill: University of North Carolina Press, 2002), 62.

11. Haydn, "The Cleveland Strike," 2336.

12. See M. W. Beacom, "Proceedings of the Eleventh Annual Convention of the Boiler Manufacturers' Association held at Cleveland, O," *Proceedings of the American Boiler Manufacturers' Association* (July 1899): 17–18.

13. Robert Bionaz offers a fine description of this case. See Bionaz, "Streetcar Politics and Reform Government in Cleveland, 1880–1909," *Ohio History* 119 (2012): 14–15.

14. Bionaz, "Streetcar City," 159. On the demand for the civic center, see Paul Boyer, *Urban Masses and Moral Order in America, 1820–1920* (Cambridge, Mass.: Harvard University Press, 1978), 264.

15. Shelton Stromquist, "The Crucible of Class: Cleveland Politics and the Origins of Municipal Reform in the Progressive Era," *Journal of Urban History* 23 (January 1997): 192–220.

16. Bionaz, "Streetcar City," 2.

17. "Move to Get More Police," *Cleveland Plain Dealer*, November 27, 1900, 5.

18. John D. Buenker, "Cleveland's New Stock Lawmakers and Progressive Reform, *Ohio History* 78 (Spring 1969): 117.

19. On Johnson, see his autobiography, Tom L. Johnson, *My Story* (Kent, Ohio: Kent State University Press, 1993). Numerous historians have written about him. See Robert H. Wiebe, *The Search for Order, 1877–1920* (New York: Hill and Wang, 1967), 172; and Daniel T. Rogers, *Atlantic Crossings: Social Politics in a Progressive Age* (Cambridge, Mass.: Harvard University Press, 1998), 138. For more comprehensive studies of Johnson's political career in Cleveland, see Carl Lorenz, *Tom L. Johnson: Mayor of Cleveland* (New York: A. S. Barnes, 1911); Robert L. Briggs, "The Progressive Era in Cleveland, Ohio: Tom L. Johnson's Administration, 1901–1909" (Ph.D. dissertation, University of Chicago, 1961); Jon Teaford, *Cities of the Heartland: The Rise and Fall of the Industrial Midwest* (Bloomington: Indiana University Press, 1993), 113–18; Kenneth Finegold, *Experts and Politicians: Reform Challenges to Machine Politics in New York, Cleveland, and Chicago* (Princeton, N.J.: Princeton University Press, 1995), 6, 82–100; Kim K. Bender, "Cleveland, a Leader Among Cities: The Municipal Home Rule Movement of the Progressive Era, 1900–1915" (Ph.D. dissertation, University of Oklahoma, 1996); Stromquist, "The Crucible of Class"; and Ronald R. Weiner, *Lake Effects: A History of Urban Policy Making in Cleveland, 1825–1929* (Columbus: Ohio State University Press, 2005), 74, 82–92, 104–11, 121, 133–49.

20. Such pressure was especially clear during a multi-workplace machinists' strike in 1907. The strikers sought a nine- rather than a ten-hour day. Most of Cleveland's employers stood firm, though one briefly succumbed to the demanding unionists. According to a report in *The Iron Trade Review*, "The one member of the Metal Trades Association who granted the demand for a nine-hour day has since reconsidered the action and has placed the shop on the former 10-hour basis." See "Cleveland Strike Ended," *The Iron Trade Review* 40 (June 27, 1907): 1027.

21. On the city's centralized labor bureau, see William English Walling, "Can Labor Unions Be Destroyed?" *World's Work* 8 (May 1904): 4758.

22. Quoted in "Enlarge The Employers Association Is the Keynote of the Annual Convention," *Ohio Architect and Builder* 13 (March 1909): 45.

23. "To Speak on Child Labor," *Cleveland Plain Dealer*, November 25, 1906, 11. The Bucyrus Company's dredging equipment was used in the construction of the Panama Canal. See Harold F. Williamson and Kenneth H. Myers, II, *Designed for Digging: The First 75 Years of Bucyrus-Erie Company* (Evanston, Ill.: Northwestern University Press, 1955); and Julie Greene, *The Canal Builders: Making America's Empire at the Panama Canal* (New York: Penguin, 2009), 56, 82.

24. On Cleveland's philanthropists, see Laura Tuennerman-Kaplan, *Helping Others, Helping Ourselves: Power, Giving, and Community Identity in Cleveland, Ohio, 1880–1930*

(Kent, Oh.: Kent State University Press, 2001). On Eells, see "To Speak on Child Labor," *Cleveland Plain Dealer*, November 25, 1906, 11. Eells served as NMTA president in 1914. For more on Eells, see Willimson and Myers, *Designed for Digging*, 61–78.

25. "Lorain and the Molders Camp," *Iron Molders' Journal* 36 (September 1900): 509.

26. Ibid.

27. Quoted in "Correspondence," *Iron Molders' Journal* 36 (November 1900): 663.

28. "A Card of the National Founders' Association," *Iron Molders' Journal* 36 (September 1900): 527–28; "Bonds Plan to Break Power of Unions," *New York Times*, November 18, 1900, 15; Margaret Loomis Stecker, "The National Founders' Association," *Quarterly Journal of Economics* 30 (February 1916): 359. At the NFA 1900 convention, delegates elected to fund the costs associated with breaking the strike. See "To Keep Up Fight on Molders," *Omaha Daily Bee*, November 16, 1900, 1.

29. "A Card of the National Founders' Association," 527.

30. "The Cleveland Strike," *Iron Molders' Journal* 37 (January 1901): 18.

31. "Bloodshed in Cleveland," *Iron Molders' Journal* 36 (October 1900): 589.

32. Ibid.

33. "One of Penton's Tricks," *Iron Molders' Journal* 36 (October 1900): 588.

34. "Organize," *Machinery Molders Journal* 1 (April 1888): 2.

35. "A Beautiful Piece of Work," *Machinery Molders Journal* 2 (November 1889): 3.

36. "This Is Comical," *Machinery Molders Journal* 2 (November 1889): 1–2.

37. "The Iron Molders' Union Over Ruled—Not Allowed to Expel Without Cause," *Machinery Molders Journal* 3 (September 1890): 11. Union rivalries were common in Detroit. See Richard Jules Oestreicher, *Solidarity and Fragmentation: Working People and Class Consciousness in Detroit, 1875–1900* (Urbana: University of Illinois Press, 1986).

38. "The Iron Molders' Union Over Ruled," 11.

39. On the IMU's evolution, see H. E. Hoagland, "The Rise of the Iron Molders' International Union: A Study in American Trade Unionism," *American Economic Review* 3 (June 1913): 297–305; John R. Commons, "Organized Labor's Attitude Toward Industrial Efficiency," *American Economic Review* 1 (September 1911): 465; and Frank T. Stockton, "Productive Cooperation in the Molders Union," *American Economic Review* 21 (June 1931): 260–74. For a biographical introduction to Sylvis, see David Montgomery, "William H. Sylvis and the Search for Working-Class Citizenship," in *Labor Leaders in America*, ed. Melvyn Dubofsky and Warren Van Tine (Urbana: University of Illinois Press, 1987), 3–29.

40. On one especially important case of employers' frustration with working-class solidarity, see "Molders' Strike Unbroken," *New York Times*, August 8, 1901, 2.

41. F. W. Hilbert, "Trade-Union Agreements in the Iron Molders' Union," in *Studies in American Trade Unionism*, ed. Jacob H. Hollander and George E. Barnett (New York: Henry Holt, 1912), 258.

42. "The Dangerous Strikers," *Machinery Molders Journal* 5 (November 1892): 17.

43. "John Howard, Stephen Lytle, George Kings: A Dishonorable Trio," *Machinery Molders Journal* 2 (November 1889): 15. These men apparently broke a strike at Ames Ironworks in Oswego, New York. Ames was later a NFA member.

44. Quoted in W. A. Perrine, "New York and Vicinity," *Iron Molders' Journal* 36 (November 1900): 664. Working during official strikes was a violation of Article 14, Section 3 of the union's constitution. See *Constitution and Rules of Order of the International Brotherhood of Machinery Molders of North America* (Milwaukee: Hartmann and Son, 1887), 28.

45. Members of the IMU and brotherhood voted to merge in 1893. The IMU machinery molders voted 7,628 to 208 in favor of merging. It appears that rank-and-file brotherhood members also voted in favor, but the results were not made available. See Frank T. Stockton, *The International Molders Union of North America* (Baltimore: Johns Hopkins University Press, 1921), 48–50. For more on the tension between the two organizations, see Gerald N. Grob, *Workers and Utopia: A Study of Ideological Conflict in the American Labor Movement, 1865–1900* (Chicago: Northwestern University Press, 1961), 159.

46. "The Molder," *Foundry* 2 (February 10, 1893): 37.

47. W. A. Perrine, "New York and Vicinity," *Iron Molders' Journal* 36 (November 1900): 664.

48. John A. Penton, *The Inside Story of Malleable Iron* (Cleveland: American Malleable Castings Association, 1915), 8.

49. "National Founders' Association," *The Iron Trade Review* 33 (January 8, 1900): 12.

50. "Cincinnati Convention of the National Founders' Association—A New Policy Adopted," *The Iron Trade Review* 37 (November 24, 1904): 50b.

51. On Penton Publishing Company, see Earl L. Shaner and Frank G. Steinebach, *History of the Penton Publishing Company, 1904–1967* (Cleveland: privately published, 1968); James L. C. Ford, *Magazines for Millions: The Story of Specialized Publications* (Carbondale: Southern Illinois University Press, 1969), 257–58; and William Ganson Rose, *Cleveland: The Making of a City* (Kent, Ohio: Kent State University Press, 1990), 623.

52. "Convention Notes," *The Iron Trade Review* 36 (November 12, 1903): 42.

53. "National Founders' Association," *The Iron Trade Review* 36 (November 19, 1903): 49.

54. *Facts*, June 1909.

55. *Memorial Record of the Country of Cuyahoga and City of Cleveland, Ohio* (Chicago: Lewis, 1894), 381.

56. *A History of Cleveland, Ohio*, vol. 2 (Cleveland: S.J. Clarke, 1910), 380–83, 935. One of the chief figures in Daniel R. Ernst's study, Daniel Davenport, like Dawley, spent years representing ordinary people in personal disputes. See Ernst, *Lawyers Against Labor: From Individual Rights to Corporate Liberalism* (Urbana: University of Illinois Press, 1995), 37–38.

57. Quoted in John S. Crosbie, *The Incredible Mrs. Chadwick: The Most Notorious Woman of Her Age* (Toronto: McGraw-Hill Ryerson, 1975), 224. Also see Rose, *Cleveland*, 581, 647–49, 776. On Wing's injunction, see "Picketing Prohibited," *Building Trades Association Bulletin* 2 (September 1901): 88. In the late nineteenth century, Wing joined dozens of other elite Clevelanders in the Gatling Gun Battery Company, a capitalist militia that defended the city's most privileged residents. See Larry Isaac, "To Counter 'The Very Devil' and More: The Making of Independent Capitalist Militia in the Gilded Age," *American Journal of Sociology* 108 (September 2002): 399.

58. W. D. Sayle, "Labor Conditions in Cleveland," *Open Shop* 4 (October 1905): 461–64.

59. "An Injunction at Cleveland," *The Iron Trade Review* 34 (June 27, 1901): 29; and "Injunction Against Strikers," *Building Trades Association Bulletin* 2 (August 1901), 65.

60. Sayle, "Labor Conditions in Cleveland," 461–64.

61. "Cleveland," *The Iron Trade Review* 35 (September 4, 1902): 48.

62. J. H. Webster, "The Church and the Labor Unions," *The Iron Trade Review* 39 (September 28, 1905): 26.

63. J. H. Webster, "Industrial Situation Hopeful," *American Industries* 6 (December 1, 1907): 16.

64. Five representatives from each side settled the strike after meeting on nine occasions. On the settlement, see "Cleveland Molders' Strike Settled," *The Iron Trade Review* 34 (February 21, 1901): 20–21. The IMU spent a total of $104,360 on strike benefits. See "Pres. Fox's Report to the Toronto Convention of the Iron Molders' Union of North America," *The Iron Trade Review* 35 (July 17, 1902): 36.

65. "Can Carry Revolvers," *Cleveland Plain Dealer*, May 26, 1901, 4.

66. Ibid.

67. "Arms His Non-Union Men," *New York Times*, November 6, 1906, 1.

68. "Tells Mayor of Strike Trouble," *Cleveland Plain Dealer*, November 5, 1906, 3.

69. "Threaten to Shoot Down Strikers," *Cleveland Press*, November 5, 1906, 11.

70. John A. Penton to Tom L. Johnson, November 12, 1906, Folder 9, Container 2, Tom L. Johnson Papers, Western Reserve Historical Society, Cleveland, Ohio.

71. "Move to Get More Police," *Cleveland Plain Dealer*, November 27, 1900, 5.

72. In 1910, Roosevelt called police head Fredrick Kohler, whom Johnson appointed in 1903, "the country's finest chief of police." Quoted in Thomas Kelly and George E. Condon, *The Cleveland 200: The Most Noted, Notable and Notorious in the First 200 Years of a Great American City* (Cleveland: Archives Press, 1996), 129.

73. On the support, see P. H. Frankel, "Numerous Important Activities at Cleveland," *American Industries* 4 (December 15, 1906): 9–10.

74. Penton to Johnson, November 12, 1906.

75. "A Notorious Labor Crusher Boldly Incites Strikebreakers to Deeds of Lawlessness," *Cleveland Citizen*, November 10, 1906, 1; United Trades and Labor Council to Tom L. Johnson, November 12, 1906, Container 2, Folder 9, Tom L. Johnson Papers, Western Reserve Historical Society, Cleveland, Ohio.

76. "Molders," *Cleveland Citizen*, December 1, 1906, 4.

77. "A Notorious Labor Crusher," 1.

78. "Molders," *Cleveland Citizen*, December 8, 1906, 4.

79. "Citizenisms," *Cleveland Citizen*, November 10, 1906, 1.

80. "Press Pays Printers A Tribute," *Cleveland Citizen*, November 24, 1906, 1.

81. "Molders," *Cleveland Citizen*, December 8, 1906, 4.

82. "Lawyer Chooses Common Pleas," *Daily Legal News*, February 2, 1907, 1.

83. "Lawless Employer Indicted," *Cleveland Citizen*, February 16, 1907, 1; "Printers," *Cleveland Citizen*, March 16, 1907, 4; and "Printers," *Cleveland Citizen*, May 11, 1907, 2.

84. "Sayle's Services," *The Iron Trade Review* 41 (March 21, 1907): 469.

85. *Cleveland Citizen*, May 28, 1910, 1. On the Reynolds Child Labor Law, see "Trend of Events," *Cleveland Citizen*, July 11, 1908, 1. For more on Reynolds, see Buenker, "Cleveland's New Stock Lawmakers," 126–27. On Kundtz, see Edward M. Miggins and Mary Morgenthaler, "The Ethnic Mosaic: The Settlement of Cleveland by the New Immigrants and Migrants," in *The Birth of Modern Cleveland, 1865–1930*, ed. Thomas F. Campbell and Edward M. Miggins (Cleveland: Western Reserve Historical Society, 1988), 121.

86. "Printers," *Cleveland Citizen*, April 6, 1907, 3.

87. "Garment Workers," *Cleveland Citizen*, February 1, 1908, 4.

88. "Cloak and Skirt Makers," *Cleveland Citizen*, March 19, 1910, 2.

89. Jay P. Dawley, "Extracts from Counsel's Report," *Facts*, December 1909.

90. *Facts*, May 1909.

91. Ibid. On the proliferation of company newspapers and magazines, see Stuart D. Brandes, *American Welfare Capitalism, 1880–1940* (Chicago: University of Chicago Press, 1976), 62–65.

92. Jay P. Dawley, "Extracts from Counsel's Report."

93. Jay P. Dawley, "Whom the Gods Would Destroy They First Make Mad," *Facts*, September 1909.

94. "Cloakmakers Declare Against Any Disorder; Win Attorney of Employers," *Cleveland Plain Dealer*, June 8, 1911, 1–2; and "Girl Strikers Win Aid with Recruits," *Cleveland Leader*, June 9, 1911, 1.

95. "Trend of Events," *Cleveland Citizen*, June 10, 1911, 1.

96. "Cloakmakers Declare Against Any Disorder," 1–2.

97. Quoted in "Trend of Events," *Cleveland Citizen*, June 10, 1911, 1.

98. "Girl Strikers Win Aid with Recruits," 1.

99. "Trend of Events," 1.

100. "Girl Strikers Win Aid with Recruits," 1; and "Dawley Attacks Unfair Employers," *Cleveland Plain Dealer*, June 9, 1911, 2.

101. Alice Kessler-Harris, *Gendering Labor History* (Urbana: University of Illinois Press, 2007), 223.

102. On the Triangle Shirtwaist fire and post-fire reforms, see Richard A. Greenwald, *The Triangle Fire, the Protocols of Peace, and Industrial Democracy in Progressive Era New York* (Philadelphia: Temple University Press, 2005). On the *Muller* case, see Nancy S. Erickson, "*Muller v. Oregon* Reconsidered: The Origins of a Sex-Based Doctrine of Liberty of Contract," *Labor History* 30 (Spring 1989): 228–50.

103. On Green's involvement in Ohio politics, see Hoyt Landon Warner, *Progressivism in Ohio, 1897–1917* (Columbus: Ohio State University Press, 1964), 283; Buenker, "Cleveland's New Stock Lawmakers," 126; Patrick D. Reagan, "Ideology of Social Harmony and Efficiency: Workmen's Compensation in Ohio, 1904–1919," *Ohio History* 90 (Autumn 1981): 317–31; and Craig Phelan, *William Green: Biography of a Labor Leader* (Albany: State University of New York Press, 1989), 20–21.

104. "Cloakmakers Declare Against Any Disorder," 1–2.

105. "Dynamite Outrage in Cleveland," *The Iron Trade Review* 39 (March 15, 1906): 1.

106. "General Otis to Speak," *Cleveland Plain Dealer*, June 3, 1911, 5; "Holds Union Shop Is Business Loser," *Cleveland Plain Dealer*, June 9, 1911, 2; and "Trend of Events," *Cleveland Citizen*, June 10, 1911, 1. For details on all these men, especially Drew, see Sidney Fine, *"Without Blare of Trumpets": Walter Drew, the National Erectors' Association, and the Open Shop Movement, 1903–57* (Ann Arbor: University of Michigan Press, 1995). On Otis, see John H. M. Laslett, *Sunshine Was Never Enough: Los Angeles Workers, 1880–2010* (Berkeley: University of California Press, 2012), 22, 25–33, 39.

107. "Says Intimidation Aids Strike Cause," *Cleveland Plain Dealer*, June 11, 1911, 2.

108. "Decries Lack of Union," *Cleveland Plain Dealer*, August 2, 1907, 12.

109. "Striking Cutters May Quit Union," *Cleveland Plain Dealer*, June 27, 1911, 12; "Cleveland Goods Sent to Chicago," *Cleveland Plain Dealer*, July 4, 1911, 16. Cleveland's Jewish community was split on class lines. Many of the city's garment manufacturers were

262 Notes to Pages 121–123

Jewish. On Cleveland's garment manufacturers, see Lloyd P. Gartner, *History of the Jews of Cleveland* (Cleveland: Western Reserve Historical Society Press, 1978), 72–79. Cleveland's Jewish garment-making community was hardly unique. On the broader context of Jews and the garment industry, see Phyllis Dillon and Andrew Godley, "The Evolution of the Jewish Garment Industry, 1840–1940," in *Chosen Capital: The Jewish Encounter with American Capitalism*, ed. Rebecca Kobrin (New Brunswick, N.J.: Rutgers University Press, 2012), 35–61. Their opponents, an ethnically diverse union, were early promoters of multiculturalism. See Daniel Katz, *All Together Different: Yiddish Socialists, Garment Workers, and the Labor Roots of Multiculturalism* (New York: New York University Press, 2011).

110. "Citizenisms," *Cleveland Citizen*, August 4, 1906, 1. Frankel was instrumental in defeating a 1907 machinists strike. See "Strikers Vote to Stay Out," *Cleveland Plain Dealer*, July 7, 1907, 2b; "Strikers Still Out," *Cleveland Plain Dealer*, July 9, 1907, 12; "Riveters Out on Strike," *Cleveland Plain Dealer*, July 11, 1907, 1; and "Strike for Third Time," *Cleveland Plain Dealer*, July 12, 1907, 12. Frankel's activism extended beyond Cleveland's boundaries. He helped organize the Toledo Employers' Association. See "Frankel Blossoms as Orator," *Cleveland Citizen*, February 2, 1907, 1.

111. "Import Workmen to Reopen Shops," *Cleveland Plain Dealer*, July 5, 1911, 13; and "Strikebreakers to be Brought in," *Cleveland Plain Dealer*, July 7, 1911, 12.

112. Edna Bryner, *The Garment Trades* (Cleveland: Cleveland Foundation, 1916), 58–69; Louis Levine, *The Women's Garment Workers: A History of the International Ladies' Garment Workers' Union* (New York: Huebsch, 1924), 214; and Benjamin Stolberg, *Tailor's Progress: The Story of the Famous Union and the Men Who Made It* (New York: Doubleday, 1944), 75.

113. "Labor Keeps out of Civic Confab," *Cleveland Plain Dealer*, July 20, 1911, 11; and "Ballot Urged on City-Wide Strike," *Cleveland Plain Dealer*, August 21, 1911, 12. On Newman, see Alice Kessler-Harris, "Organizing the Unorganizable: Three Jewish Women and Their Union," *Labor History* 17 (Winter 1976): 5–23.

114. Female strikers attempted to win the support of middle class women active in the suffrage campaign. The city's women suffrage party refused to endorse the strike. See Lois Scharf, "A Women's View of Cleveland's Labor Force: Two Case Studies," in *The Birth of Modern Cleveland, 1865–1930*, ed. Campbell and Miggins, 183. In other contexts, wealthy women sided with female strikers. See David Huyssen, *Progressive Inequality: Rich and Poor in New York, 1890–1920* (Cambridge, Mass.: Harvard University Press, 2014), 174.

115. "Striking Cutters May Quit Union," *Cleveland Plain Dealer*, June 27, 1911, 12.

116. "Cleveland Dubbed Union Thug Home," *Cleveland Plain Dealer*, August 17, 1911, 2.

117. Quoted in Levine, *The Women's Garment Workers*, 213.

118. "Chamber Opposes Rioting in Strike," *Cleveland Plain Dealer*, June 28, 1911, 3.

119. The International Ladies Garment Workers Union apparently claimed that the Cleveland strike was its bitterest struggle. See C. E. Ruthenberg, "The Cleveland Garment Workers Strike," *International Socialist Review* 12 (September 1911): 139. Ruthenberg was a well-known Cleveland socialist. See Stephen M. Millett, "Charles E. Ruthenberg: The Development of an American Communist, 1909–1927," *Ohio History* 81 (Summer 1972): 193–209.

120. "Rioters in Clash near City Hall," *Cleveland Plain Dealer*, July 2, 1911, 2.

121. Quoted in "Truce in Strike Today Following Loss of One Life," *Cleveland Plain Dealer*, June 11, 1911, 2.

122. "Vote on Ending Strike," *Cleveland Plain Dealer*, October 7, 1911, 9; and Levine, *The Women's Garment Workers*, 216.

123. "Prominent Lawyer Dead," *Greenville Journal*, June 15, 1916, 7.

Chapter 4. Avenging McKinley: Organized Employers in Buffalo

Epigraph: Theodore Dreiser, *A Hoosier Holiday* (New York: John Lane Company, 1916), 177.

1. Alan Trachtenberg makes a similar case in his analysis of Chicago's 1893 Columbia's Exposition. See Trachtenberg, *The Incorporation of America: Culture and Society in the Gilded Age* (New York: Hill and Wang, 1982), 208–34.

2. For more on Czolgosz's anarchism, see Sidney Fine, "Anarchism and the Assassination of McKinley," *American Historical Review* 60 (July 1955): 777–99; and Eric Rauchway, *Murdering McKinley: The Making of Theodore Roosevelt's America* (New York: Hill and Wang, 2003).

3. "Anarchy vs. Socialism," *International Socialist Review* 2 (October 1901): 248.

4. T. Guilford Smith, *Report of the Eleventh Annual Meeting of the Mohonk Lake Conference on International Arbitration* (n.p., 1905), 101.

5. The IMU and NFA offered conflicting numbers. The NFA put the number at 700 strikers; the IMU claimed that "about one thousand members of the union" participated. See "Strikes of Iron Molders, 1904 to 1908, Inclusive," *(Open Shop) Review* 6 (March 1909): 26; and Henry Launspach, "Our Buffalo Letter," *Iron Molders' Journal* 42 (December 1906): 917.

6. "Situation in the Molders' Strike," *The Iron Trade Review* 39 (June 14, 1906): 14.

7. Harold F. Peterson, *Diplomat of the Americas: A Biography of William I. Buchanan* (Albany: SUNY Press, 1977), 155.

8. "Tonnage and Appropriations," *Marine Review* 33 (May 31, 1906): 29.

9. Buffalo Forge Company, *Illustrated Catalogue of Buffalo Mechanical Draft Apparatus* (Buffalo, 1903), 9.

10. J. N. Larned, *A History of Buffalo: Delineating the Evolution of the city* (Buffalo: Progress of the Empire State Company, 1911), 13; and Lawrence V. Roth, "The Growth of American Cities," *Geographical Review* 5 (May 1918): 395.

11. William H. Gatwick, "Report of Annual Meeting," *Annual Report of the Buffalo Merchants' Exchange* (Buffalo, 1906): 12.

12. Ogden P. Letchworth, "Report of the Annual Meeting," *Annual Report of the Buffalo Merchants' Exchange* (1902): 11–12.

13. In business circles, Letchworth was immensely popular, which helped him get elected to the leadership of several manufacturing associations, including the NFA nationally, and the Buffalo Merchants' Association locally. His friends included proprietary capitalists and so-called captains of industry, Buffalonians and thriving industrialists from distant cities. In fact, he established close relationships with some of the biggest names in the industrial world, including steel masters E. W. Gary and Charles Schwab. His competitors and colleagues in professional business and employers' associations enjoyed his company, calling him "a good fellow." "Host Letchworth is Good Fellow, Foundrymen Say," *Buffalo Courier*, July 21, 1906, 8; "Dinner to O. P. Letchworth," *The Iron Trade Review* 36 (June 19, 1902): 28; and "Malleable Men Meet," *The Iron Trade Review* 39 (July 26, 1906): 12. As president of the board of the Wyoming Benevolent Society, Letchworth played a part in introducing underprivileged children to recreational and reading activities. According to a New York State report, the organization sought to help "dependent children and indigent young persons, chiefly by providing

a summer residence for children at Prospect Home Villa, and by maintaining a free public library." *Annual Report, Social Services in New York State for the Year 1893* (Albany, N.Y.: James B. Lyon, State Printer, 1894), 370.

14. R. H. Thurston, "The Steam Engine at the End of the Nineteenth Century," *Transactions of the American Society of Mechanical Engineers* 21 (1900): 200–201.

15. Frank H. Severance, "Historical Sketch of the Buffalo Board of Trade: The Merchants' Exchange and the Chamber of Commerce," *Buffalo Historical Society Publications* 13 (1909): 296.

16. Letchworth and his colleagues had much to tell visitors, and some manufacturers even published company magazines to coincide with the exposition's opening. See Howard R. Stanger, "From Factory to Family: The Creation of a Corporate Culture in the Larkin Company of Buffalo, New York," *Business History Review* 74 (Autumn 2000): 417.

17. Curt M. Treat, "Report of Annual Meeting," *Annual Report of the Buffalo Merchants' Exchange* (1901): 32.

18. Alfred Haines, "Report of Annual Meeting," *Annual Report of the Buffalo Merchants' Exchange* (1900): 37.

19. Businessmen in New Orleans and Cincinnati were the pioneers, starting these organizations in 1834 and 1839 respectively. See S. S. Guthrie, "History of the Buffalo Board of Trade," copy of speech delivered in 1870, Buffalo and Erie County Historical Society, Buffalo.

20. Haywood quoted in Guthrie, "History of the Buffalo Board of Trade."

21. David A. Gerber, *The Making of An American Pluralism: Buffalo, New York, 1825–60* (Urbana: University of Illinois Press, 1989), 56.

22. "A. F. A. at Buffalo in June," *The Iron Trade Review* 31 (March 7, 1901): 9.

23. Ogden P. Letchworth, "Report of Annual Meeting," *Annual Report of the Buffalo Merchants' Exchange* (1901): 16.

24. "American Foundrymen's Association at Buffalo," *The Iron Trade Review* 31 (June 6, 1901): 27.

25. Ibid.

26. Quoted in "Biggest Day of the Fair," *Buffalo Express*, September 6, 1901, 7.

27. Quoted in Rauchway, *Murdering McKinley*, 42.

28. Ibid., 113–17. On Czolgosz's time in Cleveland, see John C. Chalberg, *Emma Goldman: American Individualist* (New York: Pearson/Longman, 2008), 70; and Scott Miller, *The President and the Assassin: McKinley, Terror and Empire at the Dawn of the American Century* (New York: Random House, 2011), 57, 74.

29. Quoted in "Eexcution [sic] of Czolgosz," *Commoner*, November 8, 1901, 10.

30. Emma Goldman, *Living My Life* (1934; New York: AMS Press, 1970), 305–6; and Margaret S. Marsh, *Anarchist Women, 1870–1920* (Philadelphia: Temple University Press, 1981), 109.

31. Goldman, *Living My Life*, 310. Writer Candace Serena Falk notes that Goldman no longer supported violence by 1901. See Falk, *Love, Anarchy, and Emma Goldman* (New Brunswick, N.J.: Rutgers University Press, 1984), 33. Perhaps when she wrote her 1934 memoirs Goldman had in mind the 1899 Coeur d'Alene strike. On McKinley's intervention here, see Jerry Cooper, *The Army and Civil Disorder: Federal Military Intervention in Labor Disputes, 1877–1900* (Westport, Conn.: Greenwood, 1980), 173.

32. On this depression and the business community's response to it, see Leo Panitch and Sam Gindin, *The Making of Global Capitalism: The Political Economy of American Empire* (London: Verso, 2012), 29.

33. Quoted in Walter LaFeber, *The New Empire: An Interpretation of American Expansion, 1860–1898* (Ithaca, N.Y.: Cornell University Press, 1963), 192–93. For more on McKinley's relationship with organized businessmen, see Thomas G. Paterson, "American Businessmen and Consular Service Reform, 1890s to 1906," *Business History Review* 40 (Spring 1966): 89; and Cathie Jo Martin and Duane Swank, *Political Construction of Business Interests* (Cambridge: Cambridge University Press, 2012), 89–108.

34. Albion Guilford Taylor, *Labor Policies of the National Association of Manufacturers* (Urbana: University of Illinois Press, 1927), 96.

35. Kevin Phillips, *William McKinley* (New York: Times Books, 2003), 37; and Richard Franklin Bensel, *The Political Economy of American Industrialization, 1877–1900* (Cambridge: Cambridge University Press, 2000), 457–506.

36. William McKinley, "Speech at Banquet of Ellicott Club, Buffalo, New York, August 24, 1897," in *Speeches and Addresses of William McKinley* (New York: Doubleday and McClure, 1900), 38. McKinley and his supporters selectively invoked the same sort of Civil War memory and reconciliation during the 1896 campaign. See David W. Blight, *Race and Reunion: The Civil War in American Memory* (Cambridge, Mass.: Harvard University Press, 2001), 351; and Patrick J. Kelly, "The Election of 1896 and the restructuring of Civil War Memory," *Civil War History* 49 (September 2003): 254–80.

37. Quoted in "He is in Good Hands," *Indianapolis Journal*, September 7, 1901, 9.

38. "High Time," *(Kansas City) Independent*, October 12, 1901, 1.

39. "Platt on Lynching," *Buffalo Express*, September 7, 1901, 4. For more on the post September 6 anti-anarchist frenzy, see Brigitte Koenig, "Law and Disorder at Home: Free Love, Free Speech, and the Search for an Anarchist Utopia," *Labor History* 45 (May 2004): 199–223.

40. For a list of jurists, see "The Proceedings in Court," *New York Times*, September 24, 1901, 2.

41. Quoted in "Czolgosz Convicted," *Peninsula Enterprise*, September 28, 1901, 1.

42. Prior to becoming a jury member, Wendt admitted that he supported capital punishment. See "Henry W. Wendt, Juror No. 3," *Buffalo Express*, September 24, 1901, 8.

43. On the case against Czolgosz, see A. Wesley Johns, *The Man Who Shot McKinley* (New York: A.S. Barnes, 1970), 205, 233–34. Three years before McKinley's death, White edited a lengthy, celebratory book about Erie County, home to Buffalo. See Truman C. White, ed., *Our County and Its People: A Descriptive Work on Erie County, New York*, vol. 1 (Boston: Boston History Company, 1898).

44. On the railroad strike, see David Stowell, *Streets, Railroads, and the Great Strike of 1877* (Chicago: University of Chicago Press, 1999). On the grain shovelers' dispute, see Brenda Shelton, "The Buffalo Grain Shovellers Strike of 1899," *Labor History* 9 (Spring 1968): 210–38.

45. On immigration, see Virginia Yans-McLaughlin, *Family and Community: Italian Immigrants in Buffalo, 1880–1930* (Ithaca, N.Y.: Cornell University Press, 1971), 36.

46. "Status of Molders Strike," *Buffalo Express*, June 1, 1906, 9.

47. *Illustrated History of the United Trades and Labor Council of Erie County* (Buffalo: United Trades and Labor Council of Erie County, 1897), 260.

48. According to Brenda K. Shelton, Buffalo's labor movement "did not represent a dangerously radical force." Shelton, *Reformers in Search of Yesterday: Buffalo in the 1890s* (Albany: SUNY Press, 1976), 167.

49. "Industrial Notes," *The Iron Trade Review* 29 (October 27, 1898): 22.

50. "Moulders' Strike," *Buffalo Courier*, October 22, 1898, 6.

51. "Machinists' Strike," *Buffalo Courier*, October 23, 1898, 19; and "Strike is Over," *Buffalo Courier*, October 30, 1898, 19.

52. "Foundrymen's Defense Association" *The Iron Trade Review* 29 (February 3, 1898): 8.

53. Department of Commerce and Labor, "Agreement Between Buffalo Foundrymen's Association and Iron Molders' Conference Board of Buffalo and Vicinity," *Bulletin of the Bureau of Labor* 9 (1904): 428–29.

54. "Buffalo Foundrymen's Association," *Foundry* 27 (November 1905): 147.

55. Quoted in "Founders to Meet," *New York Times*, November 12, 1905, 12.

56. "News of the Labor World," *Illustrated Buffalo Express*, May 27, 1906, 22.

57. Quoted in John Frey, *History of a Criminal Conspiracy to Defeat Striking Molders: Lawless Methods of Employers Uncovered Through Court Records* (Cincinnati: International Molders Union of North America, 1907), 11. On the administrative council's resolution, see "The Present Issue is Radical Unionism," *Review* 3 (May 1906): 17–18.

58. For more on Briggs, see William Millikan, *A Union Against Unions: The Minneapolis Citizens Alliance and Its Fight Against Organized Labor, 1903–1947* (St. Paul: Minnesota Historical Society Press, 2001), 7–12.

59. Quoted in "News of the Labor World," *Buffalo Express*, May 3, 1906, 9.

60. "News of the Labor World," *Illustrated Buffalo Express*, June 17, 1906, 20.

61. "Status of Molders Strike," *Buffalo Express*, June 1, 1906, 9.

62. O. P. Briggs, "A Policy of Lawlessness—Partial Record of Riot, Assault, Murder, Coercion, and Intimidation occurring in Strikes of the Iron Molders' Union During 1904, 1905, 1906, and 1907" in *Hearings Before Subcommittees of the Judiciary United States Senate Together with Briefs and Memoranda Submitted In Connections Therewith During the Sixtieth, Sixty-First, and Sixty-Second Congresses* (Washington, D.C.: GPO, 1914): 734.

63. Ibid, 710.

64. "Molders," *Cleveland Citizen*, July 21, 1906, 3.

65. Briggs, "A Policy of Lawlessness," 734.

66. Ibid.

67. "Signal Victory," *The Iron Trade* Review 40 (February 7, 1907): 230.

68. On the Buffalo Foundry Company, see Henry Wayland Hill, *Municipality of Buffalo, New York: A History, 1720–1923*, vol. 2 (New York: Lewis Historical Publishing, 1923), 801.

69. The article read, "About twenty of these non-unionists have taken sick in the last few days and, it is said, have given up their jobs." See "Status of the Molders' Strike," *Buffalo Express*, July 17, 1906, 9. Also see "Striker, He Says, Told Him to Quit," *Buffalo Courier*, August 5, 1906, 30.

70. The Buffalo Foundry Company began operations in January, 1901. See "New Corporations," *New York Times*, January 13, 1901, 24.

71. "News of the Labor World," *Illustrated Buffalo Express*, June 3, 1906, 18.

72. A number of university professors began teaching the fundamentals of molding during the early twentieth century. In 1906, University of Minnesota professors published *Foundry Practice*. Their involvement in such training was one sign that the teaching of molding was not restricted to IMU-sponsored apprenticeship programs. See James M. Tate and Melvin O. Stone, *Foundry Practice: A Treatise on Molding and Casting in Their Various Details* (Minneapolis: H.W. Wilson, 1906).

73. Quoted in "News of the Labor World," *Illustrated Buffalo Express*, June 10, 1906, 20.

74. "Buffalo Situation Improves," *The Iron Trade Review* 39 (August 2, 1906): 12–13. Social and labor historians have long noted the importance of the police in suppressing working class activism. See Sidney L. Harring, *Policing a Class Society: The Experience of American Cities, 1865–1915* (New Brunswick, N.J.: Rutgers University Press, 1983); Gerda W. Ray, "'We Can Stay Until Hell Freezes Over': Strike Control and the State Police in New York, 1919–1923," *Labor History* 36 (August 1995): 403–25; Jeffrey S. Adler, "Shoot to Kill: The Use of Deadly Force by the Chicago Police, 1875–1920," *Journal of Interdisciplinary History* 38 (Autumn 2007): 233–54; and Sam Mitrani, *The Rise of the Chicago Police Department: Class and Conflict, 1850–1894* (Urbana: University of Illinois Press, 2013).

75. Quoted in Sidney L. Harring, "Police Reports as Sources in Labor History," *Labor History* 18 (Fall 1977): 587. Lyman P. Hubbell actually spent much of his life upholding "law and order" and defending the financial interests of privileged Americans. In addition to running the Fillmore Avenue Foundry Works, Hubbell was an active member of the National Guard and a proud Republican Party member. He began military service in 1896 and retired in 1936 as a brigadier general. During his forty-year service, he served as a captain on the Mexican border and fought in the First World War. He was an National Guard leader stationed in Buffalo in 1919 during that year's strike wave. Like many employers in the Buffalo Foundrymen's Association, Hubbell was active in several organizations, including ASME. On Hubbell's life, see his obituary, "Gen. L. P. Hubbell Dies Here, Aged 68, After Long Illness," *Buffalo News*, May 22, 1943, 11; and "Gen. Hubbell's Funeral to be Held Tomorrow," *Buffalo Courier*, May 23, 1943, 3. For more on police protection at his workplace during the 1906 strike, see "News of the Labor World," *Buffalo Express*, May 4, 1906, 9. Hubbell had previously settled conflicts relatively amiably with the IMU, but like other NFA members, had come to the conclusion that collective bargaining had become unnecessary.

76. "Strikers Attack Non-Union Men," *Buffalo Enquirer*, June 15, 1906, 6.

77. Apparently Goldman had no difficulty speaking in other cities, including Chicago and St. Louis. See "Emma Goldman Meeting is Stopped," *Buffalo Enquirer*, June 14, 1906, 4.

78. Emma Goldman, "A Sentimental Journey—Police Protection" in *Emma Goldman: A Documentary History of the American Years*, ed. Candace Falk (Berkeley: University of California Press, 2005) 187; and "May Count Noses of the Anarchists," *Buffalo Enquirer*, July 6, 1906, 10.

79. Quoted in Fine, "Anarchism and the Assassination of McKinley," 789–90.

80. Quoted in Beverly Gage, *The Day Wall Street Exploded: A Story of America in Its First Age of Terror* (Oxford: Oxford University Press, 2009), 67.

81. "Signal Victory," *The Iron Trade Review* 40 (February 7, 1907): 230.

82. Ibid.

83. Ibid.

84. "News of the Labor World," *Illustrated Buffalo Express*, July 1, 1906, 20; and "Striking Molders Go Back to Work," *Buffalo Courier*, July 1, 1906, 32.

85. On the Buffalo Forge Company's relationship with the global economy, see Hill, *Municipality of Buffalo*, 804; Buffalo Forge Company, *Illustrated Catalogue of Buffalo Mechanical Draft Apparatus* (Buffalo, 1903); and Henry W. Wendt, *"Buffalo Forge" (1877–1952): World-Wide Name in Industrial Equipment* (Princeton, N.J.: Princeton University Press, 1952). For a listing of the individuals on the NFA's administrative council, see NFA, *Members* (October 1906), 30–31. Wendt did well in the immediate post-strike period. He shipped large

numbers of forges to Japan. See "American Forges for Japan," *Manufacturers' Record* 38 (September 6, 1906): 198.

86. *Review* 3 (July 1906): 10.

87. Later leaders of the Buffalo Forge Company, including Wendt's son, offered a highly misleading account of the history of labor-management relations at the company during a meeting of the Newcomen Society in 1952. In his words, "in nearly three-quarters of a century we have had practically no labor troubles." Henry W. Wendt, *"Buffalo Forge" (1877–1952): World-Wide Name in Industrial Equipment* (Princeton, N.J.: Princeton University Press, 1952), 16.

88. "Thousand Employes of a Single Firm," *Buffalo Enquirer*, August 17, 1906, 6.

89. "Some Shops Open on 'Open-Shop' Principle," *Buffalo Evening Times*, June 12, 1906, 4; and "The Iron Molders' Strike," 1933.

90. "The Iron Molders' Strike," *The Iron Age* 77 (June 14, 1906): 1933. In some ways, this accommodation resembles the labor relations policies adopted by San Francisco's propriety capitalists around the same time. Responding to a powerful labor movement, both in work-places and in the political arena, San Francisco's businessmen apparently rejected the open-shop system for what sociologist Jeffrey Haydu calls "practical corporatism." Haydu explains that these "employers neither liked unions nor regarded them as having some fundamental right to exist. Nevertheless, most employers viewed them as natural expressions of worker interests and as organizations with whom they had to do business." See Haydu, *Citizen Employers: Business Communities and Labor in Cincinnati and San Francisco* (Ithaca, N.Y.: Cornell University Press, 2008), 121–22. But the situation in Buffalo does not neatly fit his model. Unlike San Francisco's propriety capitalists, Buffalo's accommodating employers pro-claimed allegiance to the open-shop idea, even though, unlike Wendt, Letchworth, and Hub-bell, they did not follow Briggs's advice meticulously. They had to give up something—in this case more money than they were initially comfortable with—for their month-long headaches to go away. But by publicly supporting the open-shop principle, they showed they were faithful team players, which allowed them to save face. For the compromisers, life was not perfect, but it was good enough. For other examples of what one might call managerial realism, see Andrew Wender Cohen, "Resisting Judgment," *Labor: Studies in Working-Class History of the Americas* 10 (Winter 2013): 98.

91. "News of the Labor World," *Illustrated Buffalo Express*, July 1, 1906, 20.

92. "Buffalo Strike Nearly Over," *Review* 3 (September 1906): 1.

93. "Buffalo, New York," *Review* 3 (August 1906): 3.

94. Max S. Hayes, "The World of Labor," *International Socialist Review* 7 (November 1906): 313.

95. "Banner Year," *The Iron Trade Review* 40 (January 17, 1907): 96.

96. "Signal Victory," *The Iron Trade Review* 40 (February 7, 1907): 230.

97. William H. Gatwick, "Report of Annual Meeting," *Annual Report of the Chamber of Commerce of Buffalo* (1907): 14.

98. "'Boost Buffalo,' Says the Button," *Buffalo Enquirer*, August 3, 1906, 1. F. Howard Mason had impeccable credentials as an antiunion activist. In 1902 and 1903, Mason cam-paigned against the proposed eight-hour law for government workers in front of the Congres-sional Committee on Education and Labor in Washington. At this time, Mason collaborated with several other prominent open-shop proponents, including Dayton's John Kirby, NAM's

Marshall Cushing, and NMTA's Du Brul. Mason insisted the "Government does not come in and interfere with a man in the enjoyment of his privileges." See *Hearings Before the Committee on Education and Labor of the United States Senate, First Session Fifty-Seventh Congress* (Washington, D.C.: GPO, 1903): 269.

99. "Heavy Castings from Buffalo," *Review* 4 (May 1907): 5.

100. "Buffalo," *Review* 4 (January 1907): 38–39.

101. Otis Briggs, "National Founders' Association Convention," *The Iron Trade Review* 39 (November 22, 1906): 83.

102. "Buffalo," 38–39.

103. The union had a membership of 51,588 in the beginning of the year. See James E. Cebula, *The Glory and Despair of Challenge and Change: A History of the Molders Union* (Cincinnati: International Molders and Allied Workers Union, AFL-CIO-CLC, 1976), 36.

104. NFA, "Molders' Union Calls Off Last Big Strike," *Square Deal* 3 (June 1908): 70.

105. Quoted in "National Founders' Association Conference," *The Iron Trade Review* 39 (November 22, 1906): 27.

106. "Another Lift for McKinley," *Buffalo Evening News*, January 10, 1902, 1. Buffalo was one of a number of places where businessmen led efforts to construct McKinley monuments. The first was built in Muskegon, Michigan in 1902. Toledo followed in 1903. On the McKinley statue-building craze, see Charles S. Olcott, *William McKinley* (Boston: Houghton Mifflin, 1916), 389–90.

107. On Buffalo's McKinley monument, see Mark Goldman, *City on the Edge, Buffalo, New York* (Amherst, N.Y.: Prometheus, 2007), 58.

108. Charles Evans Hughes, *Addresses of Charles Evans Hughes* (New York: Putnam's, 1916), 253–54.

109. Ibid.

Chapter 5. Making the "City of Prosperity": The Poetry of Industrial Harmony in Worcester

1. "Address of the Hon. J. H. Walker," *Worcester Magazine* 6 (July 1903): 14–17. Walker had presented himself as a defender of nonunionists and a law-and-order advocate for decades. Speaking one year after the great 1877 railroad strike, he stated, "All combination of men to prevent any other men from doing anything, in competition with themselves, are clear violations of the fundamental law of liberty and of right. Such action endangers the life, abridges the liberty, and destroys the happiness of the men combined against, and should meet condign punishment, sure and without mercy." *Common Sense Views on Political Economy, Capital, Labor, Socialism: Statements of J. H. Walker of Worcester, Mass. to the Congressional Labor Committee* (New York: American News, 1878), 43. Walker is perhaps best known as a proponent of protective tariffs. See Walker, *The Moral Aspect of a Protective Tariff: How It Helps the Wage Worker and Farmer* (Worcester, Mass.: Goddard Press, 1888).

2. "Employer and Employed," *Worcester Magazine* 7 (January 1904): 3.

3. On the city's ethnic diversity, see Roy Rosenzweig, *Eight Hours for What We Will: Workers and Leisure in an Industrial City, 1870–1920* (Cambridge: Cambridge University Press, 1983), 17–18.

4. Worcester was home to over 24 machine tool-making industries in 1900. On Worcester's business, see Charles G. Washburn, *Industrial Worcester* (Worcester, Mass.: Davis Press, 1917). On Worcester's contribution to the Second Industrial Revolution, see Philip Scranton,

Endless Novelty Specialty Production and American Industrialization, 1865–1925 (Princeton, N.J.: Princeton University Press, 1997). On mergers, see Naomi R. Lamoreaux, *The Great Merger Movement in American Business* (Cambridge: Cambridge University Press, 1985).

5. The founders of some technical schools, including the Georgia Institute of Technology, looked to WPI as a model to emulate. See James E. Brittain and Robert C. McMath, Jr., "Engineers and the New South Creed: The Formation and Early Development of Georgia Tech," *Technology and Culture* 18 (April 1977): 174–201.

6. Charles Washburn, "Technical Education in Relation to Industrial Development," *Science* 24 (July 27, 1906): 97–112; George Alden, "The Washburn Shops of the Worcester Polytechnic Institute," *Journal of the Worcester Polytechnic Institute* 19 (1915): 391–94; Herbert Foster Taylor, *Seventy Years of the Worcester Polytechnic Institute* (Worcester, Mass.: Davis Press, 1937); and Scranton, *Endless Novelty*, 67. On the relationship between early manufacturers and the city's civic institutions, see Joshua S. Chasan, "Civilizing Worcester: The Creation of Institutional and Cultural Order, Worcester, Massachusetts, 1848–1876" (Ph.D. dissertation, University of Pittsburgh, 1974).

7. Donald Tulloch, *Worcester: City of Prosperity: Sixteenth Annual Convention of the National Metal Trades Association* (Worcester, Mass.: Commonwealth Press, 1914), 156.

8. Monte A. Calvert, *The Mechanical Engineer in America, 1830–1910: Professional Cultures in Conflict* (Baltimore: Johns Hopkins University Press, 1967), 75. For a discussion of the links between engineering schools and big business, see David F. Noble, *America by Design: Science, Technology, and the Rise of Corporate Capitalism* (Oxford: Oxford University Press, 1979).

9. "Machinist Troubles at Worcester," *Iron Age* 69 (May 22, 1902): 16.

10. "The Blaisdell Drill," advertisement in *American Machinist* 27 (August 4, 1904), 95. Born in 1866, Hildreth, who inherited partial ownership of the Blaisdell Company because of his father's position, was a clubby figure active in many organizations. He played a leadership role in the city's Republican Party, which, in Worcester, could point to a proud history of late antebellum antislavery advocacy. The city's Republican Party continued to, in the words of historian Janette Thomas Greenwood, wave "'the bloody shirt' of the Civil War through the late nineteenth century to win elections." Republican mayoral candidates were mostly successful, winning twenty-nine of thirty-five elections in the years 1885–1919. One of these successful candidates was Hildreth's father, Samuel, Worcester's mayor for a year, 1883–84. Vermont-born Samuel Hildreth also served on the WPI Board of Trustees during his mayoral term. Charles Hildreth served in the Massachusetts state militia from 1892 to 1896. For the late nineteenth-century Republican Party in Worcester, see Rosenzweig, *Eight Hours for What We Will*, 19; Timothy J. Meagher, *Inventing Irish America: Generation, Class, and Ethnic identity in a New England City, 1880–1928* (Notre Dame, Ind.: University of Notre Dame Press, 2001), 133–200; and Janette Thomas Greenwood, *First Fruits of Freedom: The Migration of Former Slaves and Their Search for Equality in Worcester, Massachusetts, 1862–1900* (Chapel Hill: University of North Carolina Press, 2009), 14, 155.

11. The workplaces hit by the strike were medium-sized. Prentice, which employed roughly 270 mechanics, was especially important. According to the Worcester Chamber of Commerce, it was one of the nation's largest manufacturers of machine tools. See "Among Worcester Manufacturers," *Worcester Magazine* 5 (April 1902): 146. Also see *Illustrated History of the Central Labor Union and the Building Trades Council of Worcester and Vicinity* (Worcester: Central Labor Union and the Building Trades Council of Worcester, Mass., 1899), 82–83.

12. "Employers Ready," *Worcester Telegram*, May 20, 1902, 2.

13. "Employers Jubilant!" *Worcester Telegram*, May 21, 1902, 1.

14. The IAM newspaper described some of the Cincinnati Metal Trades Association's techniques. Here employers sent letters to unemployed men, promising them financial "bonuses" and "protection" to serve as strikebreakers. See "Sanctum Notes," *Machinists' Monthly Journal* 13 (August 1908): 536. For more on Cincinnati, see Jeffrey Haydu, *Citizen Employers: Business Communities and Labor in Cincinnati and San Francisco, 1870–1916* (Ithaca, N.Y.: Cornell University Press, 2008), 35–60, 91–111, 145–77. The IAM staged protests in numerous cities in 1901, but Worcester's members did not participate. See Bruce Cohen, "Lords of Capital and Knights of Labor," *Historical Journal of Massachusetts* 29 (Winter 2001): 95.

15. "Latest Strike News from Worcester," *Iron Age* 69 (May 22, 1902): 32.

16. "Employers Jubilant!," 1.

17. "Employers Ready," 2; and "Worcester Machinists' Strike," *The Iron Trade Review* 35 (May 29, 1902): 26.

18. "Neither Side Claims Decided Advantage," *Worcester Telegram*, May 22, 1902, 1.

19. "Help for Strikers," *Worcester Telegram*, June 9, 1902, 2.

20. "Say Roll Call Will Show 300 Men Have Left Work!" *Worcester Telegram*, May 21, 1902, 1.

21. "Neither Side Claims Decided Advantage," 1; "Latest Strike News from Worcester," *Iron Age* 69 (May 22, 1902): 32; and "The Worcester Machinists' Strike," *Iron Age* 69 (May 29, 1902): 11.

22. "More Pickets Put Out," *Worcester Telegram*, May 29, 1902, 12.

23. "Fifth Vice President Landers' Report," *Machinists' Monthly Journal* 14 (June 1902): 353.

24. "Machinists Get Pay Envelopes," *Worcester Telegram*, May 23, 1902, 2. On injunctions, see "Injunction by the Court," *Worcester Telegram*, July 1, 1902, 12.

25. Quoted in "Labor Man Is Wise," *Worcester Telegram*, June 6, 1902, 5.

26. "Signs of a Break," *Worcester Telegram*, June 11, 1902, 2.

27. "Nineteen Strikers Back," *Worcester Telegram*, June 27, 1902, 2; "Return to Prentice Co.," *Worcester Telegram*, July 8, 1902, 7.

28. "Employers Jubilant!" 1.

29. "Work for Outsiders," *Worcester Telegram*, June 12, 1902, 4.

30. "Commissioner's Report," *Bulletin of the National Metal Trades Association* 2 (July 1903): 466.

31. "Worcester Machinists' Strike Declared Off," *The Iron Trade Review* 35 (July 17, 1902): 51; "Promise to go to Work," *Worcester Telegram*, June 10, 1902, 5; and "Strike of Machinists' Union Declared Off!," *Worcester Telegram*, July 10, 1902, 1.

32. Quoted in "Worcester Industrial Notes," *Iron Age* 70 (July 17, 1902): 7.

33. "Manufacturers Jubilant," *Worcester Telegram*, July 10, 1902, 1. Two years later, in an advertisement, Blaisdell Drill Company announced the tool "is the result of 40 years' intelligent scientific experiment and endeavor to perfect a drill." These drills, used in machine shops throughout the nation, were apparently the very best: "Will you risk getting an inferior machine?" "The Blaisdell Drill," advertisement in *American Machinist* 27 (August 4, 1904): 95.

34. Quoted in "Cincinnati Metal Trades, Dinner," *The Iron Trade Review* 37 (January 21, 1904): 43.

35. Clarence E. Bonnett, *Employers' Association in the United States: A Study of Typical Associations* (New York: The Macmillan Company, 1922), 105.

36. Bonnett, *Employers' Association*, 112. For a description of labor spy activities, see Sidney Howard, *The Labor Spy* (New York: Republic Publications, 1924).

37. "A Matter of Business," *Bulletin of the National Metal Trades Association* 3 (January 1904): 84.

38. Robert Wuest, *Industrial Betterment Activities of the National Metal Trades Association* (pamphlet, n.p., 1912), 8, 15.

39. Ibid., 4.

40. A. E. Corbin, "The New England Districts," *Bulletin of the National Metal Trades Association* 3 (February 1904): 73.

41. Howell Harris, *Bloodless Victories: The Rise and Fall of the Open-shop in the Philadelphia Metal Trades, 1890–1940* (Cambridge: Cambridge University Press, 2000), 74.

42. Charles E. Hildreth, "Worcester Metal Trades Association," *Bulletin of the National Metal Trades Association* 2 (November 1903): 884–85. Perhaps some participants held the view, articulated by Marc C. Carnes with respect to nineteenth-century fraternal associations, that the "sociological benefits of membership outweighed the economic." See Carnes, *Secret Ritual and Manhood in Victorian America* (New Haven, Conn.: Yale University Press, 1989), 2.

43. Hildreth, "Worcester Metal Trades Association," *Bulletin of the National Metal Trades Association*.

44. Charles Perkins Adams, "The Worcester Labor Bureau," *Bulletin of the National Metal Trades Association* 3 (January 1904): 32–33.

45. Ibid., 33.

46. Clarence Hobbs, "Aims and Objects of the Labor Bureau," *Bulletin of the National Metal Trades Association* 2 (November 1903): 842–43.

47. Hastings followed legal developments closely, fully aware that Massachusetts laws, like those in most states, provided employers with protections against labor unrest. See "Massachusetts Law on Picketing: When Injunctions May be Had," *American Industries* 3 (January 16, 1905): 6. On Hastings's background, see Ellery Bicknell Crane, *Historic Homes and Institutions and Genealogical and Personal Memoirs of Worcester County Massachusetts,* (New York: Lewis Publishing, 1907), 510.

48. Herman S. Hastings, "The Worcester (Mass) Labor Bureau," *Bulletin of the National Metal Trades Association* 3 (November 1904): 510.

49. "The Worcester Labor Bureau," *Iron Age* 72 (July 9, 1903): 10.

50. "Changes in the Relations of Employers and Employes in 1904," *The Iron Trade Review* 38 (January 19, 1905): 48.

51. On Whitin, see Thomas Navin, *The Whitin Machine Works Since 1831: A Textile Machinery Company in an Industrial Village* (Cambridge, Mass.: Harvard University Press, 1950).

52. Hastings, "The Worcester (Mass) Labor Bureau," 510.

53. Ibid.

54. 'The Worcester Labor Bureau.' *Bulletin of the National Metal Trades Association* 3 (August 1904): 352–57.

55. "Metal Trades Association Notes," *The Iron Trade Review* 38 (January 26, 1905): 47. Victoria Employers had a proud history of union-fighting. See Norman F. Dufty, "Employers' Associations in Australia," in *Employers' Associations and Industrial Relations: A Comparative Study*, ed. John P. Windmuller (Oxford: Oxford University Press, 1984), 117–18.

56. "Worcester Metal Trades," *The Iron Trade Review* 39 (May 3, 1906): 15.

57. Hastings became commissioner of the United Metal Trades Association of the Pacific Coast in 1909. See "Foundry Day," *The Iron Trade Review* 45 (September 16, 1909): 496.

58. NMTA, *Synopsis of Proceedings of the Sixteenth Annual Convention* (New York: N. P., 1914): 47–48.

59. On Tulloch's involvement in these organizations, see *Worcester Directory* (Worcester: Drew, Allis, and Company, 1908–20); Charles Nutt, *History of Worcester and Its People* (New York: Lewis Historical, 1919), 780.

60. Tulloch dedicated the proceeds of the book "to the British born women of Worcester." See Donald Tulloch, *Songs and Poems of the Great World War* (Worcester: Davis Press, 1915).

61. "Worcester Firms Stand Alone in Refusal to Recognize Employees," *Labor News*, November 13, 1915, 1.

62. Quoted in "Tulloch Is Target," *Labor News*, May 29, 1931, 7. Anecdotal reports suggest that the city's workers genuinely feared the NMTA's widespread power. Evidence suggests that Tulloch was highly zealous in his use of the blacklist, and some were unafraid to label him a malicious union buster. Hard feelings about Tulloch were revisited in the 1930s when some city politicians proposed that Tulloch serve on the city's Parks and Recreation Commission. *Labor News* carried several melodramatic stories about men who were forced to leave the county in order to earn money to feed their families. One writer called Tulloch "the shining light in the local metal trades industry." See "Testimony of Labor Spy Hearings Directed Here," *Labor News*, January 29, 1937, 4.

63. "A Fifty-Hour Week," *Fitchburg Sentinel*, May 21, 1907, 1.

64. "Out-Door Demonstration," *Fitchburg Sentinel*, July 19, 1907, 3.

65. *Machinists' Monthly Journal* 19 (August 1907): 739.

66. Quoted in "Report of Fourth Vice President Wilson," *Machinists' Monthly Journal* 19 (September 1907): 881.

67. "Declare for Open-Shop," *Fitchburg Sentinel*, May 25, 1907, 1.

68. "No Strike Order Yet," *Fitchburg Sentinel*, June 3, 1907, 1.

69. "Three Weeks Today," *Fitchburg Sentinel*, July 29, 1907, 1. The Fitchburg strike was one of a number of conflicts that the NMTA helped defeat. See "Commissioner Wuest's Report," *The Iron Trade Review* 41 (April 2, 1908): 624. This was not Wuest's first visit to Worcester County. He had met with Worcester's employers shortly after they established a branch. See "Work of the Metal Trades Association," *The Iron Trade Review* 36 (December 10, 1903): 40.

70. "Report of Fourth Vice President Wilson," *Machinists' Monthly Journal* 20 (January 1908): 37.

71. "Object to Office," *Fitchburg Sentinel*, July 13, 1907, 1, 3. Also see "Donald Tulloch," *Labor News*, November 13, 1915, 4.

72. "Address of the Hon. J. H. Walker," *Worcester Magazine* 6 (July 1903): 14.

73. On the NMTA's support for "welfare work," see Wuest, *Industrial Betterment Activities*.

74. This line of argument is laid out nicely in Howard Gitelman, "Welfare Capitalism Reconsidered," *Labor History* 33 (Winter 1992): 5–31. See also William Littmann, "Designing Obedience: The Architecture and landscape of Welfare Capitalism, 1880–1930," *International Labor and Working Class History* 53 (Spring 1998): 88–112; Brian Kelly, *Race, Class, and Power in the Alabama Coalfields* (Urbana: University of Illinois Press, 2001), 60–64; and Howell J. Harris, "Industrial Paternalism and Welfare Capitalism: 'Where's the Beef?' or 'Show Me the Money!'" in *Public and Private in American History: State Family, Subjectivity in the Twentieth Century*, ed. R. Baritono, D. Frezza, A. Lorini, M. Vaudagna, and E. Vezzosi (Turin: Otto Editore, 2003), 459–82.

75. Quoted in "The Spirit that Saves Trouble," *Boston Evening Transcript*, June 11, 1904, 18. The statement was widely republished. "Cause of Strikes," *Commons* 9 (October 1904): 494; and "Mistakes of Short-Sighted Employers," *Public Policy* 12 (January 14, 1905): 21.

76. Leon P. Alford, "The Present State of the Art of Industrial Management," *Journal of the Worcester Polytechnic Institute* 16 (January 1913): 99.

77. George I. Alden, "Modern Socialism," *Worcester Magazine* 10 (January 1907): 38–39. Organized employers were no strangers to Carnegie's workplace policies. On Carnegie's managerial philosophy, see "Andrew Carnegie on Co-Operation," *American Industries* 2 (May 15, 1903): 1. On Alden's relationship to WPI, see "George Ira Alden," *Journal of the Worcester Polytechnic Institute* 29 (November 1926): 13–15. By the time Alden made these comments, the Square Deal meant more than open-shop workplaces. It also signified workplaces that promoted welfare work. See O. M. Becker, "The Square Deal in Works Management," *Engineering Magazine* 30 (February 1906): 660–87.

78. Quoted in Taylor, *Seventy Years of the Worcester Polytechnic Institute*, 249. Hollis's comments were hardly original. Anti-union activists regularly criticized both sides for failing to uphold the "golden rule." See "When the Golden Rule is Dead Among Employes and Employers," *American Industries* 5 (May 1, 1907): 12.

79. NMTA, *Synopsis of Proceedings of the Sixteenth Annual Convention*, 12.

80. Donald Tulloch, *Worcester: City of Prosperity: Sixteenth Annual Convention of the National Metal Trades Association* (Worcester, Mass.: Commonwealth Press, 1914).

81. Ibid., 3.

82. "Worcester—A Convention City," *Worcester Magazine* 17 (May 1914): 122.

83. On the Ludlow massacre and the reforms it sparked, see Howard Gitelman, *The Legacy of the Ludlow Massacre: A Chapter in American Industrial Relations* (Philadelphia: University of Pennsylvania Press, 1988); Howard Zinn, "The Colorado Coal Strike, 1913–14," in *Three Strikes: Miners, Musicians, Salesgirls and the Fighting Spirit of Labor's Last Century*, ed. Howard Zinn, Dana Frank, and Robin D. G. Kelley (Boston: Beacon, 2001), 5–56; Thomas G. Andrews, *Killing for Coal: America's Deadliest Labor War* (Cambridge, Mass.: Harvard University Press, 2008), 1–19; and Jonathan H. Rees, *Representation and Rebellion: The Rockefeller Plan at the Colorado Fuel and Iron Company, 1914–1942* (Boulder: University of Colorado Press, 2010).

84. For a comprehensive list of attendees, see NMTA, *Synopsis of Proceedings of the Sixteenth Annual Convention*, 274–81. On Morgan and Schwacke, see Harris, *Bloodless Victories*. On Laughlin's speech, see NMTA, *Synopsis of Proceedings of Sixteenth Annual Convention*, 242. On Merritt's speech and useful biographical information on this colorful figure, see Daniel R. Ernst, *Lawyers Against Labor: From Individual Rights to Corporate Liberalism* (Urbana: University of Illinois Press, 1995), 229–30.

85. "Audience Cheers at News from Mexico," *Worcester Telegram*, April 22, 1914, 8. On the U.S. invasion of Veracruz, see Robert E. Quirk, *An Affair of Honor: Woodrow Wilson and the Occupation of Veracruz* (Lexington: University Press of Kentucky, 1962); and Thomas F. O'Brien, *The Revolutionary Mission: American Enterprise in Latin America, 1900–1945* (Cambridge: Cambridge University Press, 1996), 264.

86. Donald Tulloch, *Worcester: City of Prosperity: Sixteenth Annual Convention of the National Metal Trades Association* (Worcester, Mass.: Commonwealth, 1914), 14.

87. Ibid., 218.

88. Ibid.

89. Ibid.

90. Ibid.

91. Ibid., 14.

92. Ibid., 298.

93. Ibid., 14.

94. On Norton's extensive programs, see "Helps in the Process of Accident Prevention," *Safety Engineering* 29 (March 1915): 281–82; and Charles Cheape, *Family Firm to Modern Multinational: Norton Company, A New England Enterprise* (Cambridge, Mass.: Harvard University Press, 1985), 131–40.

95. Rice, Barton and Fales, *A Line of Men One Hundred Years Long* (Worcester, Mass.: Rice, Barton and Fales, 1937), 58.

96. Tulloch, *Worcester*, 127. Rice, Barton, and Fales had confronted worker demands that it establish a closed shop in 1902. As the *Iron Age* explained, management remained adamant that it would recognize workers as individuals, "but not as a union." See "Worcester Manufacturing Interests," *Iron Age* 70 (September 25, 1902): 26.

97. Frances Green, "How the Rug Weavers Came to South Worcester," *Worcester Telegram*, July 2, 1982, 12–15.

98. "Worcester—A Convention City," 122.

99. "Enlarged Plant of the Royal Worcester Corset Company," *Worcester Magazine* 19 (January 1912): 86; Ida M. Tarbell, *New Ideals in Business* (New York: Macmillan, 1917), 104; Orra L. Stone, *History of Massachusetts Industries* (Boston: S. J. Clarke, 1930), 1734; and Albert B. Southwick, "David Hale Fanning Had His Own Brand of Feminism," *Worcester Telegram and Gazette*, January 20, 2002, C3.

100. "Presentation of Loving-Cup to David Hale Fanning," *Worcester Magazine* 15 (June 1911): 575–76; Tulloch, *Worcester*, 138.

101. Walter Gordon Merritt, "New Ideas in Industrial Organization," *Iron Age* 103 (June 19, 1919): 1627.

102. "Iron Molders Strike," *Labor World*, July 17, 1915, 3. Unsurprisingly, the company's 1937 hundred-year memorial book, *A Line of Men One Hundred Years Long*, makes no mention of any labor unrest.

103. "5000 Machinists Want Eight Hour Work Day," *Labor News*, September 25, 1915, 1, 8; "5,000 Men Strike in Four Big Cities," *New York Tribune*, September 28, 1915, 3; "Machinists Have Moral and Financial Backing of C.L.U.," *Labor News*, October 2, 1915, 18; and "Worcester's Open-Shoppers," *Labor News*, October 16, 1915, 4. Several scholars have written about this strike. See William Zeuch, "An Investigation of the Metal Trades Strike of Worcester, 1915" (MA thesis, Clark University, 1916); and Bruce Cohen, "The Worcester Machinist Strike of 1915," *Historical Journal of Massachusetts* 16 (1988): 154–71.

104. "Invitation by Mayor," *Worcester Telegram*, September 28, 1915, 4. The struggle in Worcester was part of a broader IAM campaign to increase membership and win the eight-hour day for machinists. Machine tool factory managers demanded increased productivity because of order increases due to the war in Europe. See "Unions Hold off Munitions Strike," *New York Times*, August 9, 1915, 1; and Cecelia Bucki, *Bridgeport's Socialist New Deal, 1915–36* (Urbana: University of Illinois Press, 2001), 21–29.

105. Kelly, *Race, Class, and Power*, 50–80.

106. For a discussion of 'yellow-dog' contracts, see Daniel R. Ernst, "The Yellow-Dog Contract and Liberal Reform, 1917–1932," *Labor History* 30 (Spring 1989): 251–74; and David Brody, *Labor Embattled: History, Power, Rights* (Urbana: University of Illinois Press, 2005), 127–28.

107. For more on Norton's union-breaking efforts, see Charles Cheape, *Family Firm to Modern Multinational: Norton Company, A New England Enterprise* (Cambridge, Mass.: Harvard University Press, 1985), 127; and Bruce Cohen, "From Norton to Saint-Gobain, 1885–2006: Grinding Labor Down," *Historical Journal of Massachusetts* 34 (Summer 2006): 91–92.

108. "5000 Machinists Want Eight Hour Work Day," 1, 8. On Newton, see Stone, *History of Massachusetts Industries*, 1746.

109. "Invitation by Mayor," *Worcester Telegram*, September 28, 1915, 1.

110. "Blacklist Favorite Weapon of Worcester Employers," *Labor News*, October 16, 1915, 8.

111. "Report of Organizer Jos. W. Barker," *Machinists' Monthly Journal* 28 (August 1916): 815.

112. "Not Told of Strike," *Worcester Telegram*, November 25, 1915, 14.

113. Quoted in "All Trade Unionists Urged to Give $1 a Week to Strikers," *Worcester Telegram*, September 30, 1915, 2.

114. "Cannot and Will Not Grant Eight-Hour Day," *Worcester Telegram*, September 27, 1915, 1.

115. "Drop Probe and Give Organizer Passports," *Worcester Telegram*, October 20, 1915, 2.

116. On the board's limits, see Cohen, "The Worcester Machinist Strike of 1915"; and "State Probe Fails to Adjust Strikes," *Worcester Telegram*, October 21, 1915, 1.

117. The city's employers appeared more uncompromising than employers elsewhere. A labor journalist noted that in Springfield, unlike Worcester, "nearly every machine manufacturer has granted the eight-hour day and an increase in wages." See "Worcester Firms Stand Alone in Refusal to Recognize Employees," 1.

118. "Report of Board Member Robt. Fechner," *Machinists' Monthly Journal* 27 (December 1915): 1124.

119. Quoted in "No Move Taken for Adjustment of Strike," *Worcester Telegram*, October 14, 1915, 5.

120. "Iron Molders' Strike Ends," *Labor Advocate*, January 29, 1916, 6. Although the union won this particular conflict, its members continued to face harassment from management. Shortly after the settlement, union spokespersons reported that a Rice, Barton, and Fales foreman "is discriminating against our members." See "Grievances," *Proceedings of the Twenty-Fifth Session of the International Molders' Union of North America Held in Rochester, N. Y., Sept. 19th to Sept. 28th (incl.) 1917* (Cincinnati: Rosenthal, 1917): 42.

121. "Invitation by Mayor," *Worcester Telegram*, September 28, 1915, 4.

122. See Meagher, *Inventing Irish America*, 279.

Chapter 6. "A Solid South for the Open Shop": N. F. Thompson and the Labor Solution

1. *Report of the US Industrial Commission on the Relations and Conditions of Capital and Labor Employed in Manufactures and General Business, Including Testimony So Far as Taken November 1, 1900, and Digest of Testimony* 7 (Washington: Government Printing Office, 1901), 756; and "Attack on Labor Unions," *New York Times*, June 13, 1900, 9. The commission took testimony from members of both labor and capital. It was not the first time the government took an active interest in the labor problem. The first such congressional investigation was held in 1883. See Amy Dru Stanley, *From Bondage to Contract: Wage Labor, Marriage, and the Market in the Age of Slave Emancipation* (Cambridge: Cambridge University Press, 1998), 70–71.

2. *Report of the US Industrial Commission*, 761.

3. Ibid., 757.

4. Ibid., 96.

5. Ibid., 756.

6. Ibid., 774–75.

7. Ibid., 775. This encounter occurred in Louisville in the early to mid-1870s, when he edited the temperance journal *Riverside Weekly*.

8. "Arbitration, Compulsory and Other," *Nation* 70 (June 21, 1900): 471. For an analysis of the *Nation*'s early decades, see Mark Koerner, "The Menace of Labor: Anti-Union Thought in the Progressive Era, 1901–1917" (Ph.D. dissertation, University of Wisconsin, Madison, 1995), 29.

9. *Machinists' Monthly Journal* 12 (July 1900): 6.

10. N. F. Thompson, "The Trust Question," *Weekly Mercury*, July 11, 1900, 8.

11. Ibid.

12. Ibid. Thompson was hardly alone in linking southern development to progress. See K. Stephen Prince, *Stories of the South: Race and Reconstruction of Southern Identity, 1865–1915* (Chapel Hill: University of North Carolina Press, 2014), 104–9.

13. Some scholars, including Bruce J. Shulman, have argued that anti-unionism "replaced" Jim Crow and racism as one of the South defining features in the 1970s. Shulman, *From Cotton Belt to Sunbelt: Federal Policy, Economic Development, and the Transformation of the South, 1938–1980* (Oxford: Oxford University Press, 1991), 162. Ira Katznelson goes back further than Shulman, arguing that racist politicians, responding to the growth of union density during World War II, began backing antiunion laws like the 1947 Taft-Hartley Act. Prioritizing race and political institutions over class, Katznelson argues that "For southern legislators, labor had become race." Katznelson, *Fear Itself: The New Deal and the Origins of Our Time* (New York: Liveright, 2013), 398. This chapter demonstrates that antiunionism, complementing Jim Crow-style racism, emerged as a central factor in the region's development decades before the post-World War II years.

14. The number comes from Fred Arthur Bailey, *Class and Tennessee's Confederate Generation* (Chapel Hill: University of North Carolina Press, 1987), 2.

15. *Report of the U.S. Industrial Commission*, 766. By highlighting examples of antebellum slavery, this chapter addresses Marcel van der Linden's call to engage seriously with the management of "unfree labor." See van der Linden, "Re-Constructing the Origins of Modern

Labor Management," *Labor History* 51 (November 2010): 509–22. Harry Braverman makes a similar point. Braverman, *Labor and Monopoly Capital: The Degradation of Work in the Twentieth Century* (1974; New York: Monthly Review Press, 1998), 44.

16. Rosanne Currarino suggests the labor question "became a question during the depression of the 1870s." See Currarino, *The Labor Question in America: Economic Democracy in the Gilded Age* (Urbana: University of Illinois Press, 2011), 11.

17. W. E. B. Du Bois, *Black Reconstruction in America: An Essay Toward a History of the Part Which Black Folk Played in the Attempt to Reconstruct Democracy in America, 1860–1880* (1935; New York: Russell and Russell, 1963), 55–83. Bruce Levine, sympathetic to Du Bois's overall interpretation, insists this uprising was hardly "an immediate and united slave rebellion." See Levine, *The Fall of the House of Dixie: The Civil War and the Social Revolution That Transformed the South* (New York: Random House, 2013), 91. 20,000 of Tennessee's slaves joined the Union army in 1863. See James Oakes, *Freedom National: The Destruction of Slavery in the United States, 1861–1865* (New York: Norton, 2013), 388. For a forceful defense of Du Bois's interpretation, see David Williams, *I Freed Myself: African American Self-Emancipation in the Civil War Era* (Cambridge: Cambridge University Press, 2014); and David R. Roediger, *Seizing Freedom: Slave Emancipation and Liberty for All* (London: Verso, 2014).

18. Quoted in "Anti-Lynching Leagues," *Weekly Mercury*, August 9, 1899, 4.

19. John Cimprich, *Slavery's End in Tennessee, 1861–1865* (Tuscaloosa: University of Alabama Press, 1985), 46; also see Stephen V. Ash, *Middle Tennessee Society Transformed, 1860–1870* (Baton Rouge: Louisiana State University Press, 1988), 106–142.

20. On these speeches, see *The Democratic Speakers Hand-Book: Containing Every Thing Necessary of the Defense of The National Democracy in the Coming Presidential Campaign, and for the Assault of The Radical Enemies of the Country and its Constitution* (Cincinnati: Miami Print and Publishing, 1868), 201.

21. *Biographical and Portrait Cyclopedia of Cambria County, Pennsylvania: Comprising About Five Hundred Sketches of the Prominent and Representative Citizens of the County* (Philadelphia: Union Publishing, 1896), 439; and John Witherspoon DuBose, *Jefferson County and Birmingham, Alabama: Historical and Biographical* (Birmingham, Ala.: Temple and Smith, 1887), 505.

22. After his senatorial career, which lasted from 1871 to 1877, Cooper invested in a silver mining operation in Mexico. He was president of the El Cuervo Mining Company in the mineral rich state of Sinaloa. In 1884, two Mexican robbers in the city of Culiacan killed the former senator. For a discussion of the expansion of mining in Sinaloa, see "Progress in Science and the Arts," *Engineering and Mining Journal* 31 (April 30, 1881): 303–4; and John R. Flippin, *Sketches from the Mountains of Mexico* (Cincinnati: Standard Publishing, 1889), 230.

23. J. Q. T., "From the South," *New York Times*, September 18, 1865, 8.

24. "The Ku-Klux and the Election," *(Shelbyville) Republican*, November 13, 1868, 3.

25. Eric Foner, *Reconstruction: America's Unfinished Revolution, 1863–1877* (New York: Harper and Row, 1988), 428. Foner's analysis of the class position and interests of Klansmen reinforces one of Richard Maxwell Brown's broader assessments of nineteenth century vigilante organizations. According to Brown, "The vigilante leaders were drawn from the upper level of the community." See Brown, "The History of Vigilantism in America," in *Vigilante Politics*, ed. H. Jon Rosenbaum and Peter C. Sederberg (Philadelphia: University of Pennsylvania Press, 1976), 89. Historian Scott Reynolds Nelson's discussion of the relationships between

Klan leaders and southern railroads also illustrates the important roles played by economically privileged whites. Nelson, *Iron Confederates: Southern Railways, Klan Violence, and Reconstruction* (Chapel Hill: University of North Carolina Press, 1999), 106–7. Complementing Foner and Nelson, Steven Hahn has pointed out that "The leaders generally had held rank in the army (and probably in the militia) and were connected to families of local prominence." Hahn, *A Nation Under Our Feet: Black Political Struggles in the Rural South from Slavery to the Great Migration* (Cambridge, Mass.: Harvard University Press, 2003), 270. Michael W. Fitzgerald's account stresses the pre-war financially privileged position of the men who joined the Klan: "In examining the prewar backgrounds of those reported or indicted as Klansmen, the bulk look anything but poor." Yet, many lost their wealth after the war. See Fitzgerald, "Ex-Slaveholders and the Ku Klux Klan: Exploring the Motivations of Terrorist Violence," in *After Slavery: Race, Labor, and Citizenship in the Reconstruction South*, ed. Bruce Baker and Brian Kelly (Gainesville: University Press of Florida, 2013), 146, 151. Allen W. Trelease, an early authority, believes that class mattered little in the recruitment of members. See Trelease, *White Terror: The Ku Klux Klan Conspiracy and Southern Reconstruction* (New York: Harper and Row, 1971). Other historians have insisted poor whites were behind most vigilante attacks. In describing race relations in slavery's aftermath generally, historian Stephen V. Ash suggests that tensions were more pronounced between poor whites and blacks than between privileged whites and blacks. Ash, *Middle Tennessee Society Transformed*, 196–97. Historian Douglas R. Edgerton takes a middle position: "White farmers who had not owned slaves before the war banded together with planters in the name of labor control, as the former feared that too independent black yeomen posed competition and the latter wished to impose greater restraints over those freedmen who had used the scarcity of labor to obtain beneficial sharecropping agreements." Edgerton, *The Wars of Reconstruction: The Brief, Violent History of America's Most Progressive Era* (New York: Bloomsbury, 2014), 289. The Klan undoubtedly attracted Confederate veterans from all classes, but there is no doubt property-owning elites like Forrest and Thompson helped lead it.

26. Quoted in "Views of Forrest, Pillow, Harris and other Ex-Confederates on the Situation," *(Shelbyville) Republican*, September 11, 1868, 1. Southern newspapers tended to depict Forrest as racially progressive. According to an obituary published in an eastern Tennessee newspaper, Forrest "was a warm friend of the colored race, over whom he exercised remarkable influence." See "Death of the Confederate Cavalry General Forrest—Sketch of His Career," *Bristol News*, November 6, 1877, 1.

27. N. F. Thompson, "A Confederate Veteran Denounces the New and Fraudulent Ku Klux Klan," *[Baltimore] Sun*, March 8, 1924, 8.

28. Quoted in "Original K. K. K. Head Denounces Present Klan," *Times Picayune*, September 10, 1921, 3. 1871 was the year the federal government passed the Ku Klux Act, which criminalized the organization.

29. As one historian noted, "A complete and authentic portrait of the Tennessee Ku Klux remains elusive and probably always will be so." Edward John Harcourt, "Who Were the Pale Faces? New Perspectives on the Tennessee Ku Klux," *Civil War History* 51 (March 2005): 34. Also, see Elaine Frantz Parsons, "Klan Skepticism and Denial in Reconstruction-Era Public Discourse," *Journal of Southern History* 77 (February 2011): 53–90.

30. William W. Turnbull, *The Good Templars: A History of the Rise and Progress of the Independent Order of Good Templars* (n.p.: 1901), 5.

31. David M. Fahey, *Temperance and Racism: John Bull, Johnny Reb, and the Good Templars* (Lexington: University Press of Kentucky, 1996), 5; and Elaine Frantz Parsons, *Manhood Lost: Fallen Drunkards and Redeeming Women in the Nineteenth-Century United States* (Baltimore: Johns Hopkins University Press, 2003), 6.

32. *Biographical and Portrait Cyclopedia of Cambria County*, 439. The Women's Christian Temperance Union emerged in 1874.

33. "Temperance Address," *Nashville Union and American*, August 31, 1872, 4.

34. "Our Paper," *Riverside Weekly* 5, July 29, 1875, 5. Thompson recalled his involvement in the organization fondly in a letter to the editor published in the *[Baltimore] Sun*; N. F. Thompson, "An Old Warrior Says that They Once Had Alcohol Whipped," *[Baltimore] Sun*, January 2, 1927, 8.

35. "A Card from N. F. Thompson," *Riverside Weekly* 5 (April 18, 1876): 4.

36. Geo. P. Rowell & Co., *Geo. P. Rowell & Co's American Newspaper Directory, Containing Accurate Lists of All the Newspapers and Periodicals Published in the United States and Territories, and the Dominion of Canada, and Newfoundland, 1876* (New York: UNT Digital Library, digital.library.unt.edu/ark:/67531/metadc9258/, accessed December 24, 2010).

37. "The Monopoly of 'Natural Products'," *World's Work* 7 (January 1904): 4290.

38. "The Mutual Gas Light Company," *Savannah Morning News*, May 7, 1884, 4.

39. N. F. Thompson, "The Church and Prohibition," *Catholic World* 37 (September 1883): 848.

40. DuBose, *Jefferson County and Birmingham*, 507.

41. Thompson, "The Church and Prohibition," 850.

42. "Temperance at Library Hall," *Savannah Morning News*, July 1, 1884, 1.

43. "Temperance Address Tonight," *Savannah Morning News*, February 19, 1884, 4.

44. J. H. Estill, *A Guide to Strangers Visiting Savannah for Business, Health, or Pleasure* (Savannah, Ga.: Morning News Steam Printing House, 1881), 14. Elite spokespersons from numerous southern cities published similar boosterish pamphlets, which C. Vann Woodward calls "promotional literature." See Woodward, *Origins of the New South, 1877–1913* (1951; Baton Rouge: Louisiana State University Press, 1974), 492–93.

45. "Open Shop in Coal Fields," *Tradesman* 55 (June 15, 1906): 47.

46. On Thompson's extensive work for industrial interests in Birmingham, see "Commercial Club," *Birmingham Age-Herald*, February 1, 1894, 2; "Commercial Club," *Birmingham Age-Herald*, April 7, 1894, 4; "Commercial Club Notes," *Birmingham Age-Herald*, September 29, 1895, 10; "Help Birmingham," *Birmingham Age-Herald*, September 13, 1895, 4; Henry M. McKiven, Jr., *Iron and Steel: Class, Race, and Community in Birmingham, Alabama, 1875–1920* (Chapel Hill: University of North Carolina Press, 1995), 89–112. Of course, Birmingham had its industrial builders before Thompson arrived. See Carl V. Harris, *Political Power in Birmingham, 1871–1921* (Knoxville: University of Tennessee Press, 1977); Daniel Letwin, *The Challenge of Interracial Unionism: Alabama Coal Miners, 1878–1921* (Chapel Hill: University of North Carolina Press, 1998), 9–30; and Glenn Feldman, *The Irony of the Solid South: Democrats, Republicans, and Race, 1865–1944* (Tuscaloosa: University of Alabama Press, 2013), 23–26. On Thompson's work on behalf of Huntsville industrialists, see "Chamber of Commerce Holds Busy Session," *Weekly Mercury*, August 23, 1899, 3; "Industrial Agency," *Weekly Mercury*, December 20, 1899, 3; "Big Land Sale," *Birmingham News*, October 12, 1899, 2; "Col. Thompson on Industrial Matters," *Weekly Mercury*, July 4, 1900, 7. A long

line of journalists and historians have noted that capitalists found many economic advantages in the South, which included access to raw materials, inexpensive transportation costs, labor's long hours and low wages, tax breaks, and a supposedly quiescent workforce. See "Cotton Mills," *Tradesman* 26 (January 1, 1892): 42; Broadus Mitchell, *The Rise of Cotton Mills in the South* (1921; Columbia: University of South Carolina Press, 2001); Woodward, *Origins of the New South*, 107–11; Melton Alonza McLaurin, *Paternalism and Protest: Southern Cotton Mill Workers and Organized Labor, 1875–1905* (Westport, Conn.: Greenwood, 1971); Gavin Wright, "Cheap Labor and Southern Textiles Before 1880," *Journal of Economic History* 39 (September 1979): 655–80; Leonard A. Carlson, "Labor Supply, the Acquisition of Skills, and the Location of Southern Textile Mills, 1880–1900," *Journal of Economic History* 41 (March 1981): 65–71; David Koistinen, "The Causes of Deindustrialization: The Migration of the Cotton Textile Industry from New England to the South," *Enterprise and Society* 3 (September 2002): 482–520; Beth English, *A Common Thread: Labor, Politics, and Capital Mobility in the Textile Industry* (Athens: University of Georgia Press, 2006). On pre-Civil War industrialization, see Curtis J. Evans, *The Conquest of Labor: Daniel Pratt and Southern Industrialization* (Baton Rouge: Louisiana State University Press, 2001); Tom Downey, *Planting a Capitalist South: Masters, Merchants, and Manufacturers in the Southern Interior, 1790–1860* (Baton Rouge: Louisiana State University Press, 2006); and John F. Kvach, *De Bow's Review: The Antebellum Vision of a New South* (Lexington: University Press of Kentucky, 2013).

47. "Commercial Club," *Birmingham Age-Herald*, April 7, 1894, 4.

48. Ibid.

49. "Fine Land Sold," *Weakly Mercury*, August 21, 1901, 7.

50. "Sells His Interest," *Weekly Mercury*, September 19, 1900, 2. Thompson was very successful as a commercial real estate agent. Some days he attended to as many as "five strangers" in one day, all of whom sought information about the possibilities of investing in northern Alabama. See "Industrial Agency," *Weekly Mercury*, December 20, 1899, 3; and "Big Land Sale," *Birmingham News*, October 12, 1899, 2. Another report pointed out that his company is "daily receiving letters of inquiry from all parts of the country asking about Huntsville and Madison County." See "Fine Land Sold," *Weekly Mercury*, August 21, 1901, 7. Thompson apparently sold land to "eastern capitalists, who represent the largest aggregation of milling interests ever located at one time in the South." See "Bell Factory Property," *[Huntsville] Republican*, June 2, 1900, 1; and "Bell Factory Property," *Weekly Mercury*, June 6, 1900, 3. Thompson was one of several well-known southern boosters and economic developers. Before he arrived in Huntsville, the boosterish and infrastructural networks were already in place, and several promoters had come to terms with the importance of luring northern capital. For more on businessmen's attempt to lure textile mills to the city in the years just before Thompson arrived, see Robert Eugene Perry, "Middle-Class Townsmen and Northern Capital: The Rise of the Alabama Cotton Textile Industry, 1865–1900" (Ph.D. dissertation, Vanderbilt University, 1986); and Whitney Adrienne Snow, "Cotton Mill City: The Huntsville Textile Industry, 1880–1989," *Alabama Review* 63 (October 2010): 243–81.

51. "Huntsville, Ala.," *American Wool and Cotton Reporter* (September 14, 1899): 1079.

52. *(Huntsville) Republican*, January 12, 1901, 4.

53. "An Object Lesson to the South," *Tradesman* 55 (June 1, 1906): 48.

54. "Even Coffin Factories Unionized," *Meyer Brothers Druggist* 21 (1900): 156.

55. N. F. Thompson, "The Trust Question," *Weekly Mercury*, July 11, 1900, 8.

56. According to Gerald Friedman, the "South has been hostile terrain for labor unions at least as far back as 1880." See Friedman, "The Political Economy of Early Southern Unionism: Race, Politics, and Labor in the South, 1880–1953," *Journal of Economic History* 60 (June 2000): 389; and Howell Harris, "Coping with Competition: Cooperation and Collusion in the US Stove Industry, c. 1870–1930," *Business History Review* 86 (December 2012): 668.

57. Daniel Letwin, *The Challenge of Interracial Unionism: Alabama Coal Miners, 1878–1921* (Chapel Hill: University of North Carolina Press, 1998), 9–30. On waterfront workers, see Daniel Rosenberg, *New Orleans Dockworkers: Race, Labor, and Unionism, 1892–1923* (Albany: State University of New York Press, 1988), 14–16; and Eric Arnesen, *Waterfront Workers of New Orleans: Race, Class, and Politics, 1863–1923* (Oxford: Oxford University Press, 1991), 34–119.

58. Merl E. Reed, "The Augusta Textile Mills and the Strike of 1886," *Labor History* 14 (Spring 1973): 228–46.

59. "Cotton Mills," *Tradesman* 26 (January 1, 1892): 42.

60. "Southern Wages for Northern Strikers," *Manufacturers' Record* 29 (April 17, 1896): 1.

61. "The Negro as a Molder," *Foundry* 19 (September 1901): 18. Of course, employers' use of African Americans to break strikes was not unique to the South. See John H. Keiser, "Black Strikebreakers and Racism in Illinois, 1865–1900," *Journal of the Illinois State Historical Society* 65 (Autumn 1972): 313–26.

62. "The State Fair," *Middleburgh Post*, July 30, 1896, 1.

63. N. F. Thompson, "No Natural Antagonism between Labor and Capital," *Public Opinion* 20 (April 30, 1896): 557.

64. A. S. Eisenstadt, *Carnegie's Model Republic: Triumphant Democracy and the British-American Relationship* (Albany: State University of New York Press, 2007), 162.

65. Thompson, "No Natural Antagonism," 557. Unsurprisingly, Thompson failed to point out that wage rates for the majority of Cambria's workers were lower in 1895 than in 1880. See David Brody, *Steelworkers in America: The Nonunion Era* (Cambridge, Mass.: Harvard University Press, 1960), 44.

66. Thompson, "No Natural Antagonism," 558.

67. See N. F. Thompson, "The South for Settlers," *New York Times*, August 25, 1897, 4. Thompson to Samuel Spencer, July 8, 1898, File 2998, Box 59, Samuel Spencer papers, Southern Museum, Kennesaw, Georgia. Spencer established the Southern Railway system with help from J. P. Morgan in 1894. For more on Spencer and his railroad career, see James F. Doster, "The Conflict over Railroad Regulation in Alabama," *Business History Review* 28 (December 1954): 332; Maury Klein, "Southern Railroad Leaders, 1865–1893: Identities and Ideologies," *Business History Review* 42 (Autumn 1968): 310. In the early twentieth century, Spencer was, one historian contends, "perhaps the most notorious abuser of the Interstate Commerce Act." See Richard H. K. Vietor, "Businessmen and the Political Economy: The Railroad Rate Controversy of 1905," *Journal of American History* 64 (June 1977): 51.

68. The company was originally called the West Huntsville Land Company and organized by Thompson and T. C. Du Pont, the well-known businessman, executive of the Johnstown Passenger Railway Company, and future U.S. senator representing Delaware. In Johnstown, Du Pont worked directly under Tom L. Johnson, who later became the famous reform mayor in Cleveland in 1901. For more on Thompson's investments, see "Construction Department,"

Manufacturers' Record 31 (June 16, 1899): 353; and "Electric Lighting," *Western Electrician* 25 (August 12, 1899): 98.

69. "Cotton Mills for the South," *Ferris Wheel*, August 17, 1900, 1.

70. James Cobb, *Selling of the South: The Southern Crusade for Industrial Development, 1936–90* (Baton Rouge: Louisiana State University Press, 1993).

71. Race-related issues were one of a number of reasons why many outsiders saw the region, as Natalie J. Ring puts it, a "problem." See Natalie J. Ring, *The Problem South: Region, Empire, and the New Liberal State, 1880–1930* (Athens: University of Georgia Press, 2012).

72. For more on Jewett, see Roger K. Hux, "Lillian Clayton Jewett and the Rescue of the Baker Family, 1899–1900," *Historical Journal of Massachusetts* 19 (1991): 13–23. Jewett's Bostonian supporters called her "the new Harriet Beecher Stowe." See "A Boston Girl," *Weekly Messenger*, July 29, 1899, 4.

73. "Anti-Lynching Leagues," *Weekly Mercury*, August 9, 1899, 4.

74. Christopher Waldrep, "National Policing, Lynching, and Constitutional Change," *Journal of Southern History* 74 (August 2008): 592; and Nelson, *Iron Confederates*, 91–92. For the broader context of pro-slavery thought in the post-bellum years, see John David Smith, *An Old Creed for the New South: Proslavery Ideology and Historiography* (Westport, Conn.: Greenwood, 1985).

75. "Anti-Lynching Leagues," *Weekly Mercury*, August 9, 1899, 4. Unsurprisingly, Thompson failed to note that state forces had consistently played a more vigorous role in suppressing strikes than in stopping racist lynchers. As Rebecca Hill explained, "Beginning in 1877, federal troops were regularly used to quell labor disturbances while federal authorities claimed constitutional powerlessness to stop lynch mobs." Hill, *Anti-Lynching and Labor Defense in U.S. Radical History* (Durham, N.C.: Duke University Press, 2008), 113.

76. *Report of the U.S. Industrial Commission*, 62. Thompson's Southern Industrial Convention colleague John P. Coffin, a Florida-based newspaper owner, made an even more explicit link between African Americans and strikebreaking before the Commission, maintaining that in black labor lies "the panacea for the wrongs frequently committed by organized labor, and a reserve force from which can be supplied any needed number of workers when the time shall come that they will be needed." Ibid.

77. Elizabeth Esch and David Roediger, "One Symptom of Originality: Race and the Management of Labour in the History of the United States," *Historical Materialism* 17 (December 2009): 4, 6.

78. Quoted in "Would Send Negroes to Work at Panama," *New York Times*, November 14, 1906, 4; "Col. Thompson Talks," *[Chattanooga] Daily Times*, November 14, 1906, 2; N. F. Thompson to John I. Cox, October 26, 1906, Folder 8, Box 15, John I. Cox papers, Tennessee State Archives, Nashville, Tennessee; and *Report of the U.S. Industrial Commission*, 769. On anti-vagrancy efforts in Birmingham, see Carl V. Harris, "Reforms in Government Control of Negroes in Birmingham, Alabama, 1890–1920," *Journal of Southern History* 38 (November 1972): 567–600. For convict labor, see Alex Lichtenstein, *Twice the Work of Free Labor: The Political Economy of Convict Labor in the New South* (London: Verso, 1996); and Douglas A. Blackmon, *Slavery by Another Name: The Re-Enslavement of Black People in America from the Civil War to World War II* (New York: Doubleday, 2008). The president was apparently unconvinced by the idea of sending African Americans to work in Panama. Nevertheless, both men believed that something had to be done about the lingering presence of seemingly

unproductive and footloose African Americans in urban centers. Julie Greene notes that many non-whites from other parts of the Western hemisphere dug the canal under awful, segregated conditions. See Greene, *The Canal Builders: Making America's Empire at the Panama Canal* (New York: Penguin, 2009).

79. Louis R. Harlan, *Booker T. Washington: The Making of a Black Leader, 1856–1901* (Oxford: Oxford University Press, 1972), 169. Also, see Nathan Cardon, "The South's 'New Negroes' and African American Visions of Progress at the Atlanta and Nashville International Expositions, 1895–1897," *Journal of Southern History* 80 (May 2014): 287–326. Councill's institution received less outside funding than Washington's school. According to a 1900 article, "the Councill School has been without the generous aid given it by rich men in the North, which has been the good fortune of the Tuskegee school." See "To Solve Race Problem," *Washington Herald*, October 26, 1906, 12.

80. "Anti-Lynching Leagues," *Weekly Mercury*, August 9, 1899, 4. For a discussion of the roles played by antiunion black elites like Washington and Councill, see Judith Stein, "'Of Booker T. Washington and Others': The Political Economy of Racism in the United States," *Science and Society* 38 (Winter 1974–75): 422–63; Manning Marable, *Black Leadership: Four Great American Leaders and the Struggle for Civil Rights* (New York: Penguin, 1999), 23–39; and Brian Kelly, "Sentinels for New South Industry: Booker T. Washington, Industrial Accommodation and Black Workers in the Jim Crow South," *Labor History* 44 (August 2003): 337–57.

81. William H. Councill, *The Negro Laborer: A Word to Him* (Huntsville, Ala.: Dickson, 1887), 7.

82. Ibid., 10.

83. Ibid., 11.

84. "The Huntsville Convention," *Manufacturers' Record* 31 (September 22, 1899): 152.

85. "Mr. Baldwin Will Come," *Weekly Mercury*, September 13, 1899, 2.

86. Washington to Thompson, September 7, 1899, quoted in "A Strong Delegation Named for Alabama," *Weekly Mercury*, September 13, 1899, 6.

87. "Booker T. Washington Delivers the 1895 Atlanta Compromise Speech," http://historymatters.gmu.edu/d/39/.

88. Quoted in "A Masterly Speech," *(Huntsville) Republican*, October 21, 1899, 2. In his revisionist account of Washington, historian Robert J. Norrell says nothing about the Washington-Thompson relationship, but nevertheless acknowledges Washington's law-and-order speech in Huntsville. See Robert J. Norrell, *Up From History: The Life of Booker T. Washington* (Cambridge, Mass.: Harvard University Press, 2008), 181–83.

89. Quoted in "A Masterly Speech," 2. The views of Thompson, Washington, and Councill resembled the opinions of other new South figures. See J. William Harris, *Deep Souths: Delta, Piedmont, and the Sea Island Society in the Age of Segregation* (Baltimore: Johns Hopkins University Press, 2001), 202–4.

90. Vagrancy laws were neither restricted to the South nor new during this time. Employers facing strikes or labor scarcity in other parts of the nation benefited from such laws. See Elizabeth Dale, *Criminal Justice in the United States, 1789–1939* (Cambridge: Cambridge University Press, 2011), 110; David Huyssen, *Progressive Inequality: Rich and Poor in New York, 1890–1920* (Cambridge, Mass.: Harvard University Press, 2014), 156; and Sven Beckert, *Empire of Cotton: A Global History* (New York: Knopf, 2014), 284, 287, 307–8. On the early

use of these laws in the South, see William Cohen, *At Freedom's Edge: Black Mobility and the Southern White Quest for Racial Control, 1861–1915* (Baton Rouge: Louisiana State University Press, 1991), 31.

91. For a list of participants, see "The Huntsville Convention," 117; "Huntsville, Ala.," *American Wool and Cotton Reporter* 13 (September 14, 1899): 1079; and "Devoted to Speeches," *Saint Paul Globe*, October 13, 1899, 9.

92. N. F. Thompson, "The Trust Question," *Weekly Mercury*, July 11, 1900, 8.

93. N. F. Thompson, *Proceedings of the Second Annual Convention of the Citizens' Industrial Association of America* (Indianapolis: CIAA publication department, 1904), 150.

94. Ibid., 151.

95. Ibid.

96. Ibid, 151–52.

97. Ibid., 152.

98. In a 1905 article in *American Industries*, Thompson noted that only 300 southerners, representing "every branch of industry," held membership in the NAM, which that year had a total enrollment of roughly 3,200. N. F. Thompson, "Dixie's Relationship to National Manufacturers and Exports," *American Industries* 3 (April 15, 1905): 6.

99. "The Alabama Law for Individual Rights," *Corporations Auxiliary Bulletin* 2 (October 1903): 316. According to historian Sheldon Hackney, most of the "Progressives" in the state senate "were hard-core anti-boycotters" and therefore voted for this law. See Sheldon Hackney, *Populism to Progressivism in Alabama* (Princeton, N.J.: Princeton University Press, 1969), 249.

100. Quoted in "The Alabama Law," 317.

101. Ibid., 316.

102. Quoted in "Do Working People Lack Intelligence," *Brotherhood of Locomotive Firemen's Magazine* 35 (November 1903): 774. Members of Colorado's fierce Citizens' Alliance viewed Alabama's boycott law as a model for what became their state's antiunion law. George G. Suggs, Jr., *Colorado's War on Militant Unionism: James H. Peabody and the Western Federation of Miners* (1972; Norman: University of Oklahoma Press, 1991), 157. The Birmingham Citizens' Alliance was also in the forefront of campaigns against "eight hour laws." In 1903, David M. Parry singled out Thompson's organization for adopting "a good" resolution opposing such laws. See Parry, *Disastrous Effects of a National Eight-Hour Law* (n.p.: 1903), 9–10.

103. "An Object Lesson to the South," *Tradesman* 55 (April 1, 1906): 48.

104. "Immigration to the South," *Tradesman* 55 (July 15, 1906): 52.

105. Quoted in "Would Send Negroes to Work at Panama," 4.

106. "Labor Unions and the South," *Tradesman* 57 (May 15, 1907): 44. Roughly 150 of Montgomery's streetcar workers staged this action because management fired several employees for signing union cards. See "Street Car Men Will Strike," *Gainesville Daily Sun*, March 28, 1907, 5.

107. "The Chattanooga Lesson," *Tradesman* 59 (August 1, 1908): 1000.

108. N. F. Thompson to John I. Cox, November 27, 1905, Folder 8, Box 15, Cox Papers. Cox established himself as a powerful foe of Tennessee's labor movement in 1905 when he sent the National Guard to break a strike staged by hundreds of miners at the Tennessee Consolidated Company in Tracy City. Cox also traveled to the community during the violent

dispute, telling its residents to respect the rights of nonunionists: "God gave labor a right to organize but no labor organization can say that others cannot work." Quoted in "Trouble at Tracy," *Sequachee Valley News*, August 31, 1905, 1.

109. N. F. Thompson to D. A. Tompkins, November 29, 1907, in the Daniel Augustus Tompkins papers, Folder 144, Box 11, Southern Historical Collection, Wilson Library, University of North Carolina at Chapel Hill. Tompkins held contradictory views about child labor. On the one hand, he believed that child labor helped build character. Yet he also thought that "As long as men are greedy men there will be need ultimately of some law to set a limit to the overwork of children." Quoted in Hugh D. Hindman, *Child Labor: An American History* (Armonk, N.Y.: M. E. Sharpe, 2002), 55. Tompkins shared several of Thompson's racial and managerial beliefs, including the view that vagrancy laws constituted a practical solution to the jobless African American problem. See Erin Elizabeth Clune, "Emancipation to Empire: Race, Labor, and ideology in the New South" (Ph.D dissertation, New York University, 2002), 74, 117.

110. "The South's Manufacturing Status," *Tradesman* 57 (May 15, 1907): 43.

111. "The Charm of Alabama," *National Magazine* 34 (July 1911): 421.

Conclusion. Creating the "Common Good": Individual Rights, Industrial Progress, and Virtuous Citizenship

Epigraph: Glenda Elizabeth Gilmore, ed., *Who Were the Progressives?* (Boston: Bedford/ St. Martin's, 2002), 3.

1. In his recent biography of William Howard Taft, historian Jonathan Lurie has complicated matters further by employing the phrase "Progressive conservative" to describe this individual. See Lurie, *William Howard Taft: The Travails of a Progressive Conservative* (Cambridge: Cambridge University Press, 2012).

2. More than half a century ago, historian Robert H. Wiebe described organized employers mainly as "militant" counter-reformists. See Wiebe, *Businessmen and Reform: A Study of the Progressive Movement* (Chicago: Quadrangle, 1962), 25, 168. Few have challenged this general assessment.

3. On anti-suffrage movements, see Susan E. Marshall, *Splintered Sisterhood: Gender and Class in the Campaign Against Woman Suffrage* (Madison: University of Wisconsin Press, 1997); and Susan Goodier, *No Votes for Women: The New York State Anti-Suffrage Movement* (Urbana: University of Illinois Press, 2013). Goodier shows that numerous anti-suffragists, including women, viewed themselves as progressives. The literature on post-Reconstruction white supremacy is extensive. See C. Vann Woodward, *Origins of the New South, 1877–1913* (Baton Rouge: Louisiana State University Press, 1951); William Fitzhugh Brundage, *Lynching in the New South: Georgia and Virginia, 1880–1930* (Urbana: University of Illinois, 1993); and Stephen Kantrowitz, *Ben Tillman and the Reconstruction of White Supremacy* (Chapel Hill: University of North Carolina Press, 2000). On nativism, see David Harry Bennett, *The Party of Fear: From Nativist Movements to the New Right in American History* (Chapel Hill: University of North Carolina Press, 1988), 159–82. On anti-populism, see Lawrence Goodwyn, *The Populist Moment: A Short History of the Agrarian Revolt in America* (Oxford: Oxford University Press, 1978), 278–79; and H. W. Brands, *The Reckless Decade: America in the 1890s* (Chicago: University of Chicago Press, 1995), 211.

4. O. M. Becker, "The Square Deal in Works Management," *Engineering Magazine* 30 (February 1906): 660–87.

5. John Kirby, Jr., "Address by Mr. John Kirby Jr.," *Exponent* 3 (February 1906): 18.

6. David M. Parry, "President's Address," *Proceedings of the Second Annual Convention of the Citizens' Industrial Association of America, November 29 and 30, 1904* (Indianapolis: CIA Publication Department, 1904): 7.

7. "Col. Thompson on Industrial Matters," *Weekly Mercury*, July 4, 1900, 7.

8. Quoted in William Millikan, *A Union Against Unions: The Minneapolis Citizens Alliance and Its Fight Against Organized Labor, 1903–1947* (St. Paul: Minnesota Historical Society Press, 2001), 32. For a broader discussion of the ways in which reformers avoided the question of class, see Shelton Stromquist, *Re-Inventing "The People": The Progressive Movement, the Class Problem, and the Origins of Modern Liberalism* (Urbana: University of Illinois Press, 2006); and Jeffrey Haydu, *Citizen Employers: Business Communities and Labor in Cincinnati and San Francisco, 1870–1916* (Ithaca, N.Y.: Cornell University Press, 2008), 108.

9. John Kirby, Jr., "The Death of James Wallace Van Cleave," *American Industries* 10 (June 1910): 10.

10. Quoted in James Weinstein, *The Corporate Ideal in the Liberal State, 1900–1918* (Boston: Beacon Press, 1968), 93.

11. On the Northern Securities Company case, see Lewis L. Gould, *Grand Old Party: A History of the Republicans* (New York: Random House, 2003), 141–42.

12. Quoted in Henry F. Pringle, *Theodore Roosevelt: A Biography* (1931; Orlando: Harcourt Brace, 1984), 381.

13. Quoted in Alpheus Thomas Mason, *Brandeis: A Free Man's Life* (New York: Viking, 1946), 352–53.

14. Of course, as a lawyer for independent tobacco associations, Brandeis had clear financial motivations. See Mason, *Brandeis*, 351; Philip Cullis, "The Limits of Progressivism: Louis Brandeis, Democracy and the Corporation," *Journal of American Studies* 30 (December 1996): 381–404; and Melvin I. Urofsky, *Louis D. Brandeis: A Life* (New York: Pantheon, 2009), 300–326.

15. Employers clearly had self-interested reasons to improve workplace safety, since fewer accidents and deaths meant greater efficiency. Mark Aldrich, *Safety First: Technology, Labor, and Business in the Building of American Work Safety, 1870–1939* (Baltimore: Johns Hopkins University Press, 1997), 92–93.

16. Perhaps most important, General Electric's Magnus Alexander, a National Association of Manufacturers and National Founders' Association leader, served as a member of the Massachusetts Workmen's Compensation Commission in the 1910s. See Aldrich, *Safety First,* 95; also, see Sidney Fine, *"Without Blare of Trumpets": Walter Drew, the National Erectors' Association, and the Open-Shop Movement, 1903-57* (Ann Arbor: University of Michigan Press, 1995), 149–51. Members of employers' associations were split on the question of child labor laws. Officially, the CIAA supported child labor restrictions, but some open-shop advocates, including Walter D. Sayle, were found guilty of breaking an Ohio law restricting the practice. Southerners like N. F. Thompson and Daniel A. Tompkins were generally intolerant of these laws. Others, like NAM leader Oscar Elsas, a top manager of Atlanta's Fulton Bag and Cotton Mills, employed a small percentage of children aged 16 or younger, but did so only after receiving signed parental permission contracts. See Clifford M. Kuhn, *Contesting the New South Order: The 1914–1915 Strike at Atlanta's Fulton Mills* (Chapel Hill: University of North Carolina Press, 2001), 46.

17. "Open Shop in Coal Fields," *Tradesman* 55 (June 15, 1906): 47.

18. William H. Pfahler, "Free Shops for Free Men," *Publications of the American Economic Association* 4 (February 1903): 183–89.

19. For a fine analysis of wageless workers' struggles in one North American city, see Gaetan Heroux and Bryan D. Palmer, "Marching Under Flags Black and Red: Toronto's Dispossessed in the Age of Industry," in *Workers in Hard Times: A Long View of Economic Crisis*, ed. Leon Fink, Joseph A. McCartin and Joan Sangster (Urbana: University of Illinois Press, 2014), 19–44.

20. "The Open Shop: An Incentive to Dishonesty," *Official Journal of the Brotherhood of Painters, Decorators and Paperhangers of America* 19 (January 1905): 10.

21. Victor Yarros, "Union Labor and the Citizens' Alliance," *American Federationist* 12 (February 1905): 69.

22. On Addams, see Rivka Shpak Lissak, *Pluralism and Progressives: Hull House and the New Immigrants, 1890–1919* (Chicago: University of Chicago Press, 1989), 21. On Ely, see Luigi Bradizza, *Richard T. Ely's Critique of Capitalism* (New York: Palgrave Macmillan, 2013), 35.

23. Clarence S. Darrow, *The Open-Shop* (Chicago: Charles H. Kerr, 1920), 13.

24. On workers' support for union recognition, see Melvyn Dubofsky, *When Workers Organize: New York City in the Progressive Era* (Amherst: University of Massachusetts Press, 1968); Bryan D. Palmer, *Working-Class Experience: The Rise and Reconstitution of Canadian Labour, 1880–1980* (Toronto: Butterworth, 1983); David Montgomery, *The Fall of the House of Labor: The Workplace, the State, and American Labor Activism, 1865–1925* (Cambridge: Cambridge University Press, 1987); Michael Kazin, *Barons of Labor: The San Francisco Building Trades and Union Power in the Progressive Era* (Urbana: University of Illinois Press, 1987); Howell Harris, "Industrial Democracy and Liberal Capitalism, 1890–1925," in *Industrial Democracy in America: The Ambiguous Promise*, ed. Nelson Lichtenstein and Howell Harris (Cambridge: Cambridge University Press, 1993), 55; Perry K. Blatz, *Democratic Miners: Work and Labor Relations in the Anthracite Coal Industry, 1875–1925* (Albany: State University of New York Press, 1994); and Rosemary Feurer, *Radical Unionism in the Midwest, 1900–1950* (Urbana: University of Illinois Press, 2006), 1–49.

25. Baker had not broken completely with the open-shop movement's leadership. In this same article, he praised Parry for his "great shrewdness" in dealing with labor issues. See Baker, "The Rise of the Tailors," *McClure's Magazine* 24 (December 1904): 138.

26. As historian Paul Street notes, the nation's wealthiest citizens continue to present their financial and managerial interests as "the public interest." Street, *They Rule: The 1% vs. Democracy* (Boulder, Colo.: Paradigm, 2014), 6.

Index

AABA. *See* American Anti-Boycott Association
Abram Cox Stove Company, 27
Addams, Jane, 14, 223
AFA. *See* American Foundrymen's Association
African Americans: employment of, 195–96; and lynchings, 199–200, 201; in open-shop movement, 6; and strikebreaking, 283n76; Thompson's view, 201, 202; vagrancy laws used against, 201, 204–5, 286n109. *See also* Councill; Washington
Aitken, Hugh G. J., 40
Alabama, 209–10. *See also individual cities*
Alabama Agricultural and Mechanical College. *See* Councill
alcohol, 191. *See also* temperance movement
Alden, George I., 170–71, 174, 178
AMCA. *See* American Malleable Castings Association
American Anti-Boycott Association (AABA), 10, 47, 173
American Foundrymen's Association (AFA), 24–26, 130
American Malleable Castings Association (AMCA), 102
American Society of Mechanical Engineers (ASME), 37, 156
anarchists, 18, 133, 143; Czolgosz, 18, 126, 127, 131–32, 133, 134; Goldman, 127, 132, 133, 142–43
anthracite coal mine strike, 57–61, 70, 75, 82
antimonopoly ethos, 220, 229n23
antiunionism: in South, 186, 194, 277n13; Thompson's, 192, 193–94. *See also* nonunionizing process; open-shop

movement; union avoidance; union-breaking
apostasy, 92. *See also* Dawley; Penton
apprentices, 137–38
Asian community, 69, 81, 82
ASME. *See* American Society of Mechanical Engineers
associations, belligerent, 36
Australia, 71, 165

Baehr, Herman C., 122
Baer, George, 57, 59, 60, 70
Baker, Ray Stannard, 58, 60, 64, 223–24
Baldwin, William Henry Jr., 203
Barnes, J. M., 62
Bates, W. O., 44, 46
Bates Machine Company, 44
Beckert, Sven, 30
Birmingham, Ala., 19, 193, 209
Birmingham Citizens' Alliance, 209, 285n102
Bishop, Joseph, 122
Black, Eli, 110, 111
blacklisting: of Czolgosz, 132, 222; effects, 222; by labor bureaus, 163, 164; legitimization, 14; by Tulloch, 167; of union leaders, 160
Blaisdell Drill Company, 271n33
Blatz, Perry, 59
Bliss, William Dwight Porter, 12, 78–79
Blue, John, 50
boarding house owners, 140
Boetcker, William J. H., 66
Bonnett, Clarence E., 36, 46
bonus/premium system, 76, 177
boosterism, 16–17; after urban disasters, 239n75; of Buffalo, 128–29; of Cleveland, 113–14; of Huntsville, 281n50; of New

Acknowledgments

I have spent more than a decade working on this project. And during this time, I have received an enormous amount of help. I am happy to acknowledge many individuals and institutions.

A number of scholars have read my work at various stages. I would like to thank the following individuals for reading versions of early chapters: David Hochfelder, Brian Kelly, Amy Murrell Taylor, and especially Gerald Zahavi. I must also express my great indebtedness to the readers for the University of Pennsylvania press: the anonymous external reader and series editor Pamela Walker Laird. The reader offered excellent suggestions for improvement. Pamela, one of the historical profession's sharpest and kindest members, has read my work carefully over the last several years and has taught me a great deal in the process. I cannot thank her enough for her generous support and feel very fortunate to count her as a friend.

I am also indebted to the scholars and comrades who share my interest in the history of employers' associations. Rosemary Feurer has helped me to think through many of the central issues I raise in the book and, in general, has taught me much about power relations. I am grateful for our on-going collaborations, and sincerely admire her involvement in raising awareness about labor history, both in the academy and beyond. I am also very thankful to Howell Harris, one of the world's great scholars of management history. Howell has been very generous with me over the course of more than a decade. He has provided me with useful documents and has consistently been one my toughest critics. I have learned much as a result. I would also like to recognize my good friend Howard Stanger. I appreciate that Howard, an excellent scholar of industrial relations, is always willing to read my work and to talk shop.

Many other historians have demonstrated their generosity by offering valuable comments on various parts of this work: Sven Beckert, Agatha

Beins, Mary Blewett, Andrew Cohen, Bruce Cohen, Matthew Coulter, David Cullen, Colin Davis, Melvyn Dubofsky, Rebecca Hill, Vilja Hulden, Richard John, Thomas Klug, Mark Lause, Allen Lessoff, James Livingston, Laurie Marhoefer, Norman Markowitz, Jim Maroney, the late David Montgomery, Kim Phillips-Fein, Clark Pomerleau, Steven Reich, Mark Rose, Shelton Stromquist, Heather Ann Thompson, Jennifer Jensen Wallach, Kyle Wilkison, Michael Wise, and Robert Woodrum. Thanks also to Craig Phelan, *Labor History* editor and R. Douglas Hurt, former *Ohio History* editor. I would like to acknowledge the individuals connected to these journals for allowing me to republish revised portions of my work here.

Portions of Chapter 3 were published as "A Tale of Two Men: Class Traitors and Strikebreaking on Lake Erie, 1886–1911," *Ohio History* 115 (2008), copyright © 2008 Kent State University Press, reprinted with permission. A few portions of Chapter 5 were published as "Making the 'City of Prosperity': Engineers, Open-Shoppers, Americanizers, and Propagandists in Worcester, Massachusetts, 1900–1925," *Labor History* 45 (2004), copyright © 2004 by Taylor & Francis, reprinted with permission.

Others have assisted in more informal ways, and I would like to recognize the following people for their support: Tom Alter, Laila Amine, David Anderson, Charles Bittner, John Kvach, Evan Lampe, Sam Mitrani, Bryan D. Palmer, Joan Sangster, Larry Stern, Michael Thompson, Steph Waring, and Priscilla Ybarra. I have spent the last four years working at Collin College, a highly supportive environment. Thanks to my terrific colleagues: Sharyn Art, Matthew Coulter, David Cullen, Gary Hodge, Joan Jenkins, Melissa Johnson, Michael Phillips, Ruth Payton, Samuel Tullock, Keith Volanto, Roger Ward, David Weiland, and Kyle Wilkison.

I must also acknowledge the great librarians and research assistants. Lindsey Allen tracked down many useful documents as I revised my chapter on Worcester. And I'm thankful to Elizabeth Hogan, Brian Kiss, Susanna Leberman, Delores Morrow, Elizabeth Spalding, and Shane Stephenson for helping me find photographs of a few of the nation's great open-shop activists. The Southern Labor Archives at Georgia State University funded some of my research, and I'm grateful to Traci Drummond and her colleagues for their support.

I have used the services of many libraries and historical societies while working on this project. I thank the archivists and reference librarians at the following institutions: Alabama A & M University's State Black Archives

Research Center and Museum, the Birmingham Public Library, the Brooklyn Public Library, the Buffalo and Erie County Public Library, the Buffalo Historical Museum, Case Western Reserve Historical Society, the Chattanooga Public Library, Clark University's Robert H. Goddard Library, the Cleveland Public Library, Collin College's Spring Creek Library, the Fitchburg Public Library, Georgia State University's Southern Labor Archives, Harvard University's Baker Library, the Huntsville-Madison County Public Library, Johns Hopkins University's Sheridan Libraries, the Louisville Free Public Library, the Montana Historical Society, the New York Public Library, the New York State Archives, the Princeton Theological Seminary Library, Rutgers University's Alexander Library, the Southern Museum of Civil War and Locomotive History, Syracuse University's Bird Library, the Tennessee State Archives and Library, the Wisconsin Historical Society, the Worcester Historical Museum, Worcester Polytechnic Institute's George C. Gordon Library, the Worcester Public Library, the University of Alabama at Huntsville's Salmon Library, the University of North Carolina at Chapel Hill Library, and the Yale University Library. Additionally, I am thankful to the interlibrary loan staff from Collin College, the University of Alabama at Huntsville Salmon Library, and the University at Albany.

It has been a great honor to work with the good folks at the University of Pennsylvania Press. Bob Lockhart has been a wonderful source of encouragement, which I greatly appreciate. I would also like to acknowledge Hannah Blake and Amanda Ruffner for answering my multiple logistical questions. Many thanks to Alison Anderson and Scarlet Wynns for their terrific copyediting work. Thank you to proofreader Parvin Kujoor and indexer Amy Murphy.

Finally, I would like to extend my love and thanks to my wife Sandra and to my daughter Lucia. This book is dedicated to them.